The Electronic
Media and the
Transformation of Law

D0026517

M. Ethan Katsh

New York   Oxford
OXFORD UNIVERSITY PRESS
1989

Oxford University Press

Oxford New York Toronto
Delhi Bombay Calcutta Madras Karachi
Petaling Jaya Singapore Hong Kong Tokyo
Nairobi Dar es Salaam Cape Town
Melbourne Auckland

and associated companies in
Berlin Ibadan

Copyright © 1989 by Oxford University Press, Inc.

Published by Oxford University Press, Inc.,
200 Madison Avenue, New York, New York 10016

Oxford is a registered trademark of Oxford University Press

All rights reserved. No part of this publication may be reproduced,
stored in a retrieval system, or transmitted, in any form or by any
means, electronic, mechanical, photocopying, recording, or otherwise,
without prior permission of Oxford University Press.

Library of Congress Cataloging-in-Publication Data

Katsh, M. Ethan.
   The electronic media and the transformation of law / M. Ethan
Katsh.
      p. cm.
   Bibliography: p.
   Includes index.
   ISBN 0-19-504590-4
   1. Telecommunication—Law and legislation—United States. 2. Mass
media—Law and legislation—United States. 3. Law—United States.
I. Title.
KF2765.K37 1989
343.73'0994—dc19
[347.303994]   88-25576

9 8 7 6 5 4 3 2 1
Printed in the United States of America
on acid-free paper

The Electronic Media
and the Transformation of Law

October 1, 2003

To Jeffrey!
A pioneer in cyber law
e-commerce

[signature]

To my parents
Estelle and Abraham Katsh

Acknowledgments

I have benefitted considerably from the assistance and generosity of a number of individuals and institutions. I am particularly grateful for the advice and encouragement I received from the following persons, who read all or part of the manuscript: Arthur S. Miller, Saul Touster, Harold Berman, George McKenna, Stephen Arons, George Gerbner, and David Papke. I am indebted also to the following: my colleagues in the University of Massachusetts Department of Legal Studies, for creating an environment that has supported the development of new perspectives on law; Myrtle Blanchard and Claude Shepard, the extraordinarily efficient staff of the department; Susan Rabiner, Irene Pavitt, Niko Pfund, and Martin Stanford, Valerie Aubry, at Oxford University Press, for their interest, enthusiasm, and guidance; the East-West Center, the Modern Media Institute, and the Annenberg School's Washington Program, for the opportunities provided me to enhance my knowledge of law–media issues. My greatest debt is to my family, to Beverly and to Rebecca, Gabriel, and Gideon, for their love and for the sacrifices they made so that this book could be written.

Contents

Rules of Ev
- commerce

The Electronic Media
and the Transformation of Law

The study of the legal system takes us straight to the central problems faced by the society itself.

ROBERTO UNGER
Law and Modern Society

Once mankind has created a printing press, a musket, a cotton gin, a telephone, an automobile, an airplane, a television, each of these takes on a life of its own.

DANIEL BOORSTIN
The Republic of Technology

Introduction: Law as a Process of Communication

There is an old story of an ax that had been in a family for many generations. Each generation inherited the ax, used it, and, as a cherished family heirloom, passed it along to the next generation. Recently, an old drawing of the ax was discovered, showing it as it had been originally. To the surprise of the current owners, the original was much smaller, perhaps one-half the size of what it is now, and with a smaller blade as well. Other records indicated that in the past 200 years, the ax handle had been replaced ten times and the blade five times.

In many ways, the law is our ax. It has been a useful, important, and powerful tool. It is an heirloom, an item that we cherish and take pride in. It is also extremely different from what it once was, although we have difficulty understanding how different it actually is. What we call law is not the same concept that our ancestors had in mind when they used the term.

The main theme of this book is that broad changes are occurring to the law, to what it is and how it works, and that these changes are linked to the appearance of new methods of storing, processing, and communicating information. We are the first society in history to have the ability to communicate electronically. Because of various qualities of electronic communication that will be described below, the control of information, the organization of information, and the movement of information are no longer the same as they once were. This will have a considerable impact on an institution, such as the law, whose foundation is the processing of information but whose goals, values, capabilities, and modes of operation are tied to the older methods of communicating.

Some of the areas of ferment in the law that are discussed in this book have been observed by others. Richard Abel, for example, has asked,

3

Do the following phenomena have anything in common: the attack on professionals, the state, and bureaucracy, calls to deregulate the economy, the advocacy of decentralization, demands for the decriminalization and delegalization of private behavior (drug use, divorce), deinstitutionalization (in education, care of the mentally ill, restraint and punishment of the delinquent and criminal), the preference for informality in hearing complaints and processing disputes? What is it that is really changing: ideology, substantive norms, processes, or institutions? Is the ambit of state control contracting or expanding? What impact will these changes have on fundamental social, economic, and political structures? Or is it all a lot of talk, with minimal significance for anyone except those who manage the legal system.[1]

Another scholar has suggested that "the law is becoming more fragmented, more subjective, geared more to expediency and less to morality; concerned more with immediate consequences and less with consistency or continuity."[2] The main contribution of this volume is to suggest why and how these and other seemingly unrelated or isolated facets of law are being affected by modern developments in the transmission, storage, and processing of information. Marshall McLuhan wrote that when "a new technology comes into a social milieu it cannot cease to permeate that milieu until every institution is saturated."[3] This book is an attempt to identify some of the ways in which law, an institution that has relied greatly on print, writing, and the spoken word, is highly vulnerable to the influence of new means of communicating information that possess very different qualities.

In 1886, when twenty-three-year-old Guglielmo Marconi tried to carry his small black box past British customs agents, the cautious and uncomprehending officials examined it and then smashed it to pieces. The customs personnel feared violence and revolution. They finally allowed Marconi to enter England, not comprehending that the box was indeed revolutionary, although not of the kind that they had imagined. When his rebuilt black box evolved into the radio several years later, society began a journey toward a way of life that is vastly different from what it was at the end of the last century.

Radio, television, and computers, the principal forms of electronic communication, have had an enormous impact on our basic institutions. Many of the changes brought about by the new media are already known. Modern multinational corporations could not exist were it not for the ability of the computer to facilitate management of worldwide corporate empires. The television has largely replaced the political party as the vehicle for organizing and persuading voters. In summarizing the findings of scholarly research on the impact of television on American life, Dean George Gerbner has asserted that "it has reshaped politics, changed the nature of sports and business, transformed family life and the socialization of children, and affected public security and the enforcement of laws."[4]

Of all the important institutions just mentioned, law appears to have been affected the least. The traditional nuclear family is hard to find; some business empires are now larger than many nation-states; and politicians employ a style of campaigning that would mystify the Founding Fathers. The development of the electronic media may not be the only explanation for these developments, but it is a significant contributing factor and has been the subject of much scholarly research. The number of studies of the impact of the electronic media on the nature of law and its role in society, however, is negligible.

On the surface, the law appears to be relatively immune from the effects of the new media compared with these other institutions. A judge of 1889 who was transported through time to a modern courtroom would undoubtedly be mystified by many cases brought before him. But he would be far more understanding of what was transpiring than a businessman, an athlete, or a politician who underwent a similar experience. A judge of a century ago who found himself in the Supreme Court of the United States today would need some orientation, but the process being used would not be totally alien. Imagine, however, how bewildered a business executive of a past age would feel on entering the floor of the New York Stock Exchange during a day of heavy trading.[5]

Law's appearance today will not be law's appearance tomorrow. The law's resistance to the persuasive charms of the new media is nearing an end. Anyone who reads professional legal journals, particularly the advertisements in such magazines, knows that the high-technology invasion of the legal process is in full swing. What is not recognized is that law cannot remain unaffected by large-scale changes in the communication of information. The law is an institution built on the creation, storage, processing, and communication of information. It has even been defined as "ethical control applied to communication."[6] It can resist change and has done so more effectively than the other institutions just mentioned. It perhaps has understood instinctively that not resisting would lead to deep and permanent change. Yet the era of resistance appears to be over, and it is appropriate to examine what parts of our system of law are most susceptible to change and what these changes will mean to us. The law is about to catch up to the rest of society and, in so doing, become as different as the electronic businessman, the electronic politician, and the electronic athlete are from their predecessors.

Law is an organism whose lifeblood is information and media of communication are the veins and arteries that channel the information through the system. Harvard law professor Harold Berman has written that a legal system requires that there be a "belief in the power of certain words, put certain ways, to bring about certain effects denominated as legal. This kind of magic is necessary if law is to work."[7] Manipulation of information underlies the way legal institutions work, how legal doctrines are applied, and how social and moral values are translated into legal values. Law is a response to information received *from* the public. Law is also information that is communicated *to* the public. Law is the result of judgment and decision making involving the evaluation and organization of information. As Professor Marc Galanter has observed, law

> usually works not by exercise of force but by information transfer, by communication of what's expected, what forbidden, what allowable, what are the consequences of acting in certain ways. That is, law entails information about what the rules are, how they are applied, with what costs, consequences, etc. For example, when we speak of deterrence, we are talking about the effect of information about what the law is and how it is administered. Similarly, when we describe "bargaining in the shadow of the law," we refer to regulation accomplished by the flow of information rather than directly by authoritative decision. Again, "legal socialization" is accomplished by the transmission of information. In a vast number of instances the application of law is, so to speak, self administered—people regulate their conduct (and

so, to develop laws on new technologies will alter the tech, perhaps

judge the conduct of others) on the basis of their knowledge about legal standards, possibilities and constraints.[8]

The information-processing aspect of law is rarely noticed by legal scholars, by journalists who write about law, or by lawyers themselves. Yet this facet of the legal system is as important to law as the central nervous system is to human beings. Without such a system, both the human being and the legal process would be paralyzed and nonfunctioning. What a general once claimed about the military is true of law as well: "If you ain't got communications, you ain't got nothing."[9] Or as legal philosopher H. L. A. Hart stated in a more scholarly style, "If it were not possible to communicate general standards of conduct, which multitudes of individuals could understand, without further direction, as requiring from them certain conduct when occasion rose, nothing that we would now recognize as law could exist."[10] The new media, however, the means by which much of this communication occurs, are radically different from the old, and as information begins to be handled by different means, those facets of law that are reliant on the older media will change or disappear. Since so much of law is dependent on the uses of the traditional media, the end result for law will be very substantial change.

It is considerably easier to understand the transformation of the ax than it will be to comprehend how the law will change or how the new media will exert their influence. For the ax, we have not only hindsight, but also a process of change that is discrete and an object that is easily identifiable. The law, on the contrary, is something that different people perceive in different ways. It resists definition even among legal scholars. While at a particular moment we may grab hold of it and try to use it to our advantage, looked at from afar it is a process that is in motion and whose form and qualities are somewhat blurred.

To understand the significance of the new media to law, it is necessary to discard some of the images and definitions that both law and media evoke. Typically, when law is referred to, the focus of attention is either on legal rules or on legal institutions. Law is considered to be a set of rules located in a book or library; a place, such as a courthouse; or a group of people, such as lawyers or police officers. These are, however, merely the visible parts of the system. They are the end products of a complicated process that the public does not see and therefore tends to ignore. To look solely at rules or institutions is like looking only at the words coming out of an individual's mouth and not understanding that there is something important going on inside the head that makes the external manifestation possible. In evaluating an individual's behavior, we make great efforts to understand not only what he or she does, but also the goals, perceptions, values, and choices that underlie human behavior. We need to adopt the same approach to our examination of law.

The philosopher Iredell Jenkins has warned against accepting the visible facets of law as a complete or adequate description of law:

> Law is very like an iceberg; only one-tenth of its substance appears above the social surface in the explicit form of documents, institutions and professions, while the nine-tenths of its substance that supports the visible fragment leads a sub-aquatic existence, living in the habits, attitudes, emotions and aspirations of men.[11]

What sits on the surface of the legal iceberg is undeniably important in ordering our lives and in making educated predictions about the resolution of problems. It is not, however, particularly reliable as a predictor of the long-term evolution of the legal process. The method of this book is to explore some of what lies hidden from view: the values, goals, and functions of law in our society; the habits of thought that underlie various legal concepts and approaches; and the symbols and myths that affect public perceptions of law. Significant occurrences in the law's deep structure can reveal developments that will be visible to the public later.

A central theme of this book is that changes in the means used to communicate information are important to law because law has come to rely on the transmission of information in a particular form. Law does not simply consume or produce information; law structures, organizes, and regulates information. The effectiveness and operation of law depends on controlling access to some information and highlighting or directing attention to other information. It has been observed that "organizations are networks of information flow; therefore, directing flow to the right places, filtering it in useful ways, and even preventing it from flowing to certain locations improves organizational performance. . . . the primary goal from this perspective is not to produce more information, but rather to reduce the amount that any one subsystem must process."[12] Some of the ways the law channels information have been consciously developed, but many of the patterns and traditions of information use result from limits built into the media of communication that have been employed. Law, which one scholar has labeled "the science of inefficiency,"[13] has been conditioned in many ways by various characteristics and constraints of traditional modes of communication, particularly print. It has come to depend on information being organized and communicated in a particular form. The introduction of new forms of communication that possess different qualities will not simply extend trends that are associated with print. The electronic media are not to be considered merely as more powerful versions of print. They have different mechanisms for transmitting and processing information, some of which will pressure the law to change course and become a different and not simply a more efficient institution.

Although this book is about media and about law, it is not strictly about media law. We often read about cases involving libel and slander, broadcasting regulation, obscenity and pornography, and similar issues where, because of some conflict, the involvement of law has been felt to be necessary. The development of new forms of communication has caused the field of media law to be an area of great growth and activity. Legal cases in this area often involve powerful people, large sums of money, or disputes affecting deeply held values. Such cases are newsworthy, attract our attention, and dominate public discussions about law and media. Yet media law, no matter how important it might be, reveals only a small part of the relationship between law and the new forms of communication in our society. It informs us about newly developed legal rules and changes in traditional doctrines, about how law is trying to exert its authority on the means of communication. But it reveals relatively little about how the new media are changing the general process of law, the institutions of law, the values of law, and the concepts of law in our society. While we shall inevitably touch on many topics of media law, our main concern is broader and will also reach some areas of law that are not normally thought of as being related to the media.

Media, the means we use to communicate, and law, the process we employ to settle conflicts, establish values, and secure liberties, are two of the most basic parts of society's structure. They both influence the operation of institutions that are central to our society. When these two forces clash publicly, media law is the result. When they struggle quietly—sparring, adjusting, and accommodating each other in less visible ways—the end result may be change that is broader, more pervasive, and more significant, albeit less newsworthy. This book is mainly about the quiet struggle, the one that is generally not considered newsworthy enough to be reported by either print or broadcast journalists. Its purpose is to look beyond the pressing media law problems of the day and explore the wider impact of the new media on law. It is intended to illuminate new challenges that will affect the resolution of all cases rather than to analyze the details of particular cases.

When we examine our system of communication, there are also areas of activity that are visible and above the surface and others that get less attention and are often hidden from public view. The tip of the iceberg, for many researchers and for the public, is television, particularly the content of commercial television. Much research in the area of communications is based on the theory that measuring or determining the content of a televised message will reveal to us the impact of that communication on the individual or group that receives it. Some studies that measure the amount of violence on television, for example, employ this model. They assume that there is a connection between the amount of violence viewed on television and the level of violence in society.

This approach regards television or any medium of communication as being similar to a moving company.[14] Its job is to gather, pack, and dispatch messages from sender to receiver; its impact results from the combination of pictures, words, and sounds that the viewer sees and hears. While television may affect the speed at which something is moved, it is presumed to have no effect on the information itself. Whether a car is shipped by truck, train, airplane, or boat, for example, does not change the car. Similarly, it is thought, whether one sends a message to consumers by television or by carrier pigeon does not affect the content of the message. Under this view, the medium seems largely irrelevant.

This is a model that appears plausible, particularly given our personal experiences and contact with television programming. When one sits in front of a television set watching a program, it is natural to assume that the sounds and images being seen on the screen are more influential than any other aspect of modern communication. Yet when one moves away from the television and one's range of vision becomes wider, it can be seen that the communication of information in society, particularly within institutions, involves a great deal more than the television program of that moment. If we were able to peer into many homes at once, each of which had a television set on, we might begin to think more about the process of watching television and less about what program was being watched. And if, while observing all these homes, we saw some people watching television, some talking on the telephone, some reading a book or newspaper, some talking with someone else face to face, and some transmitting data across the country through a personal computer, we would think even less about the content of the television program that some were watching. We would realize that we spend much of our lives engaged in the process of communication and being affected by communication about us, that many forms of communication are employed, and that how we communicate can influence our existence considerably.

Although I believe that television programming can and does influence viewers,[15] the emphasis in this volume will be less on the current content of that medium and more on the novel qualities which most media that transmit information electronically share. The economist Harold Innis, more than a decade before McLuhan became popular, stressed that "the materials on which words were written down have often counted for more than the words themselves."[16] This is a more restrained and, therefore, more accurate statement than McLuhan's famous assertion that "the medium is the message."[17] It suggests that the instruments carrying information are worthy of study and that we should explore the effect of a shift from a medium with certain qualities to a new form of communication having other qualities. This is particularly true for an institution, such as law, whose reliance on the printed word has been substantial.

Technologies of communication are being recognized by more and more scholars as being more than mere containers for carrying information.[18] Societies and cultures have been influenced independently of the content being communicated by their media. The long-term impact of our new modes of communication, therefore, may be deeper and more widespread than the words, pictures, or sounds being communicated would suggest. What is lurking below the surface of the new media iceberg are vast differences in the storage of information, in the movement of information, and in the presentation of information to the consumer. For example, some media allow information to travel faster than others. Some reach wider audiences. Some preserve information more effectively than others. Some encourage copying, change, and the growth of information. Some can store more information than others. Some are more easily accessible. Some are easier to use. Some communicate some kinds of information more efficiently than others. Some use images and sounds instead of text. These qualities affect the information we receive and how we perceive problems and solutions. They influence our individual thoughts and actions, and shape the organization, operation, and perception of our institutions as well.

As we look at law during the past few centuries, we shall find that our model of law has coincided with the age of the printed word and is an outgrowth of it. Law as we know it would not be possible without the special properties of print. We expect certain things from it because the technology of print structured the capabilities and functioning of law in various ways. It is not "fine print," as much of the public believes, that characterizes the law, but print itself. Print affected the organization, growth, and distribution of legal information. The processes of law, the values of law, and many of the doctrines of law, most notably the First Amendment guarantee of free expression, required a means of communication that was vastly different from writing and a society that used something other than manuscripts to store information. Law before Gutenberg was different from law today and was different in significant ways.

To explain the changes in law over long periods of time, this book has a historical orientation as well as a contemporary focus. Law is viewed more as a changing historical concept than as a clearly defined generic concept. Law is considered not merely "as a body of rules but as a process, an enterprise, in which rules have meaning only in the context of institutions and procedures, values and ways of thought.''[19] Change over time has involved ideas about law and habits of thought as well as practices and doctrines. Many of the former changes occur gradually, are almost imperceptible when they are taking place, and are often taken for granted. As two eminent English legal historians once wrote in connection with an earlier shift in communications, "the habit of preserving some written record of all affairs of importance is a modern one. . . . But it is so prevalent and so much bound up with our daily habits that we have almost forgotten how much of the world's business, even in communities by no means barbarous, has been carried on without it."[20] In each chapter, therefore, I have tried to provide a background for understanding how modern law is different from what existed previously and how the electronic media differ from speech, writing, and print. The historical material is employed to try to ascertain where change occurred when there was a shift in modes of communication and which areas of law are most likely to be vulnerable today.

Our society is already heavily reliant on the new media. Many of the vast changes that are occurring in our ability to obtain information, process it, and communicate it are obvious. Power failures, for example, create more than just temporary darkness. When electricity stops moving, the flow of information grinds to a halt and the financial and political implications can be serious. A growing percentage of information moves electronically, and much of this information is economically and legally significant. Most mailboxes contain more letters "written" by a computer than by the human hand. Even what appears to be printed, such as the morning newspaper, was probably "printed" electronically, and not in traditional ways.

What does a transformation in law entail? In confronting this issue, I have begun by focusing on some of the functions we expect law to perform. Chapter 1 examines the vital role played by the traditional media in fostering a public belief that law is stable and predictable as well as flexible and adaptable to changed circumstances. Modern law promotes stability and limits the process of societal change by placing a heavy emphasis on maintaining links with the past. This function of law and the methods the law employs to regulate change are tied to the qualities of print. The chapter explores why the concept of precedent evolved into its present form only after the invention of printing, how modern attitudes toward change are different from expectations of change in the past, and how the electronic media threaten the law's current techniques of maintaining both tradition and change.

Chapter 2 examines another important function of law, the settling of disputes and conflicts. This may be the oldest and most traditional of the law's functions. Yet there has been considerable variation in how much different cultures have relied on law to reduce conflict. Part of our affection for legal techniques of dispute resolution, I believe, has been encouraged in subtle ways by print. As other means of communication are used in lieu of print, our attitudes toward the kinds of techniques that should be used to settle problems are likely to change. The chapter explores how dependence on law to resolve conflict has evolved in the past and why other techniques may now seem more desirable.

Chapters 3 and 4 analyze the relationship between the new media and legal doctrines that concern information. One theme that is developed is that state or institutional control of information will be much more difficult in an era of electronic media than is generally assumed. As a result, all legal doctrines that concern information are in a state of flux. Legal doctrines that are designed to foster the movement of information, such as the First Amendment, will be less threatened than they were in the past. Other legal doctrines, such as copyright, obscenity, and privacy, which are designed to restrict and regulate communication, will be increasingly challenged.

Chapter 5 examines the relationship between the legal profession and the control of information. What lawyers do and what they are are changing as a result of new modes of obtaining and processing information. The idea of a profession is based at least in part on control of a body of information. As knowledge is organized differently, this task will be considerably more difficult than it was in the past. Changes occurring in the organization and structure of legal practice have already begun to occur. The new technologies of communication have been welcomed enthusiastically by the profession, but their consequences may be very different from what is expected.

Chapter 6 explores how law is an institution that not only embodies what we do, but also reflects what we think. It focuses on the perception of the individual and on the use of abstract concepts, both of which are very different now than they were in premodern legal systems. The changes that occurred in these areas in the centuries following Gutenberg allowed for the growing use of rights and the framing of social and political problems in legal terms. The use of electronic media in lieu of print threatens to change the meaning and use of rights and other abstract legal concepts. The "rights revolution," which, for the past thirty years, has been generating new rights and legal protections for previously disenfranchised groups, may turn in a new direction in which substantive ends are stressed. The new media, for example, add pressure for securing real equality instead of legal equality, equal treatment and not merely equal rights, a system with perhaps less law but more justice. Conversely, the value of a right and its perception as a highly stable and secure form of legal protection may erode as information is stored in a more transitory form and is continually processed and reprocessed.

In one of his most famous comments, Justice Oliver Wendell Holmes observed how human experience, not abstract thought, conditions and shapes the law.

> The life of the law has not been logic; it has been experience. The felt necessities of the time, the prevalent moral or political theories, intuitions of public policy, avowed or unconscious, even the prejudices which judges share with their fellowmen, have had a good deal more to do than the syllogism in determining the rules by which men should be governed. The law embodies the story of a nation's development through many centuries, and it cannot be dealt with as if it contained only the axioms and corollaries of a book of mathematics. In order to know what it is, we must know what it has been, and what it tends to become.[21]

There has been increased attention in recent years to the "experiences" that affect law. The roles of economics, politics, and religion have been explored, but the impact of the communications environment in which law operates has been neglected. This is particularly unfortunate in an era of emerging technologies and changes in the use of traditional forms of communication. Law, while it is a powerful mechanism for exerting power over others, is itself affected by other forces in society. One of these, I hope to show, is the manner in which information is communicated.

Owing to our tradition of free expression, we have not resisted

the development of the new media, as some other cultures have
done when faced with a shift in their system of communication.
After the development of writing in ancient Greece, for example,
Lycurgus, the chief lawgiver of the Spartans, is described as having

> strictly forbade that the fundamental laws of his people ever be written.
> If you must write the law in order to remember it, the spirit of the law
> has already been forgotten; and if you must think the law in order to
> respect it, you confront the law as any mere stranger confronts it who
> is subject to it in an alien encounter. The only proper tablet of the law
> is the cultivated human soul. For law is secured among men not by
> tablets of stone but by habits of loyalty, by the settled habits of the
> citizen for whom the law has become, out of old and careful discipline,
> a simple echo of the soul.[22]

The ancients may have understood that a new form of communication ultimately leads to deep-rooted change, but they were
not cognizant of the opportunities that such an occurrence also
presents. Plato warned,

> If men learn [writing], it will implant forgetfulness in their souls,
> they will cease to exercise memory because they rely on that which is
> written, calling things to remembrance no longer from within them-
> selves but by means of external marks; what you have discovered is a
> recipe not for memory, but for reminder. And it is no true wisdom
> that you offer your disciples, but only its semblance; for by telling them
> of many things without teaching them you will make them seem to
> know much, while for the most part they know nothing; and as men
> filled not with wisdom, but the conceit of wisdom, they will be a burden
> to their fellows.[23]

One of the lessons of the era of print has been that new media do
not simply threaten old ways of doing something. They also open
up new opportunities. The analysis that follows suggests that there
is reason for optimism as well as for concern. The process of legal
readjustment that will be necessary in the future may prove painful
to those who idealize the current model of law, who mistakenly
associate the rules of law with the rule of law, or who do not
understand that what we have now is not perfect and has never
been static. For those who do recognize the likely direction of
change and the unique qualities of the new media, the new possibilities that will be opened up may be a welcome as well as a
formidable challenge.

1

The Erosion of Precedent and the Acceleration of Change

> We value poets for their creative breaks from the past; We ask judges to adhere to established rules and principles.
>
> DAVID COLE
> "Agon at Agora," *Yale Law Journal*

> Adherence to the past, which was the core meaning of the traditional view of law and of constitutions, no longer is possible.
>
> ARTHUR S. MILLER
> *Social Change and Fundamental Law*

"It cannot be helped," claimed Justice Oliver Wendell Holmes, "it is as it should be, that the law is behind the times."[1] It is neither novel nor unusual for law to be criticized for being slow moving and anachronistic. It does not happen very often, however, that the legal process is praised for being out of date. Is Holmes correct that such a state of affairs "cannot be helped" and, even more importantly, that this "is as it should be"? We like to be up to date in dress, in technology, in ideas, and in almost every other aspect of modern life. Why not in law, too?

Holmes's most likely response would be that the law, or at least our form of law, has concerns and goals that are more important than keeping up with the times. If the law were to pay more attention to what is new, it would begin to focus less on the past and what is old, and this would be too large a sacrifice for the law to make. To bring law up to date would require that it be revised constantly, so that it would always be consistent with the newest knowledge on any subject. The pace of change within the law would have to be accelerated. Doing this, however, would change the nature of law radically, so that it would no longer be what it has been for the past few centuries. It would lead to a significant shift in one of the primary functions of the legal system, that of promoting a sense of stability and predictability. The degree of historical continuity provided by the law would diminish.

The theme of this chapter is that the new media are leading the law in just this direction. Certain basic characteristics of the law are being reoriented. The law possesses a way of looking at the world and approaching the problems it is supposed to solve. One of the effects of the new media is to reshape the personality of the law and make it less concerned with some things that have been important to it. In this chapter, we shall explore one facet of the law's personality, its concern with history and the past.

The purpose of maintaining links with the past is to restrict the pace of change and to provide citizens with a sense of regularity and stability. This is considered to be at least as important a goal as some of the law's other major functions, such as the achievement of justice or the settling of disputes. Justice Louis Brandeis once wrote that "in most matters it is more important that the applicable rule of law be settled than that it be settled right."[2] Another writer, asserting that "the essential features of law are uniformity and consistency,"[3] was stating a theme that can be found in many analyses of law[4]—that the law has more than one function to perform in society and that justice is often sacrificed for the sake of these other ends. The late William Seagle wrote,

> In other fields and aspects of human affairs history is merely fable and story. It is a record—frequently inaccurate—of the ideas, practices, and events of past generations. In the law it is part of the very methodology of the science, which is devoted to the preservation of precedents. As Robert M. MacIver has said: "The law, faced with new situations, applies ancient formulas." The continuity of legal history requires that the case which arises today shall be decided in the same way as the case of yesterday. Durability and tenacity are the most striking characteristics of the law. . . . it is a common saying that the law is always at least a generation behind the times. Indeed the law

has been declared to be the government of the living by the dead. . . . Jurists have declared upon innumerable occasions that it is better that the law be certain than that it be just. The classic reason for not doing something desirable in a particular case is that it will set a bad precedent in a future case, which may never arise.[5]

What these declarations about the purposes of law share is an understanding that the law takes the past very seriously. Looking backward in time and getting guidance from the past is one of the chief techniques the law employs to limit change, a state of affairs that could threaten the law's stabilizing function. The legal philosopher Lon Fuller, in his book *The Morality of Law,* asserted that too much change in the law "does not simply result in a bad system of law; it results in something that is not properly called a legal system at all."[6] Fuller illustrated his contention with a story about a hypothetical king, Rex, who assumed power and recognized the need for change. Rex, we are told,

came to the throne filled with the zeal of a reformer. He considered that the greatest failure of his predecessors had been in the field of law. For generations, the legal system had known nothing like a basic reform. Procedures of trial were cumbersome, the rules of law spoke in the archaic tongue of another age, justice was expensive, the judges were slovenly and sometimes corrupt. Rex was resolved to remedy all this and to make his name in history as a great lawgiver. It was his unhappy fate to fail in this ambition. Indeed, he failed spectacularly, since not only did he not succeed in introducing the needed reforms, but he never even succeeded in creating any law at all, good or bad.[7]

Among the many mistakes that the well-intentioned Rex made was to amend his legal code so frequently that planning became difficult, predicting outcomes of disputes impossible, and knowing the state of the law at any one time uncertain. Rex's law was up to date, but it could not be relied on. This degree of uncertainty led Rex's subjects to complain that "a law that changes every day is worse than no law at all."[8]

As a society, we have had almost no experience with Rex's problem. The law has not had any difficulty in the past in achieving the goal of preserving historical continuity[9] or in being a "force for predictability and regularity."[10] Indeed, one of the most frequently made complaints against legal systems throughout the ages has been that law is too rigid and inflexible and that it perpetuates the status quo. We therefore have few studies of the impact of rapid change on law.

During the past five centuries, the law has had an unrecognized ally in working toward its goal of managing the pace of change. This silent partner, which has assisted in fostering a public image of law as an institution that is both predictable and flexible, is the communications medium that has dominated the legal process for the past 500 years, the medium of print. The degree of change in society, as well as the law's ability to regulate change, is related to the media that are used to communicate information. As the new media begin to take on some of the duties performed by print, one of the consequences will be to upset the balance that the law has worked diligently to achieve over several centuries.

The medium of print is an integral component of the legal machine. As will be explained below, transmission of information via print has affected the pace of change and assisted in preventing the extremes of too much change or no change at all. The special qualities of the medium of print have at times functioned as a catalyst that has stimulated change and, at other times, performed as a built-in braking system, retarding the pace of change. Print provided the means for developing one of the fundamental building blocks of the common law, the process of precedent. Law may appear to move too slowly and awkwardly for some and too quickly for others. Yet what legal scholars have failed to understand is that attitudes toward change and expectations about change derive partly from the forms of communication that a society uses.

The development of the electronic media threatens this balancing act and may tip the scales toward a much faster pace of change. While this may be desirable from the point of view of social or economic justice, it does entail a threat to the prevailing conception of law. Since change occurring at too fast a pace has not been a problem that many societies have faced, it has also not drawn very much analysis. It has been recognized that a major function of law is to "maintain adaptability" and "redefine relations between individuals and groups as the conditions of life change."[11] Yet the implications of a major shift in communications media on the process of maintaining adaptability and redefining relations have not been explored.

Our attitude toward change and the legal system's perspective on what is an appropriate balance between stability and change is different from what existed before Gutenberg or in preliterate times. To understand the probable impact of the new media, it is necessary not only to describe the unique qualities of the new media, but also to explore how the expectations of modern societies are different from attitudes toward change in earlier societies. Law is a force that both reflects and shapes the society it is a part of. The techniques that are now used by law to manage change are not the same techniques that were used before Gutenberg provided us with a system of movable type. These techniques changed as public expectations about the nature of progress changed, and the law then used the new medium of print to fashion a system for managing change that was consistent with these new beliefs.

The Nature and Influence of Media

Why should a new system of communication accelerate the process of change? How do changes in the way information is communicated get translated into important societal changes? And which of the many qualities of a medium are most relevant to change in the process of law? The interaction between media and society is complex, and it is appropriate to begin by identifying some of the differences among media before exploring the consequences of these differences.

Four of the ways in which the electronic media differ from the traditional forms of communication are in the amount of information they can store, the speed with which they can transmit information, the ease with which information can be reproduced accurately, and the speed with which information can be revised or modified. For example, in an oral or a preliterate society, one that relies only on speech, information important to the society can be communicated among the members fairly quickly (since such societies are very small), but it is difficult to store or remember large amounts of data. Once this information is stored in living memories, it takes a great effort to accurately pass it on to others. The great cultural effort devoted to the process of storage and transmission makes it extremely difficult to objectively consider, analyze, or modify any of it.

After writing was invented, the speed of communicating important societal information actually declined. Societies became larger; copying was time consuming; and transmission of written documents was dependent on modes of transportation. Writing's great contribution was its ability to be carried over great distances. In terms of storing information, writing provides an enhanced capacity over living memory. The ability to copy, however, still remained a major problem. What was being copied was generally longer than what, in an earlier age, had to be remembered, and copying by hand almost always led to errors being present in the copy. Hand copying, therefore, actually led to less accurate copies than occurred in an oral society that relied on a variety of devices to perfect memorization and facilitate transmission via speech.[12]

With the invention of movable type, the problem of copying errors was gradually eliminated. All copies of an edition were uniform. In addition, information could be communicated more rapidly and more widely than in the age of scribes, since many copies could be distributed. Finally, the great explosion in the number of books produced led to an increase in available information and, as will be described shortly, a change in both the ability to modify stored information and the desire to do so.

The development of television and computers has further changed each of these qualities. The electronic quality of the new media permits the transmission of information at electronic speed and in a manner that is not dependent on modes of transportation. The computer can store incredible quantities of information. It can also reproduce and revise stored material more impressively than any of the traditional media. Reproducibility has become so easy that the copyright laws, designed to restrict copying, are virtually unenforceable.[13] For the computer, the ease and speed with which old information can be modified or replaced is equally astonishing and influential.

The effect of the qualities just described is not simply to increase the quantity of information available in a society. The adoption of a new system of communication does more than make us more knowledgeable or our institutions more efficient. It also leads to the creation of new relationships and, most importantly, changes our attitudes, expectations, and ways of thinking about law. If a citizen of ancient Greece or Rome, for example, were to be transported to the twentieth century, the most confusing aspect of modern law probably would not be our rules or the processes we have developed to enforce the rules. Rather, what might perplex the ancient visitor most of all would be our attitude toward law and the goals we set for it.

Ancient societies that depended only on speech had a radically different outlook on using law to achieve change. In preliterate societies, if something new were discovered and proved to be beneficial, it might be employed and adopted for continued use. Certainly such cultures, in order to survive, adapted to changes imposed on them. But, most modern scholars agree, the "idea of progress had no existence before modern times."[14] The contention in Ecclesiastes[15] that there is "nothing new under the sun" or Marcus Aurelius's similar belief that "our children will see nothing fresh, just as our fathers too never saw anything more than we,"[16] reflected the outlook of those societies not only in philosophy but also in law. In ancient societies, which depended only on speech, change was not an option. It was not simply that change or progress was considered undesirable. By trying to preserve the group as their ancestors had done and by orienting themselves toward the past, such societies precluded consideration of change and the use of law as a device to regulate change. As the anthropologist Ruth Benedict has concluded, such societies were overwhelmingly conservative and hence profoundly antiprogressive when seen through the framework of our contemporary culture.

> The growth of culture has not been as continuous and as purposeful . . . as we often imagine when we talk of progress. Our ideas of progress are themselves cultural inventions of restless modern man avid for improvements. In the modern world in one generation we adopt and learn to manipulate the automobile or the aeroplane or the telephone or the radio or the techniques of mass factory production. We do not pray: "Oh Lord, keep us as our fathers were." Even in finance or art, we invent freely, with our eyes on the future rather than on the past. We even create new religious cults by the dozen. It is easy, therefore, for us to picture human progress as if man had always reached out for a new idea or new invention and had adopted it whenever he saw it.

> History is full of examples of apparently simple discoveries that were not made even when they would have been surpassingly useful in that culture. Necessity is not necessarily the mother of invention. Men in most of Europe and Asia had adopted the wheel during the Bronze Age. It was used for chariots, as a pulley wheel for raising weights, and as a potter's wheel for making clay vessels. But in the two Americas

it was not known except as a toy in any pre-Columbian civilization. Even in Peru, where immense temples were built with blocks of stone that weighed up to a ten tons, these huge weights were excavated, transported, and placed in buildings without any use of wheels. . . . Necessity is not only not the inevitable mother of invention, it is not possible to assume that a people will adopt new inventions or accept discoveries others make.[17]

Such groups tended to orient themselves toward the past and tried to preserve the group as their ancestors had done. There were few deliberate efforts to discover new methods or processes. The merits of change were not debated or discussed the way we might do, since the culture did not recognize the need for change or the possibility of change. Anthropologist Christopher R. Hallpike notes that "we frequently find that primitives believe that their knowledge is inborn, or was created ready-made."[18] They assumed that "the body of knowledge was conceived to be as finite as the cosmic order within which it was contained. It came into the world ready made and ready to use, and could be augmented not by human intellectual experiment but only by further revelation by new or old deities."[19] In such a society, change occurred infrequently and no separate institution was required to promote, restrict, or manage change.

Change was not a priority in such cultures because the members of such groups believed that important skills and knowledge had "been established by the previous experience of generations."[20] In a study of boatmen in the Caroline Islands, for example, it was found that the fact that

all inputs of information and outputs of decision are so to speak prepackaged or predetermined, means that within the navigation system there is little room or need for innovation. Navigation requires the solution of no unprecedented problems. The navigator must be judicious and perceptive, but he is never called upon to have new ideas, to relate things together in new ways.[21]

In such societies, the "primary goal is to preserve what has been."[22]

Why was the attitude of nonliterate societies toward change so different from that of later societies? Such a cultural outlook was at least partly due to the limitations of speech, the only available means of communication in such societies. Speech discouraged

careful examination and analysis of information the group possessed and considered important. An oral society faced a great
challenge when it tried to make everyone aware of what the society
expected of them or when it endeavored to pass on the traditions
of the group from one generation to the next. These tasks required
constant effort, since they often involved matters of survival. They
left few opportunities for carefully and consciously analyzing the
current state of affairs and for planning change. Their energies
were expended more on conserving existing knowledge and preventing its loss than on building new bodies of information.

Societies dependent only on speech devoted enormous cultural
energies to remembering past events and repeating and reciting
stories about them as a means of instructing the young on how to
behave and conform to societal ideals. If something was forgotten
or if change occurred, it happened inadvertently, when the medium
of speech failed for some reason to transmit information perfectly,
and not because change was consciously desired. If change did
occur, it probably happened accidentally or was forced on the
group by some occurrence of nature, rather than because it was
planned or pursued.

Speech, since it depended on human memory, was an imperfect
medium for storing, analyzing, and revising large amounts of data.
In ancient societies, there was no process for modifying culturally
important information because the process of analysis was too
risky. It might result in the loss of this information. Preliterate
societies expended such great energies on remembering what they
believed needed to be known that they would not risk tampering
with the information or the process for passing it on.

As a result of their technique of transmitting traditions and other
basic elements of their culture, oral societies looked more to the
past than to the present or future. This overriding concern for the
past has been ingeniously analyzed by Eric Havelock in his studies
of Greece during the period when writing was introduced. Havelock was intrigued by the question of how Greek culture and tradition had been passed down from generation to generation prior
to the introduction of the written alphabet into Greece. He notes
that "a collective social memory, tenacious and reliable, is an
absolute social prerequisite for maintaining the apparatus of any
civilization. But how can the living memory retain such an elab-

orate linguistic statement without suffering it to change in transmission from man to man and from generation to generation and so to lose all fixity and authority?"[23]

Havelock's answer is that poetry, although used in a fashion that is totally different from the way poetry is employed in modern literate societies, served this function for the early Greeks. Poetry in an oral society was a means of public education and had a moral purpose rather than an aesthetic one. "The poet," he writes, "is a source on the one hand of essential information and on the other of essential moral training."[24] The epic stories of ancient Greece were memorized and performed those

> functions which we relegate on the one hand to religious instruction or moral training and on the other to classroom texts, to histories and handbooks, to encyclopedias and reference manuals. This is a way of looking at poetry which in effect refuses to discuss it as poetry in our sense at all. It refuses to allow that it may be an art with its own rules rather than a course of information and a system of indoctrination.[25]

Remembering the epics of Homer, which were the key sources of cultural values, required using rhythm, syntax, and sound as aids in remembering the actual words. It was not possible to add new lines or information because the whole pattern of recitation would be disrupted and everything might be forgotten. Changing one item could make remembering the whole much more difficult. Since memorization was the main technique of preserving the culture, alteration would not be risked. Havelock suggests that we consider the features of a modern nursery rhyme in order to understand how so much could be preserved orally and why the method of transmission was resistant to change.

> Take as an example "Sing a song of sixpence, a pocket full of rye." The verses of this familiar ditty illustrate both the primary and secondary levels of storage language, that of linguistic propriety and also that of rhythmic determination. Linguistic propriety forbids that the queen rather than the maid should be the person hanging out the clothes, though the rhythm would permit this. It forbids that the blackbirds be baked in a sty rather than in a pie or in any receptacle not designed for cooking. It requires that a dish set before a king be dainty or accompanied by an adjective of equivalent approval. But rhythm, together with rhyme, alliteration, assonance, themselves all varieties of rhythm, alone guarantees that the song be of "sixpence" rather than

"tenpence"; that "rye" be present to rhyme with the "pie," that the baked objects are blackbirds, that the sequence in the narrative descends from king to queen to maid, that the queen eats "honey" rather than caviar, and so forth.[26]

The limitations of speech as a vehicle for storing large quantities of data encouraged great cultural efforts to maintain traditions and links to the past. The Greek epics provided not merely stories or entertainment, but also models of appropriate behavior and a means for maintaining social order. In the period before writing, Greek culture, like other oral societies, emphasized continuity with tradition and preservation more than change. If attention was not focused on remembering the past, the culture would not be able to maintain itself. After all, the past had been proved to be workable and tinkering with it involved great risk.

Where was the law in such a society, and what was its function? It did not have to regulate the process of change, as it must do in our society, because change was minimal. It did not have to decide whether some new law was required because legislation was rarely practiced in such societies. There were no cries "there ought to be a law" because that was not the way the society dealt with its problems.

In such societies, it was not necessary for law to fulfill the stabilizing function we expect of it. Because change was minimal, the need for law was not great and an unsophisticated system of law or even a culture relying primarily on custom was possible. It was not that such societies were harmonious and without conflict. Rather, they had effective nonlegal methods of enforcing standards of behavior and of dealing with deviant behavior.[27] They were more effective than we are at preventing deviance. Conflict was not perceived as providing anything positive for the group, and concern with the past and the pressure of the group to conform to traditional values ensured a preference for continuity rather than for change.

Writing

In preliterate societies, every adult member "was the Text—a Walking Book."[28] With the advent of writing, these ambulatory tomes now needed to deal consciously with issues of societal change. Writing created something that was tangible and could be modified. Writing, according to anthropologists Jack Goody and Ian Watt, "brought about an awareness of two things: of the past as different from the present; and of the inherent inconsistencies in the picture of life as it was inherited by the individual from the cultural tradition in its recorded form."[29] Change became more possible with literacy. For the first time, we find codes of law that specifically prohibit making additions or changes, a sure sign that there had been efforts to do just that.[30]

Writing fostered thinking about change but generally did not create societies in which much change occurred. Although writing could be revised in ways that were not possible in oral traditions, it created several barriers that hindered the development of a process of easy modification. Literacy, for example, was a skill that relatively few people possessed prior to the invention of printing.[31] As we shall see in Chapter 3, writing was a tool for acquiring power; hence societies reliant on writing tended to be hierarchical and inegalitarian. Change was resisted, therefore, not because it would affect the whole culture or group, as in an oral society, but because it threatened the few who had managed to acquire power.

Writing made change possible but also unlikely. The skill needed to change important cultural documents was in the hands of the few, and important information was often "etched in stone," a substance that resisted easy change. In societies that had only writing, there were few basic documents and these were meant to last. Hammurabi's Code, the Ten Commandments, and the Roman Twelve Tables may reflect different time periods, cultures, and values, but all were written on stone. In each case, the medium communicated the same message—that change was not desirable.

By using stone as the medium for the fundamental laws of their society, the ancient Babylonians, Hebrews, and Romans emphasized values that are characteristic of almost all legal systems that rely on writing. Such societies are resistant to change. Change can occur only by shattering the stone and substituting something new in its place, not by revising and amending it. When it occurs, change in such societies is total and complete, not partial. Revolution, not evolution, is characteristic of such societies.[32]

When a less permanent substance was used, a process of limited change did creep into documents. But the process of change in these documents and in the practices of the society was more often than not inadvertent and unintentional. Writing engendered an attitude opposed to change and supportive of the status quo. This attitude is traceable to the inability of scribes to make perfect copies of books and other important information. When books and other documents were preserved by copying, and any substance other than stone was used, it was impossible to preserve an accurate record of the past. Copying books or documents inevitably led to errors. Making multiple copies meant that the final copy would be different from the original. The kind of distortion that today creeps in during the oral transmission of a rumor or gossip, so that what the last person hears may be the opposite of what the first person actually said, is similar to what happened to written material during the age of scribes.

The problems associated with copying and the unreliability and untrustworthiness of written documents generated a cultural attitude that discouraged change. Old versions of a work were preferred over recent ones because the old ones were necessarily more authentic.[33] New versions would be less valuable, since some corruption would inevitably have occurred over time. Oral proof in courts was typically considered more valid than written proof because the latter was untrustworthy and could easily have been forged.[34] Discovery of an ancient version of a valued document was a landmark event prior to the invention of printing not only because of historical curiosity about the past, but also because such a work would contribute to knowledge and would correct errors.[35] In such a milieu, comments on an ancient written work might be appreciated or respected more than a revision or an improvement on the work. Interpretation of an ancient text was a valid activity, but discarding the text in favor of a new one was not.[36]

This approach to words on paper reflects a way of thinking that is perhaps unfamiliar and difficult for us to comprehend. Margaret Aston, in her study of the fifteenth century, observed that

> men of learning in the Middle Ages were not accustomed to the idea that knowledge could be outdated. To their thinking the older the fact the better the fact and, with their great respect for the weight of authority, facts and opinions were not clearly differentiated. It was not only that new ideas and discoveries took time to be known, but there

is also a sense in which new ideas demand new minds to receive them. There was greater possibility of change during the age of scribes than in pre-literate Greece, but concern for the past, preferably the ancient past, made this unlikely.[37]

Another writer has noted,

> Untenable and long refuted theories were revived time after time, to be refuted and rejected once again; in general this tended to foster a mental attitude which looked to the past rather than to the future and which, on grounds that scientific truths had all been known in the past and that the only problem was to rediscover them, led investigators in precisely the wrong direction.[38]

While such attitudes toward the past are largely foreign to us, they are not completely absent in the contemporary world. It is possible today to observe such habits of thought and their influence on change in areas where special reverence for the past is called for, such as in traditional religious life. A recent book, for example, explains the attitude of Orthodox Jews toward sacred writings.[39] This book focuses on the vast amount of literature developed over a 3,000-year period, including the Bible, the Talmud, legal codes, philosophical and mystical writings, prayers, and commentaries. Yet in approaching texts, the point of reference is always the oldest work, the Bible, and the principal purpose is to discover its true meaning. "To understand the consciousness of the traditional texts in this regard," the author notes, "we must never forget the great sanctity with which they endowed the Torah itself. Torah . . . is more than just another book. The traditional writers saw Torah as God's very word and because of that, it itself is eternally 'original.' The commentators do not invent anything new; they discover what the Divine Author had always intended."[40] This attitude has been summarized by philosopher Gershom Scholem:

> Truth is given once and for all, and it is laid down with precision. Fundamentally, truth merely needs to be transmitted. The originality of the exploring scholar has two aspects. In his spontaneity, he develops and explains that which was transmitted at Sinai, no matter whether it was always known or whether it was forgotten and had to be redis- covered. The effort of the seeker after truth consists not in having new ideas but rather in subordinating himself to the community of the tradition. . . . Not system but commentary is the legitimate form through which truth is approached.[41]

To persons who accept such limits on the use of information, it is natural that the thoughts of a person living 2,000 years ago are to be considered more valid than those of someone living today. Such a person is considered more authoritative than any contemporary individual, no matter how wise or knowledgeable the person living today might be. The following description of the process of religious study reminds us that there is a connection between a society's attitude toward change and its habits of thought. Study of ancient religious texts takes place

> in a loud hectic hall called the bet midrash (study house) where students sit in pairs or threesomes, reading and discussing out loud, back and forth. The atmosphere is nothing like the silent library we are accustomed to. Reading in the yeshiva is conducted in a room with a constant incessant din; it is as much talk as it is reading; in fact the two activities of reading and discussion are virtually indistinguishable. . . . Through the study discussions, Jews actually replicate the world of the Talmud. It is as if distinctions of time and place are erased, and the participant is catapulted back to Rabbi Akiba's academy 1,800 years in the past. The learner joins in the discussions, voices his opinion, is defended or refuted by the legendary teachers and students of other ages and takes his place in the continuum of the tradition.[42]

This attitude toward ancient authority and the process of study would be readily understandable to medieval legal scholars and students, for they thought and studied in a comparable way. In his comprehensive recent historical study of Western law, *Law and Revolution,*[43] Professor Harold Berman traces the origin of modern law back to the finding of an ancient manuscript in Italy at the end of the eleventh century. This manuscript was a long-lost copy of legal materials compiled by the Emperor Justinian almost 500 years earlier. Again, it is not easy to identify with the attitude of the people who studied and revered this work. Berman notes,

> The law that was first taught and studied systematically in the West was not the prevailing law. . . . Roman law as such, that is, as a system, had a very limited validity in Western Europe when Justinian's work was discovered in Italy. The texts had disappeared. The terms had acquired new meanings. There were no Western counterparts to the Roman magistrates (praetors), legal advisors (jurists), or advocates (orators). The prevailing legal institutions were largely Germanic and Frankish. Thus it was the body of law, the legal system, of an earlier

civilization, as recorded in a huge book or set of books, that formed the object of Europe's first systematic legal studies.

It was of critical importance that the jurists who studied these ancient texts believed, as did their counterparts generally, that that earlier civilization, the Roman Empire, had survived until their time, in the West as well as in the East. . . . They took Justinian's law not primarily as the law applicable in Byzantium in 534 A.D., but as the law applicable at all times and in all places. They took it, in other words, as truth—the way they took the Bible as truth and the works of Plato and (later) Aristotle. Although, for example, what was written in Justinian's compilation about ownership of land had nothing to do with the regulation of feudal property rights prevailing in 1100 in Tuscany or Normandy, this did not mean that it was not "the Law." . . . The discovery in about 1080 of a copy of Justinian's compilation was received in the same spirit as that in which the discovery of a long-lost supplement to the Old Testament might have been received.[44]

The fact that this manuscript was perceived to be useful, even though it was 500 years old, is traceable to the way writing was perceived before the development of print. Justinian's Code quickly became the centerpiece of legal study and did lead to change. But this happened only because of an accidental discovery of a full-blown work. The general medieval approach to written works would have prevented a contemporarily written work from being the basis of change and having the impact that this ancient work had. Neither writing nor law was future oriented or change oriented. As law professor John Dawson has noted in connection with Roman jurists, "their assumptions were fixed, the main purposes of the social and political order were not to be called into question, the system of legal ideas was too well known to require much discussion. They were problem solvers, working within this system and not called upon to solve the ultimate problems of mankind's needs and destiny."[45] Thus "when the society and the law are relatively static, litigation and adjudication can consist for the most part of a repeated 'unpacking' of the same concepts in response to stereotyped conflicts, and this can be done quite covertly, much as experienced bridge or poker players can play for hours without ever mentioning a rule."[46] Similarly, the English legal historian J. H. Baker has suggested that the transformation in the role of the judge in the late medieval period might be clarified by comparing the medieval judge to a referee in a football game:

There is no great body of referee-jurisprudence continually refining the laws of the game, perhaps because teams are not represented on the field by counsel, but more likely because the ethics of the sport demand clear rules which the layman can grasp and which cannot be easily bent. . . . The medieval attitude toward litigation was not dissimilar. The parties were the contestants, and so long as they adhered strictly to the rules—which everyone knew—they were left to play the game unimpeded. No one looked to litigation as a means of creating or refining legal rules, any more than one watches chess matches in the hope that new or more sophisticated rules of chess will emerge. The law of the land, like the laws of chess, was there to begin with.[47]

Printing

As the scribal age was drawing to a close, Chaucer described in the general prologue of his *Canterbury Tales* (ca. 1387) a legal throwback to the age when many persons were walking books. Chaucer's "Sergeant of the Lawe, war and wys [wary and wise]," is no ordinary lawyer, but a high court officer appointed by the king, one who "knew in precise terms every case and judgement since King William the Conqueror, and every statue fully, word for word."[48] Less than a century later, when the age of printing began, a revolutionary change in attitudes concerning the past and present and the value and meaning of words on paper also began. Printing "replaced precarious forms of tradition (oral and manuscript) by one that was stable, secure and lasting; it is as if mankind had suddenly obtained a trustworthy memory instead of one that was fickle and deceitful."[49] Because of printing, the "sequence of corrupted copies was replaced by a sequence of improved editions,"[50] and "the immemorial drift of scribal culture [was] not merely arrested but actually reversed."[51]

Printing effectively brought about a complete shift in the ability to preserve the past and in the attitude toward revised copies of an older work. As a result, "it produced fundamental alterations in prevailing patterns of continuity and change."[52] As indicated above, in "scribal culture" the oldest version of a document was considered to be the most perfect. After print, the most recent version was most appreciated and considered most valuable. In the manuscript era, it was impossible to be certain what the original author had written because "every copy was unique, with its own variations."[53] The more a book was copied, the less authentic it became.[54]

How did printing, which was often on poor quality paper, preserve the past so much more effectively? The answer lies in its ability to reproduce a large number of uniform copies. Thomas Jefferson once wrote,

> Very early into my researches into the laws of Virginia I observed that many of them were already lost, and many more on the point of being lost, as existing only in single copies in the hands of careful or curious individuals, on whose death they would probably be used for waste paper.... How many of the precious works of antiquity were lost while they existed only in manuscript? Has there ever been one lost since the art of printing has rendered it practicable to multiply and disperse copies? This leads us then to the only means of preserving those remains of our laws now under consideration, that is, a multiplication of printed copies.[55]

Printing, unlike writing, allowed a society to build on the past with a confidence that each step was being made on a firm foundation. Printing generated confidence that new information was an improvement over the old. The revolution in the ability to accurately reproduce works fostered an understanding that progress can occur through a process of revision and improvement. As David Hume is reported to have written to his publisher, the "Power which Printing gives us, of continually improving and correcting our Works in successive Editions, appears to me the chief Advantage of that Art."[56]

In her authoritative study of the influence of printing, Elizabeth Eisenstein attributes the increase in new scientific theories during the sixteenth and seventeenth centuries to a willingness on the part of printers to revise old works and include new data. She describes how a sixteenth-century encyclopedia, Sebastian Munster's *Cosmography*,

> which was first published in 1544, went through eight editions in its author's lifetime and thirty-five more down to 1628. As each edition became bigger, more crammed with data, and more profusely illustrated, each was also provided with more tables, charts, indexes which made it possible for readers to retrieve the growing body of information that was being stored in the work. Editors worked conscientiously to

keep each edition updated and to provide more thorough coverage for regions that had received short shrift in earlier versions. . . . This rapid accumulation of data, it should be noted, was itself spurred from the workshops of master printers who issued reference works of various kinds. Sixteenth-century editors and publishers, who served the Commonwealth of Learning, did not merely store data passively in compendia. They created vast networks of correspondents, solicited criticism of each edition, sometimes promising publicly to mention the names of readers who sent in new information or who spotted the errors which would be weeded out. . . . The requests of publishers often encouraged readers to launch their own research projects and field trips which resulted in additional publication programs. Thus a knowledge explosion was set off.[57]

While Eisenstein provides substantial data on how change occurred in the worlds of science and religion, she touches only briefly on the impact of printing on law. Its influence, however, was enormous. As social and political change accelerated, a secular legal process gradually became a recognized instrument for managing change. In England and later in this country, the technology of print also supplied one of the means through which the law has worked to balance stability and change. This method is the modern concept of precedent, one of the cornerstones of our system of law. As one author has recognized, "English justice, if it were not to remain fluid and unstable, required a strong cement. This was found in the common-law doctrine of precedent with its essential and peculiar emphasis on rigidity and certainty."[58]

The most unfortunate omission in discussions of precedent is the lack of attention paid to the fact that the judicial decision has been a printed report for the past 450 years. This corresponds roughly to the era of the modern form of precedent. The law's attitude toward the use of prior judicial decisions has changed over time, and the way in which law today looks at prior cases would be unintelligible to a judge who lived before Gutenberg.

Precedent is generally understood to mean that earlier decisions of courts should control later decisions.[59] If it were taken to mean simply that some continuity or consistency with past decisions should be encouraged, all societies would qualify as having a form of precedent and the replacement of writing by print or print by computers as the method for storing the decisions of the past would be unimportant. Precedent, however, as our legal system understands it and uses it, means that the *printed* decisions of judges carry weight. We assume that the printed case report *is* the decision and give the printed words written by the judge supreme authority. If the reality of the decision-making process is different from what is reported in the printed opinion, or if the judge has personal knowledge of the prior case, the printed opinion still has authority. Lawyers are trained not even to think of the reality of the case and, therefore, to pay attention to only the printed version of what occurred. As a result, over time, it has been forgotten that the printed opinion is only a representation of reality.

It is only in modern times that those involved in the legal system began thinking in this way. For legal systems in the pre-print age, the relevant reality and the relevant authority were something different. Oral societies and societies that used writing desired consistency, but decisions in cases never became binding on later judges. To attribute greater significance to a later decision than an earlier one would have required an attitude toward the written word that was the opposite of the way writing was generally perceived before Gutenberg. After printing, "a book was sensed as a kind of object which 'contained' information, scientific, fictional or other, rather than, as earlier, a recorded utterance."[60] In addition, as explained earlier, scribal culture attributed greater authenticity and authority to older works than to newer works. Ancient works were revered, while recent editions of the same work were considered to be corrupted versions. One could not, therefore, expect a legal system to rely on a written copy of a report of a case. Each old case, after all, would be based on an even earlier work, and each would be assumed to be based on a record in which errors would be present due to the process of copying.

Scholars have frequently noted that in England in the centuries before Gutenberg, written case reports were considered in later cases.[61] What was controlling, however, was not the written ruling but the judge's knowledge of what English custom required. As historian T. F. T. Plucknett has written, "In the Year Book period cases are used only as evidence of the existence of a custom of the court. It is the custom which governs the decision, not the case or cases cited as proof of the custom."[62] One judge in the fourteenth century noted, "We will not and we cannot change the ancient usage."[63] While this may seem peculiar to modern minds, it can probably be explained by the fact that in those days what was passed on orally or was common knowledge among judges was considered more reliable information than what had been written about the case. In general, written records were distrusted, since they might be forgeries or contain errors.[64] An oral report of something someone had firsthand knowledge of or a judge's recollection of a case he had been involved in would carry more weight than anything written about the case. It is not surprising, therefore, that instead of using custom to assist in interpreting law, as sometimes happens today, the opposite occurred. The decisions of medieval courts were viewed by judges as "merely adding to the body of customary rules in force."[65]

The beginning of the idea of using written case reports to guide future decisions is attributed to Bracton, a judge in England in the late twelfth century. Bracton wrote that "if any new and unwonted circumstances . . . shall arise, then if anything analogous has happened before, let the case be adjudged in like manner."[66] It is clear, however, that Bracton did not intend prior cases to be controlling on later cases and that he was "not actuated by any of the modern ideas of case law."[67] Rather, he was pointing out the advisability of taking prior decisions into account.[68] They were an indication of what the law was but were not to be considered to be *the* law or to be cited in court.[69] They were to guide judges but not to shackle their discretion. British legal scholar C. K. Allen notes that in this period, "to speak of a system of precedent . . . would be an anachronism."[70] Until the sixteenth and seventeenth centuries, "precedents were useful in showing what the law was; they were not binding in any sense."[71]

The form of the report or record of a case is influential, and the way in which court records were kept in Bracton's day would have made any general use of them impossible, even if anyone had wished to do so. The earliest written reports of cases, called *plea rolls,* are sketchy notes about a case recorded by the clerk. They were filed away and generally were inaccessible to the public.[72] Bracton "alone of all the lawyers in England sought and obtained access to the plea rolls; there were no copies until he made one for his own convenience. . . . Any use of cases along Bracton's lines by the profession at large, or even by the bench alone, would have been manifestly impossible."[73] Indeed, Bracton himself had great difficulty getting access to them and was ordered to return them before he had completed his work.[74] With such an information system, "there is no possibility of any system of case law developing when the cases are inaccessible to the profession."[75] As anthropologist Lloyd Fallers has observed, "The use of writing serves to improve record-keeping with respect to 'facts,' but it does not . . . increase the explicitness of communication with and about legal concepts."[76]

In the mid-thirteenth century began a new system of reports about cases, the *year books*.[77] These were publicly available but could not be expected to create the kind of faith in the written record that is necessary for a system of precedent. These are reports about cases, not the written opinions of judges. They resembled professional newspapers and contained gossip and anecdotes about the parties as well as information about legal issues and the style of arguments.[78] Reliance on them was a problem because "there were frequently found to be two, three, four or even more versions of one case, so different that collation was impossible."[79] When a lawyer in one recorded dispute happened to cite a case, the judge is reported to have replied that he had four other written reports of the same case which stated that the opposite result had been reached.[80] Even when another version of a cited case was not known to the parties, there was the possibility that one existed. In such conditions, a judge was

> not going to be told what the law was by the citation of this or that case from a manuscript, nor that it was their professional duty to accept such a case or to show some good reason for departing from it. How could it be otherwise? The Year-Book manuscripts differed from one another again and again. "Every citation would begin a new dispute." Bench and bar must rely on their own memories for earlier cases, and the Year-Books themselves show us case after case in which no one in court utters a word about any previous precedent.[81]

Historian A. W. B. Simpson concluded that "unlike modern law reports, year books were not of much value as authorities, nor were they conceived of as such. . . . The fifteenth-century common law lacked both the modern concept of 'authority' and . . . the notion of binding precedent."[82]

Printing was introduced into England in 1476.[83] Five years later, the first law books were printed, and in 1485 the printing of parliamentary session laws began. The year-book period ended in 1535. Toward the end of the year-book period, which coincided with these early years of printing, reports of cases became more formal and uniform, with fewer different versions of the debates between the parties. In 1537, the first printed reports appeared.

The printing of reports led to a clear change in the legal authority of a report of a judge's ruling. The first printed reports contain growing numbers of references to prior cases.[84] By the end of the sixteenth century,

> reporting had still a long hill to climb, before it became the scientific affair it now is. But the lawyers, with the Year-Book Abridgments on the one hand and the numerous collateral reports on the other, had a string of easily accessible authorities. . . . "I have seen," "I remember," "This has already been adjudged"—all such vague phrases tend to disappear. There is no need to trust any longer to the accident of an accident, and to hope that by chance the judge who is trying the case also tried the case cited, and that by chance he will recollect it.[85]

By the eighteenth century, the printed word had acquired sufficient reliability that "each single decision standing by itself had already become an authority which no succeeding judge was at liberty to disregard."[86] In 1765, Lord Campbell stated, "If it is law, it will be found in our books. If it is not to be found there, it is not law."[87] In his famous *Commentaries on the Laws of England,* published in 1776, Sir William Blackstone asserted, "The doctrine of law then is this: that precedents and rule must be followed, unless flatly absurd or unjust: for though their reason be not obvious at first view, yet we owe such a deference to former times as not to suppose they acted wholly without consideration."[88] By 1794, Edmund Burke could validly assert that "to put an end to the Reports is to put an end to the law of England."[89]

Electronic Media

The printing of reports in 1537 began an evolutionary process that has culminated in the form of the modern case report and the modern attitude toward precedent. What needs to be understood is that the form of legal information has been a substantial influence on the authority that our legal system ascribes to precedent. Through its effect on the concept of precedent, print has contributed to public expectations that law can be used to achieve progress and that revolutionary change is unnecessary and inappropriate. It has fostered a belief in both the desirability of change and, at the same time, a "myth of certainty."[90]

Due to the use of computers, various aspects of the information available to the profession and to the public can be expected to change. It is extremely unwise to pretend that the stability of law and the authority of prior decisions will remain constant under such conditions. This change in communication has already accelerated the pace of change in society. For law, such a shift in communication is likely to increase public demands for resolving pressing current problems and to diminish public desire for law to maintain the kinds of links to the past that it has developed in recent centuries. The tensions that are accompanying change in society at large, in other words, can be expected to lead to similar pressures on the process of law.

The rapid process of change that is evident in almost every facet of modern life is a result of some of the special qualities of the new forms of communication. For example, the speed of the electronic media permits new information to be disseminated more quickly than ever before. This new knowledge can be taken into account by persons working on similar problems. Bottlenecks and delays that were previously caused by the slow movement of information or by a lack of communication are being eliminated. Data can be manipulated more quickly than in the past, and solutions to problems are publicized more rapidly. New products appear on the market more rapidly, partly because the process of publicizing discoveries is accelerated.

One of the consequences of speeding up the distribution of information is that we tend to be more interested in the present and the future than in the past. New information is constantly replacing old information, and old information appears to be less and less relevant to the solution of modern problems. Because of their focus on the present, the new media tend to neglect the past. Critics of television are correct in feeling that attention to history is interfered with by broadcast programming and television viewing. But it is not simply the viewing of nonintellectual programs that is at fault. If the only programs watched were the news, the effect would probably be the same. What is on the news today becomes of greater concern than what appeared yesterday. What is on the news next week makes today's issues seem like "ancient history." The concept of "news" implies a continuous replacement of the "olds." Modern journalism assumes a continuous updating,[91] modifying of information, and shifting of emphasis. The underlying message is one of impermanence, and old information becomes as disposable as old goods. We are familiar with new products that are designed to be disposable and to have a short existence. It is not often recognized that the same process of accelerated obsolescence is in operation with information, ideas, and institutions.

"In an environment of rapid information flow," Quentin Fiore has written, "ideas and institutions rapidly become obsolete."[92] Such a pace of rapid change tends to bring with it conflict and instability. Conflict results from the creation of new products and the establishment of new relationships and patterns of behavior that interfere in some way with what has been traditional. The problems that the new media are posing to the law's ability to resolve disputes will be discussed in Chapter 2. In terms of dealing with instability, rapid change creates challenges for a system that is oriented toward an orderly and moderate pace. Our law is designed to prevent too much change, what might be considered revolution, and too little change, which merely maintains the status quo. In liberal societies, law is designed to be a force of moderation, working to ensure that change is neither too fast nor too slow. The phrase "with all deliberate speed," which the Supreme Court used in 1954 when it found school segregation unconstitutional,[93] is a pace of change that the law, as well as the particular justices in that case, is comfortable with.

When society and the public have accepted an accelerated pace of change, is it possible for the law to maintain its old ways? If it is not capable of retarding change, or if more rapid change is desired by the public, will old mechanisms be discarded and will new ones be developed? An examination of the impact of the new media on the concept of precedent suggests that what has been developed over the past few centuries will need reworking and refashioning and that the end result will be a system of law that is more accepting of change and more accepting of instability and uncertainty within the legal process. It will be more up to date but less of a force for preserving continuity with the past.

We have seen that precedent is a device that has had different meanings in different eras and that legal systems have had different orientations to change in different historical periods. These perspectives have corresponded to characteristics in the system of communication used in a society. Law in the pre-print era had no pressing need for a doctrine of precedent, since societal change was not a significant problem at the time. Judges did not have to follow and interpret written case reports because their personal knowledge of prior cases was respected as much as any written document.[94] The legislative process also was not often needed or used to deal with changed circumstances. "The desire for continuous legislation," Maitland wrote, "is modern. We have come to think that year by year, Parliament must meet and pour out statutes. . . . It was otherwise in the Middle Ages."[95]

The history of court reporting has proceeded from notes about the proceedings (plea rolls) to summaries of the discussions in court (year books) to more complete transcripts of proceedings (early reporters) to printing judges' opinions (modern reporters). These opinions of judges contain the purported reasons for the judges' ruling in a case. Large sections of libraries are set aside for the thousands of volumes of these case reporters. When precedent is desired for some legal point, this is where lawyers look for it.

Precedent is a device that the legal process has developed to accommodate legal change to the pace of change in society. If law is to become more tolerant of change, the role of precedent will necessarily continue to evolve. It will not disappear as a concept, but it will not be the same concept that judges and lawyers have been accustomed to. This will not occur by a vote of any judicial body, and it may even be denied that a significant change is taking place. Yet the forces leading to such an important change can be seen at work today. The bottlenecks in the legal informational system[96] that have tended to act as a brake on the process of change are becoming more and more vulnerable.

During the past fifteen years, two computerized legal research systems have developed. LEXIS, owned by the Mead Data Corporation, and WESTLAW, operated by the West Publishing Company, allow access to case materials previously available only in printed form in libraries. Before considering what this means for the concept of precedent and for the perpetuation of the "myth of certainty," it is important to understand how different a computerized case-retrieval system is from the printed system. These differences can be summarized as follows:

1. Computerized systems, unlike print systems, have virtually unlimited storage capacity. They arrived on the scene when the growth of printed reporters threatened to become unmanageable for libraries.[97] The increase in cases and volumes posed serious logistical and financial problems.

2. Computerized systems allow the distribution of court opinions within hours or days rather than months. Potentially, they allow access from any computer terminal no matter where it is located.

3. Computerized systems have searching capabilities that are not present in print-based systems. Finding relevant cases in a library required some knowledge of legal concepts and a generally time-consuming trial-and-error process. Finding cases through LEXIS or WESTLAW can be done by thinking of a relevant word, phrase, or list of words. Legal research can also be done much more quickly using a computerized system.

4. Computerized systems are expanding the amount of legal information available to researchers. Case reporters, in order to be made accessible and usable, were divided into state, regional, and other categories. Lawyers limited their search for cases by the reporters they decided to use. Computerized systems do not contain these barriers to conducting a search. Print has also not dealt very efficiently with statutory or regulatory material, which is more difficult both to locate and to retrieve. Different research skills are needed to use these materials. These areas, in which precedent is not as important a consideration, are increasingly important areas of law, and the computer promises to make them as accessible as judicial decisions. They will be as easy to gain access to as court decisions are, since the skills needed to gain access will be similar.

5. Computerized systems are expanding the amount of nonlegal material available to lawyers. The computerized law library is very different in content from the print law collection. Although LEXIS and WESTLAW began by storing cases, they have greatly broadened the information accessible from their terminals. In addition

to legal material, for example, LEXIS allows access to NEXIS, a full text library of general and business publications, to MEDIS, a full text service of medical publications, and to bibliographic indexes and abstracts in more than a hundred subject areas. It is as though a variety of nonlaw libraries have been moved into the law library, a place that in the recent print era has always been physically separated from general-purpose libraries. This new form of library not only is growing larger, as electronic interconnections are established among different systems,[98] but also is less distinctively legal and less oriented to habits of thought and practice fostered by print.

The almost unlimited capacity of computers to store, communicate, and search for information poses an enormous threat to the authority of precedent, yet it is a completely unrecognized threat. The replacement of print by computerized systems is promoted to the legal profession simply as a means to increase efficiency. The substitution of one system for another, however, also creates pressures for change that will touch fundamental building blocks of law. Precedent and the concern of the law for retarding rapid change can be expected to be affected for several reasons.

1. A system of precedent is unnecessary when there are very few cases that are accessible; it will be unworkable when there are too many cases. "One of the main conditions for the success of the system of case law," observed the eminent British legal historian William Holdsworth, is a limit on the number of case reports.[99] Similarly, an American legal scholar has written that "when the number of printed cases becomes like the number of grains of sand on the beach, a precedent-based case-law system does not work and cannot be made to work. . . . The theory of precedent depends, for its ideal operation, on the existence of a comfortable number of precedents, but not too many."[100] In the past, the nature of printing technology imposed some limitation on how many cases could be printed and how quickly they would be published. Local libraries contained only local cases since cases from other jurisdictions were not considered to be as significant as local ones. Until the late nineteenth century, collections of cases were manageable even though they lacked efficient indexing systems for locating cases on common topics.

Concern arose in the late nineteenth century because the

number of volumes of American case reports had increased from 18 in 1810 to 473 in 1836 to 3,800 in 1885. As a result, "there was a feeling that the multiplication of law reports would one day destroy the law as it was known."[101] One commentator in 1882 wrote that

> the ratio of increase in the published volumes is constantly accelerating. . . . That the number of courts whose opinions are being reported and the number of judges writing opinions are constantly increasing, is beyond doubt. . . . And yet . . . the system of law reporting may be said to be in its infancy. . . . Unless some means shall speedily be devised of checking this appalling number of publications, it is within the bounds of moderation to assert that lawyers now in practice at the bar may live to see the number of volumes . . . exceed twenty thousand.[102]

The solution to the increase in cases in the late nineteenth century was the system of digests developed by the West Publishing Company, which is still the backbone of the case-reporter system. It made the increases in cases manageable for lawyers. It organized the law into subject areas, and a "key number" system divided the law into categories and gave every point of law within an area a number. The result was not only a practical system, but one that probably also subtly shaped the attitudes of generations of lawyers and law students about the degree of order that existed in the legal system.

Computerized legal research systems appeared when the digest system seemed to be reaching its limits. The same arguments about the difficulty of conducting legal research that were raised at the end of the nineteenth century could be raised about doing research using the printed digest system. The computer, with its miraculous searching capabilities, has allowed the system to avoid a public breakdown as a result of overload.[103] The cases being stored in LEXIS and WESTLAW at a faster and faster rate are easily and quickly retrievable.

The main threat to precedent today is that the lawyer who is searching for relevant cases now has more and more cases to choose from and can obtain such cases more and more quickly. The effect of this is to change the nature of legal argument and to diminish the authority of prior cases. Such a system, Holdsworth reminds us, will not work so satisfactorily if the number of courts, whose decisions are reported, are multiplied. The law is likely to be burdened with so great a mass of decisions of different degrees of excellence that its principles, so far from being made more certain by the decisions of new cases, will become sufficiently uncertain to afford abundant material for the infinite disputations of professors of general jurisprudence. A limitation is needed in the number of reported cases. . . . English lawyers have hardly realized that it was a condition precedent for the satisfactory working of our system of case law.[104]

The multiplicity of cases now available and easily accessible gives lawyers greater opportunities to find "helpful" precedents.[105] There are more cases available to use as building blocks for an interpretation of the law that is desirable for the client. The legal historian Samuel Thorne, in discussing the tendency of one of the English court reporters of the sixteenth century to sometimes report a long list of cited cases, suggested that "the longer the list of authorities reconciled, the greater the divergence from the cases cited."[106] The more building blocks that are accessible, the greater the flexibility in the creation of a legal argument and the more tenuous the link to any one prior case.[107] In future litigation, there will be more and more decisions cited on both sides of an issue, providing even more opportunity than there currently is for every party to a case to construct a legal argument supported by a host of cases.

2. The authority of case law is promoted by a process that does not rapidly modify reported decisions. "Landmark" decisions not only settle a particular point of law, but add to the general authority of judicial decisions because they seem to settle a problem with some finality. Today, opinions are being added to the computerized database more and more quickly. This increases the pressure to use recent cases and to continually modify and add to arguments in pending cases. Such a trend is a natural response to pressure to be less behind the times and to make use of the increased accessibility to cases. It will also lead to a perception of the judicial process as a system in which questions are not settled finally but are continually raised for reconsideration.

This is not an inaccurate image of the law even today. Legal decisions are an end point only for the parties actually involved in the case. For the rest of the public, every decision is a stopping point in a travel that includes the present case and future cases. It is a journey that never ends. A British jurist has observed that

a decision of even a final court, when pronounced, has only begun its life as a full constituent of the full corpus of the law. It is a mistake, just because it is final, to think that the matter is then closed. On the contrary, it has been handed over to the care of the profession. It will be chewed over by barristers and solicitors, commented on in the law journals, made the subject of moots and law lectures, reviewed by the writers of the legal textbooks. It will be read in the light of previous decisions, upon which it is itself a commentary: and it will be read in the light of later decisions, to which itself it forms a text.[108]

As a result of this process, "there is an uncertainty principle at work in the judicial process: any attempt to achieve certainty regarding any important constitutional issue is unlikely to succeed and—even if does succeed in the short run—will inevitably create uncertainty as to more issues than it settles."[109] We perceive decisions as end points because it is convenient to do so and gives them authority they might not otherwise have. The process moves sufficiently slowly so that the fiction can survive. Yet we should not assume that how we perceive decisions is inevitable. Rather, as the expression "it is a closed book" suggests, public perception of this quality of law is a culturally based phenomenon that is partly related to print. The application of computer technology to this process threatens to change the image, just as animation techniques in film can transform a set of discrete and fixed images into a cartoon with figures that appear to move.

3. Many of the goals of law have been achieved by limiting the use of some kinds of information.[110] In the application of precedent, for example, consistency has been fostered by severely limiting the use of nonappellate case material. The traditional law library has been an accomplice in this task by making appellate cases the heart of the law collection. Nonlegal materials are effectively excluded from use in law school by separating law school libraries from general university libraries. Within law libraries, case reporters are typically given easiest access.

Computerized research facilities, unlike print libraries, facilitate access to nonlegal sources. They threaten to undermine the categorization of information that lies at the core of the precedent process. Broadening the reach of the legal researcher involves more than a change in research techniques. It creates competition for the case as the building block of the legal process. Since much of the other information accessible via the computer relates to current topics, the focus of attention can begin to shift away from the past and lead to a reorientation of the authority of the judicial decision.

These are probably not the only ways in which the new media are weakening the law's links with the past. Some additional consequences of this shift, such as its effect on rights and liberties and on the reordering of traditional constitutional categories, will be dealt with later. What I hope has been made clear is that a rapidly changing society and a rapidly changing communications environment cannot leave the legal system untouched. Too much of legal scholarship assumes that law can be the master of its fate and of society's fate. As we shall also see in the following chapters, law is far from being omnipotent. It is vulnerable and subject to change from outside forces, just as it has been throughout its history.

2

Law, Media, and Conflict

> There's no question of justice, or right and wrong. The law
> seeks order...
>
> WILLIAM GADDIS, *JR*

Anthropologists Laura Nader and Harry Todd have written that

> law has many functions. It serves to educate, to punish, to harass, to
> protect private and public interests, to provide entertainment, to serve
> as a fund-raising institution, to distribute scarce resources, to maintain
> the status quo, to maintain class systems, and to cut across them, to
> integrate and disintegrate societies—all these things in different places,
> at different times, with different weightings.[1]

The focus in Chapter 1, how law endeavors to promote stability,
was on an important but often unexplored function of law. The
role of law in helping society to adapt to changing conditions is
also a responsibility that the legal process has acquired fairly recently. It has been a goal of law only since change became one of
society's priorities. In trying to foster links with the past, law,
during the last few centuries, has been mirroring and responding
to societal developments that were stimulated by qualities of the
technology of print.

Probably the oldest and most familiar role of law is to settle
disputes and grievances. Every community since the Garden of
Eden has "wrestled with the problem of maintaining internal peace
and harmony"[2] and developed means of settling conflict. Dispute
resolution may be both the original role of law and the most fundamental of the law's functions. Karl Llewellyn, an eminent legal

philosopher, argued that conflict and dispute settlement was at the heart of law:

> What, then, is this law business about? It is about the fact that our society is honeycombed with disputes. Disputes actual and potential, disputes to be settled and disputes to be prevented; both appealing to law, both making up the business of law.... This doing something about disputes, this doing of it reasonably, is the business of law.[3]

While the public may overlook the role of law in managing change, the assertion that law is used to deal with conflict needs no justification or explanation. Law may perform several functions in our society, but, at a minimum, it is understood that "law exists in order to keep the peace in a given society."[4] Professor Alan Watson has argued that dispute settlement is the "essential purpose of legal process"[5] and that

> the basic function of law is ... order, which is an end in itself. Law may, and at times certainly does, have an end beyond order, but this end, however desirable it might be, is subordinate to order. If one considers justice, liberty, the channelling of social behavior, in terms of functions of law, then one has to say that they are necessary to law only in so far as their absence would cause a failure of this essential function of order.[6]

There may be considerable disagreement about the appropriateness of some public expectations about law, such as whether law should be employed to further certain moral values or promote economic equality, but, at least until recently, there has been relatively little controversy about whether law is a suitable means for settling grievances. Indeed, in the public mind, law has been not only an appropriate technique for dealing with conflict, but an indispensable one. It has been the societal institution that is considered necessary to prevent conflict from overwhelming society. The public generally would agree with the character of Sir Thomas More, who exclaims in Robert Bolt's play *A Man for All Seasons:*

> And when the last law was down, and the Devil turned round on you—where would you hide, Roper, the laws all being flat? This country's planted thick with laws from coast to coast—man's laws, not God's—and if you cut them down—and you're just the man to do it—d'you really think you could stand upright in the winds that would blow then?[7]

As an institution with ancient roots and as the institution that is presumed to stand in the way of anarchy, law has acquired an almost sacred status. While better laws are often asked for, a society without law is, for most people, unthinkable. This faith in law as a means of creating order is even embedded in our language. The word *lawless*, for example, is defined as being either "unrestrained by law" or "unbridled."[8] A lawless society is one that is not only without law but without order as well. Given the ability of language to influence thought, the widespread public belief that any prelegal stage or nonlegal stage must have lacked the capability to effectively deal with conflict in a peaceful and rational manner should not be surprising.

Because we are a culture that relies greatly on law both to resolve conflict and to achieve other ends, we tend to emphasize its virtues in settling problems, minimize its flaws, dismiss other means of resolving conflict, and label earlier cultures that did not have law as primitive, savage, and the like. Most critically, we sometimes consider law to be the same tool for resolving conflict that it has always been, subject only to some plastic surgery and surface changes. Because the law has changed in the past only over fairly long periods of time, we do not recognize how the role of law and the procedures of society for handling disputes are substantially different from what they once were.

The means used to settle conflict today are not the same techniques that were used in ancient or medieval cultures. When law is viewed in an evolutionary or a comparative perspective, it becomes evident that it has not always enjoyed the revered status it has attained in the West. Other cultures, for example, have rejected the idea of "a government of laws, not men" and believed that "better than the rule of law is a kind of rule of man."[9] There are many techniques for resolving disputes without law, and both the kinds of methods that are used in a society and the attitudes about what methods are appropriate are affected by the communications media that are used in that society. The main thesis of this chapter is that writing and print are the structural supports for the modern ideal of dispute resolution and have contributed to law's growth over time, to our reliance on law, and to the authority of law. This is important today because as societies become increasingly reliant on electronic forms of communication, some of these structural supports are being eroded.

People who have disputes with one another have many possible choices as to how to settle the problem. They can talk it over and possibly reach a settlement; they can flip a coin and agree to abide by the fate of fortune; they can physically fight and allow force to prevail; and they can seek guidance from a friend, relative, clergyman, or someone else who might suggest some way to patch up their differences. Or they might go to a court of law. Most of these options can be considered *nonlegal,* in the sense that they do not involve the application of rules or the use of a formal institution. They are certainly not illegal, and they may be highly effective. Historically, as will be explained below, nonlegal methods were often preferred over legalistic processes of dispute resolution. While we revere the "supremacy of law," other societies, with different needs and characteristics, promoted dispute settlement through nonlegal means. This was true in most oral cultures and even in most societies in which writing existed. What we label "alternative dispute resolution" was once supreme, while the law, which we consider supreme, would have been treated as an alternative.

There are large differences among societies in the amount of conflict that is generated, in the kinds of disputes that occur, in the efforts made to prevent conflict, and in the means used to settle conflict. That law is now a major participant in all aspects of this process is obvious. The role of media, both now and in the past, is probably less clear. Yet without an understanding of the role that the communication of information plays in generating conflict and resolving it, we cannot fully understand either the history of dispute resolution or the future challenges to law in this area. Resolving conflict through law is a technique that is heavily reliant on attitudes and procedures that have been conditioned by qualities of writing and print which are threatened in an age of electronic communication.

One of the differences among the various techniques of dispute resolution concerns how information is used. When a solution is reached through force, for example, information about the nature of the conflict is not used at all (although communication about how force was employed may affect future disputes). When a dispute is resolved by flipping a coin, all information is irrelevant except which side the coin lands on and the prior agreement by the parties about what this will mean. In mediation, on the contrary, any information considered relevant by the parties is listened to. If peer pressure or public opinion induces a settlement, information supplied by anyone may have an effect.

How does law compare with these forms of handling disputes both in the information it attends to and in the information it refuses to consider in making a decision? In one respect, the process of law most resembles flipping a coin. The parties to a coin flip agree that there is a rule, such as whoever calls "heads" wins and whoever calls "tails" loses, and that this rule will be applied to the fact of how the coin lands. All information other than how the coin lands is considered irrelevant. Law is similar to this process in that it is a means of resolving disputes that also consciously restricts and limits the kind of information that is employed in reaching a decision. By agreeing to use law to settle their dispute, the parties agree that only information relevant to the appropriate rule may be used. While the model is obviously not as mechanical as coin flipping, it does require the participants to accept the fact that much information which a party might think should be considered will be excluded from the process. As will be explained in more detail below, the formality and procedures that are so essential to the legal process are also the means for focusing attention on rules and ensuring that only "relevant" or "admissible" information is considered in making decisions.

The acceptance of a method of conflict resolution that is based on structuring communication in the decision-making process, on focusing attention on rules, and on restricting the use of other information in reaching a decision has been greatly influenced by printing. Printing expanded information and knowledge in ways that made word-of-mouth less effective for preventing conflict and for shaping solutions to problems. As traditional processes were interfered with, printing also provided a means for communicating rules in an identifiable, tangible, reliable, and trustworthy fashion. As will be described later, attention became more focused on rules in printed form, on the meaning of law, and on the role of the judge, all of which changed from what they had been earlier. This contributed to the modern concept of "supremacy of law" and to our cultural preference for using law to settle important conflicts.

The appearance of electronic forms of communication threatens

to undermine some of the faith that has been placed in the processes of law, to generate new kinds of conflicts, and to change
the means for dealing with them. By transforming how information
is stored and communicated, new and different techniques of settling conflicts may become more attractive than law. In assessing
why the legal mode of settling conflict is vulnerable to change from
electronic forms of communication, it is important to understand
how the methods that our society uses today to settle disputes are
different from what they once were. Modern law has qualities that
it did not always have, and some of them are due to changes in
the means used to transmit information. The development of new
media in the past opened up new possibilities for law, enhanced
its power, affected the way in which law was perceived by the
public, and modified the values that were inherent in the methods
that were being employed. The novel qualities of the new media
suggest the likelihood of similarly substantial change occurring in
our time.

Speech

Societies without written legal codes have often been portrayed as
violent, conflict ridden, and warlike.[10] Hobbes wrote that "it is
manifest, that during the time men live without a common Power
to keep them all in awe, they are in that condition which is called
Warre."[11] Similarly, Sir Henry Maine claimed that "it is not peace
which was natural and primitive and old, but rather war. . . . What
does seem clear to trained observation is the universal belligerency
of primitive mankind. Not only is war to be seen everywhere, but
it is war more atrocious than we, with our ideas, can easily conceive."[12] Yet while a high level of conflict and a breakdown of
order occurred in some of these societies,[13] it is more likely that
"most 'primitive' peoples of mankind . . . show by our standards a
level of morality, sociability and peacefulness much higher than
most of their economically advanced fellowmen."[14] Or as an earlier
writer observed, "many of the jungle peoples of Asia, living under
the simplest conditions possible, appear to be peaceful, gentle folk,
quarrelling and fighting but little among themselves, and if they
have no regular law or government, scarcely seeming to feel the

need."[15] Indeed, "among the lessons to be learnt from the life of rude tribes is how society can go on without the policeman to keep order."[16]

One of the factors that significantly influenced the success of such groups in avoiding and dealing with conflict was effective use of the spoken word. In the language of the Bible, both "death and life are in the power of the tongue."[17] When speech moves within a small group, it is a very fast means of communication. Both secrecy and privacy are more difficult to achieve in such societies because information moves quickly, and what is known to one will often become known to all. All the resources that the law employs in our society to make citizens aware of its power and to deter illegal conduct are much less necessary in groups that have more effective means of communicating group expectations.[18] Anthropologist David Tait observed in one African group he studied that concern was heightened when "some acts by individuals and groups impede communication and disrupt the steady running of the parts. When such acts occur, then countervailing action may be taken to restore communication."[19] The rapid movement of information fosters group concerns and discourages acts that would stress individual differences. "Alternative life styles," in other words, are not characteristic of such societies. Nor, as we shall see in Chapter 6, are individual rights and civil liberties. The qualities and pattern of oral communication reinforce the homogeneity and conformist tendencies of such groups and deter conflict.

Oral communication worked effectively both to limit the outbreak of conflict and to bring about solutions to problems that occurred. Particularly when individuals had both blood relationships and other ongoing contacts, considerable pressure was exerted to avoid any behavior that could be considered deviant or threatening to the group. The norms, customs, and traditions of the group were known by all, and the consequences of violating any norm were generally understood. Such groups tended to be small and homogeneous[20] and did not often seek territorial expansion. The tendency in such groups was to be concerned with and knowledgeable about local affairs.

The frequent exaggeration of the amount of conflict within such groups stems partly from a lack of understanding of the nature and power of oral communication. Such societies may not have had a highly structured legal process, but they did have a potent conflict resolver in the communications medium that was dominant in that society. Thus in the absence of law, they did not necessarily resort to force, but found an effective tool in the spoken word. The use of speech promoted conformity, deterred innovation, and sacrificed individual concerns for what would help the group survive. Such groups were, however, less concerned than we are about these issues. They could emphasize the control of conflict with a singlemindedness that is not possible where the law is expected to achieve a variety of ends in addition to settling disputes.

Some discussions of preliterate societies attribute the ability to minimize conflict to custom. William Seagle, for example, concluded that "custom is king" and that

> while there is no automatic *submission* to custom, there is automatic *sway* of custom. Somehow, marvelous to relate, the savage recognizes the binding character of his customs although they are not backed by specific judicial sanctions of a repressive character, as in civilized society. In primitive society custom has a force of its own. It is obeyed merely because it is the custom.[21]

Elsewhere, he wrote,

> What is important, and, from our point of view, quite remarkable, is that rules of conduct were recognized as binding on the members of the community, although they were not supported by external sanctions of a repressive character as in politically organized civilized society. The community relied on natural factors of social cohesion. . . . Many customs—and sometimes the most tyrannical—were obeyed for no other reason, apparently, than that they were the customary modes of behavior. This sovereign sway of custom seems to us as mysterious as instinct. Accustomed as we are to believe that anarchy would ensue tomorrow if suddenly all the courts, police stations, and jails were closed, we are not likely to regard the sovereign reign of custom with equanimity.[22]

The emphasis on custom is not inaccurate, but it is incomplete in that it fails to recognize that much of the power of custom is traceable to the power of speech. Custom is obeyed not for any miraculous reason but because the custom is indeed enforced and reinforced by discussion within the community. The power of custom derived from the potent qualities of oral communication. As

Paul Bohannon has observed, "It is not law that is kept in force by . . . reciprocity and publicity. It is custom."[23] It is difficult to imagine written custom because writing changed and limited the movement of information. In fact, in those instances in which custom was written down and transformed into law, it lost some of its power and society became less orderly.[24]

The potent qualities of speech that assisted in the prevention of conflict also guided the settlement of disputes. Whereas we recognize the "supremacy of law," such cultures typically relied on nonlegal means for managing conflict and can be considered to have had a system in which oral communication helped to shape the outcomes of many disputes. They believed in the power of the spoken word and exploited its qualities in most of their methods of conflict resolution. Their processes of conflict resolution often substituted speech for force, violence, and the exercise of judicial or state power, which did not exist in most such societies. If, as some anthropologists assert,[25] law can be found in such societies, it would be law that would be considered the secondary or alternative form of dispute resolution, while the spoken word would be supreme.

What were the techniques that such societies used in lieu of courts? The following summary suggests that the rapid movement of information and the force and power of the spoken word were indispensable elements for managing conflict in a society where law was weak or nonexistent and which possessed a limited arsenal of communications media.

Public Opinion

A major technique for settling problems was simply talking. Complaints were not brought to a judicial official, as in a legalistic society, but they were brought to someone with the intention that this person would talk to someone else about what had occurred. This process can be labeled "shaming,"[26] "gossip,"[27] "ridicule,"[28] or "derision,"[29] but the essence of what occurred is similar. Anthropologist Simon Roberts has stated,

> Within any social group talking must be a principal means whereby trouble is avoided and through which efforts are made to resolve it when it does arise. Through talk people get to know what others are

thinking and going to do, as well as how their own actions are perceived, and are enabled to arrange their affairs accordingly. Where trouble does crop up, talking in the first instance provides a vehicle through which anger can be expressed and released, and then a means through which those involved can feel their way towards a settlement.[30]

Speech, in such communities, was a highly effective means of both communicating and enforcing group norms. The power of methods of dispute resolution that involve talking have certain parallels in modern times. Publication of stories in "the media" can be an effective means of bringing about the settlement of a dispute today, but only in the rare instance when the community seems agreed on what an appropriate outcome is. Yet such occasions today also pose problems, since going to the media is a different kind of process than going to law. It involves asking different questions and looking at different issues. Media-related resolutions of disputes, both then and now, are less concerned with what is legally required and more concerned with satisfying the immediate concerns of the people. Anthropologist Edward Winter, for example, noted in his research that village hearings

are of great importance for the airing of public opinion. . . . It is quite clear from the procedure followed, the relative importance accorded to various cases, and the judgments given that the paramount aim of these proceedings is the restoration of breaches of solidarity. To put it briefly, when one man commits a wrong against another, what concerns the village is not so much the wrong itself as the ill feelings which it has generated between the parties involved. Thus the principal goal is the restoration of good relations between the men concerned, rather than the administration of justice in some abstract sense.[31]

These different concerns are illustrated in the following story by anthropologist Colin Turnbull of the way a dispute was handled by the Pygmies.

Disputes were generally settled with little reference to the alleged rights and wrongs of the case, but chiefly with the intention of restoring peace to the community. One night Kenge slipped out of our hut on an amorous expedition to the hut of Manyalibo, who had an attractive daughter, one of Kenge's many admirers. Shortly afterward there was a howl of rage and Kenge came flying back across the clearing with a furious Manyalibo hurling sticks and stones after him. Manyalibo then took up a position in the middle of the clearing and woke the whole camp up, calling out in a loud voice and denouncing Kenge as an incestuous good-for-nothing. Actually Kenge was not at all out of order, though marriage might have been. Several people tried to point this out to Manyalibo, but he became increasingly vociferous. He said that it wasn't so much that Kenge had tried to sleep with his daughter, but that he had been brazen enough to crawl right over her sleeping father to get at her, waking him up in the process. This was a considered insult, for any decent youth would have made a prior arrangement to meet his girl elsewhere. He called on Kenge to justify himself. But Kenge was too busy laughing and only managed to call out "You are making too much noise!" This seemed a poor defense but in fact it was not. Manyalibo set up another hue and cry about Kenge's general immorality and disrespect for his elders and strode up and down the camp rattling on the roofs of huts to call everyone to his defense.

Moke took the place in the center of the camp where Manyalibo had stood, and where everyone stands who wants to address the whole camp formally. He gave a low whistle, like the whistle given on the hunt to call for silence. When everyone was quiet, he told Manyalibo that the noise was giving him a headache, and he wanted to sleep. Manyalibo retorted that the matter was more serious than Moke's sleep. Moke replied in a very deliberate, quiet voice, "You are making too much noise—you are killing the forest, you are killing the hunt. It is for us older men to sleep at night and not worry about the youngsters. They know what to do and what not to do." Manyalibo growled with dissatisfaction, but he went back to his hut, taunted by well-directed remarks from Kenge and his friends.[32]

Turnbull adds that "whether Kenge had done something wrong or not was relatively immaterial. Manyalibo had done the greater wrong by waking the whole camp and by making so much noise that all the animals would be frightened away, spoiling the next day's hunting."[33] Most importantly, the dispute was settled quickly, the interests of the group were asserted, and the solution desired by the group was accepted.

Mediation

Mediation, a technique for resolving disputes that is being used increasingly in the United States,[34] has ancient roots. It is a process that relies almost entirely on the spoken word, yet it does not, like the mechanisms just described, encourage public participation.

Mediation sessions are private, thus restricting communication to and from nonparties and encouraging communication between the disputants. Spoken communication between the parties is the essence of the mediation process, and preventing the breakdown of communication is a chief function of the mediator. Resolutions of problems do "not come from authoritative decision, but through agreement resulting from discussion and negotiation between the parties which are in conflict."[35] Mediators traditionally do not impose settlements on the parties. The effectiveness of mediation lies, in large part, in allowing each side to express its perception of the problem, its feelings about it, and its beliefs about what would be an appropriate resolution of the problem. This is an inquiry that would lose something if the transmission of information between parties occurred through written messages. Some feelings, emotions, and facts would not be communicated as fully. Similarly, by using nonprofessionals as mediators, there is less likelihood that the process will be affected by some printed "professional body of knowledge," for example, rules, or that solutions reached in prior cases will be cited. The mediator is not obligated to certify that the agreement reached by the parties conforms to a particular rule.

Ritual and Ceremony

Ritual and ceremony, whether they are of a magical or a religious nature, differ from the use of public opinion in that these techniques involve a large behavioral component. Yet it should also be recognized that much ritual is aimed at preventing or handling conflict and that ritual also involves exploiting the power of oral communication. It has been noted that "a significant function of ritual is precisely that of communication, of labeling acts so that there can be no mistake as to their meaning."[36] While the focus of attention may be on symbolic communication through pageantry and activity, there will also generally be a verbal component that is important. In other words, it is a mistake to assume that rituals appeal only to the sense of sight and not to the sense of sound as well. Public opinion is effective simply because of what and how information is being communicated. Ritual and ceremony may use some different means, but the goal of both is the transmission of information. In one society, for example, where the word for "knowledge" is essentially the same as the word for "speech," it was observed that "all knowledge in this sense is acquired not necessarily by means of speech (much ritual, much dance, is acquired by action, imitative action), but with the accompaniment or intervention of speech."[37]

The sound that is a part of the ritual or religious process often reflects a belief in the ability to communicate orally with unseen forces. In a description of sorcery, Mary Douglas has written,

> The sorcerer is the magician who tries to transform the path of events by symbolic enactment. He may use gestures or plain words in spells or incantations. Now words are the proper mode of communication between persons. If there is an idea that words correctly said are essential to the efficacy of an action, then, although the thing spoken to cannot answer back, there is a belief in a limited kind of one-way verbal communication.[38]

Part of the efficacy of speech in this context came from a different attitude that existed toward spoken language. J. David Bolter has found some evidence of such attitudes in ancient Greece even after writing began to be used. He claims that the

> age was alive to the incantatory and resonant qualities of the spoken word. The Greeks had already progressed far enough to be free of the grosser superstitions of primitive cultures but not so far as to forget the primitive's admiration of the power of language. In the Greek epics, characters speak "winged words"—suggesting that words themselves and the ideas they embody are as real as birds and spears that also fly through the air. Two hundred years later, the audience of Aeschylus's plays, if not Euripides', could still manage to believe that a curse uttered upon a king could bring destruction to him or his progeny.[39]

Ritual and ceremony, therefore, may be viewed as partly oral processes for communicating a message to members, "a story they tell themselves about themselves."[40] They were central components of processes used in lieu of law to settle conflicts. Societies that lacked formal legal procedures and institutions and needed effective devices for molding behavior found rituals to be effective and powerful devices for influencing thought and behavior.[41] "Religious controls function in place of law,"[42] and "magic, the use of the supernatural for moral ends, long remains the handmaid of the law, mopping up where the broom of the law fails to sweep clean."[43]

Faith in the power of speech is also evident in the use of oaths and ordeals to resolve problems. Such appeals to divine justice[44] were often the culmination of a discussion about the dispute. Oaths and ordeals occurred

> not just after "declaratory rituals" but after the issue for probation had been isolated and clarified through discussion. Ordeals may have helped to establish the results of consensus but they were not apparently the primary method of reaching consensus. That was done in the judgment which preceded them and which itself emerged from a discussion which was presumably no less rational than most human discussions. In fact, it was probably more rational than many, since it was conducted in solemn circumstances by responsible people who worked within an agreed framework of customs and values.[45]

Similarly, historian Paul Hyams has argued that

> modern courts seek to establish whether or not certain specific acts have been committed, then whether these constitute some crime of the accused or some actionable tort, and finally what the law should do. But in this more localized world of the ordeal, the goal is as much to "make the balance" and reestablish a workable peace within the community as to redress any specific grievance. The strategies vary according to the desired ends. They may aim to effect a compromise between the disputants on honorable terms, for example, or even to eliminate a troublemaker from future calculations by deprivation of civil rights, expulsion, mutilation, or death. Ideally, the court inches cautiously toward the best practicable solution, and attempts to lower the emotional temperature in thrashing out the problem aloud. En route, it exposes much material in open court (and also, less formally, outside) that today's practice and the rules of evidence would conceal. Passions are more open, audience involvement closer, than most modern judges would permit. The presiding judge here cannot force his preferred judgment down the court's throat. He can merely guide the deliberations through meanderings that strike an unprepared observer as aimless, until a satisfactory conclusion gradually emerges. The court then declares the proof to be attempted, and now at last comes the moment for God's participation.[46]

Possibly the most interesting example of exploitation of the spoken word for the purpose of settling disputes is the song duel of the Eskimos. Individual grievances can be settled by a process in each contestant sings songs criticizing, ridiculing, and insulting the other party and recounting the nature of the injustice. These contests take place in front of the whole group, which determines who sang with the greatest skill. This is another example of a group confronting problems using the media resources that it has available. It reveals oral communication being employed for a discrete purpose, the reduction of the level of conflict. Legal and moral standards are not explicitly dealt with, there is no overt concern for establishing a standard for future behavior, but "the litigants (contestants) feel relieved—the complaint laid to rest—a psychological satisfaction attained and balance restored."[47]

Writing

Oral societies, it has been seen, did not often have to confront conflicts that occurred as a result of technological or social change. Nor did they have to be very concerned about conflicts involving challenges to authority or to traditional values. Such conflicts were rare or nonexistent. These preliterate cultures, moreover, seemed to understand that the spoken word was a powerful tool for influencing behavior, and they often exploited its abilities in novel and creative ways. Speech moved rapidly but locally, and this combination was generally sufficient to both prevent and settle disputes. When necessary, supernatural, ritualistic, or more forceful measures were employed. Law, if it existed at all in such societies, was one technique among many and was less important than most others. As an old Vietnamese proverb puts it, "The customs of the village are stronger than the law of the emperor."[48]

The main question, in societies that had writing, was not whether law existed but what its role was and how important it was in the process of handling disputes. Such societies had law in the sense that they had courts, judges, and written codes. Yet it would be an error to assume that they typically dealt with disputes in a legalistic manner or that law meant then what it means now. Law remained one among many methods of settling conflict, and, with few exceptions, traditional oral techniques remained prominent. The encoding of law in written form, sometimes in stone and in prominent locations, was more often significant as an indication of who had power in that society than as an instrument to be widely used in the settling of common disputes.[49] Writing was employed more often to promote awareness that some *person* was powerful and authoritative than that the *law* was independently powerful and authoritative. For two main reasons, processes of dispute resolution in most ancient societies that had writing remained largely as they had been in the past. First, because writing did not encourage continual social change, there was little need to adopt new techniques of dispute resolution. Second, because writing was not widely used, it did not foster the kinds of attitudes toward words on paper that are necessary for a legalistic mode of dispute resolution.[50]

The introduction of writing has been assumed to be a critically important event in the history of law. Seagle has written that

> in a sense, the history of law and men of law begins with the written word. In the development of the law, the written word was to prove the most fateful discovery. The history of law not only ceased to be anonymous; it became the history of the potentialities of the written word for good and evil.[51]

Psychologist Julian Jaynes has pointed to the period when "the judgments of the gods through their stewards began to be recorded. This is the beginning of the idea of law."[52] While writing was responsible for giving the law a clearer identity and, where supported by force or divine authority, an aura of power, it is important not to exaggerate its importance in the settling of conflict. Writing was a mode of communication that enabled some legal codes to achieve immortality, but this does not mean that they became more powerful or influential in controlling conflict than nonlegal methods. A modern law, even if it has a very short life expectancy, may have a greater impact on the process of dealing with disputes.

Writing, by being tangible and transportable, did encourage territorial expansion and fostered contact and conflict among groups.[53] It opened up new possibilities for communicating over long distances and provided a means for the administration, exploitation, and exercise of power over places and people with whom there had been no relationship previously. As Claude Lévi-

Strauss has observed, writing can be associated with "the creation of cities and empires, that is the integration of large numbers of individuals into a political system, and their grading into castes or classes."[54] There are isolated examples of large empires that did not have writing,[55] such as the Incas, but the spoken word had typically limited growth by focusing attention inward rather than outward.[56] Among some tribes, "persons from one village often feared to travel to the next village, much less the next chiefdom or tribe."[57] Because there might be no place outside the group to go, ostracism or excommunication, the withdrawal of communication with a person causing some problem,[58] was a particularly effective threat in such societies.

Increased contact with nonkin groups challenged some traditional arrangements that relied on shared values and expectations, on traditional relationships, and on the rapid movement of information among members of the group. And as they became larger, political entities became more heterogeneous than they had been before. In these new political structures, the ability of media from the old preliterate days to deal with new situations was limited. The spoken word became less and less able to prevent the outbreak of conflict; some traditional forms of conflict resolution proved either ineffective or inappropriate. As societies grew in size and cultural diversity, the idea of a code of written law would have become more appealing. For no longer was the culture of these societies one in which power was often shared, rules widely known, blood relationships influential, and other techniques of dispute resolution and prevention efficiently employed.

In the early 1970s, anthropologist Jack Goody returned to some villages he had studied in Ghana to see how the quality of life was affected by the advent of literacy. He found that

> one general feature of writing dominates the process of its introduction into non-literate societies: its ability to preserve speech so that communication can take place over space and over time. It is a process of distancing which affects the personal as well as the national level. . . . Social relationships inevitably get dispersed widely over the ground and writing becomes the main means by which people can keep in touch. Nevertheless, when communication can be reduced to a few marks on a piece of paper rather than take place in the more concrete ambience of the face-to-face situation, the quality of interpersonal

> relationships is inevitably thinned; the multiplex relations of the village give way to single-stranded contacts that are more functionally specific, more manipulable, more "impersonal."[59]

While writing could be transported over great distances, it could never create or impose uniformity of thought or practice. The homogeneity of many oral societies was fostered in part by the continuous movement of large amounts of information throughout the group and occurred automatically as everyone worked to know everything that everyone else knew. Writing, however, was an imperfect medium for spreading information widely. Not only was literacy limited, but distribution depended on handmade copies and poor transportation. Writing spread information over a wider area but spread it very thinly. It could be used to extend power and authority but not to convert captives to a new way of life. In the Middle Ages, for example, even the Church, the most literate and powerful institution in society, could not enforce a standard practice and ritual because writing was an imperfect means for doing so. Elizabeth Eisenstein notes that "repeated efforts to en-sure that priests mastered the rudiments of Latin, that parish reg-isters were kept in order, that various instructions of popes and councils were carried out in scattered dioceses had met with uneven success during the medieval millennium."[60]

Writing, in most ancient societies, was a scarce resource. It was not employed to share information and thus did not encourage the exchange and growth of knowledge.[61] There were relatively few books and literate individuals. Writing involved a difficult skill, and those who were able to exploit it had an ally in acquiring wealth and power. Writing was beneficial to those who possessed the skill and could prevent others from acquiring it, but we should be careful not to overestimate its power. In an interesting study of ancient and medieval empires, for example, John Kautsky has pointed out that when the limitations of writing are ignored, many mistaken assumptions are made about the power of such empires. Due to poor communications, premodern empires were decen-tralized and unable to exert great control over the lives of those who lived far from the central administration. The rulers of empires were generally satisfied to increase their wealth and did not, and could not, standardize legal and cultural elements among widely dispersed colonies. The citizens of most ancient cultures lived the same life that their ancestors had. Kautsky asserts that the power and

> functions of government in aristocratic empires are extremely limited. It is quite misleading therefore to describe such governments by conjuring up images of modern authoritarian or "totalitarian" governments. Indeed, it may be deceptive even to describe such governments as "governments," because with respect to the scope and range of their activities and the degree to which they affect the daily lives of their subjects they are very different from the governments of industrialized societies. So little does government activity in aristocratic empires matter to their subjects that most of these are undoubtedly unaware or only very dimly aware of the fact that they are subjects of aristocratic empires.[62]

This localization of power in "aristocratic empires" had its basis in the poor network of communications that effectively isolated one part of the empire from all others. Given these circumstances, every local aristocracy had no choice but to build up a pattern of decision making on its own, one that remained relatively independent of the central aristocracy.

Until modern times, most rulers of large territories did not interfere with traditional modes of dispute settlement among conquered peoples. Even Roman law generally provided that each person lived by the law of the community to which he belonged.[63] New techniques of dispute resolution, therefore, were not needed in such groups, and they could "largely govern themselves within their villages, generally in accordance with immemorial custom, and there is little conflict between villages given the lack of communication between them."[64]

In Chapter 1, it was pointed out that writing was not able to support a coherent doctrine of precedent because the written word lacked authority. Judges relied more on their personal knowledge of customary practice and of what had been decided in prior cases than on what had been written about a case. Writing also had a limited effect on the public consciousness about change and reinforced a theme that was present in ancient codes, particularly those that purported to be divinely inspired. Writing was a poor technique for challenging tradition and fostering change. Literacy was rare, and writing was understood to be an effective means of maintaining power. The desire for change could not be realized until the period following Gutenberg, when effective control over the distribution of information became much more difficult and when attitudes about information changed.

In considering the impact of writing on the processes of dispute resolution, the medium was a force of similarly limited influence. Because of the way in which writing was used and the nature of attitudes toward the written word, the appearance of written rules did not guarantee that such rules would be used as they are in modern times or that new techniques to apply these rules to conflicts would automatically replace traditional processes that relied on the spoken word.[65] It has been observed that "it is true that political institutions, independent of the kin and the supernatural, had risen to power; yet these institutions were young, weak and untried. Their encroachment on the old allegiance was perforce wary and hesitating. Social cohesion still seemed based on non-political elements, and these elements were therefore protected."[66] Similarly, Yale law professor W. Michael Reisman has pointed out that "there is substantial reason to believe that Hammurabi's code was never applied; those charged with making decisions and those seeking decisions from officials operated on the basis of an entirely different code of norms."[67] Until citizens gained greater control over the means of communication, appeal to written law for settling disputes would be restricted. Written codes may be evidence of the breakdown of some traditional processes of dispute resolution, but given some of the inherent limitations of writing, it was relatively ineffective in transforming oral nonlegal societies into literate legalistic ones.

Thus, as in discussing change, written legal codes and documents may be misleading if only their content is examined and assumptions about the use of these codes are made on the basis of modern attitudes about the authority of printed law. Given the limitations of writing, written law had difficulty gaining supremacy over practices and customs that were passed on orally. Where the ruling authority could influence the process of dispute resolution, it encouraged a more visible and hierarchical process. The power of those authorized to exercise legal authority grew, but many traditional local mechanisms of conflict resolution were not replaced. Writing could not be expected to foster automatic obedience to written rules and to courts that relied exclusively on written rules or employed modern practices of interpreting written rules. Nor did writing, of itself, foster the conception of law as something autonomous and independent, as something that could be revised by changing what appeared in the book of laws. Such a concept, as will be explained below, would require greater literacy and an attitude toward law and words on paper that did not become common until the era of printing.

The embodiment of law in written form may be viewed as an interesting example of the means of communication being more important and revealing than the information that was communicated. Written legal codes were important in the history of dispute resolution not because courts would necessarily become more rule oriented and not because these codes contained different rules than before. Indeed, the written law may have often contained the same words as the previous customary law.[68] Ancient legal codes, while presenting modern scholars with many fertile opportunities for scholarly inquiry, do not provide a great deal of insight into what law meant for these societies. Even in Rome, where the most impressive legal code existed, litigation was something to be avoided.[69] A preoccupation with the content of law, unfortunately, mistakenly assumes that such writings were used in the same way or had the same authority then that writing has today. Both on an individual level and on a societal level, however, writing was a means of communication that was perceived and employed differently before Gutenberg than it was later.

Solomon Gandz has suggested that the use of writing in a society proceeds through several stages. He argues that history

teaches us that there are four phases in the development of literature and tradition: (1) The primordial phase of oral tradition prevailing among all the nations before the invention or introduction of writing. (2) The introduction of writing and written literature. Usually, written literature sets in with a great religious book, like the Bible, the Vedas, the Quran, the New Testament, or also with a great national epic, like Homer. (3) The secondary phase of oral literature, coming after the first Holy Scriptures as a continuation of old habits, or still later, as a movement to revive and restore old customs. In the history of civilization written literature first appears as a short episode, an isolated fact, a revolutionary innovation introduced by some great founder of religion, or prince and legislator. The people at large very stubbornly continue their old habits of preserving their lore and tradition by memory. Only very slowly and gradually do they learn to read and write and to appreciate a written literature, and thus attain the stage (4) in which the use of written literature is the general rule.[70]

Most societies with written codes remained in stage 3, and dispute resolution processes continued to be largely oral. Writing had been effective in assisting individuals and states to acquire power, but it was inadequate in helping law to attain a clear and powerful identity distinct from custom and oral tradition. Custom and other orally based techniques continued to be more important than law and to take precedence over law when the two were in conflict. One author has described how, in the Middle Ages,

> there was no written law, but there was recorded law. This fact requires careful consideration; for at this point we stand at the historical dividing-line between customary law and statute law.
>
> Sooner or later, some piece or other of law will be recorded, as an aid to memory in doubtful cases, in order to stabilize tradition and to keep it unambiguous. The possessor of a subjective right, as we should call it, may, for example, have his right corroborated by the *publica fides* of the ruler or of a notary. The community may solemnly and officially put into writing some of its legal rules, so that they may be accurately preserved for posterity. Or some private person may on his own initiative write down what he knows of "objective law"—to use a strictly modern term, where medieval people would have spoken simply of the "good old law." These are the three forms of law-recording known to the Middle Ages: charters, folk-right (i.e. the authentic law of some community), and law-books; three sources of different quality, but in the medieval estimate not of such widely different quality as they must seem to us.
>
> All these recorded portions of law are, of course, surrounded by and subordinate to the living legal sense of the community, or the law transmitted by word of mouth, and this alone contains the whole of the law. The recorded law is not statute law . . . but is simply recorded customary law, as we call it; and it is never more than a fragment of the whole law which lives exclusively in the breast or conscience of the community.
>
> The character of modern statute law is very different. Modern statute law, by its very nature, must be written law, for the whole of law is contained in the verbally defined commands of authority. It is a code, which makes claim to systematic completeness, and consequently any-

thing outside this fixed law which is still to be law must somehow be deducible from this code. Even the living evolution of the law out of the legal sense of the community—for example, the decisions of our high court judges—is formally and technically only possible in so far as the constitution, or legal code, sets up an authority empowered within limits to interpret the law. In this way, all legal development is brought under the heading of the application and particularization of the law.

The contrast between customary law and enacted law may be summarized thus: in the latter, the whole law is comprised in a written code; in the former, it lies in the living sense of the people. Recorded customary law is, therefore, never more than a fragment of the whole law.[71]

Many discussions of law in the Middle Ages unfortunately do not distinguish between new written law and old written law. The word *law* is used without indicating whether the reference is to old written law or new written law. New written law during this period, however, had little authority. Old written law had supreme authority in theory but little authority in fact, since how the old code was to be applied usually turned on what the oral tradition and local custom were. Thus those authors who concentrate on theory can correctly assert that written law, by which they mean ancient written law, was supreme to custom, while those who emphasize practice can be considered correct when they claim that custom was supreme to law. For the sake of convenience, the word *law* in the following discussion is used in the sense of new written law, and the terms *custom* and *oral tradition* are essentially synonymous.[72]

In the Middle Ages, the word *law* was used often, belief in law was considerable, and judges were expected to make decisions according to law. Medieval and modern law differ, however, in where law is thought to be found, and this difference accounts for many contradictions between the two concerning the dispute resolution process. In the Middle Ages, the law that was trusted and considered supreme was largely oral and old. The "medieval mind looked to custom as the ultimate authority."[73] Age ensured authenticity, and the fact that law was oral allowed for public opinion to continue to be a large influence on how disputes would be handled. As will be explained below, statutes and change through legislative enactment were not recognized as authoritative.

The prevalence of oral traditions persisted because writing was not trusted and because its use was limited. By requiring judges to use law in resolving disputes, we have mandated that a certain body of knowledge be given priority over other information. This body of knowledge is not the same body of knowledge used in earlier times, even though the same word, *law,* is used. We assume that legal information is located in printed books and is distinct from and superior in authority to other bodies of information, such as custom, religion, public opinion, and so on, which might have something pertinent to say about the dispute and which may conflict with the law. For us, unlike our ancestors, all of law is indeed in the books, and judges are instructed to limit their attention to what is contained between the covers of the book. In our minds, books are more authentic than the spoken word, and books also focus attention away from nonlegal considerations. In the Middle Ages, however, books of written law, except for venerated copies of ancient codes, could not be perceived in this way because writing was a medium that could not be trusted to provide reliable and accurate information. Written documents often suffered from intentional forgery and unintentional copying errors. We approach the written word with an attitude that was unusual before printing. "In modern history," it has been noted, "oral tradition has to be confirmed by written documents. In the olden days, written documents had to be confirmed by oral testimonies."[74]

The transition to more modern legalistic methods of dealing with conflict required a series of interrelated changes in both law and communications. It involved changes in procedures employed by courts, in modes of thought, and in attitudes toward words on paper. The end result was a recognition that the function of courts and judges was not simply to settle disputes in accordance with generally accepted custom but to achieve this task through law and rules that had been designed for particular kinds of problems. The model of modern law assumes that the settling of disputes through attention to autonomous rules is the heart of the judicial process. Although in reality "law may settle conflicts by a variety of means (adjudication, mediation, arbitration, etc.)"[75] and although judges may interpret rules, bend rules, pervert rules, or encourage out-of-court settlements, this variety of behavior does not deny that there is a model or paradigm of what is expected of a court in handling a dispute, and of what is accepted in our society as being the legitimate and primary function of the judiciary of the state. What is suggested here is that this paradigm is a fairly modern creation and that limitations of writing had to be overcome before this model could evolve.

Law, as a method that employs rules to settle disputes, is a process which "makes total sense when you have it"[76] but which is not easily or quickly acquired. "In a primitive society," it has been observed, "men do not naturally go to law to right a wrong."[77] The growth and increased use of legalistic modes of dispute settlement required not simply the existence of writing, but an expansion of literacy and of writing generally. When this occurred in the late Middle Ages, orally based methods became less effective and the opportunity for a more legalistic mode of dispute resolution increased. This period in England began in the twelfth and thirteenth centuries when "the first foundations of the common law were truly laid."[78] This was also an era in which a significant change in communications occurred. There was substantial growth in the use of writing, in literacy rates, and in reliance on written documents.[79] Paper and eyeglasses began to be used in Europe. European society began to overcome many of the limitations of writing and to set the stage for the development of printing.

The relationship between law and writing in England in the 400 years between the Norman Conquest, in 1066, and the development of printing is a particularly interesting period because one of the goals of William the Conqueror had been to bring "the conquered people under the rule of written law."[80] The compilation of the Domesday Book was intended to codify existing law and create a record of landholdings to facilitate taxation. Yet William's purpose was partially frustrated because the Domesday Book was rarely used during the two centuries after the Conquest.[81] The idea of relying on or consulting a written document was not common at this time. Memory was considered to be more trustworthy than anything in writing, and "practical questions were answered by oral testimony and not by reference to documents."[82] In other words, if there were a dispute over land ownership and a written charter needed interpretation or was contradicted by what was remembered, memory took precedence over written proof.[83] The "principle that 'oral witness deserves more credence than written evidence' was a legal commonplace."[84] During the latter half of the twelfth century, however, an enormous increase in the use of writing for official purposes occurred.[85] By the middle of the thirteenth century, there was apparently more trust in written records, and court records begin to show reliance on the Domesday Book for proving ownership of land.[86] After two centuries, the book began to have practical as well as symbolic value.

Historian Susan Reynolds has pointed out that "law between the tenth and early twelfth centuries was the undifferentiated, indeterminate, and flexible law appropriate to a society that was for many practical purposes preliterate, and it must be understood in those terms, not in the terms of later professional or academic law."[87] Customary law was supreme, and "no clear boundary was perceived between customary law and customs in a more general sense, between right and law, or sin and crime, or between new legislation and the confirmation of existing law."[88] Judicial verdicts were "less an indication of who was right and wrong than a compromise between plaintiff and defendant. The real function of the court, the jurors and the public was mediation."[89] The twelfth century, however, "brought many changes. The development of government began to transform law by emphasizing one source of authority and enforcement among others. . . . Law became more differentiated, less diffused. Meanwhile the keeping of records made custom less flexible."[90]

Most historians give credit to Henry II (1154–1189) for inaugurating the English common law system. Henry was not only literate, but a "champion of literary culture."[91] More scribes were employed and more letters written than during the reigns of his predecessors.[92] The plea rolls and other important national records began during this period. The centralized legal machinery was "established on the basis of fixed rules of practice, which its series of records had made it possible to create."[93] Most importantly, Henry created new courts and the system for issuing writs to compel a party to appear in court.

The designation of Henry's reign as representing the origin of the English common law system, however, should not be construed as signifying that either the old processes of handling conflict or the old legal doctrines were completely replaced with new procedures or doctrines. Henry provided new opportunities for justice and enhanced royal power by employing writs—for example, writing—in a skillful manner. Yet as the word *origin* indicates, this was only the beginning. Prior to Henry's reign, "*general* jurisdiction over *ordinary* legal matters had been confined to local and feudal courts, which were not professional courts but assemblies of neighbors and of members of the manor. What Henry did was not to abolish local and feudal jurisdiction, but rather to create a *concurrent* royal jurisdiction in ordinary cases involving particular types of claims."[94] Thus there was a new court and new procedures, but, in the sense that *common* law means a law and/or process that all English people share, there was little common law in Henry's time. As Professor J. H. Baker has concluded, "The common law was not all invented in a day, or a year, but arose out of a long process of jurisdictional transfer in which many old customs were abandoned but many more were preserved."[95] What Henry set in motion was a struggle between traditional modes of settling conflict and a more formal system of royal courts. He employed writing in a way that gave the new system authority and power. However, the limitations of writing also may be considered responsible for the inability of the common law courts to quickly or completely overcome traditional practices or give the state a monopoly over the dispute resolution process. "The coverage of the common law system of remedies," Professor John Dawson has written,

> was for long severely limited. In the ordering of English society it was a matter of the utmost importance that the crown acquired early a monopoly over prosecutions for major crime, but there remained an enormous range of minor offenses that were punished in the hundred courts, the courts of the manors and towns, and later by the justices of the peace, over whom the central courts exercised a control that was at most sporadic. Civil litigation dealt with the affairs of the relatively prosperous. For most of the population the 40 shilling limit of value on actions brought in royal courts was an effective barrier. . . . Disputes over land between unfree tenants, like most disputes of other kinds, were settled in the local courts of county, hundred, manor, and town. Many types of disputes were wholly excluded because no royal writ had been devised. Altogether one can say that at the time of its creation the common law system was remarkable for its range, its impact on English society and for the power that it mobilized, but that it captured only the key controls, over matters of paramount impor-

tance to the crown. In later centuries the emphasis shifted, new types of interests were recognized, and the coverage of the writs expanded somewhat. But the expansion was gradual and through most of the later Middle Ages the disputes and misdeeds of most Englishmen were still remitted to local courts.[96]

Over the next two centuries, the increased use of writing in the common law courts laid the foundation for the modern attitude of what law is and of where courts must look in order to fulfill their responsibility to resolve conflict according to law. At the beginning, court procedure "operated almost completely through the spoken word,"[97] and the judge's "knowledge of English law did not come from books"[98] but from experience in and out of court. Most of the part-time justices were also lay persons.[99] The court process consisted of a "hearing" in which a litigant spoke on his own behalf and in which an advocate, if the litigant had one, stated the pleading in the necessary form.[100] The advocate was also a storyteller who would tell the story in a form favored by the court. The end result was a process that had some ritualized elements, but in which "legal rules . . . rarely figure in litigation."[101] Holdsworth has noted that the "system of oral pleading had one great advantage over the later system of written pleadings. It made for far greater freedom in the statement of the case."[102] Reliance on written documents shifted the emphasis to what was written, and cases could be lost by deviating even in a minor way from the prescribed form of the written pleading. By the end of this period, the legal process had become more formal and complex, judicial institutions were acquiring a distinct identity, and law in the sense of a legislative act or judicial interpretation had begun to replace the medieval vision of law as something "inscribed in the hearts of men."

The changes that occurred during these centuries are initially changes in court procedures. Henry II's major innovation was to require that anyone who wished to initiate legal proceedings had to obtain a "writ." This was a document with the royal seal ordering someone to appear in court. Prior to the late twelfth century, persons had been summoned to appear in court by "criers" rather than by a written document. Requiring the use of writs was the essence of the new procedure and added to the authority of the king, who controlled the issuing of writs.[103] Different writs were obtained depending on the nature of the problem, and the writ designated what kind of proof would be required to prevail in the case. As new problems arose, new writs were created by the king.

While the process began with a written document, most of the rest of the procedure was oral and fairly traditional. The transformation in English law that has been called the beginning of the common law actually had nothing to do with changing the substantive rules. The changes that took place in the twelfth century had

> furnished no substitute for the old substantive law and scarcely any addition to it. At the end of the reign of Henry II it was possible to try a case to judgment and execution with hardly any use of the old procedure; but it was not possible to try it without constant recourse to the old substantive law as defining and determining rights and obligations. Upon such subjects as the holding, transfer, renting and inheritance of land, the property, inheritance and dower rights of women, debts, contracts and distraint, personal status, the obligations of the warrantor, the right of advowson, and many such topics of substantive law, the new law had nothing to say. It might be true that there was here and there during the period some modification of the law of these things, made generally by special enactment, but such modifications were by the way, of minor importance, and they were not necessary parts of the new whole. That provided new courts and new remedies but not new definitions of right.[104]

In spite of the fact that the substantive law was not directly affected, the writ system, in which writing was introduced into the court process, began to narrow the options for settling problems. As the use of writing increased, the flexibility that had been part of the oral process gradually decreased.

One reason why Henry did not attempt a complete revision of substance as well as procedure is that there was no mechanism for doing this. There was only so much that he could do with "a stroke of the pen." Parliament, which had begun its life as a court and not as a body that would make new rules, was not yet accepted as a legislature. The role of courts was to settle disputes in accordance with the judge's concept of law, but this did not include the idea of a legislative body that could change law and direct the judge to consider something new. In instances in which new law had to be made, judges made the law themselves.[105] Courts, as late as the fourteenth century, found it difficult to discover what a statute was. Could they "be certain that any particular document was a statute? Who could say, even, what the actual words of an acknowledged statute really were?"[106] They did not believe "that a statute is something imposed upon a court from without."[107] When legislation became more frequent, judges were often unaware of statutes relevant to cases and ignorant of what Parliament had done.[108] They sometimes misquoted statutes[109] and refused to apply them.[110] They often did not accept the authority of Parliament to change the common law.[111] Acts of Parliament were considered to be "analogous to judgements of a court, and were therefore not treated by the judges as inviolable rules made by an omnipotent Legislature, but merely as the judgements of another court, which might be disregarded if they contravened this fundamental law."[112] There was no theory about how to interpret a statute or to determine the intention of the legislature since judges often had participated in enacting the statute.[113] There was no need "to distinguish adjudication from legislation. If the two functions could be conveniently performed together and by the same routine, then they were, and no theory of the separation of powers was in existence to force a separation."[114]

A change in this state of affairs could occur "only when parliamentary statute law acquires, by gradual stages, a position of mastery."[115] In his study of legislative activity in the fourteenth century, Theodore Plucknett therefore concluded that there could be no

> highly developed science of interpretation until the courts are conscious of their isolation; when no outside help is to be expected from the legislature or the executive, and when the judges no longer take so much part in the functions of government other than judicature, then the courts will have to accept statutes as the commands of an authority external to themselves whose will is known to them only as expressed in the written word.[116]

Yet a large part of the problem was due to "the *written* word." Writing provided an underlying communications system that was unreliable and functioned poorly.[117] The

> situation is difficult for us in these days to imagine; that legislation of vast importance should only be published in a few manuscript copies (mostly unofficial), and perhaps also by proclamation, would certainly account for widespread popular ignorance of its provisions; but the courts themselves seem to have been dependent on memory rather than on writing for their knowledge of statute law.[118]

Existing statutory law therefore needed and was accompanied by an effective oral tradition, and local customs continued to be a strong influence "even when a law common to all England had come into being."[119]

In addition to the limitations that writing imposed on the practices of the common law courts, it is important to recognize that there were various bodies competing for business with the common law courts. The late Middle Ages was a period in which there were many courts in addition to those of the king.[120] The royal courts that emphasized the common law did not have a monopoly and were employed less frequently than is apparent from many general histories of English law.[121] Church courts, for example, continued to handle many cases.[122] For most Englishmen from 1370 to 1529, "contacts with the law, either as litigants in civil suits or as defendants in criminal proceedings, were more likely to be in one of the local courts than in the central ones at Westminster."[123] There were town courts,[124] manorial courts, and even private citizens authorized to hear cases.[125] "It is relevant to point out," Paul Hair has observed,

> that in earlier centuries the common man was accustomed to social discipline communicated, interpreted and enforced through a variety of tribunals. He was subject not only to the king's courts, and to the church courts, but also to the manorial (or otherwise, town) courts, which apart from correcting such social offenses as hedge-breaking and nuisance-depositing, were tribunals of convenience for registering various obligations and intentions. He was therefore in attendance at some court regularly, and appearance on a matter of social discipline was probably less of a singling-out and a humiliation than it would be today.[126]

These agencies "did not try actions started by writ but, borrowing from the practice of church courts, offered ostensibly no more than to hear complaints brought by petition (bill) and arbitrate equitably between the parties."[127]

One study of the late fifteenth century concluded that, even at that late date, "the common law and its courts were largely irrelevant to ways in which behaviour was directly regulated."[128] Local, secular courts

> spent much of their judicial time actively and directly applying customary law and local enactments in a wide range of day-to-day affairs.

By Henry VII's reign these courts were still the most effective because they were most immediate to the community. There was a regular amount of legislating at this level in the form of juries declaring old custom or, along with local councils, consciously creating new. Parliamentary statute is almost never cited here probably because local rules were normally adequate to local needs.[129]

Even in criminal matters, "three centuries after Henry II reserved felony prosecutions to the crown, the whole legal machinery remained totally dependent on local initiatives, local juries of presentment and of trial, as well as on appeals of felony (which came outside royal control) and liberal amounts of condoned self-help regarding rights of entry."[130] Viewed in another way, it might be concluded that writing, even when employed in a royally sanctioned and organized manner in an era of growing literacy, had not been able to erase completely much older oral traditions and practices.

Printing

In 1848, a judge wrote, "I would sooner trust the smallest slip of paper for truth, than the strongest and most retentive memory ever bestowed on mortal man."[131] While this statement may be an inaccurate statement of the law of evidence, it is indicative of the profound change in attitudes that occurred after the development of print. It reveals an approach to words on paper that would have been incomprehensible to persons living in the early Middle Ages. At that time, people trusted what they knew, and knowledge came more from hearing and talking than from reading. It is with the spread of printing that, for the majority of the public, the phrase "seeing is believing" begins to make sense concerning information that has been seen in a book and that was not experienced personally.

The growing credence paid to words in print led to diminished authority for oral traditions and thus had significant consequences for what judges did. When judges sought solutions to problems in printed works, they found something different from what earlier judges might have discovered in an ancient code or an oral tradition. Law in print, when compared with written law, tended to be both more recent in origin and less tied to the norms and values of other institutions in the society. Courts acquired a different status, and law itself became conceived of differently as the attention of judges was focused on collections of positive law. During this period, as Professor Roberto Unger has argued, law became autonomous. It could be considered to be a body of rules that was more than a "mere restatement of any identifiable set of non-legal beliefs or norms, be they economic, political, or religious."[132] Courts, whose political nature was once accepted, were now more obligated to enforce laws and rules than to accommodate the parties to a solution that was amenable to them and to other interested persons.

Significant changes in the nature of law had already occurred in the centuries prior to the development of printing as the universities grew, as scholars carefully studied the recently discovered Roman legal texts, and as the Church monopoly over copying books was broken. Centralized royal authority appeared, new systems of courts developed, and a professionalized judiciary and legal profession began. The status quo of the early Middle Ages had been disturbed, and new institutions were struggling to deal with new conditions. Yet the oral tradition had not been completely supplanted. Medieval qualities were still present,[133] and the modern character and form of the new institutions generally did not become dominant until the sixteenth, seventeenth, and eighteenth centuries. In the centuries following Gutenberg, courts became more exclusively judicial in character, and the law that was used in these courts was recognized to be that which was enacted by legislative bodies and published by printers. Law and politics became more clearly recognized as being different processes. Rules of evidence became needed. Judges acknowledged that it was legitimate to interpret statutes but not, as had occurred previously, to participate in enacting statutes. Courts recognized that statutory law was authoritative and that they were obligated to follow it. While such thoughts had already surfaced in England, the limitations of writing had interfered with their realization.

The sixteenth and seventeenth centuries were particularly important for the new meaning acquired by the phrase "supremacy of law." These words had been used in the early Middle Ages. Kings were not considered to be all powerful, and public belief in law was high. Supremacy of law, in that context, meant that "there might be fundamental laws, which could not be changed by any person or body of persons in the state."[134] Such laws were authoritative and resistant to innovation because they were assumed to be of ancient origin and embodied the community's values, particularly its concept of justice. In this model of law, "right and justice are the same as right and law."[135] In the sixteenth century, legislation proliferated and law became "more of a secular tool to be addressed to the needs of the community at large."[136] Out of the clash between Parliament and the king came a new vision of what was supreme. As the eminent English historian William Holdsworth concluded, "It is clear that the supremacy of the law . . . has come to mean, not the supremacy of an unchangeable law, but the supremacy of a law which parliament can change."[137] As a practical matter, what became supreme were rules in printed form.

This change came about as communication in printed form became more authoritative than information transmitted orally or in writing. Particularly when statutes were printed and widely distributed in the vernacular, the attention of judges was focused in a new direction. Printed law competed with the oral tradition and ultimately supplanted it. In earlier times, written law needed an oral tradition to keep it up to date and responsive to changed conditions. The oral tradition remained strong even as writing was used. Walter Ong has noted that

> scribes learned how to commit discourse to writing, but basically composition as such remained an oral matter. Early written prose is more or less like a transcribed oration, and early poetry is even more oral in its economy. From antiquity through the Renaissance and to the beginnings of romanticism, under all teaching about the art of verbal expression there lies the more or less dominant supposition that the paradigm of all expression is the oration.[138]

The change in the late Middle Ages had been "not so much from oral to written as from an earlier state, predominantly oral, to various combinations of oral and written."[139] Written law had worked together with the oral tradition, not instead of it, and thus did not demand a court's exclusive attention. The oral tradition and the written law had supplemented each other, and judges could continue to find solutions to problems in the traditions of the community.

Because both writing and print use similar symbols and marks on some tangible surface, we tend to think that there is a close and natural relationship between these two modes of communication. They are classified together as being visual media that use the sense of sight. Yet this is a modern way of looking at these forms of communication. Print, unlike writing, was able to foster new habits of thought toward words on paper. It reduced the authority of oral communication in ways that writing had not been able to do. Since the introduction of printing, words on paper have enjoyed the respect previously reserved for ancient tradition passed down orally or written works presumed to have a divine origin. Printed works, such as statutes, benefitted from this change, and, as a result, the roles of courts and legislatures became more defined and distinct.

Part of the reason why writing, unlike printing, had difficulty replacing oral traditions was that writing had not been viewed by many as a visual medium, as a totally new and distinct form of communication. Prior to the development of printing, the written word was more often heard than seen. Reading was "linked in the medieval mind with hearing"[140] because books or documents were intended to be read aloud. It was generally a group experience in which persons listened to what had been written. Even individuals who could read, read aloud to themselves. Reading was rarely the silent and solitary act that it became after Gutenberg. Publication, communication, and application of law implied speaking, hearing, and remembering, such as when laws were "published" by having criers proclaim them before large groups or when populations were enjoined that "the book of the law shall not depart out of thy mouth."[141] M. T. Clanchy has observed that

in non-literate cultures the skills of eye and hand are associated primarily with craftmanship and the visual arts, while the skills of language, which depend on the transmission of sound, are identified with mouth and ear. Although writing had the potential, in medieval England as elsewhere, to change the perception of language by making it visual as well as auditory . . . preliterate habits of mind persisted long after documents became common. Books and letters continued to be read aloud and listened to, instead of being silently scrutinized by the eye, and authors went on thinking of composition in terms of dictation rather than of manipulating a pen. The skills of reading and writing therefore remained distinct, because reading was part of the mastery of speech whereas writing was one of the manual and visual arts.[142]

Printing was significant, therefore, because "the history of the progress from script to print is a history of the gradual substitution of visual for auditory methods of communicating and receiving ideas."[143] The development of print profoundly altered traditional methods of reading and fostered the modern notion that writing, like print, is visual in nature. The printed book, which gradually came to be read silently, was more distinguishable from the spoken word than writing had been, and it was natural for the dispute resolution process to give greater attention to rules in print than it had given to rules in written form. Law in printed form was not a second-rate substitute for law as it existed in the minds of the people, for common knowledge. Rather, law in printed form was something that might even be superior, something that could contain common law for persons in widely separated places. Although law itself might be something abstract, it could now be found in something tangible. All printed books could be trusted to contain the same information, unlike written works, and could contain large quantities of data that might overburden memory. The law had been growing larger and more complex, and

> the time had passed for ever when law and procedure could be modified by the simple machinery of instructions, written or even oral, privately given to the King's Justices as they set out upon their eyre. The magnitude of business passing through the King's Courts and the technicality of the rules governing its conduct, made it necessary for future changes to be in a definite [form].[144]

Laws of Parliament were printed shortly after the introduction of printing in England,[145] and there was great demand for them.[146] Their publication focused attention on legislative enactments in a way that had not been possible earlier. The process of handling disputes during the sixteenth and seventeenth centuries increasingly required consulting books, not simply to learn the rules of procedure, as in earlier times, but to discover the nature of substantive law. More than one-third of the cases in Plowden's reports of the late sixteenth century deal with the application of acts of Parliament.[147] This was a period of accelerated legislation,[148] and

"English lawyers were beginning to think of their law in substantive terms."[149] Attention was therefore frequently focused on one work, *The Statutes at Large*, "which contained all the statutes that were then in force and were the ultimate authority."[150]

Plucknett has observed that "one of the most significant themes in the study of legal history is the growth of the power to think of law apart from its procedure."[151] This is a striking statement, considering how comfortable the modern mind is with thinking of law in substantive terms. Because of the increased importance of statutes and substantive law, "the history of statutory interpretation begins in the sixteenth century. Before that time the courts had tended to regard statutes as isolated rulings enacted to supplement the common law; now lawyers came increasingly to regard them as the supreme authority."[152] The highest priority in the past had been to settle a problem in a way that was acceptable, not necessarily in a manner that conformed to a substantive rule. What occurred was a "shift of emphasis from doctrine (common learning) to jurisprudence (or judge-made law)" as the body of law became larger and more complex. An increased emphasis on substantive law occurred when law was changing and was no longer widely known. As Harold Berman has observed,

> Before the professionalization and systematization of law, more scope was left for people's attitudes and beliefs and for their unconscious ideas, their processes of mythical thought. This gave rise to legal procedures which depended heavily on ritual and symbol and which in that sense were highly technical, but by the same token the substantive law was plastic and largely nontechnical. Rights and duties were not bound to the letter of legal texts but instead were a reflection of community values.[153]

The authority and distinctiveness of printed law was also assisted by the publication of books of commentaries on the statutes. Printing, in law and in other fields of knowledge,[154] encouraged thought to be given to basic organizing principles and concepts. Like modern books but unlike manuscripts, printed volumes were indexed and paginated and provided a common frame of reference for readers. As Elizabeth Eisenstein observed,

> The systematic arrangement of titles, the tables which followed strict alphabetical order, the indexes and cross-references to accurately numbered paragraphs all show how new tools available to printers helped

to bring more order and method into a significant body of public law. Until the end of the fifteenth century, it was not always easy to decide "what a statute really was" and confusion had long been compounded concerning diverse "great" charters. In "Englishing and printing" the "Great Boke of Statutes 1530–1533" John Rastell took care to provide an introductory "Tabula": a forty-six page "chronological register by chapters of the statutes 1327 to 1523." He was not merely providing a table of contents: he was also offering a systematic review of parliamentary history—the first many readers had ever seen.[155]

Print focused attention on collections that were believed to be complete and error free and allowed comparisons among related works and the publication of findings. The new qualities of printed works "helped to reorder the thoughts of all readers, whatever their profession or craft. Hence countless activities were subjected to a new 'esprit de système.' "[156] The period from 1485 to 1640 saw "the development for the first time of the historical study of law and legal institutions, and a heightened awareness of 'system' and the need to present law as a rational discipline."[157] Medieval legal scholars, for example, who had studied and analyzed Justinian's text did not have a manuscript of the whole text in front of them and thus did not try to relate sections of the *Corpus Juris* to the whole thing.[158] After "the brilliant thirteenth century" in England, Maitland has written,

> a long dull period . . . set in. The custody of the common law was now committed to a small group of judges and lawyers. They knew their own business very thoroughly, and they knew nothing else. Law was now divorced from literature; no one attempted to write a book about it. The decisions of the courts at Westminster were diligently reported and diligently studied, but no one thought of comparing English law with anything else.[159]

Earlier attempts had been made to analyze the nature of English law, yet these attempts had been sabotaged by the limitations of writing. As a result, some of these books had their greatest impact when they were printed centuries after they were written. The most famous of these works, Bracton's treatise from the twelfth century, "exercised its greatest influence in the sixteenth and seventeenth centuries."[160] When it had first been written, Bracton's book had been widely copied but "after a century his work became less popular. . . . It was only centuries later that the printing press was to establish Bracton's position in English legal literature."[161]

Part of the problem was that copying by hand had led to copying errors so that forty-six partial or complete versions of the manuscript were in existence.[162]

The embodiment of law in printed form did not simply replace law in written form. Rather, it replaced a system of dispute resolution that had often involved written law and oral tradition working together. Printed law, therefore, emphasized decision making according to rules more than some previous systems because attention was focused on rules in a way that had not occurred earlier. In this respect, it is important to recognize that print also brought about a narrowing of the judge's focus. Judges in earlier periods had been able at times to escape rule-oriented decisions because their attention was not bound to a printed or even a written text. They had options that were not available to later generations of judges whose decisions had to be made "by the book."

In England, the establishment of the supremacy of printed law brought with it an increased business for the common law courts and, as a consequence, a growing attention to rule-oriented solutions. One of the striking developments of the sixteenth century was the rapid increase in litigation in the common law courts. In the early part of that century, "common lawyers had been worried that empty courts would put them out of business. From the reign of Elizabeth I the concern was rather that there were too many suits."[163] There was an increase in the jurisdiction of the central courts and a "greater willingness on the part of royal courts (including Parliament) to decide points of law which had not been settled or raised before."[164] Between 1560 and 1640, "there was a great, and probably unprecedented, increase in the amount of litigation entertained by the two main common-law courts at Westminster, the King's Bench and Common Pleas."[165] From 1490 to 1640, the number of cases in these two courts increased from 2,100 to 28,734.[166] Part of the reason for this was the publicity given to the activities of Parliament. Particularly when, in the 1520s, complete collections of the statutes began to be printed in English, rather than in Latin or law French, as in previous times,

> literate Englishmen now had what learned judges and serjeants even had lacked in Fortescue's and Littleton's time: ready access and reference to the texts of statutes on which their cases and problems turned. To encounter . . . what the scarcity of manuscript copies of the statute law had meant in the fourteenth and fifteenth centuries is to grasp

something of the Tudor's excitement, relief, and sense of wonder, at
the Great Books: 300 years of the reigns, councils, Parliaments, statutes, in full sweep. In English, tabled by chapters. . . . *The Great Boke*
and *The Boke of the Magna Carta* thus were powerful factors in creating
the Tudor image and tradition of constitutionalism.[167]

Print was particularly suited to fostering the authority of the
common law because it was a technology that could transmit the
same information widely. Information actually shared by everyone
was not possible, but standardized information was. The connection between the publication of statutes and increased litigation in
common law courts was noted by an observer in 1580 who wrote,
"Many suits have arisen in the comen courts, among subjects . . .
since our statute lawes were published in the English tongue to
the common sort of people. And for this only cause, some . . .
would have the knowledge of our common laws obscurely held
from the common sort of people, as they are now."[168]

Electronic Media

One of the principal qualities of the printed word that benefitted
law was its stability. Books and other printed materials could be
revised, but this required the publication of new editions. What
was between a book's covers did not change between editions.
Print thus promoted a model of resolving disputes in which rules
could reliably be found in books and then applied. Even among
large populations, therefore, print supported the ideal of a law
that was public and applied to all, a common law that could overcome barriers of both time and space.

During a period of expanding knowledge, print was also a means
for keeping the attention of the legal community focused on legal
information rather than on the growing body of nonlegal information. Print was a tool employed to respond to both increasing
levels of conflict and increasing amounts of information. The production of large numbers of standardized copies enhanced the
authority of legal rules in books and supported a redefinition of
the meaning of written law. Printed works were also an effective
point of reference and served to organize and shape the use of
information within the judicial process. They directed attention to

law and assisted rule-oriented procedures to become the state's favored means of dispute resolution.

Because law involves using information to control behavior, challenges to existing legal processes can be expected to occur either when levels of conflict increase or when information is used differently. Electronic communication, which is being used increasingly as a substitute for print, differs significantly from print in how information is stored, presented, and communicated. Both the level of conflict and the means used to deal with conflict will be affected, and, as a result, a reorientation will occur in how we think about law and how and when we turn to law to solve problems.

The new burden on the conflict-resolving institutions of our society and the threat to the legal model of dispute resolution fostered by print result from some of the basic and most novel qualities of electronic communication. These include the speed of communicating electronically, the distance over which information can efficiently be transmitted, the ease with which electronic information can be copied and revised, the digitalization of writing and print, and the prodigious storage and processing capacities of computers.

Copying and the Information Chain

Electronic communication encourages not only the growth of information, but also its storage in a much more dynamic form. One who looks at words on a computer screen or even at words on paper that have emerged from a "printer" may think that he or she is seeing print, but the "typecast," static, or fixed quality of print (and of law) is gradually being lost as information is encoded in electronic form. One of the principal reasons this is occurring is that copying is an automatic part of the electronic communication process. In this regard, communication via a computer differs radically from writing and print. When one sends a letter through the mail, for example, one has the option of making a copy of the original or of not doing so. When one sends someone a book, the book leaves the possession of the sender and becomes the property of someone else. In communicating electronically, however, the process is reversed. What the receiver gets is always a copy, never the original. If the sender and receiver are seeing the same images on their screens, then there are two copies. "All digital machines," it has been written, "copy in order to communicate. They are essentially repeaters, able to regenerate perfect copies with abandon."[169] To say that a file is sent from one computer to another or that electronic mail is sent is to use an anachronistic metaphor. It is always a copy of a file that is transmitted. Corresponding through a computer, or even broadcasting a television signal, involves keeping the original and sending a copy of the source information to the person who requests it.

The current system is not inevitable, but it is efficient and safe. Any other process of communicating would risk losing the material in transmission. When one "loads" a program or data into a computer, the same process of copying the program or data into the computer's memory occurs for the same reason. The copying of electronic information is quick, and the risk of losing data that were moved off a disk as it was "loaded" would be too high.[170]

It might be responded that copying is also the basic element in print technology. The strength of print is indeed its ability to create a specific number of identical copies. Where electronic communication differs is that one who receives an electronic copy can often make another copy or alter it and communicate the new version. Print has operated on the basis of published editions of a certain number of identical copies. Publishers can control the content of the book and the number of copies published; if a book is purchased, passed on to twenty-five friends, and then returned, the book that is given back to the original purchaser will be the same, except perhaps for some fair wear and tear, as the book that was lent. If information in electronic form is lent to someone and then follows the same route as the book, however, the process of transmission will be different and what is returned to the original owner may not be the original copy. If each borrower makes a copy of the information, there may be twenty-five copies instead of one. Even more importantly, each user may modify the information in some way so that it will meet some need that he or she has. In its new form, the information can be passed on by each of the twenty-five people to another group. Richard Solomon has asserted,

The switching store-and-forward machines of telecommunications networks cannot be considered to be mere neutral transmitter-repeaters, as in telegraph systems. Rather, they are duplicators extraordinaire, linked together in a huge system of distributed intelligence. . . . The point is that reading of an electronic text on a computer does not necessarily involve a human. It does imply copying—copying many times over. There is no way for an originator of electronic information on an open network to control what reading or copying takes place somewhere down the line. At any one time there may be multiple copies of a text spread through a multi-machine network. Some copies may be transitory; some may remain until the space they occupy is needed for another purpose.[171]

Similarly, the chief counsel of the Information Industry Association has described how

most companies today, in their daily business, are part of what you might call an "information chain." And that means that a major part of their business involves taking information from a variety of sources, doing a variety of things to it—such as manipulating it using a computer—and either using it to gain a competitive edge, selling it, or passing it on in some way.[172]

Law's silent and faithful ally of print had assisted modern law in achieving its exalted status. This ally is changing, and law in the new form may not have the same authority or status. While the electronic media have many potent qualities, they are not powerful in the same way that print was. In some important ways, indeed, the power of the electronic media are undermining the authority of print. Just as public belief in "written law" was altered by print, print is being altered by electronic communication. As Ithiel de Sola Pool recognized,

One change that computers seem likely to cause is a decline of canonical texts produced in uniform copies. In some ways this change will signal a return in print to the style of the manuscript, or even to the ways of oral communication. . . . A small subculture of computer scientists who write and edit on data networks like the Arpanet foreshadow what is to come. One person types out comments at a terminal and gives colleagues on the network access to the comments. As each person copies, modifies, edits and expands the text, it changes from day to day. With each change, the text is stored somewhere in a different version.[173]

This is a perception of textual data that may take some time to pierce the public consciousness. It is a change of great significance but not one that is easily measurable. This shift from stability to volatility, as the following section argues, is fostered by the treatment of all data as numbers. Its effect will be to blur one of the main focal points of the law and to replace a single point of reference with multiple images.

The Digitalization of Writing and Print

One of the forces that is accelerating the movement of information along the "information chain" is the placing of data in digital form. Digitalization is a process in which some record of reality is broken up into many parts, and each part is assigned a numerical value. Pictures, for example, are not treated as whole images but as thousands or millions of dots, each of which can be identified by number. A picture can be communicated electronically, therefore, by placing it into a machine that performs this numbering process, converts the numbers to electronic signals, sends the signals to some other place, and then reverses the process and transforms the signal back into the original.

Moving information electronically does not simply transport data faster and over greater distances than other media but transforms it in the process. Most of the time, the transformation is imperceptible to the receiver. When compared with print, however, the process is less trustworthy and open to some doubt. The process of breakdown and restoration always has the possibility of intentional or accidental misuse. Digitalization thus has two equal potentials: to copy and communicate the original in a highly accurate manner; to distort reality so profoundly but imperceptibly that the receiver of the communication cannot know whether the copy as received is the same as the original or, if different, different to what degree from the original. Charles Krauthammer has observed that

once chopped into numbered bits, reality can be manipulated with unnatural ease and in an infinity of ways by microprocessors. Digital is ideally suited to crunching, shaping and twisting by modern computers. Hence such dazzling achievements as synthetic speech, computer-assisted design and the visual effects that the most modest

TV station can produce with the flick of a switch: images wrapped and flipped and squeezed and sometimes turned like pages.[174]

What is often not understood by the general public is that the impressive feats of creating "special effects," sounds and images that do not exist in nature, can be matched by the manipulation and alteration of existing sounds or images. The assertion that "seeing is believing" is, as a result, in some jeopardy. A *New York Times* story, for example, about old-fashioned ice-cream parlors in New York City included a photograph of some people sitting at a counter sipping sodas. Several days later, the *Times* admitted that

> an illustration on the front page of The Living Section on Wednesday that accompanied an article about ice cream showed six people at an ice cream parlor counter with sodas and sundaes.
>
> The illustration was made up of a drawing of the counter and photographs of the people with sodas and sundaes. The drawing and photographs were combined in a way that made it appear that all the people were photographed together at the counter. The photographs of the people were, in fact, made in different places.
>
> As a result, the illustration was misleading and contrary to a policy of *The Times* to make any such combination of artwork and photographs clearly an artist's conception rather than a photographic portrayal of an event.[175]

It is not clear whether the *Times* in this case altered the image electronically, but the fact that today almost all information in print is actually a copy of information that was once in electronic form inevitably will raise doubts that did not exist before. We are still in a stage where the printed word looks like print always did and is assumed to have all its traditional qualities. Yet almost all printed pages, such as the one you are now reading or the front page of your morning newspaper, were once in electronic form.[176] There is no technological reason why this book could not be sold in printed form for those who like the traditional book form or be available in electronic form for those who prefer it that way. The same information can be distributed on paper, on the screen, in big or small type, with accompanying music or pictures if desired, or in some other fashion. Communications scholar James Beniger has pointed out that the progressive digitalization of mass media and telecommunications content begins to blur earlier distinctions between the communication of information and its processing (as implied by the term compunications), as well as between people and machines. Digitalization makes communication from persons to machines, between machines, and even from machines to persons as easy as it is between persons. Also blurred are the distinctions among information types: numbers, words, pictures, and sounds, and eventually tastes, odors, and possibly even sensations, all might one day be stored, processed, and communicated in the same digital form.[177]

What is important to recognize is that placing information in electronic form increases the number of options that are available for distributing and receiving the information. Information need not be presented any longer in uniform and standardized form, since many of the constraints of print have been lifted. This is not a change that should be ignored because the presentation of information in stable and reliable form, as I have argued, has been one of the structural supports of the trust that has been placed in law. Law benefitted from the belief that seeing was believing and that what was printed was as trustworthy as anything else one might see. Law may, just as easily, be hurt by a process of communication that is open to doubt, is changeable, and is not always subject to easy verification.

Information Storage and Processing

In the age before printing, it was common to possess and study parts of manuscripts that were large and scarce. Print contributed to the creation, analysis, and comparison of larger bodies of knowledge by allowing complete texts to be owned and by facilitating the study of more information about a subject. Yet while print overcame the shortcomings of writing, it had its own built-in limitations. Editorial judgments became important as publishing became a profitable commercial enterprise, and decisions were made about what kinds of books should be published and what should be included in books and what should not. As already noted, law proved to be a convenient and popular category for publishers. As legal works proliferated in print, the use of these materials for processing disputes was encouraged. Equally important, print neglected nonlegal modes of dispute resolution, which suffered as consequence. The line between legal and nonlegal modes of dispute resolution became greater and greater, and law, as an important state activity, was emphasized. Other forms of conflict resolution received less attention in print and less attention generally. Most of them depended primarily on the spoken word and were relegated to the status of nonstate activities.

Electronic information can be stored in much larger quantities than print. It is also organized and accessed differently. The book, J. David Bolter has observed, is a

> carefully designed structure of words on a page, but it is a frozen structure, and it is linear. Most printed books have a sense of direction and development; they expect the reader to follow the flow of events and ideas described from beginning to end . . . elements of data in a computer memory system are not limited to one rigid order. Put the elements in a random-access device and the user can examine them in any order he cares to define. . . . In short, because we define and redefine the structure of our data, we break free of the fundamentally linear order imposed by the mechanical technology of the book. Our structures have two or more dimensions, as is indicated by the multidimensional trees and other diagrams we draw to represent them. The computer memory offers us in a strict sense a "new dimension" in the representation of information. In building such structures, computer memory is associative rather than linear. It allows us to follow our networks of association in our data, as indeed human memory does.[178]

Electronic communication and information processing breaks down some of the barriers between bodies of information that print had established. It increases the number of avenues for obtaining information and encourages the seeker of knowledge to try new paths that are continually being created. It allows individuals to enlarge or reduce categories of information as they see fit. It encourages, in other words, an interaction with data that is different from reading a book. It expands options and, as a result, does not filter out legally irrelevant information or nonlegal information in the same way that print did.

This presents a threat to law because limiting and structuring the use of information are fundamental parts of the legal process. Compared with other techniques for resolving disputes, rule-oriented processes require thinking with a restricted focus. Public opinion, ridicule, and gossip are effective at preventing and dealing with conflict because there are many participants, and each feels free to raise issues that he or she considers relevant. While culture and custom will create a concept of what is appropriate and relevant to discuss in different types of cases, they will typically have a broader focus than what is found in a legalistic process.[179] Discourse in court is expected to conform to what is considered to be relevant to the rule, not to what the parties consider to be relevant to the facts. Lawyers, it has been written, have a "trained incapacity in letting the parties decide what they think is relevant."[180] While law encourages attention to what the rule means or requires, nonlegal processes are freer to consider moral and policy issues. John Dickinson, for example, has noted that legal rules guide

> the attention of the adjudicating official to certain particular issues rather than others. . . . In the absence of rules, the attention of the official would be free to wander at large over the manifold elements of the case so that the ultimate decision might be reached on the basis of any factor or factors which for the time being loomed largest to the judge's mind. The operation of rules is to make certain factors the primary elements before the judge's attention, and to push other considerations into the background until he has reached conclusions on those which the rules single out as primary. It thus helps him decide without making the ultimate decision for him; it supplies a structure for his thought to follow, it draws a sketch map for him of the way into and through a case.[181]

Because the attention to rules restricts the way in which information is used, law is not a process of settling disputes that will appear to be desirable, appropriate, or natural to all cultures. Societies that create rules and wish those rules to be observed must recognize that such a process imposes restrictions on those who are responsible for applying the rules. We limit the power of judges by restricting the information they may consider.[182] The legal mode of resolving conflict is generally more limited in the questions it can answer than a media-based process that imposes few restrictions on the scope of the inquiry. It is different from the group that considered its chief to be "like a rubbish dump. Anything can be brought to him and he must listen."[183] For a group that is accustomed to settling disputes by talking about them and by exploring all the causes of the grievance and the ramifications of various settlements, law will appear to be restrictive and, perhaps, irrational.

While law often appears to be confronting the most complex of issues, it manages to do so only by performing an informational sleight of hand that the public typically does not see and that is intended to reduce the scope of what is discussed and considered about the dispute. In our society, law is asked to answer many significant issues and appears to most of the public to do so. Legal literature frequently refers to Toqueville's observation that "scarcely any political question arises in the United States that is not resolved, sooner or later, into a judicial question."[184] In many of these cases, however, what the public thinks is happening and what is actually occurring are not the same. A simple example of how and why the law's model for answering questions will differ from the approach of a non-law-oriented person is provided by a religious dispute that occurred in Norway in the early 1950s. As described by the sociologist of law Vilhelm Aubert, a liberal Norwegian bishop named Schjelderup publicly voiced serious doubts about whether there was such a thing as eternal damnation in hell.[185] This was followed by an extremely hostile attack by an influential Protestant theologian. Schjelderup felt that his position as a bishop of the Norwegian state church was being undermined and complained to the governmental department responsible for religion and education. In response, the department asked a constitutional lawyer for a legal judgment on the issue raised by the debate about hell.

The lawyer's opinion, when it was published, supported Schjelderup and appeared to the public to confirm the doubts he expressed about eternal damnation. In reality, the public perception was wrong because the law obviously could not answer such a question. What the lawyer did, and what the law frequently does, is change the question into one that the law is able to answer. The legal opinion in this case actually examined whether Schjelderup had violated his duties as an official of the Norwegian state church by expressing his opinion. Aubert comments,

> The reason why law can answer all questions, albeit in a specific and restricted way, is that it creates its own reality. It does not permit any problems to be legitimately raised other than those it can answer. All other questions are legally irrelevant, even if lawyers will have to admit that they are far from insignificant. . . . From a legal point of view, Hell

both exists and does not exist. This opinion is of limited use to the sinful believer who is nagged by fear of eternal pain in Hell, but it may be of considerable assistance to liberal theologians who are anxious about whether they can be true to their own convictions and yet remain safely within the broad confines of the Church. It concerns their rights as preachers, the freedom of the pulpit. . . . The incident shows that it is possible to terminate or temper a conflict by legal arguments, notwithstanding the fact that the source of the tension may lie in a question as intractable to rational argument as one could possibly find.[186]

Law appears to answer all questions only because it first forces litigants into presenting courts with the kind of questions that are suitable for legal consideration. Lawyers must frame issues properly and in a form that they believe the court will consider to be legally relevant and answerable. This is an indispensable prerequisite for any litigation and a critical part of the legal process. Law professor Bruce Ackerman has perceptively observed that defendants "are not free to rationalize their position by offering any and every reason that might conceivably legitimate their legal position. Instead, each legal culture should be conceived as a vast conversational filter that allows only a small fraction of possible justifications into the legal conversation provoked by the question of legitimacy."[187]

Law's imposition of a narrow focus and of restricted options is evident also in the range of preferred solutions to disputes. The process of focusing attention on rules and of limiting knowledge of other information tends to foster a dichotomous mode of thought. Anthropologist Lloyd Fallers has observed that

it is characteristic of the legal mode of social control that rules are used to arrive at simple, dichotomous moral decisions—"yes" or "no" decisions that in other contexts would seem intolerably oversimplified morally. The legal process does not ask: What are all the rights and wrongs of this situation—on both sides? Rather, it asks: Is John Doe guilty as charged? John Doe may be utterly depraved—may be shown to have treated Richard Roe abominably—but if he cannot be shown to have violated the rule as charged, he (as far as the legal process is concerned) goes as free as if he were a saint.[188]

The process of using and becoming reliant on written rules, of assessing whether or not the rule applies, and of deciding whether or not it has been violated tends to encourage a belief that one party is right and the other wrong. If attention to rules is increased and other information is not permitted to be considered in the adjudication process, compromise becomes less likely and an outcome in which fault is shared begins to seem less appropriate. While acknowledging that the following model may not be followed in practice, Simon Roberts has concluded that

> the ideal relationship between rule and decision is clear-cut: the facts lead the judge to the appropriate rule in the repertoire, which in turn indicates the decision: Rule determines outcome. . . . One important element which flows from such a system of rule-based adjudication is that little element of compromise is encouraged. Once the issue is before the judge he is expected to decide the matter, rather than act as a mediator between the two disputants. . . . Also inherent in this method of adjudication is the result that one party wins and the other loses. . . . it is not an objective of the system that both parties should go away feeling that they have won, or even that honours have been shared.[189]

Reliance on rules, therefore, tends to limit the range of options available to a judge. Solutions to problems cannot be imposed simply because the judge believes that they are fair or is confident that they will repair a damaged relationship. The judge is expected to pay attention to what is legal more than to what is just.

Law is sometimes praised for a commitment to "blind justice." In reality, the legal mode of dispute resolution is myopic rather than blind. It carries out its task of deciding disputes by limiting its vision and the scope of its inquiry. "Legal training," Nils Christie has written, "is a training in limiting the area of factors accepted as relevant."[190] Similarly, rules of evidence have been called "the most careful attempt to control the processes of communication to be found outside a laboratory."[191] In this regard, therefore, law may be compared to a racehorse that wears blinders during a race. Such horses run faster when their vision is partially obstructed. They can achieve their goal when opportunities for distraction are removed. What blinders accomplish for such horses, procedure accomplishes for law. Different legal cultures may vary in what is considered legally irrelevant information, but a commitment to law cannot be taken seriously if there is no set of procedures or mechanisms that in some way pressure the judge to pay more attention to the rules than to any other factors. This was acknowledged in a most eloquent manner by a professor of law, Robert Cover, who pondered how Justitia, equipped as she is with a sword and scales and standing upright with blindfolded eyes, obtained her job.

> Consider, a moment, a possible myth that might lie behind our well-known icon. Each God's hand is set against her neighbor. The Gods, amidst heated disputes leading to a cosmogenic crisis, search for the route to peace and with it the end of the cosmic travail. The obvious solution, an impartial arbiter to the various differences, is dashed on the rocks of personalities as each and every applicant for the job is put to a test. One young, strong God comes forward and seems fearless and undaunted before threats but is seduced from his vocation by a beautiful nymph. An old and wise man is impervious to chicanery and immune to the allures of sex, but quivers before the fist of the strong. The tests go on until Justitia steps forward. Self-consciously, she ties her scarf to her eyes and with effort of will she sees not. Seeing not, she fears not. No form attracts her. Her very invention of the gesture has a superficial attractiveness about it. She is obviously attuned to the need to keep much from herself and the very fact that she is cognizant of the import of keeping out information makes her a more suitable candidate than one who rashly or stupidly tries to overcome.
>
> Justitia is chosen as their judge and her story portrays the "para-digmatic gesture" repeated by all judges who are worthy of the name. It is a tale of purposeful interposition of a makeshift screen between reality and decision, an interposition which obstructs direct knowledge. . . .
>
> Our icon is Justitia blindfolded, not Justitia blind, and therein is suggested a critical dimension for procedure. Political cartoonists have often seized upon this dimension of the icon and portrayed Justitia "peeking" in order to illustrate the willful failure of impartiality. The blindfold (as opposed to blindness) suggests an act of self-restraint. She *could* act otherwise and there is, thus, an everpresent element of choice in assuming the posture. The temptation to raise the blindfold may not be the temptation to cheat. Indeed, the strongest temptation for persons of quality is the temptation to *see*—to overcome the elusiveness of indirection.[192]

Cover concludes by suggesting that "procedure is the blindfold of justice."[193]

One of the few books that has explored the meaning of a change in communication for a process that has great social importance

is John Ziman's *Public Knowledge*. Ziman, a professor of theoretical physics, believes that modern science began after the invention of printing and was influenced by habits of thought
conditioned by print. He contends that

> our experience of the form that such knowledge can take is so limited
> to verbalizations and formulae—to written and printed words and sym-
> bols—that we instinctively frame our definitions of Science within the
> framework of such forms. Our theories and explanations have to pass
> through this filter, in which causes are only allowed to act singly, and
> effects can only be observed in one dimension at a time. A photograph,
> a tape-recording, an electronic device, can react to many causes si-
> multaneously, and yet record the consequences, as a complex pattern,
> accurately and reproducibly. It thus permits us to entertain theories
> and explanations whose workings and consequences cannot be rep-
> resented by symbols placed in order on the page. The very nature of
> scientific thought must be modified by this development.[194]

Law, like science, reflects certain assumptions that have been
encouraged by the nature of printed information. Law has its own
editorial process that filters out certain information in order to
make the process operate efficiently. This is easier to do when
one's eyes are focused on the printed page than when one's attention can be diverted to other objects. The process of law, for
it to work according to plan, must structure and limit the mind of
the judge. Faith in law is faith in a process that is successful when
it suppresses one's natural instinct to consider all the complexities
in a dispute. The nature of the printed word, therefore, and its
use in the training and work of the judge, has been very important
in the willingness of the judiciary to accept restrictions that are
now ingrained in the process of law. The explosive growth of
information is a serious challenge for law if it will diminish the
effectiveness of the means employed by the law to suppress the
information that may enter the legal process. Herbert Simon has
pointed out that "many of the efforts to design information systems
for municipalities and corporations fell into the fallacy of thinking
that 'more information is better.' They took over, implicitly, the
assumptions of a past society where information rather than attention was the scarce resource."[195] Such programs did not realize
that institutions often require "the destruction or ignoring of information in order to facilitate its processing."[196] The legal com-

munity seems equally unconcerned with how increasing quantities of information and expanding sources of information will affect the myopia that the law has worked so hard to achieve.

Conflict and the Resolution of Conflict

In *The Laws,* Plato wrote,

> The first and highest form of the state and of the government and of the law is that in which there prevails most widely the ancient saying, that "Friends have all things in common." Whether there is anywhere now, or ever will be, this communion of women and children and of property, in which the private and individual is altogether banished from life, and things which are by nature private, such as eyes and ears and hands, have become common, and in some way see and hear and act in common, and all men express praise and blame and feel joy and sorrow on the same occasions, and whatever laws there are unite the city to the utmost,—whether all this is possible or not, I say that no man, acting upon any other principle, will ever constitute a state which will be truer or better or more exalted in virtue.[197]

This utopia, in which individuals "see and hear and act in common," relied on perfect communication among citizens. Plato understood that such a society had to be based on the spoken word, a means of communication that was accessible, that was relatively uncontrollable by any single person in the group, that was highly influential in a face-to-face context, and that implicitly limited the growth of information and the size of the group. As will be explained in Chapter 3, Plato regarded writing as a divisive and destructive force that interfered with the acquisition of knowledge, the attainment of truth, and the achievement of justice. He regretted the recent introduction of writing into ancient Greece and believed that it created more disunity than unity and made the teaching of traditional values more difficult.

While Plato may be guilty of distorting the past and of glorifying uniformity, his sensitivity to the wide ramifications of a new form of communication should not be dismissed, particularly in this era of emerging electronic media. The history of writing and print, and our brief experience with electronic media, indicate that the degree of consensus that once existed in small groups will not be matched again. Each new medium of communication—by expanding group horizons, by increasing the knowledge base of the group, by influencing individual habits of thought, and by promoting new intergroup and interpersonal interactions—has moved us farther away from the pristine state of affairs that Plato longed for. While there are occasional and highly publicized instances in which the electronic media appear to unite countries, these occurrences are inevitably brief. The more common condition of society in the future will be one of heightened diversity and competition and will present a growing challenge to traditional means of preserving order.

A recurrent theme in this book is that, contrary to what is popularly believed, electronic communication is exceedingly difficult for the state to control. In the following chapters, it will be explained how the electronic media promote First Amendment values while interfering with other legal doctrines, such as copyright, obscenity, or privacy, that rely on restricting the flow of information. In a less direct way, perhaps, the degree of conflict in our society will also be affected by the fact that the movement of information is being expanded and accelerated and the use of information cannot be manipulated, as it once was. Courts and other law-oriented institutions that need to direct attention to rules and away from other categories of information will thus face serious obstacles in the new environment and will be forced to change as a result.

To suggest that the electronic media promote fragmentation and heterogeneity rather than uniformity and homogeneity is to contradict some popular beliefs about the effect of television in particular and, more generally, about the movement of information in an electronic environment. Largely as a consequence of the power of McLuhan's vision of a "global village" and of our personal experiences with television over the past fifty years, the new media have been feared for promoting uniformity and stifling creativity. That the new media were creating a "global village" was one of McLuhan's most controversial and publicized assertions. He wrote that "postliterate man's electronic media contract the world to a village or tribe where everything happens to everyone at the same time."[198] However, while the new media are certainly global in character and have as one of their most influential features the ability to transmit data across incredible distances, the village part of the analogy has some serious flaws. The pattern of communication, for example, in the "global village" is very different from the flow of information in the tribal group. As Plato recognized, the essence of conflict prevention in the small group was that everyone knew everything that happened. Uniformity and homogeneity were based on shared values and perceptions that came about because change was slow and information moved quickly among the whole group. This condition, however, began to break down with the advent of writing and was destroyed by printing. As Jack Goody and Ian Watt have noted,

> The literate mode of communication is such that it does not impose itself as forcefully or as uniformly as is the case with the oral transmission of the cultural tradition. In non-literate society every social situation cannot but bring the individual into contact with the group's patterns of thought, feeling and action: the choice is between the cultural tradition—or solitude. In a literate society, however, and quite apart from complexities arising from the scale and complexity of the "high" literate tradition, the mere fact that reading and writing are normally solitary activities means that in so far as the dominant cultural tradition is a literary one, it is very easy to avoid; as Bertha Philpotts wrote in her study of Icelandic literature: Printing so obviously makes knowledge accessible to all that we are inclined to forget that it also makes knowledge very easy to avoid. . . . A shepherd in an Icelandic homestead, on the other hand, could not avoid spending his evenings in listening to the kind of literature which interested the farmer. The result was really a degree of national culture such as no nation of today has been able to achieve.[199]

The tribal village was an environment of limited information and fast communication. The electronic global village, however, provides access to increasing amounts of information and encourages the creation of new information. Yet it is not shared information in the sense that the growing body of information will be learned by all even if it is accessible to all. Most of the potential audience for any particular information will typically not acquire it. The electronic media thus continue a trend that has been occurring since the introduction of writing. As Mary Douglas has asserted, "Progress means differentiation. . . . Advance in technology involves differentiation in every sphere, in techniques and materials, in productive and political roles."[200]

In a country that has been dominated by broadcast television, it is not surprising that some aspects of other forms of electronic communication are frequently ignored. In his otherwise remarkable book, *No Sense of Place,* for example, communications theorist Joshua Meyrowitz describes television as a "system that communicates everything to everybody at the same time,"[201] that has created a "shared arena"[202] of information. In addition, "compared to print, television tends to include people of all ages, educational backgrounds, sexes, professions, religions, classes, and ethnic backgrounds into a relatively similar informational world. The differences between 'types' of people are muted."[203] While this seems to be a reasonable conclusion to anyone who has grown up with television, the ultimate effect of communicating electronically, as even Meyrowitz seems to realize elsewhere in his book,[204] will be just the opposite. The movement of information by electronic means tends to highlight differences and thus be divisive. New groups can form among people who can identify others, no matter where they are located, who have some characteristics in common. Information can be refashioned by individuals or groups in accordance with personal or group interests. The overall impact of communication of this type is to promote heterogeneity and diversity rather than homogeneity and unity. The world, as Vine Deloria has observed, is becoming increasingly "not a global village so much as a series of non-homogeneous pockets of identity."[205]

Television has fostered an illusion of homogeneity because of its blandness, its appeal to mass audiences, and its one-way communication and because all viewers learn about some major events—such as the Chernobyl nuclear disaster, the *Challenger* space shuttle accident, or presidential assassinations—at the same time. As electronic communication increases, however, as change accelerates, as new information replaces old, as interest grows about what is occurring in other parts of the globe, and as cable systems and prerecorded communication expand, we will be able to know more than our predecessors but a smaller percentage of what is available to be known. We may be able to find out those things that we wish to know, but we will all know less of all those things that could be known. The end result will be greater diversity, fragmentation, and, in all likelihood, conflict.

Our understanding of electronic communication has been hampered by an almost exclusive focus on television as it has been used in the past and by an image of computers that tends to ignore their communicative capabilities. Computers are generally perceived to be machines that store information and occasionally process it. The public is far more aware of the storage and processing functions of computers than it is of the communicative powers of computers. This is highly unfortunate, since the storage of information usually occurs as a precondition to its being processed or communicated. Information in electronic form can be moved over greater distances with greater speed and in greater quantities than information in any other form. As a result, the "marketplace of ideas" is becoming internationalized,[206] as is the marketplace for conflict. In such an environment, it is inevitable that stress is felt by the means that are currently employed to resolve conflict.

In a best-selling book, John Naisbitt stated that

> an industrial society pits man against fabricated nature. In an information society—for the first time in civilization—the game is interacting with other people. This increases personal transactions geometrically, that is, all forms of interactive communication: telephone calls, checks written, memos, messages, letters, and more. This is one basic reason why we are bound to be a litigious-intensive society.[207]

While Naisbitt's analysis of the impact of the new media on the generation of conflict is valid, his assumption that the end product will inevitably be litigation is doubtful.[208] His conclusion that our society will become "litigious-intensive" assumes that courts will be used the same way in the future as they are today and does not take into account how the development of electronic communication is changing both our attitudes toward law and the manner in which law and courts are employed.

Naisbitt unfortunately does not ask whether the legal process is a desirable, appropriate, or effective vehicle for dealing with the trend he identifies. The new media are not simply affecting the number of problems in society, but also influencing expectations about how problems should be settled and creating difficulties for a system of conflict resolution, such as law, that relies on techniques, approaches, and modes of thought that are tied in many ways to print. The accelerating quantitative growth of information and the increasing volatility of information are fostering cracks in the law's perceived monopolization of the dispute resolution process and are weakening the hold of law on the public mind. Law will certainly not disappear, but it may not have the same status it has been enjoying and it may be different in some important ways. The expanded options in acquiring and communicating information will cause a shift in what courts do, in what the public thinks courts do, and in what the public wants courts to do. The direction of change, I believe, can be illustrated by a comparison of two models of courts. The first model is described in a story by Franz Kafka, while the second is included in a project of dispute resolution that has attracted considerable attention in this country.

In Kafka's story, which is part of his book *The Trial,* a priest tells K, the central character in the book, how

> before the Law stands a doorkeeper on guard. To this doorkeeper there comes a man from the country who begs for admittance to the Law. But the doorkeeper says that he cannot admit the man at the moment. . . . The doorkeeper gives him a stool and lets him sit down at the side of the door. There he sits waiting for days and years.[209]

At the end of the story, the priest relates that the man dies, never having attained access to the law. This summary clearly does not do justice to the parable and to the nuances and subtleties that are present in the original. What is interesting from my point of view, however, is that the man had only a single goal and that there was only a single point of access to the court. The attention of the man from the country was narrowly focused on a single door, that of the law. When the door was not opened, there were no options other than sitting and waiting and, ultimately, dying. He tries various maneuvers to get in the door but does not seem able to imagine any alternatives to the door or to the law.

Like K, we often assume that there are no other options. The communications process of print had supported basic qualities of the legal mode of dispute resolution and habits of thought that fostered public acceptance of law. Both print and law encouraged thinking and seeing in "black and white." The qualities of electronic communication that I have described create new areas of knowledge, blur the lines separating some categories of information, and, in general, expand the options that are available for seeking and obtaining information. Information that had been accessible only through one door may now be acquired in several different ways. As a result, "supremacy of law," in the sense that law is preferred and respected over other techniques of settling disputes, may be very vulnerable.

In stark contrast to the vision of Kafka's "man from the country" are the organizers of an experiment in dispute resolution that has been labeled the "multi-door courthouse."[210] The essence of this concept is a building that is "not simply a courthouse but a Dispute Resolution Center."[211] Various agencies that deal with disputes that might now be located in different places would be housed in "a building with many rooms. In each room disputes could be resolved by a different process."[212] As illustrated in Figure 2-1, behind each door one would find a different method used, such as mediation, arbitration, and the like. The multi-door concept represents an attempt not simply to improve access to law, but to "make multiple paths to justice a reality."[213] By changing what a court is and does, it therefore poses a threat to the "paradigm of legal centralism"[214] and to the way of thinking and the model of dispute resolution described in Kafka's parable. It is also a development that is consistent with the analysis of the qualities of the new media presented earlier.

The attractiveness of many of the alternatives to law is enhanced by the fact that they are not affected by "information overload" in the same manner as rule-oriented processes are. They do not rely on suppression of information, a goal that is more difficult as the movement of information expands and accelerates. As information becomes less controllable, the narrow vision that is inherent in the legal process and in the public's acceptance of the legal process will gradually erode. New options can be expected to challenge existing procedures and lead to a rearrangement of preferred alternatives.[215] While the state may try to maintain control by including these options inside the courthouse,[216] the ultimate result is that the attention given to law is diluted and the authority of law becomes more open to question.

The most astute recent analysis of the relationship between information and conflict is James Beniger's *The Control Revolution.*[217] Beniger argues that "a society's ability to maintain control—at all levels from interpersonal to international relations—will be directly proportional to the development of its in-

Figure 2-1 Multi-Door Dispute Resolution Flow Chart

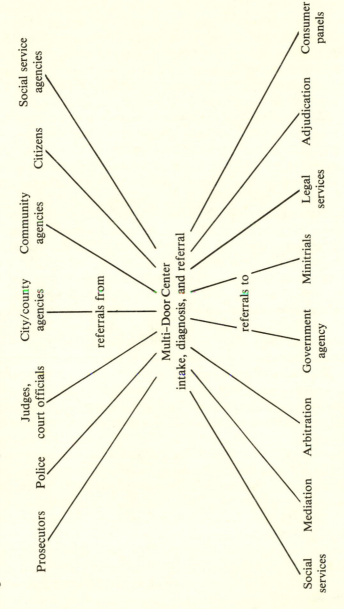

Source: "Toward the Multi-Door Courthouse—Dispute Resolution Intake and Referral," *NIJ Reports,* July 1986, p.3.

formation technologies."[218] Beniger views new information technologies as possible solutions to problems in organizing and controlling information that have resulted from the widespread industrialization that has been occurring for more than a century. The growth in the movement of information has brought about a "crisis of control"[219] for institutions that manage information. This is a special crisis for an institution, such as law, that is concerned with order and that has to control information to be successful. State support for alternatives to law, therefore, may be viewed as a twofold attempt: first, to maintain state control in an era in which it is increasingly difficult to do so through law; second, to assert control over the whole range of means for settling conflict, not simply the legal mode.

One consequence of the growing willingness to accept a variety of options for settling disputes will be some pressure to develop novel techniques for resolving problems that directly employ the electronic media. The computer is a processing device in addition to being a communications technology. It is conceivable, for example, that a new door could be added to the multi-door courthouse which would contain a computer that could offer several services that might influence how disputes were settled. The specter of a computer that would render final judgment for the parties[220] is more remote than the appearance of a computer that could answer particular kinds of questions, one that could help parties in a dispute to clarify what their argument is about and what kinds of solutions are possible, and one that could guide them through the problem-solving process.[221] In this role, the computer would be a consultant or an adviser and, at the very least, an answerer of questions. An even more creative use for the computer would be to develop simulations in order to assist in decision making and to serve as a more active ally in the dispute resolution process than print has been in the legal system. Computer scientist Herbert Simon has urged greater awareness of the fact that "with the development of information-processing technology, we have a growing capacity to consider interactions and tradeoffs among alternatives and consequences; to cumulate our understanding of fragments of the whole problem by embedding these fragments in comprehensive models."[222]

The acceptance of the computer's presence in the courthouse

may also change some of the traditional alternatives to law. Unlike law, many of these methods are effective because they are handled in private. No formal record of the process or outcome need be distributed. Because there are no established channels for communicating information about cases handled in this manner, such methods do not set standards for persons who are not parties to the dispute. Legal adjudication, on the contrary, affects nonparties by setting in motion an "information chain" in which the decision or the report of the decision is transmitted to persons who have an interest in it.[223] Marc Galanter has observed that

> the impact of courts on disputes is to an important extent accomplished by the dissemination of information. Courts produce not only decisions, but messages. Their product is double: what they do and what they say they do. Messages about both are mediated through various channels to different audiences. These messages are resources which parties and others use in envisioning, devising, pursuing, negotiating and vindicating claims (and in avoiding, defending and defeating them). . . . Since courts, like other legal institutions, have far more commitments than resources to carry them out, their capacity to conduct full-blown adjudications is limited to a fraction of potential cases. The social effects they produce by communication must be far more important than the direct effects of the relatively few decisions they render. Law is more capacious as a system of cultural and symbolic meanings than as a set of operative controls. It affects us primarily through communication of symbols—by providing threats, promises, models, persuasion, legitimacy, stigma, etc.[224]

In many cases, this means that the legal mode will alert persons who have a similar grievance to bring it to court. Imposing confidentiality on mediators has the effect not simply of facilitating a settlement by the parties, but also of reducing discussion by nonparties of how the settlement was reached. The powerful transmission capabilities of the new media are assumed to be unused by nonlegal methods, and the discussion of outcomes of settlements reached by such means will, therefore, not be as high as in disputes handled by legal processes.

If such reasoning implicitly or explicitly underlies some of the attractiveness of the proliferating alternatives to law, those in control may be disappointed. Such a view assumes that nonlegal techniques, which have privacy and confidentiality as part of the process, can effectively remain private in the new communications environment. While there is currently a great imbalance in the efficiency of the communications system that exists for communicating legal outcomes and that which exists for obtaining information about nonlegal settlements, this may be changed by the spread of information by new means.

The expansion of options for communicating in an electronic era opens up possibilities for acquiring previously unavailable information. Those interested in a problem that has been settled nonlegally behind one of the new doors of the courthouse will eventually find that it is possible to consult an electronic storehouse of information and discover some information about the case and its resolution. It may be, therefore, that nonlegal methods will not be as private as they once were, and as information about them flows through some channel of communication, they will have the practical effect of influencing the future behavior of nondisputants. Because of the new media, it will be less possible "to view each new dispute as a unique phenomenon"[225] that can be handled in an ad hoc manner that is completely unrelated to similar disputes that have occurred. The expansion of the new media, therefore, should not be considered irrelevant even to those alternatives to law that appear very similar to processes used by ancient nonliterate groups.

The "electronic village" is different from the tribal village. The presence in courthouses of alternatives, such as mediation, that seem to rely more on the spoken word than on futuristic high-tech electronic oracles of justice should not obscure the significant long-term change that is currently taking place as a new communications infrastructure is being put into place. Electronic communication, even if it is ocurring in the background, has begun to affect our practices and expectations. As a result, the role of law will continue to change, and the meaning, purpose, and operation of courts will once again evolve into a new form.[226]

3

Freedom of Expression:
Rights and Realities

> "To the future or to the past, to a time when thought is free, when men are different from one another and do not live alone—to a time when truth exists and what is done cannot be undone:
> From the age of uniformity, from the age of solitude, from the age of Big Brother, from the age of doublethink—greetings!"
>
> GEORGE ORWELL,
> *1984*

The act of writing these words was, for Winston Smith, the main character in George Orwell's *1984,* an act of courage and rebellion. These first words of his diary, written with a quill pen on old paper, represented his resistance to a system that used technology to maximize state power and strip the individual of liberty and freedom. In such a society, even the most personal and least threatening form of communication, such as a secret diary addressed only to future generations, was illegal. The goal of the state was to restrict not only speech and writing, but thought as well.[1]

Orwell's fictional society is an appropriate starting point for an examination of the influence of the new technologies on the "first freedom,"[2] freedom of expression. His vision has colored much of our thinking about technology and freedom during the past forty years and has heightened our society's concern over the misuse of technology and information. The images of *1984* are referred to frequently,[3] resonate powerfully within us, and effectively evoke

113

thoughts of past and present totalitarian regimes. The book has been valuable as a reminder of how deeply the effects of a new medium can be felt and of the fact that information is power and not simply data or knowledge.

While *1984* has been highly effective as a warning concerning abuses of technology and potential assaults on the human psyche, it is less successful if viewed as a realistic guide about the nature or power of the electronic media. It is misleading and damaging if it is assumed to be an accurate prediction or a valid reading of the qualities of the new media. The electronic media can be expected to be a potent influence on individual expression and democratic values, but the future society that Orwell describes is unlikely to come true. As will be explained, an examination of the qualities of electronic communication suggests that the existence of a totalitarian state whose foundation is control over information is less probable in an era of widespread electronic communication than at any previous time. Rather than being an ally of state power, the new media are more likely to be a force that will undermine state control and authority.

It is not surprising that Orwell would assume that electronic communication would have a monolithic quality that would play into the hands of a totalitarian state.[4] He was aware of the effective way Hitler had used radio before and during World War II.[5] He had worked for the British Broadcasting Corporation during the war, and this radio experience had been the breeding ground for many of his ideas about state control of the new media. In reviewing Orwell's wartime experiences, W. J. West concluded that "the totalitarian atmosphere of *Nineteen Eighty-Four*—of universal censorship that alters the past as well as the present and even attempts to alter the mind—was the ultimate development of Orwell's experience of censorship at the BBC."[6] Most of the other technologies that are relevant to this discussion were either in a primitive state or had not even been invented in 1948. Television, for example, was just beginning its period of great expansion in 1948, the year *1984* was completed. In that year, the number of television sets in the United States increased from 100,000 to 1 million.[7] Computers at that time were essentially military secrets[8] that filled huge rooms[9] and served only governments.[10] The transistor was invented in 1948 but was not yet in production, and the first commercial Xerox machine, a large failure at first, was not introduced until 1949.[11]

The most critical error Orwell made was to assume that information in electronic form could be controlled and monopolized by the state. As will be described, contrary to what Orwell thought and contrary to much of what the public still believes, the new media are an imperfect tool for exercising power over the flow of information. Information in the future will frequently be *out of control* rather than *in the control* of any one individual or institution. Thus the new forms of communication ultimately will be more of a threat than an ally to political institutions that developed during the age of print and that relied on control of printed information to enhance their power. For any legal doctrine whose purpose is to restrict or regulate the movement of information, whatever difficulties of enforcement and execution now exist will grow even more serious.

Orwell assumed that the new media would merely extend trends that seemed to be occurring at the time the new forms of communication were being introduced. "Oceania" was not really a new society with new ambitions, institutions, and values but a composite of totalitarian societies that Orwell was familiar with, albeit with an enhanced ability, owing to the new media, to carry out its programs. The old forms of communication had been inefficient and had inherent limitations that prevented complete subjugation of citizens. In the hands of the rulers, he was suggesting, the new media would allow intrusions into personal space that had never before been possible. As he had written in 1939, "the terrifying thing about modern dictatorships is that they are something entirely unprecedented. . . . The radio, press-censorship, standardized education and the secret police have altered everything."[12]

A new form of communication, however, is not simply a more powerful form of what had existed in the past, and it is wrong to assume that the new medium will inevitably be used in the same way the old one was. "New information does not necessarily threaten an ensconced power elite. But a new medium does," William Kuhns has argued.[13] A new medium and a change in the movement of information and access to it are more likely to disturb the status quo than to preserve it. Those individuals or institutions that have acquired power or achieved a high status in any society have been able to exploit and manipulate the currently dominant medium. Power is enhanced whenever one can manipulate who receives or does not receive certain information. There is no guarantee that those with the skills to exploit the old system of communication will either recognize the nature of change being fostered by the new medium or be as adept at exploiting its qualities. The novel qualities of any new medium almost guarantee that new patterns of communication will evolve, and, as a result, ongoing social, economic, political, and legal trends will change course.

The movement of information is the primary focus of many legal doctrines. The law has implicitly understood that to achieve certain goals it is necessary to encourage the movement of information, while to accomplish other ends, the flow of information has to be restricted and regulated. Thus to encourage a vigorous intellectual environment and a democratic political process, the First Amendment contains a basic policy that expression should be encouraged or at least not penalized. Yet there are also a whole host of rules restricting not simply when and where something may be communicated but what may be expressed. One may be punished for expressing libelous statements, for communicating information that invades someone's privacy, for publishing obscene literature, for printing something that someone else has already copyrighted, and for releasing information that violates the espionage or securities laws. These doctrines touch on different aspects of individual and social life, but they are similar in that they achieve their goals through the same means, by regulating in some way the movement of information. Because the new media are changing the flow of information and the ability to control information in society, all these doctrines are being disrupted. The new media have qualities that interfere with the successful operation and enforcement of most of these rules of law.

All these information-related legal doctrines are considerably different from anything that existed prior to Gutenberg. All these doctrines are also experiencing considerable stress and for essentially the same reasons—more information is moving by electronic means, and electronically stored or communicated information is more difficult to control than information in printed or written form. Information in an electronic mode, it will be seen, rarely stays put in one place or in one form. Efficient use of electronic information encourages it to be revised, copied, and transmitted. Information in an electronic environment tends to proliferate, just the opposite of the contraction of information and knowledge that occurred in Oceania.[14] As a result, it will be seen that many values associated with the First Amendment are probably more secure in the new environment than they were in the old. Conversely, those legal doctrines that attempt to restrict the flow of information are finding it increasingly difficult to achieve their goals.

The main purpose of this and the following chapter is to explore the likely impact of basic qualities of the electronic media on those legal doctrines that are designed to foster or restrict the movement of information. These areas of law involve some of our most important legal doctrines. They are designed to protect democratic political values (the First Amendment), liberal legal ideals (privacy), moral values (obscenity), and creative endeavors and property rights (copyright). The primary doctrine of this type, of course, is the constitutional guarantee of free speech and press. This chapter explains how intimately the First Amendment is tied to the medium of print and why the new media are likely to change our system of fostering expression through law. Chapter 4 analyzes the sources of the difficulties that other legal doctrines relating to information are now experiencing.

The First Amendment and the Concept of Free Expression

"Contemporary case law reflects concepts born of the Gutenberg revolution," one commentator has astutely observed.[15] Yet this same author also asserts,

> The information society is not likely to compel a wholesale reappraisal of First Amendment law. True, the advent of new communications technologies such as cable television, Xerox copiers, and teleprocessing have had a sweeping impact on the laws of copyright and privacy. And other applications of electronic technology may force change elsewhere, too. Electronic eavesdropping by foreign agents may, for instance, become intolerable and may give rise to the passage

of protective statutes or negotiated international conventions. But just because there will be more abundant and versatile means of communication in the information society does not necessarily mean that the courts will find it necessary to fundamentally rethink all the rules.[16]

As we explore the history of legal concern about expression and assess the limitations on expression in our society, I think it will become clear that a significant reorientation involving the First Amendment must inevitably take place. The new media are changing both the movement of information and the meaning of information in our society. They do not promise to restrict communication, but they do threaten the communications environment that fostered the idea of a law to protect expression. We may, for example, have both more freedom and a more explicit system of regulation. These are not necessarily contradictory or undesirable states of affairs,[17] but they are also not wholly consistent with the way the First Amendment has been considered in the past.

The following analysis concentrates more on the qualities of the new and old media than on particular court decisions affecting either the First Amendment or legal doctrines that do not seem to be working as effectively now as they did in the past. The purpose is not to determine whether any individual court decision was wise or foolish but to develop a theory about why a whole set of legal doctrines is undergoing change. This approach also makes it possible to see that the new media are not simply extensions of the old media. The new media do not merely have some novel qualities that require some tinkering or revision of old doctrines. Rather, they are different kinds of organisms that move information in new ways and in new forms and that raise questions about all legal doctrines linked in some way to the movement of information. Most of the doctrines discussed would not exist if printing had not been invented. With the development of the electronic media, both those doctrines that foster communication, such as the First Amendment, and those that restrict communication, such as those listed earlier, will go through a process of change. The new media not only raise discrete problems that must be resolved, but also pose new questions about the nature of information and the relationship between citizen and government, two issues that lie at the foundation of First Amendment law and theory.

To understand the changes that are taking place, it is important to recognize that the phrases "free expression," "freedom to communicate," "free speech," and "free press" can be looked at in two ways. These phrases can be considered, first, as legal rights or, second, as describing the degree of freedom actually prevailing in a society. How judges and lawyers think of rights has colored most public discussions of free expression, and this has caused at least one problem. The legal or judicial view of a right is that it is something that is either present or not present. It exists or it does not exist. By definition, there are no half rights. Judges interpreting the First Amendment in individual cases, for example, treat freedom of expression as an either/or question, and the activity in question can only be constitutional or unconstitutional.[18] There is no in-between status.

Because most public discussion of free expression takes place in the context of court rulings involving constitutional rights, it is easy to forget that in practice, there are varying degrees of control over expression and subjective differences among individuals about the degree of freedom that is perceived to exist in society.[19] Our pride in the First Amendment tends to obscure the fact that all societies tolerate some freedom to communicate and all, ours included, tolerate some censorship. There may be considerable differences about how much or how little is censored. But, as one historian has observed, "the relevant question at any stage of human history is not 'Does censorship exist?' but rather, 'Under what sort of censorship do we now live?' "[20] As indicated earlier, copyright, privacy, obscenity, and espionage laws all restrict communication and, therefore, could be considered to be examples of censorship in our society. One commentator has argued that "a censorship-free social environment would not be a social environment at all, it would be a maniac's nightmare."[21]

Law is generally considered to be the determining factor of whether expression will be protected or restricted. Pnina Lahav, in comparing press regulation in different countries, has asked,

> What makes the press "free"? Can there be a free press absent the inclusion of a commitment to press freedom in a constitution? Can a society have a statute that clearly defines the privileges and obligations of the press and still maintain a "free" press? Can the press be free under a regime of censorship? Can the state interfere with editorial

discretion, by providing for a statutory right of reply, for example, and still maintain a free press? Can the press fulfill its role as watchdog of the government and yet be sued by public officials?

In the United States, the conventional answer to these questions in all probability would be that the First Amendment is essential for press freedom, and that a special statute which regulates the press, censorship, and the right of reply, or a defamation law which ignores the importance of uninhibited criticism of public officials, are all incompatible with the notion of a free press. Indeed, the American legal system reflects just this set of answers to the questions posed above.[22]

As a result of this attitude, it has rarely been recognized that legal doctrines related to expression are vitally affected by the communications environment of a particular society. We view law as a means to restrict or protect expression and as a result do not perceive that the kind of law we have and the degree of freedom we enjoy are deeply affected by the kind of media we have. The flow of information in a society is not merely an outgrowth of its laws, but also a result of the means used to communicate in that society. The inability to communicate can, in fact, sometimes be remedied more efficiently through a technological improvement than through a legal change. The form of communication in a society can affect enforcement of legal controls, extend or restrict the capacity for communication, and, ultimately, influence the nature of the legal restrictions on expression in the society. Most importantly, the kind of media used in a society can affect the meaning and value placed on information and thus color a society's perception of the need for regulation. Law, even in the form of a constitutional guarantee, is important and perhaps necessary, but it is not all important or all powerful. We are trying to adjust to a new communications environment that is becoming dominated not by values fostered by print but by a different medium with different qualities. As this occurs, our thinking about information will change and expectations and attitudes about the First Amendment will change as well.

Even in a society with a constitutional guarantee, free expression, both as a legal right and as a state of affairs, has a dynamic and elastic quality. Change occurs continually. These changes in the law and in the ability to communicate do not involve complete elimination or complete freedom but a stretching or contraction, a change in what may be said and how easy it is to say it. A new medium can directly expand or restrict the actual process of communication and indirectly influence the legal doctrines whose job it is to regulate this process of communication. Historian Herbert Muller has observed that

> freedom is more than a political matter. Although men brought up in a consciously free society generally assume, with good reason, that rights or civil liberties guaranteed by law are its essential condition, I assume that a historian in particular has to consider it in relation not only to government but to mores, technology, commerce, art, religion—the culture as a whole. Thus the rise of civilization made political power a problem ever after, but it also widened the range of man's choices, gave freer reign to his creative powers, made possible a fuller range of his potentialities, and eventually produced the higher religions, philosophy, and science, which cannot possibly be ignored in a history of freedom.[23]

If we look at earlier societies, we find that they enjoyed varying degrees of free expression and that the medium of communication used was a significant contributor, along with the law of that society, to the conditions under which communication occurred. What is clear is that law alone does not provide a true picture of the communications environment of a society. Purely oral societies tended to have a high degree of free expression, even though there were no laws guaranteeing a right to speak freely. After the invention of writing, there were still few censorship laws but, unlike in oral cultures, there was more restricted communication. Following the invention of printing, censorship laws were enacted frequently and yet, as a state of affairs, there was significantly more communication than there had been centuries earlier when there were no censorship laws. The explanation for all this is that the different media used in these societies had inherent qualities that thwarted or encouraged the movement of information. In addition, different media created different attitudes toward the nature of information and the uses to which information could be put. By looking at some facets of these different cultures and by understanding the differences in media qualities and how these differences have contributed to the evolution of doctrines relating to communication, we shall better understand what the direction of change will be in modern society.

Speech

In a small group, the spoken word moves very quickly and, as a result, is difficult to control. Before the development of writing, this quality was an important influence on the nature and degree of expression in most societies. Dorothy Lee has written that "as a concept or as a recognized value, freedom is seldom if ever present in non-Western cultures, but the thing itself is present and carefully implemented."[24] Most oral cultures lacked a concept of democracy and of free expression but possessed some qualities that are characteristic of democracies. Power, for example, was often exercised by the group rather than by one individual. There were few formal controls on expression, and, in a subjective sense, communication was more free than in most later societies. What is most important to recognize is that the limits on expression that existed in such societies were traceable not to consciously designed laws but to custom, to taboo, and to the inherent difficulty in controlling the spoken word.

In these local groups, speech was a communications medium that discouraged hierarchy and encouraged equality.[25] What people said was not easily regulated by those who wished to exercise or acquire power. "In the linguistic sense, all oral societies had to be functionally democratic."[26] Behavior by someone else that was perceived to be threatening to one's interests or to the group's interests could be criticized, if not outright and in the open, then by starting rumors and gossip, the ancient equivalent of "leaking information to the media." The spoken word, in a small group, is a fast medium, and complaints and criticisms spread very quickly. The inability to control speech or to trace the source of what was being said about someone gave the individual a measure of political power that, with the advent of writing, citizens would lose for centuries.

While speech was encouraged in such societies and was indispensable to the maintenance of the group, it should not be thought that there was anything resembling "freedom of speech" in a modern sense. Speech in preliterate societies was not intended to satisfy the goals that we have when we assert that expression is important both for the individual and for society. Professor Thomas Emerson, one of the most respected First Amendment scholars, has suggested that free expression is necessary for the following reasons:

1. It facilitates self-fulfillment.
2. It is an essential tool for advancing knowledge and discovering truth.
3. It permits individuals to be involved in the democratic decision-making process.
4. It is a way to achieve a more stable and adaptable community. It provides a safety valve.[27]

In most preliterate societies, the first two of these goals typically were irrelevant. As was seen in earlier chapters, such societies stressed continuity with the past, not experimentation and change. What was most critical was maintaining the harmony and survival of the group and not fostering the success of individuals. While a certain degree of free speech existed, it was not designed to promote individuality or advance knowledge. And truth did not have to be discovered, since it was assumed to already exist and to have been handed down from previous generations.

The last two goals identified by Emerson appear to be more relevant. If a democracy is defined as a system in which everyone is entitled to play a role (even though in fact some persons or groups may be excluded) and in which power is diffuse, one could call such societies democratic.[28] Anthropologist E. Adamson Hoebel, for example, has asserted that "the simplest primitive societies are always democracies; rarely does dictatorial political leadership crop up among savages."[29] He concluded that

there is no tribal state. Leadership resides in family or local group headmen who have little coercive authority and are hence lacking in both the means to exploit and the means to judge. They are not explicitly elected to office; rather, they lead by the tacit consent of their followers, and they lose their leadership when their people begin no longer to accept their suggestions—when they begin to accede to the ideas of some other man. As it is, their leadership is confined to action in routine matters. The patriarchal tyrant of the primitive horde is nothing but a figment of nineteenth-century speculation. The simplest primitive societies are democratic to the point of near-anarchy. But primitive anarchy does not mean disorder. Anarchy as synonymous with disorder occurs only temporarily in complex societies when in a social cataclysm the regulating restraints of government and law are suddenly and disastrously removed.

In the pristine state where all social relations are face to face, where the meager economic resources are open to all and shared by all, where interests are simple and common, basic order is maintained through the primary mechanisms of social control. There is little recognized need for any extensive suprafamilial authority. In the words of Murdock, "United by reciprocal relations and bound by a common culture, the members of the community form an 'ingroup' characterized by internal peace, law, order, and cooperative effort. Since they assist one another in the activities which gratify basic drives and provide one another with certain derivative satisfaction obtainable only in social life, there develops among them a collective sentiment of group solidarity and loyalty which has been variously termed synergism, we-feeling, *esprit de corps*, and consciousness of kind."

Whenever special questions of moment arise, we find that the issue is discussed at length by all the adult males of the group until a consensus is arrived at. The legislative halls of civilization have their foundations in the "town meetings" of the primitive groups.[30]

The governing processes of such societies were critically dependent on expression. Yet I think it is also fair to say that speech did not and could not perform the functions that Emerson had in mind. In modern times, the purpose of being "involved in the democratic decision-making process" is to achieve for the larger society what expression accomplishes for the individual. It is to contribute to policy making, to deal with changed conditions and circumstances, and to advance societal knowledge. What was primarily lacking in oral cultures was a developed "marketplace of ideas."[31] While these societies may have had free speaking, they did not have free thinking, and because of this the potential range of politically critical speech was limited.

At the risk of oversimplifying, preliterate societies did not need speech to assist in making policies for the future because this was not what the group did. The process of adapting to changed circumstances typically occurred informally rather than as a result of deliberate selection of one choice from among several. While expression was an important part of preliterate societies, fostering open discussion was not a conscious policy or something that the group decided was necessary in order to protect certain values or political processes. It existed both because it had served the interests of the people in the past and because speech had certain qualities, the main one being that control over the medium was difficult, if not impossible. There is a lesson about free expression to be learned from this kind of a society, but it is more a media lesson than a legal one. It is that media qualities can encourage the process of expression even when there is no formal law to protect it and restrict expression even when there is no formal or visible censor.

Free expression was used in those societies mainly to settle conflict, to function as a "safety valve." Survival of such groups depended not only on resolving conflict but on preventing it. As a byproduct of the dispute resolution process, however, the special qualities of speech had a significant effect on the values and organization of the group. Speech gave individuals a means to limit political power, to thwart those who would have desired to centralize authority and create a hierarchy. While this end was not always achieved, the power of speech enabled the group to accomplish some of the goals that the legal "right" of free expression would hope to achieve millennia later.

Were such societies places where free speech existed? There were no formal censors, yet there were a host of nonlegal pressures that effectively censored what was said and thought to a degree that might have impressed the rulers of an Orwellian society. The constraints, however, were not formal, visible, and the kind that would appear to be repressive to the members of the group. Individuals from this century would find the atmosphere and attitudes stifling, but it would not be easy to find the censor because every facet of the culture acted to limit deviant thought, deviant expression, and deviant action. In such circumstances, as Maurice Bloch has observed, " 'control' is not seen as control since it is not consciously compared to situations where such control might not exist."[32]

Writing

The development of writing had significant consequences for both the community and the individual. Writing led to societies that, in comparison with those which had been monopolized by the spoken word, were larger, more complex, and less homogeneous.[33] They were also less egalitarian and more frequently contained a group that exercised power over another.[34] In this new social and political environment, the spoken word became very different from what it had been in the past. It became recognized as an instrument of power and as something that could be threatening to those in authority.

Anthropologist Claude Lévi-Strauss has noted that writing's first uses were "connected first and foremost with power. It was used for inventories, catalogues, censuses, laws, and instruction. In all instances, whether the aim was to keep a check on material possessions or on human beings, it is evidence of the power exercised by some men over other men."[35] Another scholar has asserted that "making records is initially a product of distrust rather than social progress."[36] Whether the original aims of such activities were or were not innocent, the effect of using writing for such endeavors typically led to the growth of hierarchy.[37] Unlike speech, which required no special skill or training, writing was possible only for those who could read or write or could employ someone who was literate. Thus whoever could use data that was in written form tended to move into a position of power.

It had been difficult to acquire power in an oral society because speech, public opinion, and the flow of information in such societies were difficult to control. The group maintained its power and achieved consensus by moving information among its members quickly and efficiently. With the introduction of writing, some information began to move not horizontally, as before, but vertically. The movement of written information in such societies paralleled the exercise of power. Written communications moved from those at the top of the hierarchy to those down below and occasionally back up to the top. Lacking writing skills, neither individuals nor groups could effectively communicate in writing with other individuals or groups that, living in different places, might have similar interests or complaints about the prevailing authority. The skill required to write and the ability needed to control the flow of some information were, therefore, the means for securing and exercising power.

At the same time that writing was promoting the restructuring of groups and political entities, it was having an unanticipated effect that did not benefit those who were intent on enhancing their power. It was fostering new ways of thinking and was stimulating questions about the status quo. Owing largely to the durability and transportability of the written word, political administration over large areas and over different groups became possible. Military conquests led to larger, less uniform, and less homogeneous societies. Harold Innis has written that "the sword and the pen worked together. Power was increased by concentration in a few hands, specialization of function was enforced. . . . The written record signed, sealed, and swiftly transmitted was essential to military power and the extension of government."[38] One side effect of expansion over territorial space was that individuals and groups came into contact with other individuals and groups having different ideas, traditions, and practices. As groups became larger, the quantity of information potentially available to an individual increased, and one could compare other traditions with one's own.

Because writing encouraged political expansion and the growth of empires, it eventually brought the society new knowledge and information. New ideas did not come directly from information that had been put in written form, since few individuals were literate, but the overall effect of the new medium and the ways in which it was used contributed to a growth of knowledge nonetheless. Writing made possible the administration of empires, and as soldiers moved to different places, they carried not only weapons but word of what they saw and heard. Journalist Ben Bagdikian has observed that "any massive change in personal travel is a significant event in communications."[39] As noted in Chapter 1, the passage from an oral society to one with writing created a different attitude toward knowledge and a different perspective about using information to create change. As a result, there was not only an increase in the quantity of information present in the society, but also a greater willingness to assess the information and use it.

In the changed communications environment brought about by the introduction of writing, speech itself acquired new capabilities. Earlier societies had tolerated free speech because speech contributed as much to the solution and prevention of problems as to their creation. It was not threatening to the government, since there were no formal governing bodies and rulers. There were built-in controls that effectively limited what was thought and what was said and ensured that speech would not be critical of the basic values or practices of the group. In such an environment, speech was more of a conflict-resolver than conflict-producer, and there was little need or desire for formal controls over communication. As Eugene Black has noted, "Where habits of mind control behavior, law and formal regulation are unnecessary. Social discipline suffices and legal discipline is redundant."[40]

As Eugene Black has noted, "Where habits of mind control behavior, law and formal regulation are unnecessary. Social discipline suffices and legal discipline is redundant."[40]

In literate societies, speech became a potential weapon not only because the societal structure had changed, but also because the role and outlook of the individual were different from what they had been in smaller oral cultures. As writing spread and as societies became larger, the individual became less involved with the group, less indispensable to the success of the group, less identified with the group; gradually, the individual began to emerge from the domination of the group.[41] As a result, he became more of an individual and began to be able to differentiate his personal interests from that of the group.

Writing was a means for some to achieve power and authority over others, but it was not a technology that could foster the same degree of control or unity that the spoken word had been able to do in earlier times. Writing was a reasonably effective tool for administration, for acquiring power, and for controlling some behavior. What individuals thought about, however, could not be as easily regulated. One of the consequences of "the individualizing tendency of a literate technology"[42] was to remove some of the limits over thought that had existed in strictly oral societies. As the range of inquiry and ideas available in the society increased, what was liable to be said changed as well. These messages were not particularly threatening in written form, since few could read and fewer could write. Ancient societies did not have high literacy rates.[43] As M. L. Finley reminds us,

> One cannot say often enough or emphatically enough that in classical antiquity (and indeed anywhere before the invention of printing) the number of books in circulation and the numbers of readers of books were infinitesimal and insignificant outside the small world of professional philosophers and intellectuals. . . . Books and pamphlets played no part of any consequence in affecting or moulding public opinion, even in elite circles.[44]

As a result, the written word rarely suffered from censorship. This fact, however, was not attributable to any belief that information, in either written or spoken form, was deserving of protection. There was no notion "of an inalienable human right of freedom of speech: no ancient state recognized so anachronistic a concept, not even Periclean Athens. If the state did not censor, that was only because writings as such were without sufficient effect."[45]

Yet the fact that in some societies there could be a "small world of professional philosophers and intellectuals" reveals that the impact of writing went far beyond the numbers of books or readers. Philosophy is an endeavor that requires one to ask questions that would not occur to a member of an oral society.[46] While censorship of writings may not have been necessary, the broadening of the content of thought made the spoken word a potential problem. Speech became, therefore, an object of greater concern to authorities than the written word and was subjected to formal restrictions that had not been employed prior to the development of writing.

The development of writing led to the first concrete examples of censorship and restrictions on speech. This occurred particularly often in religious communities.[47] The Ten Commandments, for example, may be a noble expression of eternal ethical concerns, but they are also repressive in terms of expression. Two of the ten establish prohibitions on communication.[48] Exodus 20:4 commands that "thou shalt not make unto thee a graven image," and Exodus 20:7 enjoins individuals that "thou shalt not take the name of the Lord thy God in vain." Insofar as these prohibitions were designed to protect values that were handed down to the people rather than developed by the people, they were typical of how societies that had a writing system tried to protect those who were in authority. In selecting the media of art and speech as the objects of legislation, but not writing, they also reveal which media were perceived as being influential and in need of control.

In such societies, there was more understanding of the nature of the spoken word and more fear of it than previously. While the spoken word was not often threatening in an exclusively oral society, because of the nature of that society and the numerous cultural pressures that affected the content of what was said and thought about, such was not necessarily the case in a society in which writing existed. In these societies, there were persons holding power and, therefore, speech could result in a loss of power.

The censorship laws that arose in ancient societies illustrate both the desire of groups in power to maintain their authority and the fact that they had some difficulty doing so. There is no evidence that any ancient society tolerated what would be today considered to be seditious speech,[49] but the fact that censorship laws were sometimes needed and that speech was a greater threat than writing makes it clear that ancient rulers had problems with seditious speech and were not able to eradicate it. Ancient censorship laws and acts of censorship suggest the beginning of a struggle between the popular will of the people and state authority, a struggle that is still continuing.

In societies that employed writing, neither writing nor speech nor the combination of the two was a serious match for those in power. Speech was perceived to be a potential problem, but the spoken word was generally not capable of being used to forge alliances among groups that had common interests but were separated by distance. Writing was mainly a weapon for those in power and did not foster a pattern of communication that would have suggested to observers any political concept of free speech or any political value in free speech. Writing did have many "liberating consequences for the mind,"[50] but these effects of the shift from orality to literacy occurred in subtle and gradual fashion; more significantly, the political implications of writings were not obvious even to the most perceptive observers of the time. Although censorship laws indicate that the authorities recognized that expression was a threat, there is no evidence that they understood that the new medium of writing contributed both to their own status at the top of the hierarchy and to the potential threat to that status from the derivative effects of a literate society.

The most instructive ancient writings on the cultural and individual impact of writing are found in Plato. The Socratic dialogues show us both an individual, Socrates, and an ancient society, Athens, coming to terms with the differences between expression in an oral society and expression in a literate one.[51] In particular, the combination of effects that writing produced and their impact on the development of a policy of free speech might be clarified by looking briefly at some apparent contradictions in statements of Socrates and at the reality of free speech in ancient Athens, a community that prided itself on the protection of free expression. If we can understand why Socrates was a critic of the poets and what remained of the oral culture, why he was a critic of free expression as it was then practiced in Athens, and why he was also a critic of the relatively new medium of writing, the effect of writing on the spoken word may become clearer.

Socrates was an enemy of Greek poets, with their uncritical acceptance of the lessons of Homer and the other poets.[52] Memorization and repetition of the Homeric epics, he believed, "are the ruin of the hearer's mind."[53] Such practices promoted the solidarity of the group but restricted the opportunities for individual exploration in new directions and stood in the way of philosophical inquiry. Poets, in Socrates' view, were not involved in creative or truth-seeking activities. Rather, they performed the function of censors who accepted and transmitted the past as ultimate truth. For Greeks in Socrates' time, Homer provided all the answers, even about practical matters and appropriate conduct, as becomes evident in this conversation between Socrates and Ion of Ephesus, a public reciter of Homer.

SOCRATES: Well, since you understand military matters, do you do so as being a bit of a general, or as being a good reciter?

ION: I think there's no difference.

SOCRATES: How's that—no difference? Do you say that reciting and generalship are one art, or two?

ION: One, I think.

SOCRATES: Then whoever is a good reciter is also really a good general?

ION: Certainly, my dear Socrates.

SOCRATES: Then whoever is really a good general is also a good reciter?

ION: No, I don't think that.

SOCRATES: But you do think that whoever is a good reciter is also a good general?

ION: By all means.

SOCRATES: Well, you are the best reciter in Hellas?

ION: Much the best, my dear Socrates.

SOCRATES: Then you are also the best general in Hellas?

ION: Yes, I assure you, Socrates; and I learnt it all from Homer.[54]

Yet while the most obvious remnant of Greek oral culture was the object of most of Socrates' mocking, he also criticized writing and was distressed about its limitations. A famous passage in *Phaedrus*, for example, contains the following:

SOCRATES: He would be a very simple person . . . who should leave in writing or receive in writing any art under the idea that the written word would be intelligible or certain; or who deemed that writing was at all better than knowledge and recollection of the same matters?

PHAEDRUS: That is most true.

SOCRATES: I cannot help feeling, Phaedrus, that writing is unfortunately like painting; for the creations of the painter have the attitude of life, and yet if you ask them a question they preserve a solemn silence. . . . And when they have once been written down they are tumbled about anywhere among those who may or may not understand them, and know not to whom they should reply, to whom not; and, if they are maltreated or abused, they have no parent to protect them; and they cannot protect or defend themselves.

PHAEDRUS: That again is most true.

SOCRATES: Is there not another kind of word or speech far better than this, and having far greater power—a son of the same family but lawfully begotten?

PHAEDRUS: Whom do you mean, and what is his origin?

SOCRATES: I mean an intelligent word graven in the soul of the learner, which can defend itself, and knows when to speak and when to be silent.

PHAEDRUS: You mean the living word of knowledge which has a soul, and of which the written word is properly no more than an image?

SOCRATES: Yes, of course that is what I mean.[55]

While Socrates expressed distaste for both the oral culture and the medium of writing, he placed the highest value on learning through the spoken word. His own technique and the educational method he prescribed for training rulers was based on exploring issues through dialectic and conversation. Yet while the spoken word was to be preferred over writing and might lead some persons to the truth, Socrates also saw little value in a policy of free speech or a democracy built on free speech. Quite the contrary, his statements on censorship, and the need for it, are very clear. He was not attracted to a democracy where "liberty and free speech are rife everywhere."[56] While Socrates certainly understood the relationship between speech and learning for some individuals, on a societal basis he perceived free speech as leading only toward anarchy. "The poet," claimed Socrates, "is to create nothing that differs from the city's conventional and just version of the beautiful or good things; he may show none of his creations to any of the nonexperts before he has shown them to the judges appointed in these matters as well as to the Guardians of the Laws, and met with their approval."[57]

Some of these inconsistencies become explainable if we understand that the introduction of writing did not merely add a new and perhaps exotic mode of communication to Greek life but changed the nature and use of the spoken word, the prevailing method of transmitting knowledge. Socrates was an individual with the psychological and cultural habits of thought of the literate mind,[58] but he had little practical experience to suggest that writing could be politically beneficial or worthwhile to the individual. He was sensitive to the significance of a change in the way communication took place but was not aware of the many ramifications of this new medium or even of how it had already affected his own thought. While, as a result of the introduction of writing, the censorious shackles of speech on thought had been broken, it was not clear to him that the fact that speech could now be used as a tool for philosophical inquiry and knowledge was attributable to some of the qualities of writing. For all his sensitivity to the special qualities of different media, Socrates may not have comprehended that his own philosophical inquiries and approach to life could not have occurred in a purely oral society. While he frowned on the inadequacies of writing, his habits of thought are more typical of a literate personality than an oral one.[59]

The introduction of writing began the process of developing the individual's potential but only because it interfered with the manner in which the old medium had been used. Socrates was liberated from the way speech had censored both the imagination and the creativity of individuals and saw speech as the most worthy of activities. He even welcomed death because heaven would bring eternal conversation and discussion.[60] For Socrates, learning was primarily through dialectic, not reading and writing, and the opportunities that would later be available for learning through printed books were unimaginable to a person of his era. Socrates was "poised between an oral past fast disappearing and a literate consciousness now coming into its own."[61] Writing had changed what some thought the mind was capable of achieving, but there was as yet no faith in the capacity of the individual to contribute positively and freely. Given the limitations of writing, it is not surprising that the hierarchical structure of *The Republic* rather than a democracy would appear to be a more feasible option for society. An oral culture placed extreme limitations on individuality, but writing imposed separate problems. Socrates prized speech, at least if it was oriented toward discovering philosophical truth, but writing itself did not appear to have great value.

The lifting of restrictions on individual thought had parallels in Athenian political institutions. Part of the reason why Socrates and many Greek playwrights[62] were critical of Athenian democracy and the exercise of free speech is that during the fifth century B.C. the content of speech had changed considerably. Socrates was able to view "the endless ferment of new ideas at the end of the fifth century in Athens, and the growing skepticism about religion and ethics."[63] We would probably characterize such changes as constituting an expansion of speech and, therefore, of opportunities for expression. But there had been no legal change to account for this change in the content of debate. What was occurring during this period was that some cultural values and customs became less powerful forces in Greek life. As these cultural inhibitions or censors were lifted, the range of expression at public forums became broader.

Socrates perceived two groups of wordsmiths in society as his primary enemies: the poets, whose practices and thinking stifled thought in ways that were common in the oral society; and the Sophists, whose rhetorical tricks and manipulations of ideas suggest that the mental bonds of the oral society had been lifted but no other widely shared values or limits had replaced them. One recent classicist has noted that by the fifth century,

> the technology of writing, together with other cultural forces, brought forth a new point of view. The infamous Sophists, of whom Plato was so critical, were itinerant orators and philosophers who specialized in verbal pyrotechnics and cynical attacks on the established order. These

Sophists relied as much as anyone on the power of the spoken word, for they were debaters and orators. Most of them, however, taught their students to regard language as something to be manipulated arbitrarily for their own purposes, whether philosophical or monetary. For the Sophists, words had lost the awesome power they possessed for earlier generations of thinkers."[64]

This "awesome power" was the power of the spoken word in an oral culture. Until the fifth century B.C., as F. M. Cornford wrote,

the claim of authority to regulate the citizen's conduct had not been explicitly challenged. However much or little individual conduct conformed in fact to the customs and laws of society, it had been tacitly acknowledged that those customs and laws embodied an absolute obligation, beyond dispute. But in the time of Socrates some of the Sophists began to cast doubt on this basic assumption with a daring which seemed to conservative minds to threaten the whole structure of society.[65]

What discussions of Athenian democracy frequently omit is that the expansion of freedom came at the expense of traditional Greek values. Pericles reportedly had said, "We are a free democracy, but we obey the laws, more especially those which protect the oppressed and the unwritten laws whose transgression brings shame."[66] Freedom under law at the beginning of the fifth century B.C. did not mean freedom under written law but freedom under custom or unwritten law, which was an infinitely more important force at that time than written law. It meant freedom within the traditional Greek cultural virtues of moderation, restraint, and avoidance of excess,[67] those values that allowed oral societies to survive. Freedom expanded during the fifth century B.C. at the expense of many of these virtues, virtues that are more typical of oral cultures than literate ones.

Socrates lived in the only ancient society that valued free expression,[68] yet he was put to death for what he said and taught. Although the official complaint against Socrates was "impiety," this charge merely

served as an easy way to reach a religious offense that was little more than an exercise of free speech by a strong-minded intellectual whose politics, like his religious views, were objectionable. Athens honored its cultural leaders who celebrated its values. Those who challenged its values risked the charge of impiety, especially if their expression had an unpopular political coloration.[69]

Socrates' execution has been considered to be evidence of the lack of free speech in Athens.[70] Yet in Athens particularly, and even elsewhere, the spread of writing broadened the content of thought. There was more externally imposed censorship, but there was less internal or nonlegal control over ideas and thought. During the era of the written word, political repression became harsher, but habits of thought changed and the growth of knowledge increased. Writing itself was mainly a means of acquiring and exercising power but was not a threat to power. Those in power did not worry about it or have to censor it. But writing, because of its impact on individual habits of thought, brought into clearer focus the political power of speech. At least for some in the society, expression began to perform more of the individual functions of free expression identified by Emerson. For those in power, expression became a threat that it had not often been before.

It is in this context that laws repressing expression should be considered. Such laws do not only illustrate the power of a ruler or the desire of a ruler to wield power. More frequently, they are an indication of a struggle for power between the ruler and the ruled. Such laws reveal that there had been challenges to the ruler, that informal measures for preventing deviant expression were not functioning perfectly, and that the degree of resistance had reached such proportions that rules and censors had to be resorted to. Looked at in this way, writing began the struggle for using expression to counteract political power. It was not, however, a medium that was conducive to winning such a struggle. Success would have to wait for a form of communication that was less easily controlled by those in power, such as printing.

Print and the First Amendment

The analysis thus far suggests that speech and writing affected both what people thought and what they communicated. Oral societies seemed to tolerate free speech but did not have much to fear from a system of free expression, since the medium also effectively censored thought. Different cultures, Thomas Kasoulis has noted, differ mainly not "in inherent thinking patterns, but from differences in what is thought about."[71] Writing, by expanding the possibilities of what might be thought about and then communicated, transformed speech and energized it into a potentially more threatening medium. Writing brought about the beginnings of a struggle between the state and citizens. In this contest, however, those in power generally were able to increase their authority by asserting control over the use of the new medium. While speech in the new communications environment might on occasion be more threatening, political communications in general were more controllable.

One noteworthy consequence of the ability of those in power to effectively monopolize the flow of information was the rarity of formal censorship laws. According to Ithiel de Sola Pool,

> Before printing, there had been no elaborate system of censorship and control over scribes. There did not have to be. The scribes were scattered, working on single manuscripts in monasteries. Moreover, single manuscripts rarely caused a general scandal or major controversy. There was little motive for central control, and control would have been impractical.[72]

In preprint societies, religious authorities enacted prohibitions against blasphemy and heresy,[73] but there were few legal prohibitions imposed by the political authorities. The lack of censorship laws does not, however, suggest that free expression was permissible. Indeed, vocal public criticism probably would have been dealt with harshly.[74] In this instance, the lack of law reflects the lack of a problem and the lack of a need for law on the part of the authorities. The nature of the medium of writing made it both an impotent weapon in the hands of an individual and an infrequently used weapon, and it was, therefore, unnecessary for the ruling powers to be concerned about seditious writings.[75]

The spread of printing in the last half of the fifteenth century created a new communications environment that undermined the authority of powerful institutions. Those whose power derived from their ability to control the written word were threatened by a reduced ability to control the new medium of print. As a result, many censorship laws were enacted, trials held, and punishments meted out. By the late sixteenth century, "censorship of the printed word had become the universal practice of the lay and church authorities throughout Europe."[76] What is often forgotten when attention is focused on historically famous trials is that there was still much more active communication during this period than before Gutenberg, when few formal restrictions on expression existed. At the same time that the state was becoming increasingly active in censoring communication, the invisible censors of the medium of writing were being lifted, new patterns of communication were being developed, and the flow of information was being accelerated.

Generally, legal scholars either ignore the fact that there are other censors besides the state or assume that there is little the law can or should do about such nonstate restrictions on communication. Censorship is usually defined as being what the state does or does not do. Indeed, governmental action to remedy nonstate censors and promote more vigorous public discussion runs the risk of being unconstitutional if it interferes with a traditionally protected interest.[77] This is not an inevitable way of looking at the issue. Rather, it is partly an outgrowth of "the modern struggle against censorship by the state, and the libertarian ideology that developed in and out of that struggle."[78] It is a consequence of the growth of state power over the last few centuries, of the nature of law in a liberal society, and of the pride that we take in the First Amendment. In the present era of communications change, however, this creates a blind spot. Lack of understanding of the interaction between law and media and of the differences among media leaves us unprepared for changes that are likely to occur as the result of a changed communications environment.

Most contemporary scholarship on the First Amendment deals with recent cases, cases earlier in this century, or the Revolutionary period. There were no significant First Amendment cases in the federal courts in the nineteenth century. It may be, however, that the greatest insights into what will occur over the next ten to twenty years can be derived from looking back even further, at the period after printing was introduced. This was the era when the modern struggle between individual expression and state control over expression was forming. It may be that more can be discerned about the future of free expression, about attempts by government to control a new medium, and even about the likely direction of

Supreme Court decisions by looking at the spread of printing and by comparing the qualities of print and the qualities of the new media, than by analyzing either the trend of court decisions or the thoughts or intentions of the framers.

Forty or fifty years ago, the lack of attention to changes in the flow of information following Gutenberg would have been an unfortunate omission but not one with any serious practical consequences. Given the changes that are now occurring in our communications environment, this is no longer the case. What happens out of court ultimately affects the evolution of legal doctrine and the content of legal decisions. Thus to understand why the modern concept of free expression surfaced in the seventeenth century and why protection of speech and press seemed appropriate for inclusion in our Constitution, it is necessary to look at more than the intent of the framers of the Constitution, at more than the writings of Milton and others who discussed free speech, and it is crucial to examine something other than the landmark cases, such as *Zenger*. This is particularly important in an area such as freedom of expression where the extremely restrictive nature of the law on the books following the spread of printing might lead one to an incorrect view of what the communications environment actually was.

The most obvious change brought about by the new communications technology of print was in the production and availability of books. One writer has suggested that "a man born in 1453, the year of the fall of Constantinople, could look back from his fiftieth year on a lifetime in which about eight million books had been printed, more perhaps than all the scribes of Europe had produced since Constantine founded his city in A.D. 300."[79] Other estimates calculate that 12 million to 20 million books were printed before 1500 and that 150 million to 200 million copies were printed in the sixteenth century.[80]

The expansion in the number of available books was only the most obvious effect of Gutenberg's invention. Consider the following:

1. As noted earlier, books gradually came to be more accepted as authoritative sources of information. Because all printed versions were the same, one did not have to worry about scribal

errors. The reader could be certain that what was read was actually written by the author. The printed word had greater authority than manuscripts.

2. The flow of information changed. Printing made it possible for an individual to communicate with a larger number of individuals and over a greater distance than was possible before.

Print affected both habits of thought and the flow of information and, as a result, might have been perceived to be a threat to any institution whose power rested on the restrictive qualities of the written word. If the hypothetical fifty-year-old individual in 1503 had understood these powers of print and the consequences of introducing a new medium of communication, what reasonable predictions might he have made?

If the individual had been especially insightful or clairvoyant, he might have suggested that the most vulnerable institution of the day was the Church. Given the fact that the Church was the most powerful institution in Europe at the time printing was invented, that "in the latter part of the fourteenth century Christendom was more meaningful than Europe,"[81] such a suggestion would probably have been regarded as more ludicrous than blasphemous. On the surface, the Church seemed fairly secure. It had consistently overcome various heretical movements. It also seemed to be the main beneficiary of the new technology. The first book printed by Gutenberg was the Bible, and the largest single category of books printed before 1500 was religious.[82] After all, "what subject was more likely in the eyes of printers to sell at a time when most readers were clerics?"[83] During this period, one cardinal called the new technique a "divine invention"[84] and "the technique was seen as divine, God-given for the purpose of enlightening humanity."[85] "Numerous monasteries also welcomed printers into their midst and some monks even did printing."[86] From the point of view of the content of the new medium, early printing appeared to be a "conservative force."[87]

Yet the key to the future of the Church was not to be found in the content of early printed works or in the Church's investment in printing. More important than any of these activities was the fact that the Church was both a "heritage that was transmitted by texts"[88] and an institution that had successfully restricted the process of writing by limiting the acquisition and use of the skill. Its power derived in large measure from its control over sacred texts and from an attitude toward sacred writings that was fostered by their scarcity. From an early period, therefore, the Church also attempted to control the use of the printing press. In 1485, Berthold von Henneberg, archbishop of Mainz, announced that

> we take it to be our duty to act as the guardian of this art and to protect the purity of our divine books. We therefore order clerics and laymen alike to refrain from translating books from Greek, Latin and any other foreign tongue into German, and from buying directly or indirectly translated texts unless they are approved by the faculty of the universities of Mainz and Erfurt. We furthermore decree that books to be exhibited at the Frankfurt fair are to be examined and to be approved before they can be sold.[89]

Yet neither the Church nor Martin Luther, whose attack on the Church left it forever changed, realized that "the Church could not assume in this age of printing the same role as in the age of manuscripts, when she had been able to control the distribution of texts."[90]

It is no coincidence that the most momentous challenge to the medieval Church occurred shortly after the development of print. The Protestant Reformation would not have occurred as it did without the invention of movable type.[91] In 1519, Martin Luther tacked his complaints about the Catholic Church to the church door in Wittenberg, Germany, a university town where he was a professor. More significantly, however, the Ninety-Five Theses were printed and circulated widely. Elizabeth Eisenstein has written that

> when Luther proposed debate over his Ninety-Five Theses, his action was not in and of itself revolutionary. It was entirely conventional for professors of theology to hold disputations over an issue such as indulgences and "church doors were the customary place of medieval publicity." But these particular theses did not stay tacked to the church door (if indeed they were ever really placed there). To a sixteenth century Lutheran chronicler, "it almost appeared as if the angels themselves had been their messengers and brought them before the eyes of all the people." Luther himself expressed puzzlement, when addressing Pope Leo X six months after the initial event: It is a mystery to me how my theses, more so than my other writings, indeed those of other

professors, were spread to so many places. They were meant exclusively for our academic circle here.[92]

For Luther, the increase in the size of the audience and the speed of communication gave his message an impact it would not have had 100 years earlier. It has been estimated that in the three years following his historic act, more than three hundred thousand copies of Luther's writings were sold.[93]

Printing not only fostered new ideas, but also enabled these ideas to be distributed more widely and efficiently than was possible in the age of scribes. Richard Friedenthal has noted that

> the great controversies of the Middle Ages, though no less bitterly contested, had been fought out on parchment—with a very limited number of copies available—and confined to the universities, which in most cases meant only Paris. Now printing presses had been set up everywhere, often in the most out-of-the-way places, and were disseminating the writings, for and against, of the contestants in slim volumes and pamphlets, illustrated with satirical woodcuts. Everything was printed, immediately pirated and circulated; every eulogy to a friend and fellow thinker, every piece of personal spite or revenge, every begging letter and every defense of everything. . . . The dismemberment of the Holy Roman Empire had at least one good result: there was almost complete freedom of the press, not because no censorship existed but because each town reserved the right of censorship to itself. A work forbidden in one place was immediately published in another.[94]

The examples of censorship that are commonly cited in legal histories should be understood as responses to a new communications environment in which dissatisfied individuals possessed a capacity for finding allies or reaching others in ways that had not existed previously. Censorship laws were an attempt to use law to regulate what had earlier been controlled by the inherent qualities of writing. Licensing laws about who could publish[95] can be viewed as an attempt to foster only books that promoted the values or interests of the authorities, something the scribal system did automatically. Early libel laws that allowed no criticisms of the state had a similar purpose.[96]

The speed with which censorship laws grew and the prosecutions that occurred, however, should not be viewed as clear illustrations of state power or as signs of victory by the state. Quite the opposite was often the case. What these laws actually depict is a situation in which the authorities were under frequent attack.[97] An escalated response or a publicized prosecution symbolized growing weakness and vulnerability. Hannah Arendt once noted that "since authority always demands obedience, it is commonly mistaken for some form of power or violence. Yet authority precludes the use of external means of coercion; where force is used, authority itself has failed."[98] What the history of censorship laws suggests is that during the early period when such laws were growing, the power of the state, as embodied in these laws, was struggling with the power of the new medium. Convictions of authors or printers slowed the pace of change, but the power of the medium was such that significant change in most of Europe was inevitable. In England, for example, as Leona Rostenberg has observed in her study of the underground press in the sixteenth and seventeenth centuries, "the official attempt to stifle the minorities in England failed. Long after the defeat of the Armada the orthodox movement persisted in England. The 'Puritannicall spirits' so abhorred by James I triumphed completely and mastered the realm bequeathed by him to his son."[99]

The essential point to understand is that the first authors to advocate free speech were reacting not only to oppression and their ideas about free expression had not developed in a vacuum. John Milton and other advocates of fewer restrictions on communication also had more experience with a more active process of communications than any earlier generation. Their genius lay in drawing conclusions about the benefits of a system of free expression from their own experiences and from what accessibility to information meant to their own development.

This analysis does not deny that authors and printers were severely punished or that at various periods the state did not exercise considerable control over what was published. It is clear, however, that the state was not nearly as powerful as one would think if one looked at only the laws on the books or the famous cases or the instances of book burnings or the catalogues of banned books or the infamous Star Chamber. The author of the most respected study of freedom of the press in England in the sixteenth and seventeenth centuries recognized that "in spite of the stringent regulations and the multiplicity of agencies of enforcement, there continued to flow from the presses a stream of publications which in that day and age were considered either seditious or offensive."[100] Printing was a technology that "was for once on the side of liberty,"[101] since the medium of print was not as controllable as writing. "Liberty and the printing press are inseparable. One has no meaning, the other little use, without its partner."[102] Enforcement of censorship laws, therefore, was much more difficult than most constitutional historians realize. If one looks at the struggle between the medium and the state from the perspective of what was being published and distributed, even when the state was actively attempting to suppress information, then one's predictions about the future are different from what they would be if the sole focus of attention were on the laws on the books.

The main problem for the authorities was that enforcement of censorship laws was exceedingly difficult. "Evading the censor developed into a fine art," Steinberg notes.[103] The state might get the author or printer of the work in its grasp, but the work itself was more elusive. "The attempted control and regulation of printing (or rather, the failure of such attempts) constantly, from the 15th to the 18th century, encouraged the multiplication of pirated editions and, consequently, the development of a more or less underground book trade."[104] It is convenient to ignore the illegal and clandestine flow of information and the frequent avoidance of censorship laws, but such myopia misleads us into believing that print was successfully controlled whenever the state wished to do so. It is more accurate to conclude that prosecutions revealed the tip of the iceberg in unlawful publications, in much the same way that an obscenity prosecution today does not really reveal the nature or extent of the obscenity trade. In eighteenth-century France, for example, underground and foreign presses were especially important in evading the combined efforts of state censors, the police, and a monopolistic guild of booksellers, which "attempted to contain the printed word within limits set by the official orthodoxies. When it conveyed heterodox ideas, the word spread through the underground. . . . most of what passes today for eighteenth-century French literature circulated on the shady side of the law in eighteenth-century France."[105] L. Febvre and H. Martin, in a classic study of the French book trade in an earlier period, note that forbidden tracts and pamphlets were smuggled into France with ease, even into the gaols where the Huguenots were imprisoned. Everywhere underground organizations formed to trade in illegal books. Often the officials of the Booksellers' corporation whose job it was to inspect imported crates of books were accomplices in the trade. In practice they took action against smugglers only when they had no choice in the matter. How, in any case, particularly given the administrative limitations of the governments of the period, could one hope to put a stop to the smuggling of books, which were small objects and easily concealed? Consequently the prime outcome of the policy of rigorous official censorship was the establishment, around the French borders in the 18th century, of a series of printing businesses producing pirated editions and editions of banned books in complete freedom. The works of the *philosophes* were printed by these firms. Sometimes indeed the Chancellor had the disagreeable surprise of discovering his coachman bringing pernicious books to Paris concealed in his own carriage. Soon, under Malesherbes' influence, the officials in charge of censorship sought to relax the regulations, granted tacit permission for the pub-lication of certain books and were tolerant in other ways. It is evident that official censorship as it was then understood had proved to be ineffectual.[106]

This lengthy quote suggests that the law is both a reflection of reality and a creator of reality. Demands for legal protection for expression arose out of some experience with an active process of communication, and legal protection for expression was typically more a recognition of the difficulties of controlling communication than it was an acceptance of arguments about the philosophical and positive benefits of freer communication. In France, as one scholar has noted, "establishment of the *permission tacite* register in 1718 may well have legitimized a fait accompli. It also legitimized the fact that the French reading public, a full generation before the *philosophes,* had gone beyond the canons of taste established even by relatively tolerant censors."[107]

The basis for the relaxation of censorship laws in England also was "due not to any philosophical conclusion concerning the advisability of a free press but primarily to an inability to devise an enforceable system of regulation capable of achieving the results desired."[108] In 1694, the Regulation of Printing Act was not renewed by Parliament, and licensing of printers ceased. In an eighteen-point document that the House of Commons sent to the House of Lords supporting its opposition to renewal, every argument made was one of "expediency rather than of conviction on moral or philosophical grounds."[109] Frederick Siebert concludes that "the reasons which prompted a majority of the members of Parliament to reject the Act for the Regulation of Printing were surprisingly enough the practical reasons arising from difficulties of administration and the restraints on trade."[110]

Our constitutional guarantee of free speech and press, too, is attributable not merely to the logic, idealism, or persuasive rhetoric of the framers of the First Amendment but to the framers' experience with the communications environment in this country in the late eighteenth century. The most thorough research on what the framers actually believed about free expression is found in Leonard Levy's *Emergence of a Free Press,*[111] a recently published revision of his *Legacy of Suppression,*[112] published in 1960. The core of Levy's thesis is that the framers did not intend to abolish the crime of seditious libel, which made it a criminal act to criticize the government. The crime of seditious libel, for example, was what John Peter Zenger was charged with.

Levy's thesis when it was first published was novel in that he asserted that the framers "did not believe in a broad scope for freedom of expression, particularly in the realm of politics."[113] He denied that the framers had had a comprehensive theory of the relationship between free expression and democratic government and claimed that their intentions had been not particularly libertarian. He concluded that "the American experience with freedom of political expression was as slight as the theoretical inheritance was narrow."[114]

In the recent edition of his book, Levy does not change his main thesis, that the framers' concept of free expression was very limited, but he does recognize that he erred in how he had described the actual colonial experience with seditious speech and publications.[115] Several reviewers had criticized the first edition for not recognizing the vitality of the colonial press.[116] While still insisting that "the Bill of Rights in its immediate history was in large measure a lucky political accident,"[117] he now admits that "from a far more thorough reading of American newspapers of the eighteenth century I now know that the American experience with a free press was as broad as the theoretical inheritance was narrow."[118] Levy explains:

> My original interest lay with law and theory; I had paid little attention to press practices. I had searched the newspapers only for statements on the meaning of freedom of the press and had ignored the nearly epidemic degree of seditious libel that infected American newspapers after Independence. Press criticism of government policies and politicians, on both state and national levels, during the war and in the peaceful years of the 1780s and 1790s, raged as contemptuously and scorchingly as it had against Great Britain in the period between the Stamp Act and the battle of Lexington. Some states gave written constitutional protection to freedom of the press after Independence; others did not. Whether they did or did not, their presses operated as if the law of seditious libel did not exist. To one whose prime concern was law and theory, a legacy of suppression came into focus; to one who looks at newspaper judgments on public men and measures, the revolutionary controversy spurred an expanding legacy of liberty.[119]

Because Levy had focused his research on what the framers wrote, on the law on the books, and on actual prosecutions for seditious libel, he had titled his book *Legacy of Suppression*. Actually, as he now admits, there was also in existence a legacy of expression.[120] There was a contest between state authorities and what is today referred to as "the media." As we have seen, the contest had changed as a result of the new medium of print and the fact that print was a medium that was more difficult to control than was writing. The First Amendment was not a "historical accident," if this is the way one views the contest between the state and the medium. The framers may not have been able to agree on a coherent set of goals for free speech or press, but they "knew what the press was, knew how crucial a role it could play in shaping government, and knew the multitude of ways in which the journalistic function could be undermined."[121] The medium was exerting pressure on the law to adapt to a new communications environment and was much more active than one might assume simply from examining the laws of the time.[122] Indeed, the most recent study of this historical period concluded that the "colonists were publishing and justifying aggressive journalism for decades before the Revolution. . . . By the time of the First Amendment, Americans had forged a general libertarian press ideology that was incompatible with the idea of seditious libel. The components of this theoretical perspective came from practical experience as well as from radical Whig and Enlightenment thought."[123] The particular words chosen for the First Amendment may have been fortuitous or accidental, but the evolution of a law that was more protective of expression than anything that existed pre-Gutenberg was not. As William Mayton has perceptively observed, "One determinant of the 'American idea' of speech and government was that in the society that approved the constitution the press had in practice become free."[124] The new media had provoked the authorities into enacting censorship laws, but it was inevitable that a model would evolve that would consider the properties of print to be of value.

Electronic Media

In a noteworthy speech delivered at Yale in 1974, the late Supreme Court Justice Potter Stewart suggested that the guarantee of a free press should be viewed more as a process than as a set of rules listing what the press may or may not do:

> So far as the Constitution goes, the autonomous press may publish what it knows, and may seek to learn what it can.
> But this autonomy cuts both ways. The press is free to do battle against secrecy and deception in government. But the press cannot expect from the Constitution any guarantee that it will succeed. There is no constitutional right to have access to particular government information or to require openness from the bureaucracy. The public's interest in knowing about its government is protected by the guarantee of a Free Press, but the protection is indirect. The Constitution itself is neither a Freedom of Information Act nor an Official Secrets Act.
> The Constitution, in other words, establishes the contest, not its resolution.[125]

Stewart's description of the press–government relationship in this manner is both helpful and misleading in explaining the implications of the electronic media for free expression. It is helpful in that it highlights the ongoing and dynamic character of constitutional doctrine. A court decision in the area of expression will settle a particular conflict and set a standard for some future activities. Yet other activities, or even similar activities under slightly different circumstances, may remain legally ambiguous and generate new cases. The image of a continuing contest, therefore, is an accurate one. The First Amendment is not simply a fixed set of rules but a process in which boundaries of permissible behavior are established and then modified, and then modified some more.

What is misleading about Stewart's approach is his assertion that the Constitution "establishes the contest." The theme of this chapter has been that a contest has been occurring since ancient times. The nature of the contest is, of course, very different from what it was in earlier times, but that is due both to the invention and spread of printing and to the adoption of legal protection for speech and press. The First Amendment developed out of a communications environment that had changed the flow of information dramatically and had done so in spite of numerous attempts to censor and control. If the First Amendment had actually established the contest or was truly the beginning of the modern era of freedom of expression, then the development of the electronic media would be an interesting but not a particularly critical development. However, if the First Amendment was itself a response to changes in how information was communicated and would not have been enacted if these changes had not occurred, then the arrival of the new media becomes vitally important. It is important because the process in which the law reorients itself so that it is in tune with contemporary shifts in the movement of information is likely to occur again.

The key question in our era is: How will the electronic media affect Stewart's "contest"? Are those who are trying to restrict or control the flow of information most likely to benefit from the new technologies, or will the task of managing communication be more difficult? Must the flow of information in the electronic environment—by its very nature—be as open and externally unimpeded as a computer's "binary bits moving in the most straightforward, logical path necessary to do their complex job"?[126] Or can such flow be rigidly channeled and controlled in the most Big Brotherly way? Or is electronic communication not only a business in itself, but also "something that has made control impossible," so impossible that those at the top of any polity or economy "can no longer hide what they're doing"?[127]

In answering these questions, our objective is neither to assess whether any single case has been wisely or foolishly decided nor to propose the details of a regulatory policy. One of the themes of this chapter is that sometimes more can be learned about the contours of future legal doctrines by looking at what is occurring out of court than in court. The purpose here, therefore, is to emphasize what the underlying challenges are and what should be understood by those who are concerned with First Amendment values and by those who desire to regulate and develop policy in the area of expression in an era of electronic media.

The analysis of earlier societies suggested that each medium has inherent qualities that can shrink, expand, or shape the flow of information. In addition, different media create different attitudes toward the nature of information and the uses to which information can be put. When a new form of communication is developed, it does not replace the old, but it does change the media then in use so that they are used differently or are perceived differently. The medium may not always be the message, as McLuhan argued,[128] but it does have a message that is all too often ignored. The purpose of the following analysis is to urge that the new media be treated as a prominent player in the "contest" over communication and to explain why and how the novel qualities of electronic forms of communication may influence this contest.

The starting point for looking at the impact of the qualities of the new media on expression should be the differences between the old and the new. At its most fundamental level, the difference is that information in the form of coded electrical impulses is gradually replacing information represented by marks on paper. When we see words on a computer monitor or images on a television screen, the computer or television is translating the electrical impulses into a format that is meaningful to us. Television viewers or computer users can easily forget that electronic information is not communicated in the form of pictures or letters. It is the television set or computer that changes the electrical impulses into pictures or words. When they are stored and when they are communicated, electronic data consist of patterns of electrical impulses that are capable of being transformed into a familiar and recognizable form. Letters or images appear only as the last step in the electronic communications process. Computers can be described as devices that have the ability to regulate the flow of electricity. When the letter *A* is pressed on a typewriter keyboard, the letter is almost immediately imprinted on a piece of paper. When one presses an *A* on a computer keyboard, the flow of electricity is manipulated in a certain way and the end result is that an *A* appears on the screen. Each time a key is pressed, the flow of electricity is changed. Thus it is only indirectly that one changes images or words on a computer monitor. What one is really doing at the keyboard of a computer terminal is determining how the flow of electricity will be regulated.

When information assumes an electronic form, there may occur some things that are not possible with print. One of the major capabilities of electronic information is its virtual instantaneous communication over great distances. Print was vastly superior to writing in spreading information, but there are still significant time and geographical limits to the distribution process that are traceable to the nature of print. In exploring the First Amendment implications of placing information in electronic form, this new technological capability and the expansion of the potential audience for information should not be ignored.

The following analysis suggests that the movement of information at electronic speed will gradually weaken the control that can be exercised over the movement of information, particularly when compared with writing and print. The need for law and the role of law in protecting expression will be different in a society with fully developed electronic communication. If "the role of law here is to mark and guard the line between the sphere of social power, organized in the form of the state, and the area of private right,"[129] we shall find that the line between the state and the individual may be shifting, and the degree of vigilance or power that is required to protect individual and social interests and achieve the goals of free expression may be different.

How does the ability of the new media to conquer geographical barriers promote the movement of information? The problem that the new technologies pose for any institution or government desiring to limit the distribution of information might be illustrated by the following example. In early 1986, the American Broadcasting Company announced that it was halting production of a television movie entitled "Amerika."[130] The movie would have dramatized life in the United States under Soviet rule. ABC listed a number of reasons for its action, among them threats by the Soviet government to expel the ABC News correspondent in Moscow.[131]

When this decision was reported in the popular press, the newsworthiness of the story centered on the integrity and fortitude of ABC. When ABC reversed its decision two weeks later, the independence of ABC seemed to be reasonably secure and news media attention disappeared. While neither the law nor the First Amendment directly affected the outcome of this incident, the incident is relevant in a number of ways to assessing how qualities of electronic communication can affect the future of free expression. What is most significant about the case is not the case's particular outcome or that ABC ultimately resisted pressure but what it reveals about how the "contest" over free communication is changing. The context in which both court cases involving free expression and nonlegal judgments that affect communication, such as ABC's, are occurring is different because information has become able to traverse distances in ways that were not previously possible. New players, such as foreign governments and international media organizations, have entered the contest, and the interaction between the traditional participants is changing as a result.[132]

An important lesson provided by the "Amerika" incident is that once electronic information begins moving around the globe, the ability of any one government to restrict the movement of information decreases. All governments try to control the flow of information that affects them and to shape attitudes that will result from words and pictures that are communicated to the public. In this country, presidential press secretaries are often accused of trying to "manage the news," the most frequent and obvious case being the manipulation of "photo opportunities." What these successful manipulations obscure, however, is that in general it is more difficult for those in power to control the flow of information now than it used to be. As Joshua Meyrowitz has observed,

> Leaders once had easy access to others, but were able to control access to themselves. Before the 1920s, most people had never heard the voice of a President or received any direct evidence of his humanness or personality. Before the late 1940s, few reporters had access to

portable voice recording machines that could be used to substantiate quotes from interviews (and therefore quotes could be denied). Indeed, it is somewhat startling to realize that as recently as the beginning of Eisenhower's presidency the press was not allowed to quote the President directly without his permission.[133]

The simplest explanation of Soviet concern is fear that public opinion in this country would be affected by ABC's "Amerika" television program and that this would influence the policies and bargaining positions of the administration in Washington. It may, in other words, have been a case of anxiety about the power of television to shape the opinions of viewers in this country and concern about the effect of public opinion on the official policy of this country. This is undoubtedly a large part of the explanation, but there may be more. One might speculate, for example, that what is shown on United States television is relevant for the Soviets more directly. It is not simply that what is communicated in this country touches their country by affecting our national policy. Rather, some of what is communicated in this country ultimately reaches across the Soviet border and, through tourists, through the Voice of America, through tape recordings, through telephone calls, and through a variety of other channels that did not exist fifty years ago, bypasses the official Soviet information system. In other words, some communication in this country touches the Soviet public directly and no longer primarily through official governmental channels.

In the "Amerika" incident, the strategy of the Soviet government may seem heavy handed, but their anxiety is quite understandable. They are threatened by the ability of the new media to overcome the barrier of distance, and, as a result, they are entering the contest over control of the flow of information. They are entering and participating in the contest less from a position of strength than from a position of vulnerability. When information can be transmitted across borders more and more easily and as the technology for conducting this kind of communication becomes more and more widespread, it is more difficult to isolate the public from information that a government considers undesirable. The government's system of censorship becomes more difficult to enforce, and officials perceive, quite correctly, that movies produced thousand of miles away can have consequences internally. As Ben Bagdikian has observed,

> A population that requires insulation from uncontrolled information is living in the wrong era; for the last few centuries this insulation has become increasingly porous, and regimes that have used it for social control have lived precarious existences. There have been massive tragedies associated with authoritarian regimes and the dictatorships that marked the earlier stages of newer nations. But it has gone almost unnoticed that among modern, centralized governments, the regimes with the greatest longevity have been democratic, not authoritarian. There are not many monarchies left; the dictatorships mutate or die. Freedom of information is not a small part of this evolution.[134]

Similarly, Benjamin Compaine has concluded that "the proliferation of new communication processes over the years has made it increasingly difficult for any single entity or small cabal, even governments that have the will and power, to have total control over the mass media."[135]

In an insightful book, journalist Donald Shainor has revealed some of the ways in which the flow of information to the Soviet Union has been increasing, how the movement of information electronically bypasses many of the traditional means of control, and why the new media are such a threat to them. Shainor points out that there is a growing "underground telegraph" that "competes with the official media, correcting, supplementing, and often contradicting what they have to say."[136] The source of much of the information that reaches Soviet citizens comes from émigrés. They do not physically return, but many of their stories filter back. In ancient times, expulsion of a critic was an effective method of dealing with someone who was considered a problem.[137] Socrates, it should be remembered, was killed only because he refused to leave Athens. In modern times, however, because of the ability of the new media to transcend boundaries, exiles do not disappear. Shainor discovered that

> before 1973, when the third wave of Soviet emigration began, U.S. Postal Service officials estimated that the volume of mail between the Soviet Union and the United States was much less than a million letters a year in both directions. No exact records are available before 1979, when the two-way flow was already 2,599,000. It has increased dra-

matically every year since: to 3,090,000 in 1980, 7,277,000 in 1981, 10,512,000 in 1982, and 12,276,000 in 1983.[138]

Letters are supplemented by telephone calls, tape recordings, shortwave broadcasts, books, and periodicals. Even news reports sent by Western reporters from the Soviet Union can now sometimes find their way back. Dissident David Goldfarb, shortly after his release, wrote that "hearing your name on the BBC or the Voice of America is the best assurance that the K.G.B. will think twice before cracking down on you. . . . Western journalists in Moscow, whose reports are broadcast into Russia by foreign stations, substitute for a free domestic press. . . ."[139]

Recent challenges to Soviet control of information, it should be recognized, have not resulted from the use of the most advanced or sophisticated electronic technologies. Direct broadcast satellite transmissions to Soviet homes, Shainor asserts, "would constitute such a threat that the Soviet leadership probably would order the transmitting satellites shot down."[140] The Soviet government has moved very slowly in promoting the spread of small computers because it probably understands that the communications potential of the computer will undermine the ability of the government to regulate the flow of information to and among citizens.[141] A recent book recognized that "the computer is not merely an information-storing, an information-manipulating machine, but an information-furnishing machine. Can a totalitarian society live in the midst of such devices when its whole past has been based on minimal, carefully regulated information? Can a multitude of user-friendly computers have any place in a user-unfriendly society?"[142] Similarly, former Assistant Secretary of State Lawrence Eagleburger has observed,

> Mr. Gorbachev may put a computer at every school desk. He may even succeed, though I doubt it, in training the bureaucracy to use the computer as a management tool. Can he, however, permit computers in homes or individual offices, with open access to data banks and the ability to cross-talk freely? Not unless he is prepared fundamentally to change the nature of the system that promoted him to his current position.
>
> This, then, is the Soviet conundrum: make whatever use you can of the new information system technologies, but always under firm state control, thereby forgoing the advantages of a free flow of information,

or loosen the control network, free your citizens' inventive capacities and run the risk that you will not be long in power.[143]

As the newer technologies appear on the scene, publicized attempts to control information will probably increase, just as censorship laws proliferated in the sixteenth and seventeenth centuries in the West when smuggled printed matter interfered with local control. The inevitable end of the process, however, will be a realization that total control of public information is an anachronistic concept.

The beginnings of a growing, de facto condition of greater press freedom in a society with de jure censorship is most clearly seen in Poland. In addition to Radio Free Europe, Voice of America, and BBC radio broadcasts in Polish that are heard by 10 to 20 million Poles,[144] Poland has an underground press that often astounds visitors in the quantity, range, and accessibility of printed materials.[145] The ground is being laid for a future legal change. Here, too, however, the effect of electronic communications technologies is just beginning to be felt. The correspondent for *The Times* of London has observed that

> the fundamental problem is how information should flow in a closed society. Technical progress entails political risk, especially in systems where power is partly based on control of information.
>
> In computers, this is only just becoming visible. Some Polish dissidents use word processors to print out *samizdat* material. Underground pamphlets, even books, are sometimes put on floppy discs, smuggled into Poland, then printed at the press of a button. More playfully, there is even an underground video game called Zomo in which a riot policeman chases a Solidarity supporter through a maze of streets. And what if teenage "hackers" start to break the computer codes of Warsaw Pact defence ministries?[146]

An incident such as "Amerika" or the banning by the South African government of television pictures of protests or the arrest of Polish intellectuals is more a sign, on the one hand, of weakness and diminished influence by those governments and, on the other, of the power of electronic media than evidence of strength and ability to control. Although censoring may appear to be successful, any victory of this type is more likely to be temporary than permanent. It is a sign that the contest is heating up and that the two

sides are more evenly matched than before.[147] The struggle between the power of law and the power of media is reminiscent of
the struggle in the sixteenth and seventeenth centuries between
these two forces. Each side can be expected to win some victories,
but the current contest will not take two or three centuries to be
resolved. As technological abilities increase, law simply cannot be
expected to successfully control the movement of information, as
it has done in the past. For example, once news organizations have
access to what are now referred to as "spy satellites" (but are really
simply cameras in the sky), they will have the ability to acquire
pictures of events almost anywhere at any time. Such satellites are
operational now and allow photographs of places and events that
are restricted by law. We are approaching an era in which a country
could not effectively ban camera coverage of protests or demon-
strations because the camera would be on a satellite and not on
the territory of the censoring country.[148] Such cameras can now
photograph objects as small as ten meters in length and are expected to be able to take pictures of objects one meter long within
a few years. Such pictures are available for sale from private companies and, perhaps surprisingly, from various governments,
among them the Soviet Union.[149] In such an environment, efforts
by any government to suppress such photographs are futile.[150]

This discussion may seem to be interesting for its impact on
governments lacking protection for expression but to be irrelevant
to the law of this country. While the quality of the electronic media
that allows it to move quickly and escape national boundaries may
be more threatening to those societies that are more restrictive, it
is in fact a problem for all governments. One of the recent spy
cases in this country focused on an employee of a naval intelligence
agency who sold satellite photographs not to a foreign government
but to a foreign magazine.[151] Perhaps this is a better example than
the "Amerika" controversy for illustrating the problem that our
government has in common with more restrictive governments.
The new media make the line between spying and "leaking" more
difficult to draw than in the past. In this country, we do not know
exactly how many instances there have been of worthwhile news
stories that were never published because a cooperative outlet
could not be found. Whatever the number, the new media make
it more likely that what is known to a few will ultimately be known

to many. The legal doctrine of prior restraint, which allows the government to prohibit publication, historically has been a rarely used doctrine. Because the ability to limit the spread of information is less today and more information leaks out, there have been more attempts to use prior restraint in the past five years than previously.[152] What is also true, however, is that the doctrine is essentially unenforceable. The law, as was discovered in the hydrogen bomb–*Progressive* magazine case,[153] is too slow to catch up to the movement of information today and prevent publication permanently.

The fact that information can reach people who were previously isolated and that it can reach them faster is only part of the story, however. The other half is that there is an enormous growth in the quantity of accessible information and that placing information in electronic form stimulates and accelerates this process. In addition, there is probably a greater ability to obtain information that was previously inaccessible.

In early 1986, two seemingly unrelated stories about the electronic media appeared in the press; like the "Amerika" incident, they suggest that electronic information is difficult to monopolize. On January 15, 1986, Home Box Office and Cinemax began to scramble the signals they used to transmit their programs to local cable companies. The problem for these cable companies, whose income derives from fees paid by subscribers to local cable franchises, was that owners of satellite dishes were able to pick up the signals as easily as the local cable company and could watch the programs on such services for free.[154]

Several weeks after the scrambling of satellite signals began, the federal government announced that it was negotiating with universities to limit the access of Soviet scholars to supercomputers.[155] Such computers, it was asserted, could be used to design weapons or to carry out military research. As a result, the government wished to regulate scientific research in ways that had not been attempted previously.

What these two examples share is the recognition by an institution that wishes to control the flow of information, for either economic or political reasons, that the use of electronic information poses problems of control. While each of these cases could end up in the courts as a First Amendment case, they are used here to illustrate a general quality of the electronic media and a general lesson about the ability to control information in the future. Both of these examples suggest that control over electronically stored or communicated information is an increasing problem for anyone who wants to restrict or regulate the flow of such information.[156] Governments and other institutions that wish to benefit from the unique capabilities of computers will discover that there is a price to be paid in that information in this form is more vulnerable to eavesdropping or unauthorized access than information stored or communicated by some other medium.[157]

The most controllable of media is writing. There is usually only a single copy, and it can be obtained only through theft and a physical seizure of it. Prior to the development of printing, bribery, blackmail, and theft could provide access to secret documents, but the problem of copying effectively limited distribution. Monetary factors are not the only reason for not printing documents one wants to limit access to. It is implicitly understood that control decreases as the number of copies of any document increases. In recent years, the traditional ways of surreptitiously or illegally gaining access to secret documents have been joined by effective means of copying that have made actual physical theft unnecessary.

Next to speech, the electronic media are the least controllable form of communication. One of the central features of information stored in electronic form is that it is intended to be accessible and usable from a distance. Printed information has to be written, published, and distributed. For much electronic information, this is a model that does not make sense. Computerized information is not published or distributed in the same sense that printed information is. Publication of electronic information consists of placing it in a computer that can be communicated with. In the simplest form of electronic information, there is virtually no production or distribution process.[158] As Professor Ithiel de Sola Pool recognized,

> The very definition of "publishing" is changed by convergence between books, journals, and newspapers, which deliver information in multiple copies, and information services, office automation, and electronic mail, which deliver information in editions of one. A distinction between publishing and the provision of individual information was a product of Gutenberg's mass media revolution, when for the first time in history written texts could be mass produced cheaply. With contem-

porary communications technologies, singly produced copies are no longer much more expensive than mass produced ones.[159]

For most purposes, electronic information is efficient because once it is stored in one place, it is accessible and usable to anyone in any place with a computer. All it has to do is remain in electronic form in a computer that has links to other computers.

The speed with which electronic information can be transmitted encourages computers to be linked to other computers. When information is needed for some task, it is becoming more and more possible to find it in electronic form.[160] While many microcomputers today are not used to communicate, a computer without such an ability is an inefficient use of the technology. It is as though a videotape recorder were used only to play prerecorded tapes but never used to copy television programs off the air or make original recordings. Since computers are devices that can communicate information as well as store and process it, it is essentially inefficient for the computer to contain information that has to be typed in if the information is available somewhere in electronic form. There is an important byproduct, however, in using the computer in a way that maximizes its efficiency. It also has the effect of improving access to information and interfering with restrictions on the movement of information.

Shoshana Zuboff has described, in a study of the use of the electronic media in industry, how information technology differs in a critical way from earlier machine technology. She writes that "information technology, even when it is applied to automatically reproduce a finite activity, is not mute. It not only imposes information (in the form of programmed instructions) but also produces information."[161] As a result, the new media "informate"[162] as well as automate. Zuboff stresses that assumptions based on the qualities of older machines hinder recognition of the profound changes that will occur to the nature of work in the future. Similarly, I believe, in attempting to understand the control of communication in the future, one must be wary of drawing inferences that derive from the inherent logic of print.

Electronic information is designed to be usable at a distance. For such uses, it has to be moved and when it is moved, it becomes vulnerable. This is true both for signals sent through the air[163] and for computerized information.[164] It may be that most information can be controlled most of the time and that the most sensitive information can be protected all the time. But to assume that all the information in an "information economy"[165] where the use of electronic communication is growing rapidly can be secure at all times is to be unrealistic.[166] As a former director of the United States Information Agency has stated, "The only way to 'censor' an electronic network moving 648 million bits per second is literally to pull the plug."[167]

The recognition that more and more information is available in electronic form, and that such information can be easily copied, altered, and transmitted, was at the heart of an interesting and illustrative corporate reorganization involving McGraw-Hill. McGraw-Hill publishes magazines, such as *Business Week,* and financial services, such as *Standard and Poor's,* and owns four television stations. In all these ventures, information is at some point stored in electronic form.

Until 1984, the corporation was organized into book, magazine, broadcasting, and other divisions on the basis of the form in which the final information reached the public. This organizational model assumed that the goal was to distribute some publication and that once this occurred, the information in the publication would not be used again. In recent years, McGraw-Hill has recognized that the ease with which electronic information can be copied, revised, and indexed means that it is inefficient and uneconomical to give information that has been collected only a single life.

McGraw-Hill is now organized not into book, magazine, and other media-based divisions but into groups oriented around the market that is served. The hope is that the enormous amounts of data originally collected for one purpose can be placed in an electronic database that will be continually revised and added to. One executive has stated, "McGraw-Hill collects millions of bits of data each year. The idea is to use it over and over and over again. It's no revolutionary idea. It's so simple you wonder, 'Why didn't we think of it before?' "[168]

While this may not be a revolutionary idea, it is an idea that is based on the recognition of the novel qualities of the new media. It is an idea that would have been of little economic value in an age when publications were actually set in type. It highlights the fact that electronic information can, more easily than information stored any other way, have more than one life. John Milton, in the *Areopagitica,* wrote that "books are not absolutely dead things, but doe contain a potencie of life in them, to be as active as that soule was whose progeny they are."[169] Printed works did typically survive their authors, and, as noted in Chapter 1, this quality contributed to the significant growth of knowledge in many fields that occurred in the sixteenth and seventeenth centuries. Print added to "the stock of information from which members of the public may draw."[170] Electronic information is even more active and more easily manipulable, revisable, and changeable. It is changeable in ways that print is not and, by its very nature, moves much faster. The relevance of this to the First Amendment may be seen by comparing the great difficulty in retrieving printed copies of some work that has for some reason to be recalled with the impossibility of doing the same thing with electronic information that has for some reason been accidentally or illegally released.

The discussion thus far has alluded to several legal doctrines whose goal is to restrict the circulation of some information. Privacy, obscenity, copyright, and espionage laws all attempt to halt or restrict the flow of certain kinds of information. We shall see that these and other areas are currently under stress because some of the limitations inherent in print have been overcome, and, therefore, these laws cannot operate as effectively as they have in the past. The same factors that are increasing opportunities for expression generally are posing threats to those whose concerns can be satisfied only by limiting the flow of information.

The legal doctrines just mentioned are areas of law that arose or changed greatly as a result of the use of printing. They are large legal areas today, but they were not significant legal subjects prior to Gutenberg. This suggests that each medium brings out into the open new legal issues because new patterns of communication become possible and information acquires a different role in society. We are in a fairly early stage of communicating electronically, and all the values and issues that will surface and call for legal protection are not yet clear. What might be suggested, however, are the contours of the legal dilemma that we will have to face.

The expansion of communication and the difficulty of using law in the future to control information does not necessarily mean that it will not be used. For a few legal issues, alternatives to law may be experimented with, or we may decide simply to "legalize" the problem and learn to live with it. We might, for example, learn to live with less privacy or with a more limited legal definition of privacy rather than try to engage in a futile and constantly escalating series of legal wars to control the problem. For other legal areas, however, we may decide that the fight over a particular issue is necessary and that some degree of control is better than none. We have many laws that are enforced poorly, such as many criminal laws, but there are no suggestions to legalize theft or robbery or tax evasion.

What this analysis suggests is that the contest Justice Stewart spoke about is certain to heat up. The First Amendment has been labeled a "growth industry."[171] This description is based on the increasing number of cases in which some activity is claimed to fall under the protection of the First Amendment.[172] Such cases get to court because there are greater opportunities for expression, a greater demand for information in an "information economy"[173] and a lowered ability to control information. The overall increase in communication leads to conflicts with governmental authorities and individuals who feel threatened or hurt. Nonlawyers generally expect the courts to provide solutions in such situations and to articulate precise, predictable, and general legal standards. More frequently, however, court decisions that settle a conflict in a particular set of circumstances will generate litigation to determine what is lawful in a slightly different set of circumstances. The end result is likely to be a continuing and growing amount of litigation.

The mere fact that communications is a volatile legal area is very significant to understanding the law and the reality of free communication. Highly active legal areas have a less stable and more dynamic quality than less active areas. For strict civil libertarians, this is an undesirable situation for a number of reasons: first, a continuing series of battles have to be fought; second, losses and victories will be intermixed; third, the concept of a legal right as something highly stable and secure will be threatened. The image of the First Amendment as covering all forms of expression under almost all circumstances will become increasingly difficult to promote if the number of cases grows and the level of uncertainty about the outcome of particular cases becomes greater. There is considerable wisdom to the statement of Professor Alexander Bickel, who once wrote that "law can never make us as secure as we are when we do not need it. Those freedoms which are neither challenged nor defined are the most secure."[174]

In such an environment, it is important to be aware not simply of what the law says, but of what the reality is concerning the communication of information. We may be moving toward an environment that will tolerate some more explicit controls on information than we now have. Indeed, the new media are already regulated in ways that would be unconstitutional if applied to print.[175] At the same time, the actual flow of information is increasing many times, and the likelihood of any law succeeding in preventing citizens from finding out about a particular event will be less than it is now. We are certainly not at the point today where we can say that we do not need the First Amendment as critically as we needed it when there were far fewer outlets for information and any law enacted to control the flow of information could have been enforced effectively. Most of the forms of communication that will be commonplace in the next decade or two are in the experimental stage today. But the day may come in the not-too-distant future when the public will probably feel more comfortable about accepting some controls on communication that might not be tolerated today.

As the courts struggle increasingly with the problem of drawing lines between permissible and impermissible restrictions on communication, perhaps the most important task is to try to develop a consensus on what we expect from the First Amendment. Lay people would probably be surprised to read that there is "lack of agreement about what the First Amendment is supposed to do"[176] or that "freedom of the press is an elusive concept."[177] Although there has been considerable writing and debate about the purposes of the guarantees of free speech and press,[178] the lack of agreement has not had significant practical consequences until now. It has been possible to avoid the issue and to discuss it more as an abstract than as a practical problem. As the new media expand our ability to communicate and to remove some of the inherent censors of print, the law will be faced with novel and difficult decisions about limiting communication, and the lack of a coherent theory will become a more substantial problem.

To understand why the new technologies will require a clarification of the goals and purposes of free expression, it may be helpful to consider a parallel in the medical field. Advances in medical technology have extended the abilities of physicians to prolong life. As a consequence, however, doctors and researchers now have to confront issues that they previously could avoid. It is necessary now to be more precise about the definitions of life and death and about when it is permissible to stop treatments that could prolong life.[179] These issues have to be faced because the limitations of the old technology have been overcome.

In a similar manner, the development of new communications technologies places pressure on the law to clarify the purposes of free expression. Professor Emerson has written,

> The attainment of freedom of expression is not the sole aim of the good society. As the private right of the individual, freedom of expression is an end in itself, but it is not the only end of man as an individual. In its social and political aspects, freedom of expression is primarily a process or a method for reaching other goals. It is a basic element in the democratic way of life, and as a vital process it shapes and determines the ends of democratic society. But it is not through this process alone that a democratic society will attain its ultimate ends. Any theory of freedom of expression must therefore take into account other values, such as public order, justice, equality and moral progress, and the need for substantive measures designed to promote these ideals. Hence there is a real problem of reconciling freedom of expression with other values and objectives sought by the good society.[180]

Fortunately or unfortunately, the increase in the number of channels of communication will force us to confront this "real problem" more frequently, and the public will be more aware that difficult choices are being made. The Supreme Court is less able to resolve modern cases by

> determining that free speech is harmless or integral to some mysterious, unalterable evolutionary process. Instead, the Justices are now faced ... with the difficult task of deciding just how high a price our constitutional commitment to open, meaningful discussion requires us to pay in terms of such competing concerns as individual reputation, adjudicative fairness, efficient public administration, and peace and quiet.[181]

It is in large part due to the effects of an expansion and acceleration of the movement of information that there is a growing recognition of a need to "dispel the climate of uncertainty and intellectual disorder that permeates the concept and implementation of freedom of speech"[182] and find principles to guide choices and decisions in First Amendment cases.[183]

I hope that it is clear that I am not suggesting that all legal controls on communication are inconsequential or that any controls should be treated as trivial or insignificant. My vision of the future is considerably more optimistic than that of scholars whose analyses focus on the economics of the communications industry[184] or of those whose concern is with television and not other new forms of technology.[185] It may or may not be different from that of researchers who try to predict future legal trends from past court decisions. What is different is the basis of assessing what is likely to occur. This analysis rests less on who today controls the new technologies, on what recent court cases have held, or on what is happening now and more on certain differences between the new and old forms of communication. Given the rapid pace of technological development and the fact that the First Amendment itself was a product of a change in communications environments, it is unfortunate that this perspective on the First Amendment has been ignored in the past.

It is not unusual for legal scholars to pay lip service to the influence of nonlegal factors on the nature of law. In a recent examination of the First Amendment, for example, it was written that

> freedom of communication in America, as in any society, is encouraged and restrained by the interplay of many forces. The history and traditions of a people provide a pervasive backdrop. In America that history and those traditions have worked largely in favor of openness and against restraint. The temperaments of the individuals and subcultures that make up a society are also a significant ingredient. In our tremendously heterogeneous mix of racial, ethnic, and nationality groups there is much variety in the impulse to communicate. Some of us are highly expressive, others are exceptionally stoic. Physical environment, too, plays an important role. People who are crowded together on small islands, like the Japanese or English, tend to guard what privacy they can with more inhibitions on their interpersonal and

public communication styles than has been the case, for example, in the wide-open spaces of the American West. Ultimately, the law of the land, reflecting a composite of these and other forces, determines what its people will be allowed or not allowed to say.[186]

In an era in which new forms of communications are being developed, it is particularly important to focus on the "other forces." The most important of these may be the special qualities of the new media. Without an understanding of these qualities, our perspective on the future evolution of the First Amendment will be incomplete.

4

Legal Doctrines and Information: The Medium Has a Message

> Among all the things in the world, information is the hardest
> to guard, since it can be stolen without removing it.
>
> ERVING GOFFMAN

One of the most popular television adventure programs in the early 1970s, "Mission: Impossible," always began with the playing of a tape recording describing some covert action to be performed. This ritualized opening scene typically concluded with a warning by the voice on the tape that if the operation became publicly known, the government would not admit any responsibility for the activity. The tape, as the only evidence of governmental involvement, then self-destructed in a puff of smoke.

The "impossible" element in this program always seemed to be the rescue, escape, or other assignment undertaken by the group of mercenaries. Yet it may very well be that the most fantastic element in the series was the maintenance by the group and by the government of perfect secrecy. Today, more exotic feats of technology than self-destructing tapes are easily imaginable, but absolute control over information is becoming less and less believable. If a duplicate copy of the tape did not find its way to some newspaper or television station, another revealing piece of information would.

"Mission: Impossible" appeared to take place in a society in which government control of information was possible without any help from the law. It seemed to be inherent in a technology that was capable of many varieties of wizardry. The group, as in almost

168

all police or mystery programs on television,[1] was inevitably successful in obtaining any information it needed either by force or by duplicity. The society was not our society, but it may have reflected, albeit with some exaggeration, our image of technology at that time. Technology was power, and a new communications technology would inevitably translate into greater power and control for those already in power while others would become vulnerable and powerless.

In Chapter 3, I argued that any new communications medium will affect the contest over control of information and that, in the new communication environment fostered by printing, the state eventually grew more tolerant of the production and dissemination of information. The ongoing contest between government and citizen over the control of political information was redefined, at least in part, because the new medium of print had very different properties from writing. An astonishing increase in literary production and in the distribution of printed matter in the centuries following Gutenberg eventually brought about a recognition that legal control of printed information was, at the very least, more difficult than it was originally thought to be. The wide circulation of printed literature and the greater than expected difficulty in censoring communication ultimately contributed to attempts to develop a concept of free expression and were important influences on the constitutional model we are now accustomed to.

The relaxation of controls that is reflected in the First Amendment was, however, neither complete nor absolute. The three areas of law that are the focus of this chapter—copyright, obscenity, and privacy—are designed to restrict the communication of certain kinds of information. Each of these legal doctrines assumes that control of this information is both necessary and feasible. Each treats information as something that can and should be captured and controlled. Each makes assumptions about the nature of information, and each reflects attitudes about qualities of the media used to transmit the information that has to be controlled.

These three areas of law are, like the First Amendment, "growth areas" in which there is much litigation and legislative concern. The new technologies, by accelerating the movement and production of information, have, it is generally acknowledged, weakened the ability to enforce the law in each of the areas. Information is escaping that previously did not exist or was easier to suppress. Copyright law is violated daily in homes and offices with videotape recorders, computers, and copying machines. The rules of privacy are unable to cope with the collection, distribution, and processing of information by electronic means. Sexually explicit materials in a variety of media are widely available. In a time of expanding use of electronic communication, the law's ability to restrict the movement of certain kinds of information has become increasingly difficult. The law itself has not changed radically, but the communications environment has; as a result, many of the goals of the law are more difficult to achieve. Those who benefit from copyright, obscenity, and privacy laws are, therefore, threatened as the inherent controls of print are being lifted. In addition, however, the concepts themselves are vulnerable as the public acquires experience with information that was previously suppressed. While the law's short-term concern may be to find a means to restore efficient enforcement, the lesson of print is that more far-reaching change is likely. The print environment not only brought about a desire for legal regulation in these areas, but also affected how we think about creativity, erotica, and individuality, issues that underlie the legal doctrines of copyright, obscenity, and privacy. A new medium affects societal perceptions and concerns, and these may be shifting at the same time that the enforcement model is deteriorating. It is, admittedly, more difficult to describe what is occurring in our minds than in our courts and legislatures, but without being cognizant of the former, we may seriously misunderstand the latter.

All the areas of law discussed in this chapter arose only after the development of printing and can be linked to qualities of print. The history of these areas suggests several important lessons. It is, for example, a mistake to assume that legal, political, economic, philosophical, or social goals alone will determine the outcome of struggles taking place in each of these fields of law. More law, even if enforced effectively, will probably not bring about as controlled or restricted a communications environment as that which existed in the print era. If the new technologies are significantly expanding the production and movement of information, then the ultimate effect of restrictive laws will be, at best, to slow down the increase in the flow of information rather than to reduce it. It is also an error to assume that legal concepts that are widely accepted today will be unaffected by the new media. We can expect sharp revisions in traditional legal concepts as well as the emergence of new legal doctrines that reflect new concerns and values.

The meaning and evolution of any legal doctrine is neither pre-determined nor constant but results from cultural developments that may be largely unrecognized by lawmakers. Copyright, for example, is more than a means of protecting a property interest. It may be viewed as a response to a changing concept of authorship and to a condition of artistic and scientific progress that was largely absent before the print era. Obscenity laws surfaced not simply to suppress sexually explicit publications that were more widely available, but because morality was being redefined as law became secular and distinct from religious codes. Privacy law arose not merely in reaction to an intrusive press, but in support of a concern for the self that had become more valued as a result of printing's focus on the individual. Law should be seen, therefore, as a response to a whole set of experiences and not simply to a particular problem that may have triggered a public outcry.

If this analysis is correct, the most important areas of future change to copyright, obscenity, and privacy will not be the means of enforcement but the core ideas that are at the heart of particular rules of law. Each area of law developed because of the capabilities of print, and each benefitted from inherent limitations of print. Each reveals a desire both to control information and to achieve an accommodation among First Amendment concerns, property interests, and social or moral values. The definition of each legal doctrine implies a particular balance among these competing interests, and it is this balance that is currently vulnerable. The enforcement difficulties contribute to this process by presenting us with novel experiences with previously suppressed information. Whether the information was unavailable because of legal restrictions or the limitations of prior modes of communication, the ultimate effect of the new communications environment will be a new kind of accommodation, a new balance, and a new meaning.

As doctrines that involve the movement of information, copyright, obscenity, and privacy can be considered to be related to one another. Each relies on placing limits on the "information chain" described in earlier chapters. The information chain is a useful metaphor for the process of acquiring and processing information. A chain that grows longer and longer indicates that existing knowledge is used and built on. Like some children's toys in which necklaces are made by linking different colored shapes together, the chain can be re-formed and modified by substituting some links for others. A highly active and volatile chain not only gets longer, extending and adding to knowledge, but also forms new branches and fosters connections between areas of knowledge that were previously isolated. This reworking of information is a key ingredient of the information society[2] or information economy in which new information or old information processed into a new form acquires substantial economic value. What is often not noticed is that the accelerating volatility of the information chain not only encourages the growth of the information economy, but also contributes to a new attitude toward information and a new meaning for those legal doctrines that attempt to retard communication.

Copyright

Copyright, like state-imposed censorship, is a creation of the era of print. Prior to Gutenberg, there was no clear concept of ownership of written information.[3] Information was common property, and "ideas that we associate with such terms as 'plagiarism,' 'copyright,' or 'author's rights' simply did not exist and were not likely to exist until the invention of printing had revolutionized methods of production."[4] There were no copyright laws because "there did not have to be. The scribes were scattered, working on single manuscripts in monasteries."[5] The development of copyright law after printing reveals not simply a legal change, but a shift in attitudes about the influence and value of information. Elizabeth Eisenstein concludes, "Until it became possible to distinguish between composing a poem and reciting one, or writing a book and copying one . . . how could modern games of books and authors be played?"[6]

In the Middle Ages, it was "felt that all the literature that existed in their time was a fund of man's knowledge, rather than belonging to its individual authors."[7] At that time, books existed chiefly in single copies, almost like long letters from author to patron. . . . There were few lay writers and very little original writing. The ubiquitous monastic chronicler had renounced personal property, and even enterprising communities, which might have claimed some corporate right, were more interested in diffusion. Much of the work reproduced centered around the classics and long-dead Fathers and Doctors of the Church, and there was no one to dispute the freedom to copy. Even if someone had claimed an exclusive right to copy, it would have been almost impossible to enforce in the case of hand-written books. A tradition which allowed whoever possessed a manuscript to copy it grew with little opposition. . . . Rabbinical authorities held the opinion that one was allowed to copy a manuscript without the consent of the author, and it was considered a blessing to permit scribes to make copies. Christian authorities heartily agreed. One synod went so far as to declare that the lending of books to be copied was one of the works of mercy.[8]

Frequently, authors were not known, and even today we have difficulty knowing who wrote many manuscripts that have been preserved. The methods of producing manuscripts encouraged those who owned them to take liberties that might be unlawful today. In the scribal period, when a work

became famous and widely used, any careful reader might constitute himself an editor and assume wide powers of revising, enlarging, abbreviating, and rearranging the text. His aim in preparing a copy for his own use was not to preserve the *ipsissima verba* of the master, but to put between one pair of covers all of the original which seemed to him valuable, plus such additions and corrections as his learning suggested. If he felt that he could use the work better with a different arrangement, then he forthwith rearranged it.[9]

An economic interest that might have encouraged legal protection did not exist. Printing changed the economic value of authorship by making large-scale distribution possible. Techniques for faster copying of some kinds of works had been developed in the thirteenth and fourteenth centuries,[10] but through most of the Middle Ages the difficulties in copying by hand were an enormous obstacle. An average book might involve three to four months' work, and a Bible might require a full year.[11]

Copyright came into being as state censorship controls were relaxed and as the concept of authorship changed. Anglo-American copyright law is usually traced back to the Statute of Anne, which was enacted in 1709. Since Caxton introduced the printing press to England in 1476, however, it is important to understand how protection for authors and publishers was handled in the almost two and a half centuries between 1476 and 1709. During this period, copyright was intertwined with political censorship laws. English censorship laws during the sixteenth and seventeenth centuries can be considered to be both censorship *and* copyright laws. The censorship laws granted control over publication to the Stationers' Company, and only printers who belonged to the company could legally publish books.[12] Any publisher who printed a work owned the rights to it in perpetuity. Censorship served the interests of the state, and the economic interests of the publisher, who acted as "policeman of the press,"[13] were protected. Copyright, during this early period, was partly political censorship and partly trade regulation. Neither rights for authors nor encouragement of creativity was a part of the concept of copyright during its early period. While copyright protection may be taken for granted by authors today, the original model, with control in the hands of printers licensed by the state and with the publisher holding the copyright, was simply designed to protect church and state from unwanted publications.

Enactment of the Statute of Anne in 1709 was made necessary because the Licensing Act of 1662 expired in 1694 and was not renewed. Yet the new statute did not retain the old model of publisher's copyright. Rather, it recognized in law what was becoming apparent in fact, that the author was a key participant in the creation of the work. The novelty of the new law was partly separating copyright from other laws that censored printing and partly making the author the principal beneficiary and allowing the copyright to be in his name.[14] The new law "meant more than the end of censorship: it meant also the end of legal sanctions for the stationers' copyright."[15] Not only were the links between copyright and state interests weakened, but copyright gradually became a tool of authors rather than a tool of the state.

The change in meaning and emphasis that occurred to copyright law in the eighteenth century and the shift in the legal status of authors were a reflection of the more general change in the role of the individual during this period. Printing, as will be explained later,[16] may be considered to be not only a mass medium that could reach large numbers of people, but also an "individual medium," in the sense that it encouraged individual accomplishment, attention, and responsibility. The new experience of authors, as they were identified and celebrated in ways that were not possible in earlier times, was part of the growing concern for the individual in society and in law. The new opportunities for and legal protection of individual authors were part of a trend in which other areas of law touching individuals, such as privacy, were also affected. Copyright law may have given authors a new formal status in the eyes of the law, but this was partly a recognition of the achievements that individuals and authors had already attained in the public mind.

The improvement in social and economic status that the medium of print bestowed on authors as a class suggests that an even broader principle is at work in the evolution of copyright law: any basically new medium of communication fosters parallel and distinctive changes in the nature of authorship and creative activity. Thus the problem for those who wish to retain and reinforce the current model of copyright is not only that copying is easier than it was before, but that methods of creation are also changing. As will be described below, the ease of copying is part of a larger shift in the use of information in the creative process, a shift that the law will have to take into account. The value and perception of creation, it has been observed,

> is at least in part determined by our current tools for technological creativity. Indeed, what we can make in our own technological world influences our beliefs about the world of nature and how it came to be: hence the ambiguity of the term "creation," which refers to both the act of making and the world as a product of (divine) creation. Here again, technology and philosophy interact. The computer, the most philosophical of machines with its preoccupations with logic, time, space, and language, suggests a new view of human craftsmanship and creativity as well.[17]

To the extent that copyright law reflects a print-oriented model of the creative process, it can be expected to be transformed as the manner of creation and the forms of creative works change.

The dilemma for copyright law in the electronic era arises not only because increased copying occurs, but also because copying becomes a more obvious, accepted, fundamental, and even legitimate part of the creative process. The electronic media are fostering a proliferation of new creative forms, some of which require, encourage, or facilitate copying.[18] With print, the act of copying the author's work occurred in a remote factory and into a form that encouraged that it be treated as a whole. All electronically obtained information, however, is essentially information that, with some technological help, one has copied oneself. Unlike print, one participates in the act of copying and in choosing which information will be copied and which will not. The number of tasks one could perform on a printed book or article was limited. One could read it, take notes, or summarize it. Mostly, one could think about it. One could not edit it, revise it, or otherwise transform it without, at the same time, destroying it. The copying of electronic information, on the contrary, allows it to be processed, manipulated, and put to use in ways not possible with print. Copying, therefore, is often not an end in itself, not an act of piracy done solely to make a profit from someone else's work, but part of a larger process in which new tools can be applied to data in new ways.

The redefinition of copyright is inevitable because much more of the act of creation in the future will involve working with copied information. For those who use electronic information, there are opportunities to work with the material and not simply to read it or look at it, which is all that copyright lawfully allows the user. The user of electronic information is in a different position from persons in earlier generations who had the limited options of reading and writing. The digitalization of information, as Figure 4-1 reveals, allows the color, shape, position, size, and texture of images to be reworked as easily as text is edited using a word processor. Indeed, the very act of acquiring electronic information violates assumptions on which copyright is based. As Ithiel de Sola Pool recognized, "To read a copyright text is no violation, only to copy it in writing. The technological basis for this distinction is reversed with a computer text. To read a text stored in electronic memory, one displays it on the screen: one writes it to read it. To transmit it to others, however, one does not write it; one only gives the password to one's computer memory. One must write to read, but not to write."[19]

Figure 4-1 The Art of Digital Retouching

Photo credit: Pacific Lithograph Co., San Franciso CA

This demonstration of digital retouching was put together by Pacific Lithograph Co. What appears to be two separate photographs is actually only one. By digitizing the photograph of the four hikers, it becomes possible to capture and then manipulate information about color, patterns, and texture. With a Chromacom machine, a computer-driven device, it becomes a simple matter to copy the color or texture at one point and slide it over to another. Distinctive patterns are copied exactly. Thus the three people standing in the top scene were not removed; instead they were "washed over" with sky and mountain bits, taken from the scene. Each move of the cursors brings the seams of the changes closer and closer together. While requiring skill, the digitizing process appears to be almost a routine operation.

Source: U.S. Congress, Office of Technology Assessment, *Intellectual Property Rights in an Age of Electronics and Information* (Washington, D.C.: Government Printing Office, 1986), p. 140. For further details, see "Image Processing," *Byte,* March 1987, pp. 141-198.

Part of the problem in understanding the new role of copying in the creative process is semantic. Language, like law, is slow to recognize some changes. In earlier times, when books were produced in a different way, different terms were used depending on the contribution made. Elizabeth Eisenstein has noted how a thirteenth-century Franciscan, Saint Bonaventure,* described four ways of making books:

> A man might write the works of others, adding and changing nothing, in which case he is simply called a "scribe" (scriptor). Another writes the work of others with additions which are not his own; and he is called a "compiler" (compilator). Another writes both others' work and his own for purposes of explanation; and he is called a "commentator" (commentator). . . . Another writes both his own work and others' but with his own work in principal place adding others' for purposes of confirmation; and such a man is called an "author" (auctor).[20]

Completely original works are not even part of this scheme. The manner of production was so different from what we are accustomed to that those involved in literature, such as it existed, were thought of differently. The author's role became highlighted only after the spread of printing. He appeared for the first time on a title page, in a book that was no longer produced piecemeal by

---

*It is interesting that this quotation, by being attributed to a Saint Bonaventure, itself reveals some of the differences between scribal and print culture. Daniel Boorstin has observed, "There were special problems of nomenclature when books were commonly composed as well as transcribed by men in holy orders. In each religious house it was customary for generation after generation of monks to use the same names. When a man took his vows, he abandoned the name by which he had been known in the secular world, and he took a name of one of the monastic brothers who had recently died. As a result, every Franciscan house would always have its Bonaventura, but the identity of 'Bonaventura' at any time could only be defined by considerable research.

"All this . . . gave a tantalizing ambiguity to the name by which a medieval manuscript might be known. A manuscript volume of sermons identified as *Sermones Bonaventurae* might be so called for any one of a dozen reasons. . . . Was the original author the famous Saint Bonaventura of Fidanza? Or was there another author called Bonaventura? Or was it copied by someone of that name? Or by someone in a monastery of that name? Or preached by some Bonaventura, even though not composed by him. Or had the volume once been owned by a Friar Bonaventura, or by a monastery called Bonaventury? Or was this a collection of sermons by different preachers, of which the first was a Bonaventura? Or were these simply in honor of Saint Bonaventura" (*The Discoverers: A History of Man's Search to Know His World and Himself* [New York: Vintage Books, 1985], p. 530)?

separate hands, and in a manner that suggested that he was responsible for everything between the covers. Partly as a result of this, all the different kinds of copyists and scribes that had previously existed were replaced by "author" and "publisher."

Printing also fostered the belief, which underlies the copyright law, that each copyrighted work is deserving of protection because it is an independent creation. Courts have inferred a requirement of originality, but "originality means only that the work owes its origin to the author, i.e. is independently created, and not copied from other works."[21] All works granted a copyright receive identical protection, and no distinctions are made among copyrighted works based on their relative originality. One is an "author" whether one's works are literary masterpieces or pulp novels, whether one is highly creative and innovative or mundane and superficial, whether one has merely described the works of others or presented new ideas. Both the most original and the least original writers are authors with the same legal rights to their work. If a book consists of only selections from other books, the author may be transformed into an "editor," but we have no other words to describe the varying degrees of originality that may be present in different works. Both our language and our law are limited in this regard.

The properties of print have affected how we conceive of work that should be rewarded and protected by law. Anthony Smith has concluded that

> we have tended to mystify the author, to allow him to pretend that his work is semisacral, "original," the emanation of his spirit. The writer has held an exalted position in Western society since the invention of the printing press. His has been the scarce talent around which the process of publication takes place and which holds the audience together. . . . The computerization of memory causes us to perceive the nature of originality in different ways. The computer will not cause, nor change, nor bring about, but will help us to create an altered image of the author and inventor, a changed image that is growing out of the changed nature of the modern research publication process. Within the creative process it is becoming clearer that the talent lies in the refining of past knowledge, in reformulation, in recirculation, in reordering the vast human storage of information that springs from the collective intellectual activity of the species, an unencompassable totality of versions and facts. The creative task lies in being able to manipulate this ever-expanding totality. It is a new perception of crea-

tivity that is now possible—a readjustment, not the elimination of the concept.[22]

The new media are revolutionizing the means of producing works and, more slowly, changing the form in which works appear. While the copying capability of the new media is widely recognized, we will only slowly become aware of the proliferation of new creative, artistic, and literary forms. Copying and digitalization make boundary crossing between different creative forms much easier and ultimately make the boundaries themselves less distinct.[23] Traditional methods of using information will be joined by newly feasible techniques of expression. The proliferation in the means of producing works and in the kinds of works that are created challenges the restricted model of creativity that is implicit in copyright law. For example, the computer has made possible interactive fiction, in which "readers" can participate in defining characters and changing plots. The author of one analysis of this emerging genre notes that

> the fluid nature of interactive text and its computer medium explodes the traditional literary concept of the individual authorship of a printed text. In some ways, the authorship and transmission of the interactive text is similar to those of oral literature. With a printed text, we generally have the idea that there is a single "author" who "owns" the text; copyrighting reflects our views about this. But in oral literature and IF [interactive fiction], single, joint, multiple, communal, unknown, and anonymous authorships are common.[24]

The process of building on prior information and of extending the information chain exists in the print environment, but the mechanics of production ensure that it occurs much more slowly than it will in the future. When the links consist of electronically coded information, new methods of accelerating, combining, creating, and transforming them become possible. In addition, there are growing opportunities to transform a work that is in one medium into a slightly different product in a different medium. Copyright law currently states that it applies to creative works in all media, but we should recognize that it has had to deal with only very few modes of producing a copyrightable work. The new processes of creation will pose a challenge for language as well as law as more hybrid forms appear. As our experience with electronic communication is enlarged, as our language expands and creates new words to describe people whose work does not fit established criteria, the assumptions underlying the copyright model will feel even more stress than they do now.

Obscenity

"It is the prevailing social consciousness," a judge once wrote in an obscenity case, "that matters quite as much as the law."[25] With obscenity, as with other areas of law that involve the suppression of information, history suggests that the "prevailing social consciousness" can be greatly influenced by changes in the existing modes of communication. In terms of the ability to restrict obscene or pornographic works, it might also be said that "'it is the prevailing media that matters quite as much as the law." The qualities of the media used in a society will affect both public concern about sexual works and the ability of law to effectively limit publication and distribution.

The use of law to restrict obscenity is of surprisingly recent origin. Legal programs to control sexually explicit materials did not appear until the eighteenth and nineteenth centuries,[26] when expanded distribution of these materials made it clear that some existing mechanisms of control had been greatly weakened. The absence of explicit legal regulation of obscenity and pornography in earlier times should not suggest that such materials did not exist. Enough artifacts remain from ancient times to warrant the conclusion that "at every stage of its development European civilization has known both obscenity and pornography."[27] For example, paintings on vases and the dialogue in Greek plays suggest that the Athenians

> viewed sexuality in almost all of its manifestations as an essentially healthy and enjoyable fact of life. There is no indication of the kind of guilty, inhibited, and repressive feelings so characteristic of later societies in regard to this area of life. The Athenians of this era may not have been uninhibited children of nature, but their inhibitions concerning human sexuality were certainly less muddled by complicated feelings of shame and guilt than our own.[28]

Even more explicit materials remain from Roman times, some of which would probably qualify as obscene under modern legal definitions. Walter Kendrick, in a recent study of pornography, concluded that Roman poets "hit a peak of obscene polemic that Western literature would not reach again (and then only palely) until the end of the seventeenth century. Cattullus, Martial, and Juvenal regularly accused their enemies of practices which modern languages have no words for."[29]

The father of modern pornography is considered to be Pietro Aretino, who lived from 1492 to 1556. His most famous work, commonly called *Aretino's Postures,* consisted of printed pictures and text, and its content and impact were described by a contemporary as follows:

> Giulio Romano caused Marc'Antonio to engrave twenty plates showing the various ways, attitudes, and positions in which licentious men have intercourse with women; and, what was worse, for each plate Messer Pietro Aretino wrote a most indecent sonnet, insomuch that I know not which was the greater, the offense to the eye from the drawings of Giulio, or the outrage to the ear from the words of Aretino. This work was much censured by Pope Clement; and if, when it was published, Giulio had not already left for Mantua, he would have been sharply punished for it by the anger of the Pope. And since some of these sheets were found in places where they were least expected, not only were they prohibited, but Marc'Antonio was taken and thrown into prison.[30]

Aretino's notoriety was due not only to his book's erotic content, but to the fact that printing allowed the work to be "found in places where they were least expected" and thus transformed his work into something of public and not simply private interest and concern. There were at least enough copies in existence to bring a response from the religious authorities, which had not been necessary when the inherent limits of writing effectively restricted distribution. Moreover, those responsible for the work were identifiable, a situation that had not always existed when manuscripts were copied piecemeal. A "content analysis" of sexually explicit works in the centuries following the development of printing, in other words, does not explain fully the origins of a legal movement to control obscenity. The nature of sexually oriented materials may have been no more "hard-core" after the fifteenth century than it had been in earlier times. The change was less in what was printed than in how widely it was available and how it came to be perceived.

As the development of printing made sexually explicit materials more widely accessible and, particularly, as literacy increased, the law began to respond to changing methods of distribution, and the modern concept of obscenity began to come into focus.

The experience of Aretino also suggests that there were, before the development of specific legal controls, other institutional and community pressures limiting what today would be considered pornographic or obscene works. During the Middle Ages and the first two centuries of printing, the Church and later the state did exert pressure to limit some forms of sexually oriented material. There may have been no laws that banned the obscene, but there were many laws against blasphemy[31] and sedition, against criticizing the Church or the state. Erotic works that were in some way also critical of these two institutions might thus be suppressed, or at least attempts at suppression were occasionally made. As with copyright, some pressure limiting obscenity and pornography was exerted by the broader censorship laws.

In a world in which religious and political institutions were often linked, the areas of law, religion, and morals were not easily distinguished. Fears of offending Church or state shaped the kind of sexual material that was likely to be acceptable. Pressure of this kind limited sexual material with political impact in the same way that it limited nonsexual material with political impact. The end result was a situation that was almost the direct opposite of what modern law tolerates. Recent constitutional law in the area of obscenity prohibits the suppression of material that has literary, artistic, political, or scientific value.[32] Material that is purely sexual in character, that "appeals to the prurient interest,"[33] that "depicts or describes, in a patently offensive way, sexual conduct specifically defined by the applicable state law,"[34] and that has "no literary, artistic, political, or scientific value"[35] may be declared unlawful. Prior to the development of modern obscenity law, this was the kind of material that was the target of authorities least often. Many examples of ancient or medieval pornography were designed to be humorous or titillating, and the authorities were less concerned about simply erotic material than about material that, though less sexually oriented, could be considered seditious or blasphemous. The Church was more concerned with heresy than with obscenity, and the state focused on sedition more than obscenity. In one of the first attempted prosecutions for obscenity in the early eighteenth century, for example, the court dismissed the indictment, stating that "a crime that shakes religion, as profaness on the stage, &c. is indictable; but writing an obscene book, as that intitled, *The Fifteen Plagues of a Maidenhead,* is not indictable, but punishable only in spiritual court."[36] Until the nineteenth century, "immorality and immodesty apart from antireligious behavior or seditious behavior or behavior provoking violence had not been punished."[37] In the Middle Ages, "religion and bawdiness were not seen as mutually exclusive. They combined in the vividly descriptive ballads of the period, and the *Exeter Book,* a largely devotional work which constitutes the earliest example of Anglo-Saxon literature, contains obscene riddles which were collected by a monk."[38] Even the Church did not seem to regard itself as the safeguarder of public morals. While we legitimize potentially obscene works by attaching political significance to them, earlier pornographers could escape public wrath by highlighting the sexual and minimizing the political.

Printing changed attitudes about erotica by altering the conditions of distribution of and accessibility to sexually explicit materials. The limitations of writing had been a highly effective censor, restricting general public access to such materials much more effectively than law alone could have done. Law was less needed when "scarcity and obscurity provided all the necessary safeguards."[39] That no copies of *Aretino's Postures,* famous as the book was, survive to this day suggests that there continued to be informal pressures to keep such works hidden even if they were not illegal. For example, Samuel Pepys, whose diary reveals him to have been a great consumer of erotic works, made the following two entries in early 1668.

> 8 February 1668. . . . Thence away to the Strand to my bookseller's, and there stayed an hour and bought that idle, roguish book *L'escholle des Filles;* which I have bought in plain binding (avoiding the buying of it better bound) because I resolve, as soon as I have read it, to burn it, so that it may not stand in the list of books nor among them, to disgrace them if it should be found. . . .

> 9 February 1668. *Lords day.* . . . We sang till almost night, and drank my good store of wine; and then they parted and I to my chamber,

where I did read through *L'escholle des Filles;* a lewd book, but what doth me no wrong to read for information sake (but it did hazer my prick para stand all the while, and una vez to decharger); and after I had done it, I burned it, that it might not be among my books to my shame.[40]

A century after Pepys wrote, however, literacy among women and the lower classes had increased, and the hiding and burning of copies of books by individuals could not prevent previously restricted groups from obtaining access. Obscenity law, like copyright, emerged as a result of the new communications environment brought about by novel means of production and distribution. Along with many other kinds of literature, sexually oriented material became published in larger editions and, as literacy increased, became more widely accessible. Again, it was not merely that the content of sexually oriented works had changed but that the whole communications environment was different. Explicit materials that had always been available mainly to the literate elite became more widespread. As this occurred, the law became concerned with regulating morality, which began to be viewed as something independent from religion. The changing means of distribution, in other words, brought about a new set of rules, a new perspective on the dangers of such literature, and new concepts for the law to build on.

The past thirty-five years have been a period of great activity for obscenity both in the legal arena and in the marketplace. In *United States* v. *Roth,*[41] decided in 1957, the Court declared that obscene material was not protected by the First Amendment. Since then, the Supreme Court has been trying out different definitions; it is trying to find one that will allow law enforcement officials a constitutional way to determine whether or not a particular work may be banned. The current standards, which date back to the case of *Miller* v. *United States*[42] in 1973, have given the law a little more stability, if not clarity, than it enjoyed before that date. Due to a rapidly changing communications environment, however, one could argue that this period of legal stability has also been an era in which the law has been nearly irrelevant and impotent. One can ask whether, if there existed a constitutional right to publish obscene works, the marketplace would look substantially different from how it now appears. The enormous technological changes that have occurred during this period have largely overwhelmed the law. The appearance in 1953 of *Playboy,* with its circulation in the millions, may, therefore, have been a more telling indicator of future trends than the "landmark" Supreme Court decision in *Roth* in 1957. Similarly, changes in the means for producing, viewing, and acquiring sexually explicit materials in the years since 1973 may provide more insight into the future development of the law of obscenity than the words of the Court in *Miller* or subsequent Court decisions in the area.

The essential problem faced by those wishing to keep obscene materials out of the marketplace is that it is more difficult for one group to keep any information hidden from any other group. The most thoughtful general analysis of the process by which the electronic media encourage hidden information to become more public is contained in communications theorist Joshua Meyrowitz's *No Sense of Place.* Meyrowitz persuasively argues that groups throughout society are losing control of information that had previously been theirs exclusively. Individual, group, and professional identities are threatened because information can no longer be effectively monopolized. Children know more of what adults know; citizens learn many of the secrets of politicians; laypeople can more easily question professional expertise; and women are able to discover the nature of the male domain. In these and many other areas, the ability of the new media to overcome barriers of distance means that socialization into a new role can occur without "access to the group's territory and to the knowledge and information available in it."[43] Information moves faster and in new directions and cannot be as easily isolated or compartmentalized. Electronic messages, Meyrowitz writes,

> do not make social entrances; they steal into places like thieves in the night. The "guests" received by a child through electronic media no longer can be stopped at the door to be approved of by the masters of the house. Once a telephone, radio, or television is in the home, spatial isolation and guarding of entrances have no effect on information flow. Electronic messages seep through walls and leap across great distances. Indeed, were we not so accustomed to television and radio and telephone messages invading our homes, they might be the recurring subjects of nightmares and horror films.[44]

Electronic information is, as a recent government report noted, "inherently leaky,"[45] leading to a condition where "nothing could be further from the spirit of the new technology than 'a place for everything and everything in its place.' "[46]

Meyrowitz argues persuasively that the new access to information is responsible for increasing public exposure of many behaviors previously hidden from view. The visual media, in particular, are intrusive, allowing us to see places that are physically hidden from us. The increasingly explicit nature of sexually oriented works in various media is thus merely one example of a broad shift in the content of publicly available information that is affecting public expectations of what can be known and seen. As Walter Kendrick has perceptively observed,

> during the course of the pornographic era—from approximately the 1840s to the 1960s—representations of all kinds proliferated at a wildly accelerating pace in both quantity and medium. Printed books followed that path, along with every new medium invented during the period, from photography at its beginning to television near its end. The trend in all cases was toward ever wider dissemination of evermore representations, saturating the culture with words and pictures. Simultaneously, the range of content steadily broadened, in an apparently unstoppable drive toward the total availability of total detail. If the smut of fifty or even twenty years ago looks tame by comparison with today's, the reason may have nothing to do with pornography itself. Every mode of representation has become explicit in the same years, in every nonsexual realm; it has become possible to photograph the earth from outer space, a fetus in the womb, and Vietnamese children in the process of dying. The only difference in the case of pornography is that it faces steady resistance, while these other advances in explicitness win praise for contributing to the enrichment of knowledge.[47]

Obscenity law is much more concerned with content than with the form in which the content is displayed. The same legal definitions apply regardless of medium,[48] although the Supreme Court has tolerated some additional restrictions on radio and television content and, in the future, is likely to have to deal with novel modes of presentation, such as dial-a-porn. Generally, however, consideration of the qualities of the new forms of communication is considered legally irrelevant. McLuhan's assertion that "the 'content' of a medium is like the juicy piece of meat carried by the burglar to distract the watchdog of the mind"[49] describes fairly accurately the judicial attitude. It is the content of sexually explicit publications, more than anything else, that attracts both public and legal attention. Yet the absence of judicial comment on the role of the new media in shaping legal approaches to sexually explicit material does not mean that legal doctrine in this area can be forever insulated from the changing communications environment. On the contrary, in the long run, it is the qualities of the new technologies that are most likely to be responsible for the reconceptualization of obscenity doctrine.

The increasing availability of sexual materials due to the powerful distribution and production capabilities of the new media is assaulting the traditional legal model of obscenity. This does not necessarily mean that the Supreme Court will formally remove itself from judging the sexual content of works, but it is likely that sexual explicitness by itself will infrequently justify suppression of a work. There may be more materials in circulation that technically meet the criteria for obscenity in *Miller* but less likelihood of prosecution and, in general, less concern with such material. It also does not mean that attempts to control some material found objectionable by some groups, even though not technically obscene, will not occur. The recent activity over materials labeled "pornographic"[50] and "indecent"[51] provides an example of this. Some publicized attempts at control may also be tried. In general, however, the contours of the contest in the future over control of such material will leave more, not less, discretion and choice in the hands of the individual. Indeed, as electronic media become technologically more and more sophisticated and are able to make ever more complex interactive assaults on our senses and minds, the basis for judging whether a work is "pornographic" or "indecent" may center more on questions of aesthetics than on those of morality. The "prevailing social consciousness" of the future may see the whole question of obscenity—whether in books, films, videos, or whatever—from a perspective proclaimed in the era of print: "There is no such thing as a moral or an immoral book. Books are well written or badly written. That is all."[52]

This message is, indeed, implicit in the recent *Final Report* of the Attorney General's Commission on Pornography.[53] The report consists of two thick volumes containing almost two thousand pages. Its uniqueness, however, does not lie in its analysis of the spread of pornography or its recommendations of how to control it. Rather, it is most revealing in its inclusion of nearly three hundred pages of summaries, descriptions, and listings of pornographic and obscene magazines, films, books, and tapes. Readers of the report, which can be found at U.S. depository libraries located in almost every community, may or may not skip over this material. But that will be their choice. The inclusion of this material, graphic and explicit, clearly indecent and pornographic under any definition of these words, can be avoided by the individual reader. But, as is increasingly the case with such material in the larger society, little help in doing so will come from government or from the law.

Privacy

Privacy may be the most interesting and revealing of the rules regulating the flow of information. Privacy is an area of law which recognizes that the medium has a message and which distinguishes among information communicated by different means. To this day, some acts that are undeniable invasions of privacy, such as gossip, do not become illegal invasions of privacy unless the information is communicated by some medium other than speech. Large parts of privacy law punish the communication of information in print or on television but impose no restriction when the same information is transmitted orally. In many cases, the act of invasion of privacy is unlawful only if accompanied by distribution of the material to a wide audience.[54] Private information that has been discovered but that is not passed on to others or is passed on by some medium that is incapable of reaching large numbers of people may create no legal wrong.

Privacy, like copyright and obscenity, had no direct legal ancestor in the preprint era. As a legal concept, privacy is something new, a field of the law whose origin is linked to printing, although the relationship is more complex than with the areas of law already discussed. Like the other areas of law, however, it is a subject that suggests some of the conditions under which the demand for new legal doctrine will occur and how a new medium can generate distinctly new rules to regulate information.

The traditional account of the origins of modern privacy law is quite well known. It attributes privacy law to certain invasions of privacy committed by the press in the late nineteenth century. Those affected by these press activities considered the news media of that time to have Big Brother–like qualities and responded by proposing the creation of laws to protect against abuses of the press. The press was the villain and the perpetrator of activities that required a legal response. In 1890, in volume four of the *Harvard Law Review,* an article was published entitled "The Right to Privacy." The authors of the piece were two young Boston lawyers, Samuel Warren and Louis Brandeis.[55] Warren and Brandeis were concerned about the fact that

> instantaneous photographs and newspaper enterprise have invaded the sacred precincts of private and domestic life; and numerous mechanical devices threaten to make good the prediction that "what is whispered in the closet shall be proclaimed from the house-tops". . . . The press is overstepping in every direction the obvious bounds of propriety and of decency. Gossip is no longer the resource of the idle and of the vicious, but has become a trade, which is pursued with industry as well as effrontery. To satisfy a prurient taste the details of sexual relations are spread broadcast in the columns of the daily papers. To occupy the indolent, column after column is filled with idle gossip, which can only be procured by intrusion upon the domestic circle.[56]

In response, the two authors proposed the creation of something novel, a legal right of privacy to provide protection for the "anguish caused an individual where there had been no injury to property or contract rights."[57]

This review of the origin of modern privacy law, though not a false history, is an incomplete history. For modern privacy law is an outgrowth not only of press abuses but of a new conception of the value of privacy. Attempts to control privacy or to create a legal concept of privacy had not occurred in earlier times, when there was much less privacy than in the late nineteenth century. One account of the eighteenth century, for example, describes how life was lived, to a large extent, in public. One's activities were "shockingly open to one's family, friends, neighbors, enemies, clergymen, and the curious. It was not a matter of social position. At Buckingham, the young King of England, George III, had little more privacy than a Boston artisan. Nor Louis XV at Versailles. They seemed to have no more conception of privacy as a desirable thing than they had of electricity, and did not miss either."[58] To modern eyes, people in earlier times would have had serious privacy problems. Yet they did not look at the condition of their existence in this manner, and Warren and Brandeis, if they had written their article in an earlier era, would not have been very successful. What was different at the time they were writing was the existence of a clear target they could point to and an audience they could appeal to, and print was a contributor to both of these.

If one looks beyond the journalistic use of the printing press and focuses instead on some other effects of printing, a more complex picture of the relationship between printing and privacy emerges, one which suggests that printing bears some responsibility not only for making possible glaring instances of invasions of privacy, but also for two other contributions to modern society: first, the public's acceptance of a concept of privacy; second, a condition of more privacy than had existed previously. Thus print encouraged the appreciation of and the existence of privacy as well as its invasion.

The different outlook on the need and value of privacy in earlier societies is reflected in changes that occurred in the meaning of the word itself. Hannah Arendt observed that

> in ancient feeling, the privative trait of privacy, indicated in the word itself, was all-important; it meant literally a state of being deprived of something, and even of the highest and most human of man's capacities. A man who lived only a private life, who like the slave was not permitted to enter the public realm, or like the barbarian, had chosen not to establish such a realm, was not fully human. We no longer think primarily of deprivation when we use the word "privacy," and this is partly due to the enormous amount of enrichment of the private sphere through modern individualism.[59]

The Greek word for "private" was *idios*. The "noun form of *idios* is *idiotes* from which comes the English word 'idiot.' Its main meaning is a private person or individual, or one in a private station as opposed to one holding public office or taking an active part in public affairs. . . . Thus privacy in Greek carries negative overtones, implying lack of full participation in the approved social order."[60]

There are boundaries in all cultures between public and private.[61] Some cultures, however, are less willing than others to tolerate the costs, conflicts, and compromises that a strong com-

mitment to privacy can require. As philosopher Ferdinand Schoenman has pointed out, the right to privacy may be viewed as

> creating the context in which deceit and hypocrisy may flourish: It
> provides the cover under which most human wrongdoing takes place,
> and then it protects the guilty from taking responsibility for their
> transgressions once committed. The right to privacy often stands in
> the way of vigorous public debate on issues of moral significance.
> Without the shade of privacy, many practices that are arguably legit-
> imate though in fact illegal might be thoroughly and rationally debated
> rather than left unexposed and unexamined. Concern for one's own
> privacy may be regarded as a sign of moral cowardice, an excuse not
> to state clearly one's position and accept whatever unpopularity might
> ensue. Privacy may be seen as a culturally conditioned sensitivity that
> makes people more vulnerable than they would otherwise be to selec-
> tive disclosures and to the sense of comparative inferiority and abject
> shame—a sense engendered by ignorance about the inner lives of
> others.[62]

The growing concern for privacy in modern times is related to
greater opportunities for nourishing interests and concerns of the
self. Part of the reason there was less privacy and less concern with
privacy in earlier times is that the individual, the principal beneficiary of a right of privacy, did not have the same status in the
ancient world as in the modern era.[63] Privacy, one author has
observed, "rests upon an individualist concept of society."[64] It
creates a barrier that the individual may defend against the state,
other institutions, or other persons. It gives the individual control
over "the intimacies of personal identity"[65] and his "inviolate personality."[66] It "define[s] the limits and boundaries of the self. When
the permeability of these boundaries is under the control of a
person, a sense of individuality develops."[67] Similarly, Steven
Lukes, in his study of individualism, has noted that "liberalism
may be said largely to have been an argument about where the
boundaries of this private sphere lie, according to what principles
they are to be drawn, whence interference derives and how it is
to be checked. It presupposes a picture of man to whom privacy
is essential, even sacred, with a life of his own to live."[68]

The role of printing in fostering more concern with the individual
and less with the group of which one was a part is examined in
detail in Chapter 6. For present purposes, what is noteworthy is

that at the time Warren and Brandeis were advocating a new legal right of privacy, most citizens understood through experience what the value of privacy was.[69] Life was, in many ways, more private than it had been in earlier days, and this was a condition that print had contributed to. Reading, for example, was no longer done orally and publicly but had become a silent and private activity. Opportunities for individual learning and self-fulfillment were possible using accessible literature in print. Thus at the same time that writers were complaining about journalistic invasions of privacy, there was a growing experience with privacy. Print and privacy, therefore, are linked not only in the abuses that print made possible, but also in the acceptance of privacy as a desirable condition of life and as an important social value. Brandeis and Warren were not merely reacting against intrusions into Warren's life, but implicitly acknowledging a change in the value of and desire for privacy to which print had contributed a great deal.

Before there could be a publicly perceived threat to privacy, there had to be an awareness of privacy and experience with it. Justice Brandeis once wrote that privacy is "the right most valued by civilized men."[70] Given the limited legal attention to privacy in earlier eras by persons no less civilized than ourselves, the validity of this assertion is quite doubtful. As Barrington Moore has asked, "Is there such a thing as a need for privacy? If there is, it can hardly be a compelling one like the need for air, sleep, or nourishment."[71] Privacy is a legal right that is designed to protect a "socially created need."[72]

Print made it possible to invade privacy by spreading information rapidly and widely, thus reducing an individual's ability to control information about himself. Print also, however, fostered a condition of increased personal privacy and a heightened appreciation of privacy as a concept. In addition, print, in the form of newspapers, also provided a rather clear and seemingly controllable target for those interested in furthering privacy through law. The law did not focus on the spread of all private information. It was principally concerned with government and journalism, two institutions that were readily identifiable.

In considering the ultimate impact of the electronic media, a similar perspective is necessary. Our law is conditioned, at least in part, by our experiences. Privacy as a legal doctrine can expand, contract, or acquire a change in meaning and purpose depending on our appreciation of its value. How broadly the legal concept is defined will be a reflection of our ability to control information about ourselves, our desire to do so, and the societal need for the kind of information that privacy laws restrict and try to keep hidden. It is well to remember that media can contribute to the loss of not only privacy, but also other opportunities for individual thought and action, part of the reason for protecting privacy.

Instances of loss of privacy or problems in enforcement of privacy laws are part of a general difficulty in controlling information. What the difficulties now being experienced by the copyright, obscenity, and privacy laws suggest is that any institution in the new communications environment will find it difficult to keep a firm hold on proprietary information. Both individuals and governments are learning that a central feature of electronic information is that it is in motion as often as it is stationary. Each time such information moves, it is subject to copying, editing, and revising. Exclusive control of information and the power associated with that control is, therefore, difficult to achieve not only by individuals but by governments as well.

Governments, in fact, are experiencing many problems with maintaining their own private concerns. For governments, the equivalent of privacy is secrecy.[73] Governments that cannot control information face a loss of the ability to keep secrets. Individuals wishing to protect privacy and governments desirous of maintaining secrecy, therefore, face a common problem. It is that along with the novel and impressive storage capabilities of computers have come equally impressive, although less publicized, communicative powers and processing capabilities. The specter of databanks, which have ever-growing storage capacities, and long-range cameras and microphones, which can listen and see into private and secret places, have captured public imagination and largely distracted attention from what happens to the information after it is collected. This information, if it does not stay put in the large databank, will start down the path from secret to public.[74]

Discussions of privacy have tended to focus more on how information can be obtained in novel ways[75] than on what happens to it after it is captured, on the acquisition of private information rather than on its spread, although it is the circulation of private information that legally, at least, constitutes the invasion. Individual privacy and governmental secrecy are threatened not only because files can be larger or new means of spying are possible, but also because the communicative and processing capabilities of the new media provide collected information in electronic form with a much more active life than they could have expected in the age of print. As the discussion of the "information chain" in previous sections has argued, the value of information stored in electronic form is that it becomes easier to use, revise, and manipulate. Information that is only collected and stored is much less valuable than information that can be copied, used, or further processed in some way. This quality of electronic communication is the reason why privacy laws are much more difficult to enforce than they were in an earlier period. At one time, journalists were the only ones who could spread information widely. Once private information was "published," it could no longer be retrieved, but much collected information was also never published. In the case of electronic information, collection and publication occur almost simultaneously. Information is obtained, stored, copied, routed, and rerouted in many directions with almost no time lag.

The novel powers of communication and transmission that the new media possess account for the fact that government and journalism—the primary invaders of privacy in the print era—and friends, neighbors, and relatives—the principal gossip mongers of the oral age—are now being joined by new villains who are more numerous, more ambiguous, and less easy to identify. Individual privacy actually benefitted from some of the inefficiencies of print; for example, in the pre-electronic era, the news media were not interested in everyone and had the capacity to publicize information about only relatively small numbers of people. Today, electronic media make it possible, when storage and publication are almost synonymous activities, to communicate private information about much larger numbers of persons. Distribution of such information may not be as wide, but far more people are affected.

These trends are encouraged by the fact that much of the collection of private information occurs not as a result of snooping and spying but through voluntarily revealed data. When we purchase a product and then send in a rebate form, when we subscribe to a magazine, when we purchase items by mail order, and when we contribute to charities, information about ourselves is provided to others; it is not, however, simply "filed" for future reference, as it might have been in earlier times. In an "information society," such data have value. They may be provided to others and can be analyzed in ways that will yield additional knowledge to others about ourselves. The processing capabilities of computers allow the combining of discrete bits of information, each of which alone might not be considered an invasion of privacy, into a picture that has meaning and that we might be concerned about. Ruth Gavison, in an interesting discussion of privacy, provided the following story, which illustrates how this can occur:

> Consider the famous anecdote about the priest who was asked at a party, whether he had heard any exceptional stories during confessional. "In fact," the priest replied, "my first confessor is a good example, since he confessed to a murder." A few minutes later, an elegant man joined the group, saw the priest, and greeted him warmly. When asked how he knew the priest, the man replied: "Why, I had the honor of being his first confessor."[76]

This story is instructive because it shows how privacy is dependent on limiting the communication of information and keeping some information separate from other information. Rapid increases in the movement and sharing of information, however, along with new abilities in processing data, make compartmentalization much more difficult than it was previously. As our experience with private information changes, and as it becomes more difficult "to be able to control the dissemination of information about oneself,"[77] our expectations and experiences with privacy will change as well.

Modern privacy law grew out of a changed communications environment, and we can expect the future of privacy law to reflect the new communications environment. This is an environment that relies on acquiring and sharing information and on the rapid movement of information. It is an environment that expands options for individuals and, as will be described in Chapter 6, fosters new opportunities for groups. Writing and print conditioned us to think of information as being "contained" on pages of paper or in files. We expected it to stay put unless it was physically carried or sent by someone to another place. We are only gradually coming to recognize that, because of the electronification of information, the resting state of information is more temporary than it used to be. As this occurs, our expectations about "containing" information will change, and our conception of privacy, which is neither particularly clear nor very old, will change as well. It would be a mistake to assume that, even if it were possible to do so, we would desire to extend existing laws to cover every situation that might have been considered to be an invasion of privacy in the past. More likely to occur, as we become more aware of the almost continuous movement of information about ourselves, is the redefinition and reorientation of the legal concept of privacy in a way that is compatible with the promotion, protection, and enhancement of the options provided by the new media to individuals to choose and select information, to find out information about others, and, by so doing, to distinguish ourselves from others. Our experience with information, in other words, is changing and, as a result, our values and concerns are as well. This fact may be more obvious today to those concerned with the increased availability of sexually explicit materials and to those affected by illegal copying, but the same difficult challenges and decisions will have to be faced also by those wishing to use law in the future to promote individual privacy.

5

The Legal Profession

It should be clear that to talk of *the* legal profession is a misnomer; we would be better off referring, instead, to *many* legal professions. There are strong similarities between the modern American legal profession and that of fifteenth-century England. At that time there were six discrete strata of lawyers, sergeants and judges, clerks and officers of the central courts, attorneys, apprentices, utter-barristers, and solicitors and accountants. By the eighteenth century the number of groups had effectively declined to two—barristers and attorneys (later solicitors).

American lawyers are differentiated along many axes. . . . All they share is the same name, lawyer.

JOHN FLOOD, *The Legal Profession in the United States*

The legal profession of the 1980's is a profession in transition.

BARBARA CURRAN, KATHERINE ROSICH, CLARA CARSON, AND MARK PUCETTI, *The Lawyer Statistical Report*

Previous chapters have argued that the new media are fostering conflict and complexity and accelerating the process of change. It has also been asserted that control of information by any one group or institution is becoming more difficult as greater quantities of information are communicated electronically over greater distances and with greater speed than ever before. These trends are extremely pertinent to assessing the future of the legal profession. Lawyers would seem to be beneficiaries of the former developments because managing conflict, interpreting complexity, and adapting to change are services that lawyers have traditionally performed. At the same time, however, the mystique, power, and,

TABLE 5-1   Number of Lawyers: 1900–1980

Year	Number of Lawyers
1900	115,000
1945	198,000
1960	285,000
1970	355,200
1975	456,000
1980	585,000
1985	655,000

ultimately, income of the legal profession require public acceptance of lawyers as being in exclusive control of a special body of knowledge. Lawyers, in modern times, are a "profession," meaning that they can exclude others from performing the same services. At least part of the reason lawyers are a powerful profession is that they control information about law. Information in the new communications environment, however, as I shall argue, cannot be controlled as it was in the past. Traditional mechanisms for organizing information are being disrupted, and new means of access are being created, all of which threaten institutions that benefitted from and evolved with printing. The long-term impact of the new forms of communication may, as a result, cause great change to the profession and turn out to be significantly less beneficial than would otherwise be the case.

During the past thirty years, it has been asserted, the legal profession has experienced changes "whose speed and magnitude are without precedent in its history."[1] The most frequently publicized development of this period has been the great increase in the size of the profession. The United States now has more than 650,000 lawyers, almost double the number in 1970. Table 5–1 shows the increase in the number of lawyers during this century.

On the basis of the approximately 35,000 persons graduating from law school each year,[2] it has been estimated that the number of lawyers in the United States will approach 1 million by the mid-1990s.[3] These numbers prompted former Chief Justice Warren Burger to comment that "we may well be on our way to a society overrun by hordes of lawyers, hungry as locusts, and brigades of judges in numbers never before contemplated."[4]

The increase in the number of lawyers during the past thirty years has been occurring at a much faster rate than population increases. In 1951, 1 of every 696 persons in the United States was a lawyer.[5] This was essentially the same proportion that existed at the beginning of the twentieth century. By 1980, however, 1 of every 418 persons was a lawyer, and only four years later, in 1984, the number was 1 in 364.[6] Between 1950 and 1980, the total population increased by 45 percent; the labor force, by 64 percent; and the legal profession, by 150 percent.[7]

Some of the explanations for these quantitative changes can be traced to major social and political developments of the past twenty-five years. The influence of the feminist movement, for example, is reflected in large increases in the number of women law students and lawyers. The percentage of women lawyers increased from 1 percent in 1910[8] to almost 3 percent in 1970 to approximately 13 percent in 1984.[9] Unlike blacks and other minorities whose representation has increased slowly,[10] the number of women law students has grown precipitously, from 1,800 in 1963 to 45,000 in 1981, from 3.8 percent of law students to 35.3 percent.[11] Women may compose one-half of the law students by 1990 and one-third the profession by the year 2000.[12]

While the profession is larger than ever before, however, is it more powerful, more stable, more secure? How should these statistics be interpreted? Will the increased size of the legal profession make it more able to protect its status and interests? Can future trends be extrapolated safely from what has been occurring in the recent past? More particularly, what does the transition from print to electronic forms of communication, which is now taking place, suggest about the meaning of "the practice of law" and the role and work of lawyers in our society in the future?

Law professor Richard Abel of the University of California at Los Angeles has argued in a series of recent articles[13] that neither the increase in the number of lawyers nor other changes in the composition of the profession that have occurred recently are adding to the power of the profession. Among the developments that Abel believes are important are the following:

1. Decline in the number of lawyers practicing independently or in firms and an increase in the number of lawyers employed by corporations and institutions. As a result, "a profession that

was 85 percent self-employed in 1948 and about 60 percent self-employed in 1980 soon may be more than half employees."[14]

2. Elimination of some anticompetitive practices previously enjoyed by the profession, such as minimum fee schedules and restrictions on advertising.

3. Increase in the size of law firms. The largest firms now have hundreds of lawyers with offices in many states.

4. Increase in the heterogeneity of the legal profession. Owing to the recent growth of the bar, the profession is younger, with more women and minorities. There are more fields of specialization and types of practice.

These developments suggest to Abel that lawyers today "look less and less like a homogeneous category of independent professionals."[15]

It is generally assumed that economic and political factors are responsible for these phenomena. As the following analysis suggests, however, a complete explanation of why and how the practice of law is changing cannot be achieved if new developments in the movement of information are not included in the analysis. Control of the movement of information, as has been argued in previous chapters, may be more difficult in a highly volatile electronic environment. The removal of some legal restrictions on advertising, for example, may be connected with the appearance of powerful new techniques for communicating with potential clients. Similarly, fragmentation of the profession is being encouraged as the movement of information among different-size groups is fostered, while national law firms[16] and larger firms are a response to the ability to communicate instantaneously over great distances. Most important, the profession is threatened because what is considered "legal" and within the exclusive domain of the profession is shifting as a result of diminished control over a body of knowledge. The idea of a profession, which had been supported by an organized and comprehensive body of printed information, is vulnerable because of the development of a mode of storing, processing, and organizing information that employs novel principles and processes.

The current era of transition to electronic modes of communication is part of the latest phase of a lengthy historical process of definition and redefinition of who and what lawyers are. The legal profession, like the rest of law, has some ancient roots. One can find lawyers at work in Rome 2,000 years ago,[17] and the origins of the modern legal profession are traceable back to the thirteenth century.[18] Yet, as with other aspects of law, there is also a distinctly modern form of the legal profession. Lawyers are different from what they were in ancient or medieval times. They are, as will be explained, not simply an occupation but a profession, a type of employment that has acquired very special characteristics. A large part of the justification for the powers accorded to professions is due to the development of printing and the changing role of information in modern society. The evolution of the modern form of the legal profession, one that has attained monopolistic powers, required assistance from a medium of communication that possessed the special qualities of printing. The degree of the legal profession's vulnerability in our time depends on how important print has been to its modern development, how reliant it is on print currently, and how different the electronic media are from the print media.

The profession is welcoming the new media with open arms in order to improve productivity and increase revenues. Of the many parts of the world of law, legal practitioners have been the most aggressive in replacing traditional modes of processing and communicating information with electronic forms. The pages of the *American Bar Association Journal,* which ten years ago contained advertisements for the impressive-looking books associated with law libraries, today are dominated by products that make it look like an adjunct of an electronics catalogue. As the following analysis suggests, however, the perceived benefits may prove to be like the Trojan horse, welcomed at first but holding hidden and unwelcome powers inside.

Speech and Writing

In *Joseph Andrews,* the novelist Henry Fielding traced lawyers back to the time "when the first mean selfish creature appeared on the human stage, who made self the centre of the whole creation, would give himself no pain, incur no danger, advance no money, to assist or preserve his fellow-creatures; then was our lawyer born."[19] In reality, lawyers do not appear this far back in history. Although lawyers are often pictured as persons for whom speech and oratory are indispensable qualities, it is the development of writing that provided the environment lawyers needed for their development. Lawyers are not found in oral cultures or in minimally literate societies.[20] Where the rules were widely known or where disputes were settled nonlegally, a separate group of persons with specialized knowledge about rules would be unnecessary. In addition, for reasons that may be difficult for the modern mind to grasp, many earlier societies did not allow a party to authorize an agent to represent him or take his place.[21] Thus the appearance of counsel or the concept of a "right to counsel" would have been difficult to comprehend as well as unnecessary in many preliterate societies. There was both little need for legal expertise and disapproval of the idea that someone could or should be held responsible for another's words.

Some insight into the intimate connection between legal practice and the written word can be discerned in the two most famous and frequently quoted literary comments about lawyers, those from Shakespeare's *Henry IV* and from the book of Luke in the New Testament. In *Henry IV,* Shakespeare has a character propose, "The first thing we do, let's kill all the lawyers,"[22] while the Bible contains the reprimand "Woe unto ye, lawyers!"[23] What is rarely noted when such lines are quoted, however, is the nature of the complaint against the lawyers. What were they doing to receive threats of death or to risk damnation? It is interesting that in each case, the lawyers were accused of some evil achieved through manipulation of the written word.

For Shakespeare, the evil complained of is explained in the lines immediately following the exhortation to "kill all the lawyers." Cade, a leader of a revolt against King Henry, replies by proclaiming:

> Nay, that I mean to do. Is not this a lamentable thing, that of the skin of an innocent lamb should be made parchment? That parchment, being scribbled o'er, should undo a man? Some say the bee stings: but I say, 'tis the bee's wax; for I did but seal once to a thing, and I was never mine own man since.[24]

In Luke, the specification of the curse "woe unto ye, lawyers!" is as follows: "You have carried off the key of knowledge; you did not enter yourselves and have hindered those who would enter."[25] What was the "key" that could have opened these doors of knowledge and whose possession made it possible to deny entrance to others? The most reasonable interpretation is that it was literacy and the skill to read and write. The target of the curse in Luke, as many commentaries make clear, was not really a group of lawyers in any modern sense, but scribes. The charge was that the "letter of the law" was being asserted but not its spirit, a charge that a nonliterate group would be unlikely to comprehend. The functional equivalence of the words *scribe* and *lawyer* reveals, at the very least, the intimate connection that has existed between lawyers and the written word. For lawyers to exist, there was needed a body of knowledge that they could capture and control. Writing provided the opportunity for this to occur. While critical differences can be found between lawyers before and after Gutenberg, to consider the lawyer's origin to be in preliterate times is to stretch too far the definition of what a lawyer is.

As noted in Chapter 2, the origin of the common law system of courts in twelfth-century England coincided with a significant expansion in the use of writing generally. At the beginning of that period, most of the officials of the royal courts were clerics, the most literate group at that time. In less than a century, however, literacy had sufficiently expanded so that lay specialists could perform the tasks earlier performed by the clerics.[26] Literacy was important to lawyers at that time because writing was the key needed to gain entrance to the royal courts. Lawsuits in these courts began with a "writ," a document issued by the king compelling a party to appear in court. Different kinds of cases employed different writs. The procedure to be used and the remedy that might be obtained depended on which writ had been issued. If the wrong writ were obtained or if no writ existed for a particular kind of dispute, the litigation could not proceed. Books were needed to keep track of what writs were available and what kind of oral pleading was required by each writ. Such books grew more necessary as new kinds of cases appeared in court and as the number of different writs proliferated. The principal purpose for using writing in this manner may have been to enhance the king's influence over the courts, but it also had the effect of making the process of litigation more complex. It thus provided power and economic rewards to persons who could master the intricacies of the system.

The two general services provided by these individuals, services provided as well by modern lawyers, were forensic ability and interpretation. Lawyers were and are interpreters of a body of knowledge that laypeople are either unable to master or do not wish to learn. Writing fostered complexity and contributed to the creation of a specialized body of information and to a literate group with access to and control over this information. Writing was also, however, a technology that had inherent limitations. While writing provided the key to entering the courts, the process of litigation for most of the period until the beginning of printing remained largely oral. Writing added a new and important dimension to the practice of law, but its limitations also colored how the profession evolved.

During this preprint period, books were not really "published" in quantity, nor could the same kind of faith be given to manuscripts that print receives today. Completely trustworthy manuscripts were scarce and valuable. In 1500, a lawyer with a large library might have thirty-five volumes, most of which would have been religious or nonlegal in nature.[27] The library of the Sorbonne in the early fourteenth century contained fewer than two thousand volumes, and Cambridge in the fifteenth century had only five hundred books.[28] Paper, which allowed for increased book production, was introduced into Europe only in the thirteenth century;[29] it did not quickly displace parchment and probably was used less in England than in other countries.[30] Owing to various limitations, writing could not emerge as a mass medium that would communicate large amounts of uniform information to large numbers of people in many different places. Writing did not foster the sharing of large bodies of information but encouraged narrow specialties based on the manuscripts one could gain access to or the skill one possessed.

It is also important to be aware that for many people at that time, reading and writing were separate skills, almost like television viewing and production are separate functions today. In the centuries before printing, more people could read than write. Indeed, writing was such a specialized task at one time that the occupation of scrivener arose to put agreements and legal instruments into written form. The scrivener was eventually squeezed out of doing legal work by increasingly literate lawyers,[31] but his mere existence and competition for some time with lawyers suggest that writing itself was scarce and, as a result, remunerative.

The form in which legal information was communicated during this period affected the nature of legal work, the structure of the profession, and its development. Legal work involved expertise, specialized knowledge, and control over some area of information that worked to separate the emerging practitioners from the lay public. Yet, owing to the various limitations of writing, legal information in written form also lacked breadth and depth, as did the practice of law. The emphasis of the lawyer's work was on procedure and was

> so intensely practical that it is more like a trade than a profession and the best way for an apprentice to learn it is to get into the shop or court and watch how the journeymen work. This reacts upon legal literature, and makes much of it arid and disjointed judged by modern standards. The books on procedure—and there were very few books of which that was not the main theme or at least a considerable part— resemble manuals of practical engineering; they constantly assume the presence of the machine whose working they describe, they can tell you how to run it, but they have little or nothing to say as to how or why the machine was built, or what functions it serves. Books of the law are tolerably common, books about the law are comparatively rare.[32]

This perspective suggests that the nature of legal literature reflects the nature of legal practice. Practice is atheoretical, narrowly focused, and compartmentalized; and these characteristics influence what is written about law for lawyers. It may also be, however, that how law is practiced and thought about is a reflection of the medium used. The constraints of the medium of writing, in other words, may influence practice as much as practice itself influences writing. Writing has allowed the acquisition of power but has not encouraged either an accelerated movement of or an accumulation of written information. Those in control of the written word have employed it for practical ends; they have not perceived it as something that should be critically questioned. Nor has writing proved to be a tool that can distribute information widely and thereby provide a sense of unity or identity among varied fields of practice.

The modern British legal system often seems mysterious to persons from the United States because legal work is divided between two groups, barristers and solicitors. Barristers do not deal directly with clients, while solicitors do not appear in court. Barristers enter the profession through the Inns of Court, while solicitors may not belong to the Inns. In the preprint period, however, there were many more distinct groups engaged in legal practice, with labels such as pleaders, serjeants-at-law, apprentices, attorneys, solicitors, and utter-barristers. There were also scriveners, notaries, and conveyancers who were involved in some aspect of legal work.[33] During this time, while some of the legal practitioners were clearly distinct from laypeople, others were semiprofessionals whose training was neither formal nor officially recognized. Among most of the groups of legal practitioners, it was also possible for one to expand one's specialty and perform more than one role, just as today a plumber may acquire expertise as an electrician. The occupational names, which are obscure today, simply referred to a function or service, and in the absence of an organization enforcing a monopoly, one could perform one role one day and another the next.[34]

The lines between barristers and solicitors have become fixed and rigid only in the past three centuries as each group achieved control over an area of legal practice. In the 1500s and earlier, solicitors could be found in the Inns and barristers occasionally dealt with clients. Thus the practice of law was more fragmented than it is today, and the area of control of each group was more ambiguous than it is currently. Each group lacked complete control over its own specialty. What was probably not even considered possible was that some group could control some general universe called law, a feat that legal professions in most contemporary societies have managed to achieve.

Partly because of the limitations of writing, the practice of law occurred in many little legal universes with different rules, practices, and specialists. At that time, too, in spite of the common law, medieval England was characterized by a fragmented court system. One scholar has made the striking statement that even as late as the sixteenth century, "there was in the world of procedure no such thing as an English legal system."[35] The common law courts did apply the national law of the realm, and "there was a sense of unity about the substantive law. . . . But in reality, contemporaries were well aware that it was all too easy for litigants to pursue the same suit through more than one court at the same time."[36] C. W. Brooks has noted that

> early modern lawsuits very often seem as preoccupied with writs as with the issues which had originally caused the dispute. Given this, it is not surprising that there were large numbers of men associated with the courts who made their livings by issuing and handling these writs, men concerned with what contemporaries called the "practical" as opposed to the "theoretical" part of the law. These practitioners constituted a large part of what we would call the legal profession, but, apart from a common concern with procedure, they were an extremely diverse group of men who defy easy definition or categorization. . . . We must leave behind all modern conceptions of what constitutes a profession. Instead, we must enter the world of clerks and under-clerks, of parchment and writs.[37]

The "world of clerks and under-clerks, of parchment and writs" is, unfortunately, difficult to enter. Clerks, then and now, provided advice, exercised discretion, and had expertise in some area. The service they provided, however, was in a bureaucratic setting and more narrowly focused than modern professionals would be comfortable with. This was a system that was supported by the qualities of writing.

In time, with the introduction of a different means of communication—printing on paper instead of writing on parchment—a different system of legal workers would evolve. But some of the old legal tribe, given the reluctance of lawyers to part with the old and well tried, would die very slowly. Almost 400 years after Gutenberg and his invention of movable type, Herman Melville drew a portrait of a scrivener working on Wall Street in Manhattan, a living fossil in the 1850s but one still performing services from the scribal age. In the course of his story, Melville gives a clear description of the scrivener's job and temperament.

> It is, of course, an indispensable part of a scrivener's business to verify the accuracy of his copy, word by word. Where there are two or more scriveners in an office, they assist each other in the examination, one reading from the copy, the other holding the original. It

is a very dull, wearisome, and lethargic affair. I can readily imagine that, to some sanguine temperaments, it would be altogether intolerable. For example, I cannot credit that the mettlesome poet, Byron, would have contentedly sat down with Bartleby [the scrivener] to examine a law document of, say, five hundred pages, closely written in a crimpy hand.[38]

During the scribal age in the centuries just before Gutenberg, the scarcity of books and the qualities of writing affected the training of lawyers as well as their work. While lawyers may have been literate, it would be too much to expect training in such an age to have occurred principally through texts. The skills needed for legal practice in the early period were acquired mainly through apprenticeships and alliances with experienced practitioners. Later, in the fourteenth century, the Inns of Court were established and provided entry into practice for barristers. Yet partly owing to the limitations of manuscript texts, the Inns never completely controlled the education of barristers.

The Inns of Court originated as eating clubs or rooming houses for lawyers whose practice brought them to London. When they evolved into institutions responsible for certifying persons who could appear in court, learning through apprenticeship was joined by educational exercises organized by the Inns, but the use of texts was minimal. Legal education consisted of moots, arguments or trials of hypothetical cases, and "readings." The "reading," however, was not information in written form to be read by the student but a "lecture" read orally by a reader. The Latin origin of the word *lecture* is "reading," not "speaking." A "reader," therefore, was not someone who spent time reading books but someone who was considered qualified to prepare a lecture, often on one of the old statutes, which he would read aloud to students.[39] The reader might even read the same lecture a previous reader had given. The purpose of the oral "reading" or dictation was to allow students to make their own "writing."[40] This was a system that was weakened by the advent of printing and the availability of printed texts. Whereas "private reading was almost certainly no more than a supplement to and preparation for aural means of instruction before the introduction of printing, from about the 1550s onwards the position had been decisively reversed."[41] The new literature also, albeit in less dramatic fashion, threatened the fragmented structure of legal practice. The wide circulation of standardized materials in print encouraged a common and increasingly unified identity for legal practitioners.

Print and the Legal Profession

The word *lawyer* and the phrase "legal profession" have, thus far, been used very loosely. The "profession" as it developed in England before printing had a strange look to it, at least in part, because of the limitations that writing was unable to overcome. Using the word *profession* to describe practitioners of law in the thirteenth, fourteenth, and fifteenth centuries is to look at these groups anachronistically.[42] What is strange to the modern eye is that there is no single profession of law, and many types of people performe work that seems legal in nature. The dividing line between legal and nonlegal work is not very clear, and the qualities of a profession that provide status, authority, and power are not present. *Profession* is, as will be explained below, a modern word, and the phrase "legal profession" has been used thus far only because terms such as "legal craft" or "legal trade" have little current meaning.

The effect of being labeled a profession is probably more clear than the concept itself, which is difficult to define with precision and may change over time.[43] Professionals have an elevated social status and a distinct identity, and enjoy an economic advantage over other groups of workers. Professionals are granted a special autonomy by the state, possessing a monopoly over some kinds of work and having authority to limit entry to the profession. Only a "profession has the recognized right to declare . . . 'outside' evaluation illegitimate and intolerable."[44] Is it not extraordinary, Michael Joseph has asked, to be accorded the status of a *professional* person—that is, to become someone "who is not subject to competition, whose services cannot be dispensed with, and who does not find the rules particularly irksome since it was he who drew them up in the first place?"[45]

Because they are classed as a "profession," lawyers perform certain categories of work designated "legal," work that persons who are not lawyers may not perform. Had lawyering not acquired the status of a profession, nonlawyers would be more able to do some of what lawyers now do, as occurred in medieval England. The acquisition of professional status in England and in this country was assisted by the effect that print had on legal practice and on public attitudes about who lawyers are. It is important, therefore, to understand what a profession is, why the appearance of professions were assisted by printing, and how vulnerable the legal profession is as electronic communication expands.

The United States Department of Labor has classified occupations into the following seven categories: professional, technical, and managerial; clerical and sales; service; agriculture, forestry, and fishing; machine trades; benchwork; structural.[46] While the meaning of profession and the lines distinguishing some occupations from other occupations are not always clear, some of the qualities characteristic of a profession include the following:[47]

1. An organized body of knowledge. The professional possesses more than a skill. The "skills that characterize a profession flow from and are supported by a fund of knowledge that has been organized into an internally consistent system."[48] Professions are concerned with developing theoretical support for their work. Training for professional work, therefore, typically involves formal academic schooling.

2. Authority over client relationships. Professionals possess more control in client encounters than those in other occupations can exercise over customers. "Professional judgment" may not give the professional complete authority, but it implies that clients are less able to evaluate their problems and possible solutions than might be the case in some other context.

3. Control over admission standards. Professions accredit schools of training and determine the requirements for admission to practice.

4. Ethical codes of practice. In exchange for being granted independence and a monopoly over its work by the state, a profession is expected to promulgate standards of professional behavior and regulate abuses.

5. Organization. Professions have associations that promote their identity. These are not simply lobbying organizations that endeavor to protect the interests of members. Professional organizations are also designed to influence the conduct, commitment, and attitudes of members about the profession.[49]

6. Public service orientation. Membership in the legal profession

is presumed to involve "holding out to the public, the offer of public service. . . . the dedication of the call to the bar. . . . the moral duty not to refuse the client without cause or explanation."[50]

As these qualities of professional life suggest, groups cannot automatically qualify for professional status by meeting some objective criteria. A profession is, in the words of one historian of the legal profession, "a subjective value-laden concept, not a precise analytical category."[51] A group that aspires to be a profession and thus secure all the benefits that professional groups possess cannot present incontrovertible proof that it has satisfied the criteria listed above. At best, it can supply persuasive evidence that the conditions have been fulfilled. Many nonprofessionals undergo formal training, have specialized skills, are important to the public, and may even have a base of theoretical knowledge. The qualities that are used to define professional work may also be present in some nonprofessional work. There is no way to measure precisely how professional a type of work is or how close some occupation is to achieving professional status. As Professor Magali Larson has stated,

> The cognitive and normative elements generally used to define profession are undoubtedly significant; but they should not be viewed as stable or fixed characteristics, the accumulation of which gradually allows an occupation to approximate the "complete" constellation of professional features. These cognitive and normative elements are important, instead, because they can be used (with greater or lesser success) as arguments in a process which involves both struggle and persuasion.[52]

Or, as Erving Goffman has argued, "Licensing bodies require practitioners to absorb a mystical range and period of training, in part to maintain a monopoly, but in part to foster the impression that the licensed practitioner is someone who has been reconstituted by his learning experience and is set apart from other men."[53]

In the contest to acquire professional status, what becomes important is both the reality of whether certain criteria are met and the public perception of the occupational group and whether it possesses certain qualities. Groups aspiring to professional status have to believe that they meet certain criteria and have to persuade others of this. Communication is involved in various phases of this contest. For example, professionals are "agents of formal knowledge"[54] and need a means for processing, storing, and communicating this information. Media are also a force that can influence the organization of the group and how it is perceived by the public. Lawyers were one of the first occupational groups to acquire professional status, and law provides an interesting example of how a particular medium of communication can assist claims of an occupational group to special treatment.

Concerning the role of knowledge in the professionalization process, Eliot Freidson has asked:

> How is it possible for formal knowledge to have an impact on anything? In and of itself knowledge is an abstraction. Insofar as it is tangible, its "growth" over the past century or so can be "measured" by counting the number of books and journals that were published, but in order to exist in books and journals, knowledge must have human creators and consumers. How does knowledge establish a consequential relationship to the everyday world? To have any impact on either the natural or the social world knowledge must have human agents or carriers, and the impact it makes must be influenced in part by the characteristics of those agents. Thus we cannot understand the role of formal knowledge in our world without understanding the character of those who create it and apply it. This, then, raises another question, namely, What are the characteristics of those who are the carriers or agents of formal knowledge? Who are they? and What are the characteristics of the institutions that make their activities as agents of knowledge viable?[55]

Without falling into "the trap of assuming that knowledge itself is a system of domination that controls the ultimate power of the polity,"[56] it is also true that the form in which knowledge appears can influence how it is organized, who has access to it, and how the profession that depends on it is perceived. With the spread of printing, legal literature grew and its form changed, and this ultimately affected what lawyers did and what the public thought about them.

After printing was well established as a technology, legal literature changed qualitatively and quantitatively. Law was an extremely popular area for printers. In England, by 1600, there had been almost three hundred editions of the statutes.[57] In other countries, the number of legal works printed gradually surpassed those that were primarily religious in nature. An analysis of the number of private libraries possessed by lawyers and by clergymen in France, for example, suggests the effect of printing not only on law, but also on the secularization of society:[58]

	Lawyers	Churchmen
1480–1500	1	24
1501–1550	54	60
1550–1600	71	21

Perhaps more importantly, the size of private libraries increased substantially. While fifteen to twenty volumes was an impressive library in 1500, collections of five hundred volumes are not uncommon in 1550.[59]

Quantity is not an irrelevant factor. For example, the amount of material published in a particular field can affect the value placed on that endeavor. Quantity may not be a measure of true importance, but it can often reveal what the public perceives is important. An increase in book production in law highlighted the growing role of law and served, in effect, as an advertisement for the field. Law gradually began to be identified with these large collections of books. As William Seagle persuasively observed,

> To speak of law today is to speak of books, big and little books, of whole libraries of books, of books containing legislative acts, codes, digest, judicial decisions, forms of legal documents. Other arts and sciences have, of course, produced great libraries which, however, merely *record* their contributions to human knowledge. But in the books of the law the words themselves have magic properties—powers to loose and bind. The words themselves are the subject matter of the science, the words *are* the law.[60]

In the limited private libraries of lawyers in the preprint era, a surprisingly small percentage were law books. One of the most respected lawyers of his time had only four law books in his library of thirty-six volumes when he died in 1500.[61] Modern scholars have been surprised at the range of nonlegal interests and variety of fields that are represented in these early collections.[62] The apparently eclectic, humanist, and nonlegal interests of early lawyers are, however, not surprising if one recognizes that the areas of knowledge and academic disciplines that we use to categorize books either did not exist or were not as well defined at that time. In an era of limited book production, the lines between categories were not as distinct as they would become later. As book production increased and specialists needed to become acquainted with the greater quantities of material that had become available, they found it more necessary to make determinations about what should be included and what excluded in many fields of endeavor. Larger collections made it more necessary to develop a clearer organization of what was placed in libraries.

Printing not only made possible the development of more distinct, more organized, and larger law collections in libraries, but also guaranteed standardization among collections. In the preprint era, different libraries may have had books with the same title but dissimilar content. The most important legal book in medieval England, for example, was the register of writs. Before printing, however,

> a uniform copy of it could not be expected. Each official might have his own copy and transmit it to a successor who had his own idiosyncrasies, and no two copies need have been exactly alike. Indeed the collection grew at such a pace, that it would have been difficult to stereotype it at any given date, and one of the most striking things about the manuscript copies is their astonishing variation in bulk even in the same period. No doubt there is always a mass—and a considerable one too—that is common to all Registers of any particular time. No scribe would be stupid enough to omit the writ of right and its kind. But there is always a margin for difference on writs that were of less frequent occurrence. Then some writs will be dropped as obsolete from one manuscript and retained in another as just alive.[63]

Printing, therefore, fostered not only the growth of libraries, but also the growth of distinctly legal libraries, and of distinctly legal libraries with largely uniform or common collections. It became possible for the first time to refer to a volume and page with confidence that others in distant places could find the identical reference. The development of law libraries that emphasized law, excluded other areas, and had fairly large and standardized holdings allowed the library to assume a status within the legal process equal to that of the courthouse. The law library stands as a powerful symbol that law is distinctive and separate from other human endeavors. Its existence can be used to persuade the public that connected to what happens in court is a large body of information that is difficult to master but is accessible to and needed by those who appear in court. As Judge Thurman Arnold wrote in *The Symbols of Government:*

> For the layman, the entire body of legal literature represents juris-prudence, because it is here that he thinks that the fundamental prin-ciples of the law have all been worked out to be revealed to him piecemeal in the occasional decision which comes to his attention. For the lawyer, jurisprudence is that part of the law which he never gets time to read—the part adorned with learned names like Austin, Jher-ing, Pound, which is separate from, and above, the legal arguments which he uses in court. He assumes that in jurisprudence is found the bridge from one legal subject to another, the philosophy that law is a seamless web, that it is based on logical theories which are sound, that it governs society, that it is synthesized into a uniform system.[64]

The realities of legal practice may be that large academic law libraries have little in common with libraries used by practitioners, that most practitioners rely on a limited number of narrowly fo-cused and practical books, and that for 99 percent of the profession, legal work is as atheoretical as fixing a toilet or making a jigsaw puzzle. The general inaccessibility of law libraries,[65] however, con-tributes to the belief that there is a theoretical basis for law which is shared by those able to use the collections. The library of print, therefore, not only provides a resource for the profession, but helps shape public impressions of law and lawyering.

The forces that enabled law to be accepted by the public as an organized and discrete body of knowledge also assisted in the organization and formation of the profession itself. In the scribal period, information was shared locally as manuscripts were copied from colleagues and acquaintances.[66] Print, however, as the first mass medium, could reach practitioners in areas separated by great distances. Printed books emphasized to book users that they had something in common with other users of the same books, no matter where these other persons might be. The Inns of Court had begun as local clubs and had used personal contact and the spoken word to foster a clear identity among those who belonged. Print was the vehicle through which lawyers could acquire a group iden-tity that would not be limited by local concerns, that would high-light common qualities regardless of where one practiced.

The ideal of the professional association was stated earlier this century by Dean Roscoe Pound of the Harvard Law School, who wrote that "the bar association as an essential element of those practicing the profession is an essential element of professional life. It is only through organization that the spirit of public service can be developed and maintained and crucial types of public service can be rendered effectively."[67] The establishment of national organizations to foster the interests of lawyers, such as the American Bar Association in 1878, should be considered not as the beginning of a national profession but as a response to a growing common identity that was encouraged by printing. National organizations were a natural outgrowth of a spatially expanded identity that had been fostered by print. The shift from writing to print gradually encouraged the establishment of formal organizations, but the fact that a national organization of the profession could be perceived to be appropriate or realistic owes much to the spread of information via print.

The processes by which print contributed to the sense of a common endeavor among vastly different practitioners also put pressure on the numerous competing splinter groups that had existed in earlier times. The recognition of a single profession in this country or of two branches in Great Britain is consistent with the tendency of print to be useful to larger rather than smaller groups. The desire of printers to sell more copies of a work would lead them to emphasize elements that different practitioners might have in common. Organizations with the largest membership could communicate more effectively with members than some smaller organizations. While print set law apart from other endeavors, therefore, it was a unifying force for those who were already lawyers.

In the United States, the use of print to foster a common knowledge base and a common identity among persons in different places with varying interests coalesced in the law school as it has existed during the past hundred years. The founder of modern legal education, Christopher Columbus Langdell of Harvard, recognized the power of print when he stated that "law is a science, and that all the available materials of that science are contained in printed books. . . . Law can only be learned and taught in a university by means of printed books. . . . Printed books are the ultimate sources of all legal knowledge."[68] Because of printing, Langdell's new technique of studying printed cases did more than promote the idea of law as a science, as a body of knowledge worthy of a profession. The common curriculum that was almost universally adopted in law schools emphasized to prospective lawyers in whatever school they were studying that, in spite of variations of local law and practice, they were members of a single group with common experiences. The growth of printed educational materials both imparted the theoretical knowledge the profession is presumed to possess and, by initiating students into the profession, formed the basis for professional organizations. Print was one of the forces which encouraged lawyers to believe that, no matter what their particular specialty, they spoke the same language, had studied the same texts, and were justified in setting standards for what was becoming a standardized experience.

Electronic Media

The previous discussion suggested that the professionalization of lawyers was assisted by the coding and communication of information in printed form. Print served as a catalyst for the organization of both knowledge and people. Acquisition of professional status required not only the existence of special knowledge, something that had existed prior to Gutenberg, but also its existence in a particular form. The character of law and of lawyers, as historian T. F. T. Plucknett once wrote,

> is largely influenced by the technical methods used by lawyers in going about their daily business. When faced with a difficult case, the advocates and the judges have to undertake research in order to find what law will govern it. The method which they pursue, the character of the books and sources which they use, and the attitude of mind with which they approach them, all have their influence upon the shaping of the law, and upon their conception of the law itself.[69]

Print thus assisted in providing an *organized* body of knowledge that could foster a group identity and an organization among individuals in distant places. Print worked not only to unite persons at a distance, but also to distance persons from one another in the same place. In the realm of law, as in other realms of learning, large amounts of information and large numbers of people were transformed in ways not possible in the days before the technology of movable type.

The legal profession is a body whose character and identity will be different in the future. It is vulnerable to change because some of its structural supports are being eroded by rather than assisted by certain qualities of the developing forms of communication. Its distinct knowledge base and its organizational structure are being challenged by the movement of information in new ways. The end result will not be the elimination of lawyers from modern society but a reorganization of what legal work is and who will do it.

As the analysis of the electronic media in previous chapters has suggested, electronic communication has some very different properties from print, which will affect traditional patterns of both transmitting and organizing information. For example, information can now be employed by bodies that are smaller than as well as larger than those groups that benefitted from print. Information can move more easily both among small groups and across national boundaries. It can be both a mass medium for huge numbers of people and a group medium for smaller numbers separated by great distances.[70] In addition, as larger amounts of information can be processed, traditional categories of information are revised and attitudes toward information change. There is a reorganization of knowledge that creates new specialists based on new categories of information.

In a recent popular book about the new communications technologies, it was asserted that "in the final analysis, the raw material of a modern profession is nothing more than information, and the professional expertise lies simply in knowing the rules for handling or processing it."[71] Some writers, noting easier public access to larger amounts of information stored electronically, have assumed that citizens will be able to use information which had been available previously only to professionals. The ability of the new media to provide information in new ways, it is argued, will allow previously guarded information to escape into the hands of citizens. Professional knowledge is presumed to be secret knowledge, and the new keys provided by, for example, self-help videos and electronically accessible databanks will allow laypeople to find information that was previously supplied by doctors, lawyers, and other certified professionals.

To a limited extent, there is validity to such assertions. Some professional expertise is based not on information that is inherently complex or theoretical, but on the control of the means of access to certain information. The new media can be expected to be threatening to those lawyers who have benefitted from what might be labeled "artificially created complexity." Information that the profession has successfully hidden or kept secret but that does not require expert interpretation will be more difficult to control in the future than it has been in the past.

The conflicts that will arise as such information is distributed to the public will undoubtedly generate publicity about and litigation over the boundaries of what kind of legal information may be circulated in the mass market. While such cases may lead to some decline in the amount of business handled by lawyers, it can be expected to be offset by increasing complexity in other areas of law and by new abilities to reach potential clients. The kinds of cases that are likely to make headlines will, therefore, probably be no more devastating to the profession as a whole than statutes, such as those permitting no-fault divorce, that removed one profit-making activity from a large galaxy of such activities. As Eliot Freidson has commented, "The success of occupations like midwifery and real estate sales in infringing on the prior jurisdictions of medicine and law means little for the future of those professions if it is contained at the fringes while new areas of work are being invented."[72]

If there is a serious long-term threat to the legal profession from the new media, it will result less from suddenly empowered laypeople than from a gradual and subtle change in the knowledge base of the profession and in the role and makeup of the organized bar. The influence of the new media is being felt not only in who will have access to information, but in what kind of information is being produced and, most importantly, in how this information is being organized. The knowledge issue is more complicated than is suggested by publicized controversies over whether some book or legal software written by a layperson constitutes the "unauthorized practice of law." The new media, by weakening both the internal organization of legal information and the boundaries between legal and nonlegal work, will raise serious questions about what the "practice of law" means and who is entitled to perform it.

One of the most impressive feats of the computer is its ability to store huge quantities of information. How much "memory" a new computer model has or how much information it can store or process inevitably accompanies announcements of new products. Electronic files or electronic libraries have almost unlimited storage capacities compared with traditional filing cabinets or print libraries. The emphasis on size and capacity, however, masks the even more impressive fact that it is often easier and quicker to locate some item in these larger collections than it is in much smaller collections of print. One does, of course, save the time needed to walk from shelf to shelf and manually find some item. But the most important time-saver occurs because access to these files does not depend as much on prior knowledge of how they have been organized. One of the reasons electronic files can grow so large is that in order to use them, it is not as necessary to understand how electronic data are organized as it was to know how print information was. It is easier and quicker to find electronically stored information than printed data because more avenues of access exist, and knowledge of where, how, and why some item has been placed is less necessary.

To a large extent, current perceptions about how electronic information is stored are derived from how print libraries are organized. Most of us in this transitional generation are familiar with print libraries, and, therefore, we are attracted to electronic sources of information that resemble print libraries. The model of organization and use that developed because of the nature of printed materials, however, is not necessary with electronic collections. As Meyrowitz has recognized, "We need to distinguish between the inherent complexity of specific ideas and processes and the superimposed complexity of the means through which we encode and describe them."[73] Until there is greater familiarity with using electronic libraries and databases, both our methods of searching for information and our thinking about the organization of information will retain those characteristics fostered by print.

Some of the differences between the new and the old media can be illustrated by the concept of "random access." Random access means that one can move from one place to another without stopping or touching all the places in between. The contrary procedure, "linear access," requires that one travel the same route between two points every time in order to reach one's destination. Random access is an obviously faster process. With linear access, the process is slower and more cumbersome, but a lesson may be learned each time the route is traveled. At a minimum, we learn something about the structure and organization of the material being studied. Traditional models of legal research imprinted a model of organization on the user every time the system was used. Our habits of thought are probably still structured by the familiar models and categories of print, and, therefore, we do not yet think of information as it will be thought of in the future. It is inevitable, however, that new ways of thinking about information will develop, just as new means of accessing it have. As this occurs, the categorical lines and organizational boundaries that were fostered by print will be weakened.

An interesting example of how print has influenced the organization of law is provided by WESTLAW, one of the two principal electronic legal information services. More than a century ago, the West Publishing Company began its venture in indexing printed cases and placing them in legal categories. West gave every point of law a "key number," and every case West publishes contains a listing of the key numbers relevant to the case. In its "digests," West provides lists of cases that deal with each key number. It is an ingenious, albeit complicated, system that allows users to find similar cases scattered in books where cases are printed in chronological order and have no inherent organizational structure.

In the WESTLAW system, which allows electronic access to cases and many other legal materials, West has made it possible to use the traditional key numbers and categories that were employed in the printed editions. West employs editors who read the cases and decide which points of law are involved in them. This obviously has appeal to lawyers who were trained to use printed reporters and who think along the lines suggested by the printed materials. It is a selling point for some members of the legal profession, even though it is not really necessary for using WESTLAW. In print, the most comprehensive search for cases must rely on the classification scheme that West's editors developed. The electronic database, however, could be accessed just as easily by thinking of relevant words or combinations of words. WESTLAW has this capability, and the legal retrieval system that competes with

WESTLAW, LEXIS, uses only this method since it cannot make use of the West Publishing Company's key-number system. The ability of LEXIS to satisfy the legal research needs of the legal profession indicates that while West's categories may be helpful at times, they were largely fostered by print and are not a structure that is inherent in the nature of the material.

The change in the means of access to legal materials will ultimately affect how law is perceived by lawyers and by others who may have an interest in such materials. Print supported a standardized set of categories, and every case was placed into one or more categories. The internal organization of legal materials need no longer conform to such a system. Yet it is this system that, at least in part, unites lawyers by influencing how they think about law. As new techniques for finding electronic data replace the habits encouraged by print, the organization of data will begin to reflect individual users' varied views of law rather than some structure that was developed in order to use material in printed form. This new and less-standardized structure will not require that labels be placed on data or that there be any limit to how a user wishes to organize data. How a person perceives the body of data will depend more on what that person's needs are and less on what the needs of a publisher are.

If law cannot be expected to possess the same internal organization in the future, neither can it expect its external boundaries to remain as fixed as they are today. The question of what is law, which even today is often a matter of controversy, or the issue of who is entitled to dispense "legal" information will become even more difficult in the future. The definition of law has been argued about by academics for some time, but the question now promises to be one of debate for practicing lawyers. The legal profession needs clarity in terms of what law is in order to justify the exclusion of nonlawyers from the edifice of the law. If this domain is more difficult to describe in the future, there will be less justification for granting lawyers a monopoly.

Print had assisted in separating law from fields, such as politics and religion, with which it had previously enjoyed an intimate relationship. As increasing amounts of materials appeared in print, it became easier to think about law and lawyers as distinct entities. One of the contributors to this process of separating law (and lawyers) from other fields and disciplines was the manner in which library materials were organized. Any book or journal, for example, can occupy only one location in a library. It violates the rules of cataloguers for a single book to have two call numbers. Thus if there are two copies of a book in a collection, they are located in one place, even if the book treats a variety of themes. At best, such a book will be listed in a card catalogue under several different subject headings. The physical properties of printed books, however, require that they be placed in some space, and they cannot occupy more than one space at one time. This kind of violation of the laws of physics is, in a sense, possible with electronic information. Two users, for example, may find the same information while using different "electronic libraries" or information services. Each user may believe that he or she has found the data in a place that is different from where the other believes the data was found. Yet the telephone lines that provided each with access to the information may have also led each to precisely the same place.

Print had allowed the separation of law school libraries from general university libraries, and this tended to emphasize the distinctiveness of law. The physical distance between law school libraries and general university libraries was matched by the existence of negligible bibliographic links between the subject areas in the two collections. Electronic libraries, however, do not suffer from the artificial spatial barriers erected by print, and an inquiry in some area need not be as limited as in the past. As J. David Bolter has noted, "Computer memory is associative rather than linear. It allows us to follow out networks of association in our data, as indeed human memory does."[74] The removal of print's limits and restrictions, therefore, allows access to information that may have been unavailable previously and contributes to the breakdown of traditional structures and patterns of thought.[75]

The novel qualities of electronic communication present lawyers with both new opportunities and new threats. For example, as information from outside the world of law becomes more accessible, lawyers are implicitly encouraged to move beyond traditional boundaries of legal practice. At the same time, however, the legal profession can also expect to face increasing encroachment of its own domain by outsiders. The rearrangement of market boundaries is a trend that has been occurring in various fields. In the economic sector, for example, it has been observed that

> for generations (centuries in the case of many of the great financial capitals of the world) the principles guiding the financial markets have been specialization and national control. The Chicago commodity markets concentrated on futures in pork bellies and other local produce, just as the Sydney exchange dealt mainly with "greasy wool" and the Baltic Exchange in London developed the market for freight rates by sea. . . . Markets for short-term, medium-term and long-terms funds were separated, and the whole structure was traditionally buttressed by central authorities that controlled interest rates and currency movements to manage the economy better, keep a hold on the domestic money supply and ensure stability and solidity in the most crucial and most vulnerable area of the economy.
>
> Now all this is changing and changing far faster than anyone would have thought conceivable even a few years ago. . . . There is less and less distinction between type of borrowing and lending, between short-term and long-term, between national and international. There are fewer and fewer means, therefore, for governments or central banks to preserve the old separations between them. And, as the barriers come down, so the brokerage houses, the banks, the investment houses are pushing voraciously into each other's liberalized markets around the globe.[76]

In the legal world, during the last few years, some large law firms have begun to branch out, setting up subsidiaries or partnerships in nonlegal areas, such as real-estate development and economic consulting, and providing management services involving labor relations, office management, and health care.[77] Part of the rationale for beginning such profit-oriented business ventures, according to the managing partner of one leading firm, was a belief that "the lines between various professionals have dimmed. . . . People in banking, investment banking, insurance and law all do many of the same things."[78] The lawyer, who has always been an information worker, is now in competition with other information workers whose fields and expertise overlap with law. Information is a commodity of increasing value in our society, and, therefore, the erection of entry barriers at the boundaries of law has significant economic consequences. For this reason, the rules about who may do what legal work can be expected to be an area of growing conflict, particularly as the boundaries of law become less clear.

These rules, which protected lawyers and provided for special treatment, previously had an ally in the technology of print. As the influence of print is weakened and the contours of the legal profession become more ambiguous, these rules can be expected to come under considerable challenge. It may not, therefore, be possible to assert confidently in the future, as an eminent legal scholar once did, that "the most important thing about the practice of law is that it is, and in the inherent nature of things demands always that it shall be, a profession."[79]

6

Law and the Modern Mind: Orientations and Perspectives

As we think, we live.

ALFRED NORTH WHITEHEAD, *Modes of Thought*

In *Law and the Modern Mind*,[1] a well-known book written in the 1930s, Judge Jerome Frank argued that there was a great gulf between what the public thought law was and what it actually was. While the public, and many lawyers, believed that law was, or at least was supposed to be, clear, stable, and certain, Frank claimed that law possessed exactly the opposite qualities. He asserted that law was inherently unclear, unstable, and uncertain, that this was its inevitable nature, and that the public image of law could never be realized. As to why law was perceived in unrealistic ways, Frank found the cause to lie in the psychological realm. The "modern mind," according to Frank, was actually an immature and childish mind, searching for the safe world one yearned for as a child. Citizens used law for security and protection in the manner of children who are totally dependent on others.

When Frank was writing a half-century ago, the only way to expose the myths that persisted about law was to compare them with what actually occurred in the courts. *Law in the Modern Mind* was a criticism of how law existed in the modern mind. To change the modern mind, Frank tried to bring new insights and knowledge to it. He explored what actually went on in the courts and provided examples of the ambiguity of law, of judges exercising broad dis-

227

cretion, and of the inevitability of uncertainty in applying rules and finding facts. Neither Frank nor his colleagues, however, looked at the modern mind as being different from the ancient mind; nor did he look at any other causes of how the public viewed law than psychological ones.

Frank was one of the foremost members of the "legal realist" movement. He and his colleagues sought to distinguish "law in action" from "law in the books" and to reorient public thinking about the nature of law. His ideas, which were once considered radical, are no longer controversial. Most legal scholars today accept Frank's point of view about the reality of law. Yet the current state of public knowledge of law is probably no more sophisticated than it was fifty years ago. Law is still often perceived to possess the same mythical qualities that were criticized a half-century ago. We are still under the spell of law in the books. Given the influential powers of print already described in this book, this should not be surprising. Law, as it exists in our minds, has been conditioned for several centuries by this medium. Our thoughts and attitudes have been affected not only by the content of the books, but also by the form that has been used to communicate this content.

Public yearning for a purer form of law continues because the power of print and the book as symbols of law is still substantial. Legal attitudes, beliefs, and concepts, however, are not likely to remain stable very much longer. The reason for this is not that the public is "growing up" or even becoming more knowledgeable about law. Rather, as information about law is stored and communicated electronically, one of the key sources of public belief about law is being changed as well. We may not know any more about law, but we may think about it differently. To the degree that our thoughts about law affect what law is, law itself will also be different.

Public thought about law will be different because the means of communicating information are changing, and the subtle effects of print on the modern mind are being undermined. Whatever influence the metaphor of "law in the books" had is eroding as law and information become stored, processed, and communicated electronically. The electronification of information is changing the symbols of law, and, as a consequence, many of the concepts, values, and perceptions on which the law rests are being modified as well.

At the time he was writing, Frank would have had to be clairvoyant to think that a new outlook on law might develop by transforming the nature of the "books" that were the cause of much of the public's thinking about law. In the 1930s, one could point to the courts and argue that more attention should be paid to what occurred inside the institutions of law. One could also claim that far too much attention was given to the judicial opinions of appellate courts, while the trial courts were being ignored. But one could not expect to be taken seriously if one suggested that change would come as an electronic alternative to law in the books developed. He could not be expected to comprehend how differently the "modern mind" might be when law would exist not as printed characters in books but as electrical impulses in central processing units.

Professor James White has written that "the law is best regarded not so much as a set of rules and doctrines or as a bureaucratic system or as an instrument for social control but as a culture.[2] In previous chapters, it has been argued that the goals, doctrines, and institutions of law have ancient and modern forms whose differences can be traced at least in part to changes that have occurred in the movement, storage, and processing of information. As print is replaced by the electronic media, these visible facets of law are likely to exhibit new characteristics. Law is also, however, partly a set of attitudes and perceptions and a reflection of the culture of which it is a part. Modern law is different from law in other historical periods because modern culture is different from ancient culture and the attitudes and perspectives of inhabitants of modern society are different from those of ancient citizens. In some important ways, law in modern times is the result of the modern mind, of orientations, values, and concepts that have become dominant only in the past few centuries. If the "modern mind" is changing as a result of the new forms of communication, the shift is not from immaturity to maturity or from ignorance to knowledge, but from a society influenced by one means of communication to one affected by different perceptions and concerns.

Some of the differences between ancient and modern orientations toward law have been identified by Professor Roberto Unger of Harvard Law School in his book *Law in Modern Society*.[3] Unger postulated that law has existed historically in three different forms and labeled them as the customary, the bureaucratic, and the legal order. In brief, these three forms of law differ in substantial ways.

The earliest legal type, "customary," is informal and oral.[4] Individuals in a group interact with one another guided by common expectations about what kind of conduct is proper and desirable. There is no separate body whose function is to make rules. The group as a whole develops understandings about proper standards of behavior and customs. Traditions and rituals play a more prominent role than enacted law.

The second form of law, "bureaucratic," has explicit rules established and enforced by an identifiable government."[5] Law, in the bureaucratic society, is "deliberately imposed by government rather than spontaneously produced by society."[6] Unlike customary law, a bureaucratic society has a centralized authority that has most of the power in the society.

Unger's third concept of law is labeled the "legal order."[7] Like the bureaucratic form, it is characterized by the existence of an identifiable centralized government that establishes and enforces explicit rules. In addition, law in the legal order is both general and autonomous. It is general in the sense that legal equality is presumed to exist among citizens. The law is "expected to address broadly defined categories of individuals and acts and to be applied without personal or class favoritism."[8] The law is autonomous in that there is a body of rules which is considered to be more than a "mere restatement of any identifiable set of non-legal beliefs or norms, be they economic, political or religious."[9]

For Unger, the appearance of the legal order occurred for two major reasons, one sociological and one attitudinal. He attributes the decline of the bureaucratic form of law first to a growing pluralism in Western society. As a result of increased heterogeneity, no one group was presumed to have a right to rule.[10] Competition existed among social and economic groups, there was a dwindling sense of community among society's members, and behavior could not be expected to conform to implicit standards known or accepted by all. As a result, there was a higher level of instability than existed previously and a growing need for a legal process that was based on consent and exhibited egalitarian values. Unger also suggests that the appearance of the legal order was accompanied by a new belief in a "higher universal or divine law as a standard by which to justify and to criticize the positive law of the state."[11] Thus in addition to being faced with larger and more heterogeneous populations, governments had to take into account a new outlook on the purposes and nature of government. Persons came to believe that systems more just than the existing order were possible and that law could be designed to further social, economic, and other interests. In the legal order, law is conceptualized differently and different values guide the system. Although Unger does not mention printing, the "legal order" reflects qualities that were encouraged by print and that would have been difficult, if not impossible, to achieve without a means of communication such as print.

The following analysis focuses on two facets of the modern legal mind that may be under stress because of the very novel qualities of the new media. Modern law is characterized, first, by a perspective on the individual that is lacking in most premodern systems. Second, modern Western systems of law rely much more heavily on abstractions than other legal systems. Both of these qualities contributed to the development of fundamentally important characteristics of liberal legal systems, such as the protection of legal rights and fundamental liberties. The role of the individual and the use of abstract concepts are differences between modern and ancient legal systems that are often overlooked. These twin cornerstones of modern law, however, provide interesting starting points for assessing the potentially far-reaching influence of the new media on our habits of thought.

The Individual Orientation of Law

Compared with legal systems of other times and places,[12] Western law of the past few centuries possesses a very different outlook on the nature and importance of the individual. The individual, in modern times, is considered the basic unit of society, and concern with individual citizens is, therefore, the principal focus of law. In theory, at least, individuals are more important than the state or any other groups or institutions in society because such entities derive their existence and power from the consent of individuals. Associations may receive legal protection to the extent that they are composed of individuals, but they, unlike individuals, are not presumed to have any "inalienable" rights. The "individual human being remains the paradigmatic legal actor, in whose image the law is shaped and then applied to corporations and other collective entities."[13]

The emphasis on the individual that forms the cornerstone of much of the uniqueness of modern law is not present in many premodern systems. "The history of law in the West," it has been argued, "is a history of the development of the individual and the concept of the individual."[14] Indeed, "modern individualism, when seen against the background of the other great civilizations that the world has known, is an exceptional phenomenon."[15] Oral cultures, for example, where survival depended on group success, placed much less emphasis on the individual. Because control of information by any one individual was difficult in such a group, it was "collective, communal, and celebrative as the medium of communication required it to be."[16] Sir Henry Maine wrote that ancient law "knows next to nothing of individuals. It is concerned not with single human beings but groups."[17] Karl Polanyi has observed that economically, in tribal societies, the

> individual's economic interest is rarely paramount, for the community keeps all its members from starving unless it is itself borne down by catastrophe, in which case interests are again threatened collectively, not individually. . . . Such a situation must exert a continuous pressure on the individual to eliminate economic self-interest from his consciousness to the point of making him unable, in many cases (but by no means in all), even to comprehend the implications of his own actions in terms of such an interest.[18]

Similar pressures and similar consequences were experienced throughout the social realm. Individuals were not thought of as they are today and, as a result, were treated differently by the legal process.

Larger and more heterogeneous societies that possessed writing also did not exhibit great emphasis on the individual. In most systems, the individual had value not as an autonomous and independent entity but as a member of some group or class.[19] Even in ancient Greece, "the *polis* was not an aggregate of individuals or citizens who had a self-conscious awareness of themselves in opposition to an entity that was public. . . . There was no opposition between the self and the political entity of which one was a part."[20] Common rules might or might not apply to the different groups, but what was unthinkable was that one could change one's group and, as a consequence, one's status. In most of these societies, one could not change one's group or status because where one belonged defined who one was. These systems seem discriminatory and inegalitarian to modern eyes, and they are if one uses the lens of the modern mind. But the basis for practices that violate modern norms derived not merely from one group grabbing power or consciously using law to enslave others. Such systems reflected underlying differences in the relative importance of the individual and the larger group in the life of the society.[21] The supreme importance that we place in the individual resided elsewhere in those systems. As Burkhardt claimed, "Man was conscious of himself only as a member of a race, people, party, family, or corporation—only through some general category."[22]

It is important to recognize that the individual lacked rights in such societies not simply because oppressive laws were enacted for the purpose of denying some persons these rights. Such laws, themselves, were outgrowths of a vision of the individual that differed in fundamental ways from the concept of the individual in modern society. The law was not removing some right that was desired or had existed previously. It was not only a case of conscious suppression by the state, nor did individuals necessarily feel oppressed. The position of the individual derived from a world view that was different from ours and that seemed as natural and inevitable to the vast majority of persons living at the time as the idea of individual rights seems today.[23]

In the Middle Ages, for example, it was assumed that "society was one whole and was indivisible, and within it the individual was no more than a part."[24] What mattered was "not the individual, but society, the corpus of all individuals. In the high Middle Ages, thinking in the public field concerned itself with the whole, with society."[25] What was lacking for the individual was not simply the particular rights that we associate with democratic rule, but the idea of rights or the belief in them. Professor Walter Ullmann has compared the formal relationship of king and subjects at that time with that of parents and children. Individuals were assumed to be ignorant and in need of protection and guidance. He suggests, too, that

> there may well have been adequate and justifiable reasons for this view, and we should not measure this fundamental conception by modern standards. It is not necessary to exercise one's historical imagination to realize how little knowledge of the matters which were the concern of government could in fact be presupposed not only among the rural population but also among the townsfolk. In obvious contrast to modern conditions, the individual as a subject had no means to inform himself; he had not much opportunity of acquainting himself with any of the issues at stake, and he could not be expected to have an adequate grasp of the matters which the king, by virtue of his own governmental apparatus, necessarily possessed. It is against this sort of background that one can understand . . . the requirement postulated in all spheres of theocratic governments—whether papal, royal, or imperial makes no difference—the requirement of knowledge, of *scientia* with which the subjects, precisely because they were subjects, were not credited.[26]

The highest duty in such societies was obedience. Persons assumed that the law was given to them rather than made by them. They were more subjects than citizens, and "what mattered was the public weal, the public welfare, the public well-being, in brief, the good of society itself, even at the expense of the individual well-being if necessary."[27] Each individual had a specific function that he pursued for the common good. What was considered important was his membership in a group and not his identity as an individual. It has been written that

> at the basis of the self-perception of medieval *Gemeinschaft* stood not the individual but relationships, those of occupying and acting in a certain status or of belonging to a certain group, at least for the purpose in question. . . . the very distinction between private and public law had no intellectual force or material reality in these conditions—all feudal relations were both private and public. Feudal society, though rooted in an individual act of fealty, was largely seen not as a collection of individuals but as a system of special or partial—rather than individual—interests and estates, represented by *parlements,* corporations and other bodies.[28]

As a result of this outlook, one's legal obligations and legal treatment might even vary, depending on which group one belonged to. The value of an oath, for example, might depend on the estate to which the individual taking the oath belonged. Or in a decision voted on by members of a corporate body, the value of one's vote could vary, depending on the status that one had or office that one held. One could be inflicted with a punishment because the group one belonged to was being punished and not because one had committed some offense. In this perspective, collective accusations and punishments, such as blood libels or excommunications of whole villages or inquisitions, can at least be explained as an outgrowth of a system in which the individual was conceived of differently from the way he is viewed under modern liberal political and legal systems.

In the new orientation toward the individual that has surfaced in the past few centuries, print should be considered to be a contributing force. This may seem implausible because print is generally recognized as being a "mass" medium—indeed, the first mass medium. Without denying this facet of print, it is also accurate to describe print as an "individual" medium and as the first effective individual medium. Print, as a mass medium, fostered the growth of the modern state and of national legal systems; print, as an individual medium, encouraged a new perception of the individual. It provided information and opportunities to individuals that had not been possible to obtain in earlier times. As a result, the individual gradually acquired a new status, first in the minds of men and later in the pages of law. The explicit recognition of individual rights in the seventeenth and eighteenth centuries signified not only that the rules of law were changing, but also that the definition of the individual was changing. Constitutions that were enacted into law during this period and that provided for individual liberties did not begin the process of changing public views about the rights that individuals should possess but were a reflection of a new orientation toward the individual, one that had been fostered by the medium of print.

Print had a radically different impact on the individual than was possible with speech or writing. David Riesman has argued that "if oral communication keeps people together, print is the isolating medium *par excellence.* People who would simply have been deviants in a preliterate tribe, misunderstanding and misunderstood, can through books establish a wider identity—can understand and even undermine the enemies of home and hearth and herd."[29]

Persons in an oral culture, theologian Wendy Donager O'Flaherty has noted,

> know their myths so well that they *are* the text: they are the vehicles on which the disembodied myth is projected. In this way, the retelling of the myths takes on the function of *communion* rather than *communication*. People listen to stories not merely to learn something new (communication) but to relive, together, the stories that they already know, stories about themselves (communion).[30]

The qualities of the spoken word that worked to deter change and conflict also served to focus attention less on the concerns of the individual than on the interest of the group. For this reason, the "highly interiorized stages of consciousness in communal structures are stages which, it appears, consciousness would never reach without writing."[31]

In preprint societies that possessed writing, popular "literature" remained primarily in spoken form. Writing and reading skills remained limited, and much reading was done orally as part of a group activity or a drama. In ancient Greece, for example, medium and content supported a common theme, with both the Homeric epics and the classical playwrights emphasizing the supreme importance of family and city, not the individual. In the Greek tragedies, where actors wore

> carved masks which prevented facial expression and let one actor play many parts, there are no "modern" individuals in them. Conflicts are always role-conflicts. . . . For example, the characters in Sophocles' *Antigone* are trapped in their societal roles. Antigone must decide whether to bury her brother Polynices, who lies dead outside the walls of Thebes after his luckless invasion. Family duty commands burial but she is also subject to the king's edict forbidding burial for a traitor. The king is Kreon and his edict embodies hallowed custom; but he is also her uncle, head of her house, and bound by family duty. Antigone follows what she takes to be the higher law and buries her brother; Kreon does what he takes to be his greater duty and has her walled up alive. This is a tragedy without individualism or private moralities.[32]

Similarly, as Arlene Saxonhouse has pointed out, "the *polis* was not an aggregate of individuals or citizens who had a self-conscious awareness of themselves in opposition to an entity that was public. . . . There was no opposition between the self and the political entity of which one was a part."[33]

The establishment of the individual as a cornerstone of liberal legal systems was accelerated by the growing recognition and appreciation of the contributions made by individuals in the period following Gutenberg. Opportunities for individual achievement increased, as did the likelihood of being rewarded with fame, fortune, or both. The law, as the field of intellectual property grew, further focused attention on individual accomplishments. The law did not create the idea of an independent and self-directed human being, but it did reinforce and encourage it. The changing public perception of individuals and the changing legal status of individuals together allowed the individual to be seen as an entity that was distinct from other persons, from the various groups in the society, and from the state.

Printing also supported a changing concept by aiming its output at individuals. The medieval book

> had been an institutional possession, the Renaissance book becomes an individual possession. . . . The medieval book is the property of a community, of the cathedral-chapter, of the college, it belongs to the house. . . . Quite often they are chained to their cases in the library so that they should always remain available to the community; not even for a brief span of private study may the individual member take a volume to his room.[34]

Not only were more books produced by individuals, but these volumes were read silently and individually. There was a quantitative increase in volumes produced and a qualitative change in literature as the modern novel emerged and histories and stories about individuals became more popular. Artificial memory stored in printed form and subject to critical interpretation and analysis was replacing a communal history resting largely in the minds of the community. Authors of books were given more attention, and

> cheaper writing materials encouraged the separate recording of private lives and correspondence. . . . The wish to see one's work in print (fixed forever with one's name in card files and anthologies) is different from the desire to pen lines that could never get fixed in permanent form, might be lost forever, altered by copying, or—if truly memorable—be carried by oral transmission and assigned ultimately to "anon."[35]

Elizabeth Eisenstein notes that "by its very nature, a reading public was not only more dispersed; it was also more atomistic and individualistic than a hearing one. . . . The notion that society may be regarded as a bundle of discrete units or that the individual is prior to the social group seems to be more compatible with a reading public than with a hearing one."[36]

In Chapter 3, I described how the message of Martin Luther, a half-century after the development of printing, benefitted enormously from the ability of the new technology to spread rapidly hundreds of thousands of copies throughout Germany. The Reformation also focused attention on the individual in a new way, and this too was assisted greatly by the new mode of communication. Luther did not limit himself to protesting against abuses of papal authority and asking for reforms. In addition, he argued against the power and authority of the priesthood to serve as the intercessor between the individual and God. He claimed that "all believers are priests, serving each other, and each is a 'private person' in his relation to God. Each responds directly to the Bible as the Word of God."[37] Luther thus presented each individual with a new opportunity for achieving salvation through faith, and for this the group and the institution were not necessary. In lieu of *hearing* the biblical message from priests, Luther urged individuals to read and study the Bible themselves. This was an attack on the Church's control over information and thus was also an attack on its authority and power. It was an attack that succeeded at least partly because the number of Bibles available for public consumption had increased dramatically. More persons were now able to read, and Bibles were appearing in the vernacular rather than in Latin.

The new medium thus facilitated the Lutheran idea of the individual, and this had major ramifications for secular thought as well.[38] It has been observed that "the key to the renewal of law in the West from the sixteenth century on was the Lutheran concept of the power of the individual, by God's grace, to change nature and to create new social relations through the exercise of his will."[39] The attention that reading and expanded access to information focused on the capacities of the individual fortified the individual's status within the law. The liberal legal systems that resulted attempted to guarantee the rights of individuals. In doing so, they benefitted considerably from print, and they culminated in a different orientation toward the individual, toward his role in society, and toward his relationship with government.

Electronic Media

At the heart of the modern liberal legal system is a "view that society is constituted of autonomous, equal units, namely separate individuals and that such individuals are more important, ultimately, than any larger constituent group. It is reflected in the concept of individual private property, in the political and legal liberty of the individual."[40] This is a conception that print has contributed to and that is consistent with the flow of information in a print-oriented society. The electronic media, however, have different biases from print, and the role and conception of the individual may, therefore, be in some jeopardy. The new media can be used differently and in ways that were not possible with print. What is at stake, as this occurs, is the shared state–individual orientation of liberal legal systems and the legal principles that are based on a particular view of the individual.

Just as the mass media qualities of print have often obscured the fact that it was more of an individual medium than other forms of communication, the spectacular ability of the electronic media to reach worldwide audiences instantaneously has diverted attention from the support that electronic communication is providing to smaller entities that have to reach limited audiences. As a mass medium, print assisted the state; as an individual medium, it fostered greater appreciation of the individual. But print was not a tool that groups could use efficiently. The opposite is true for electronic media and groups. The novel qualities of electronic communication are easily used by those who do not wish or have to reach large audiences. As a result, they are fostering links among persons and groups who were not able to communicate efficiently before. They are facilitating the establishment and proliferation of groups, and this trend threatens the shared monopoly of the state and the individual.

The mass circulation quality of print, which provided opportunities both for the state and for the individual whose work or behavior was of public interest, also served to restrict persons or groups wishing to reach smaller audiences. This quality of print may be viewed as an invisible censor that limited the communicative and organizational abilities of such groups. The thrust of the following argument is that electronic communication is removing this censor and providing groups, organizations, and institutions with new communicative powers. In addition, the electronic media are focusing attention on groups in ways that were previously reserved for individuals. Whether or not it can now be reasonably argued that "groups are the building blocks of organizations, communities, society,"[41] it is at least plausible to argue that the attention that has been lavished on individuals is being diluted and fragmented and that this may ultimately influence those facets of law that rest on a particular view of the individual.[42]

Much public writing about the new media, particularly television, gives the impression that it is merely extending the trends fostered by print. For example, the masses reached by television are much larger than those reached by print. As with print, television also seems to be useful to at least some individuals, as the television camera becomes the means to create instant celebrities known to millions. As I have suggested throughout this book, however, early uses of a new medium do not necessarily reveal how it will be used later. Those who benefitted from print or from the early uses of the new medium may not continue to benefit from the opportunities provided by the new technology as it matures, and other entities may benefit in ways that were not possible with print.

If the spoken word was largely a group medium and print was both a mass and an individual medium, electronic communication provides opportunities for all three entities. We are experiencing a quantitative explosion in the production of information that allows huge audiences to be reached instantaneously and simultaneously and increases opportunities for individuals to obtain information and organize it according to their needs.[43] Individual access to larger bodies of information is also increasing.[44] Where the new media are qualitatively different from and not merely more powerful than print is in the new patterns of communication that are encouraged. The new media possess a linking power that often escapes public attention, since they do not occur in as public a fashion as print or television and are less easily documented. Their effects, however, can be glimpsed in several ways and suggest that some concern for the current view the law takes of the individual is warranted.

The linking power of the new media is a function of having an enhanced ability to both locate persons with certain qualities or

interests and communicate with them. In our daily mail, for example, we are subjected to frequent appeals to purchase products,
to contribute to charities, and to join organizations. All these
solicitations suggest more than the obvious fact that someone wants
our money. They indicate that someone knows something about
us, often a great deal. It is not by coincidence that these letters
and newsletters typically come from groups to which we are sympathetic. Those who send mail-order catalogues know our tastes,
and the charities appealing for funds all seem worthwhile and
involved in work we sympathize with. We may not respond with
a purchase or contribution, but our reasons for inaction are probably strictly economic. We do not resist for ideological, political,
or aesthetic reasons because we almost always receive information
from groups that already know our preferences. We are not solicited randomly but on the basis of a considerable amount of information about us that can be obtained relatively easily.

We may not formally respond to many of the noncommercial
organizations that write to us; but in reality, we are members of
those organizations anyway. In the vast majority of cases, these
organizations represent interests we have, and what is preventing
us from appearing on their rolls is not disagreement with their
policy but economic constraints. We are a part of their constituency
even if they have not yet secured a contribution because they know
about our beliefs and interests and can probably count on some
form of support from us if it is necessary. What is important to
understand is that we do not receive appeals from every needy
charity that is in existence (although we might sometimes think
we do). If that were to occur, Republicans would be getting appeals
from Democratic groups, pro-life activists would be receiving mail
from Planned Parenthood, IBM computer owners would be sent
information about Apple products, and so on. This does not happen, at least very often, because what we like, believe, and do is
known and accessible and can be used in ways that were not previously possible.

Some support for this interpretation of the movement of information in our society can be found in statistics about recent growth
in organized group activities, most notably nonprofit associations
and political action committees (PACs) in the United States. The
number of national nonprofit associations in the United States in

1970 was 10,734. It increased to 14,726 by 1980 and reached 20,076 in 1986.[45] The rise in political action committees is even more striking, increasing from 722 in 1975, to 2,551 in 1980, and 3,525 in 1983.[46] There may be a variety of reasons for these increases, but one of the underlying contributing factors is more efficient means for communicating among individuals with particular interests. While much of the communication involving such groups appears to be traditional, such as the use of mail solicitations, the whole process of producing such letters relies on sophisticated electronic techniques for acquiring and processing data.

Group activity has been increasing because the use of electronic media permits the movement of information among much larger numbers of individuals in ways that were not possible before. Unlike broadcasting, which has been a mostly hierarchical form of communication, microcomputers allow communication horizontally to other individuals or groups with similar interests. Until now, "there have been no means for a *group* of people to adequately exchange information among themselves and reach decisions, other than to meet frequently face to face and talk it out."[47] At present, new "classes" can be identified, whether they are owners of 1982 Chevrolets or persons sympathetic to a particular policy, and communication among these groups can occur. Many of these groups exist not simply to share information, but to pursue a cause or program not shared by others. As grievances are identified and publicized, pressures for satisfying grievances can be expected to increase as well.[48]

In its advertising, AT&T has urged that the telephone be used to "reach out and touch someone." This slogan reveals that the telephone may be used to speak with someone far away and that it is limited to reaching only one person at a time. Newer forms of electronic communication conquer distance as well as the telephone but allow one to reach a larger audience, to "reach out and touch many." This particular quality provides the basis for forging links among persons and groups who are separated by great distances and were not in communication previously.[49] The ability to "touch many" has been an element in some acts of violence, such as hijackings, in which one goal was to receive publicity for a cause. Television, in such instances, has been the main focus of attention because it was perceived to be the most effective electronic medium for achieving widespread publicity quickly. What is often lost sight of is that other forms of electronic communication are also being used continually, albeit in nonviolent fashion and over longer periods of time, to organize groups and publicize claims. One can "reach many" today in an increasing number of ways and formats. Nontelevision electronic communication thus is the tool used for reaching across territorial boundaries by groups as diverse as large multinational corporations and international peace groups. Even large commercial advertisers on television have recognized that there are new and different technological means for reaching particular audiences that in many instances are superior to television.[50]

The limitations of print guaranteed that much information about ourselves was never communicated. It was private. It was controlled by us and was rarely even desired by others. In the past, our links with others and our joining of groups were based on information about a very limited number of our interests or values. Typically, our organizational relationships derived from broad political, occupational, or religious concerns. Our links were with large organizations that could overcome the economics of print or with small localized groups that did not need print. The new media are fostering the formation of associations on the basis of information that was previously secret, such as income level, or of little value to anyone, such as what type of computer we own. It has been written that "in the past, costs of organization were sufficiently high to preclude formation of potential interest groups into litigating or lobbying groups, so that the prime actors in the legal process (both statute and common law) were individuals."[51] The ease of forming links makes it possible to establish groups around relatively minor interests and concerns. As a result, the "organization man" who is affiliated with only one group will be an extinct entity. We are, as a result of the ability to process and transmit information in new ways, in touch with many organizations.

The exploitation by groups of the capabilities of the new technologies is paralleled by the attention focused on groups that in the past was generally received by individuals. Professor J. David Bolter has argued that

> computer technology is team technology. It was born through collective projects . . . [and] every new machine and most significant programs have also been products of a team effort. In this respect, too, the computer is an archetype for current technology: the twentieth century has been shaped for good or ill by great team projects in engineering,

of which the three outstanding examples are the V2 project in Germany, the Manhattan project in America, and more recently the American space program. Even as late as the nineteenth century, individual inventors could make important advances working alone. Today the man or woman who gets the credit for an advance is often simply the group's leader.[52]

Print provided the means for scientists to learn of discoveries and build on the work *of* others. The electronic media provide the opportunity for scientists to work *with* others. Group efforts are fostered by the ability to work together, even though the persons who are part of the group may be separated by great distances. Barriers to such cooperation that existed previously are being removed. In addition, the speed with which information is transmitted means that any finding or discovery will be built on more quickly than in the past. It is more difficult to recognize individual achievements than it was in the past because the pace of change is more rapid and an improvement on any one finding may occur before public recognition of the first person can be noted. In such an environment, any one discovery appears to be only part of long chain of discoveries in which groups of people have played some role rather than a novel and completely independent event.

Solo achievements are also more unlikely because of the heightened complexity of many issues and problems. It is more difficult to isolate problems, consider them narrowly, and use the perspective of only one discipline. Confronting complex challenges requires both narrow expertise on the part of each individual and an understanding that one's own findings are part of a larger picture or puzzle.

Part of our affection for individuals who achieved certain goals by themselves is that their accomplishment justifies the liberty and freedom which ultimately rests on a notion of an individual who is capable of independent action. It also justifies the responsibility that is borne by those who violate certain norms. At the heart of liberal legal systems, which emphasize the protection of rights, is a conception of the individual that received great support from the technology of print. The provision of rights would make little sense if the conception of the individual and the role of the individual had not changed in the centuries following Gutenberg. As Richard Flathman has noted:

The rights that have been our primary concern belong to and are exercised by individuals. If such rights are to be defensible—indeed if they are to be comprehensible—the individual must be an identifiable, comprehensible, and morally and juridically appropriate "unit" of analysis and assessment. Major traditions of justifications for rights . . . begin with the assumption that the individual is not only a distinguishable entity but one possessed of or characterized by natural, inherent, or intrinsic value, which demands respect and protection as such. On this mode of individualism the practice of rights is based on recognition of the intrinsic value of the individual. Particular rights recognize and accord protection to aspects or, better perhaps, manifestations of that intrinsic value.[53]

What is perhaps most significant about the new linkages being formed on a national and international scale is that they reflect a perception of the individual that is very different from the abstract, autonomous, independent, rational, and whole person whose dignity is respected and protected by the legal and political systems. The growth in the number, activities, and power of groups rests less on a concern with the whole human being as an abstract individual and more on the real interests of real people. The individual is seen as a collection of interests, values, and desires that can be fragmented and exploited. Print has fostered an idea of the individual as an entity that had some links to others through family, work, religion, politics, and employment but whose primary identity was as something distinct and, indeed, separate from others. The electronic media encourage a fragmented view of the individual in which particular interests are important but the whole is almost irrelevant. Rather than being a distinct independent entity, the new individual is primarily an appendage of one or many groups.

We are in the midst of a change in fundamentally important parts of the liberal legal model involving the relationship of the individual and the state. Most legal thinking, as Meir Dan-Cohen has pointed out, still clings to

an image of the political structure of society as consisting in the juxtaposition of two kinds of entities: the state on the one hand, and the multitude of isolated, atomistically conceived individuals on the other. . . . If the existence of organizations is mentioned at all, it is in a perfunctory manner, typically by subsuming organizations under the generic term *individuals* to which the state (or government) is juxta-posed.[54]

The empowering and highlighting of the role of organizations in modern society will eventually bring about the recognition that the legal paradigm, one which tends to assume that organizations are merely groups of individuals and can be treated as though they were individuals, is inadequate. While lawyers and judges have recognized organizations as legal entities,

> they often tend to refer to them as if they were indistinguishable, from a legal point of view, from another familiar kind of "legal person," namely the individual human being. Legal discourse often applies a unified normative vocabulary to both individuals and to organizations. Concepts, institutions, doctrines, and attitudes that originated in an individualistic context, and whose applicability to organizations is at best questionable, are frequently used indiscriminately and unreflec-tively to deal with organizations as well. The use of a unified normative vocabulary that is oblivious to differences between individuals and organizations allows the law to deal with various organizations within an essentially individualistic framework, without fully confronting or-ganizational realities and exploring their potential legal implications.[55]

The legal process is only beginning to struggle with this change in the attention demanded by groups. Perhaps the most notable existing example of what the shift may involve is contained in rulings concerning affirmative action. In such cases, courts must make choices between a person who desires some goal for reasons that concern that person, and another who seeks the same goal but whose argument requires that the group he or she belongs to be taken into account. I am not suggesting that the rulings in this area have been wrong or unjust, only that they can be viewed as involving a balancing of group interests and individual interests that is different from what it has traditionally been. The decisions may claim to be granting relief to individuals who are suffering as a result of past injustices, but they can also be interpreted as reflecting a new orientation about groups, individuals, and the "organization society." Such a shift not merely is a legal change, but may very well be indicative of a significant cultural event, a reworking of how the individual is perceived and thought of by society.

The Abstract Quality of Law

"What is happening," Alvin Toffler has written, "is not merely the breakdown of law, but, more importantly, the breakdown of the underlying order upon which law is based."[56] Throughout this book, I have argued that the new media are affecting the structure of law in subtle and often indirect ways. Like any tangible object, law is vulnerable to changes that are unseen, that are occurring beneath the visible surface, and that only gradually become noticeable to the public and the profession. Law differs from many other objects of study, however, in that some key components of law exist only in the mind. What supports the visible persons and practices of the law are abstract ideas, concepts, and habits of thought. Our system of law is thus composed of and based on a set of ideas and concepts that exist apart from the actual buildings and people of the law.

This abstract component is as important to modern law as any of its tangible parts, perhaps even more important. Indeed, the degree to which we rely on abstractions distinguishes our culture's system of law from that of other societies. There is also a close relationship between these abstractions and the manner in which primary values of our system, such as the protection of rights or the achievement of equal justice, are attained. Other societies, which have different values and goals, have been much less comfortable with basing law on a set of abstract concepts and principles than ours has been. The main theme of this concluding section of the book is that print supported and influenced the use of abstractions and that the conceptual model we rely on is threatened by very different qualities of the new media.

The fact that law is abstract rather than tangible is easy to ignore. We are aware mostly of the very real consequences that occur when rules are applied or violated. Gains and losses, and the people who cause these outcomes to occur, are the principal reality for those who come in contact with the law. If one thinks of law as consisting of lawyers, police officers, courts, judges, and so on, it is easy to ignore the abstract concepts and reasoning that underlie the whole process of law. Yet we rely as much on these creations of the mind as we do on those facets of law that can be seen or touched. Indeed, the artificial reality created by law and not the reality we actually experience is what determines what is lawful and what is not and thus conditions what lawyers do and what occurs in court. This separate legal world, therefore, is something that deserves to be treated on its own. In an era in which new means of communication are emerging, it would be an error to ignore the potential effect of the new media on how we organize and conceptualize the law.

Legal systems vary in the degree to which they rely on abstract concepts. Our legal process ranks very high in its use of abstract concepts and is premised on a mode of thought that implicitly accepts abstractions. If we were not as accepting of the law's abstract nature as we are, the whole world of law would be affected. It would be less powerful, less independent, less concerned with legal rights and the individual. Print, I believe, has facilitated the growth of our current model. Conversely, a new form of communication with different properties may make such a legal process less viable.

One of the secrets of the legal profession is the knowledge that law is less concerned with the real world we live in than with another world, a world that bears some similarity to our real world but also differs in substantial ways. The power of the law is to place into this legal world entities that are intangible and that do not exist in our world.[57] The process of law requires that before law can affect the real life of any person, it is necessary to determine how the law would apply in the special abstract world that exists only in the minds of lawyers and the books of the law. It is whether some act is lawful or not in this legal world that determines whether it will be lawful in the world in which we live our lives.

A few examples of the parts of the legal universe that have no tangible form include rights, corporations, and contracts. It is their intangible nature and the fact that they are created by law, however, that allows them to be defined according to some plan and be given whatever qualities we wish them to have. One scholar has written that "all legal relations are abstract and exist not in fact but only in contemplation of law. Rights and duties do not belong to the physical world, though the infringement of a right may involve the wrongdoer in a loss of physical goods or in a physical interference with his body."[58] When an entity appears in the legal world, we are not constrained by its natural form since it has no natural form. We thus have great flexibility in creating legal rights and in determining when a right will apply and when it will not. We can make corporate directors liable to shareholder suits or immune from such claims. We can enforce contracts for surrogate motherhood or refuse to do so. As Professor F. H. Lawson has argued,

> Legal personality is not the same as human personality, an estate in fee simple does not exist physically in the same way as the land over which it exists, nor is a contract the same as the agreement of which it is the legal manifestation . . . It is an artificial world, whose members are to some extent, arbitrarily, though not irrationally, created to serve certain purposes. Thus they can be defined with fair exactness, much more satisfactorily than the facts of everyday life. In a sense they are created to conform to predetermined definitions. Again, their relations to each other are much more clearly fixed than relations in the world of fact.[59]

The power of the law and the acts of creation that are possible in the legal world may be more clear if we look at a few objects that exist in the real world but whose legal reality is very different. Part of the power of the law is evident from its ability to create a world that actually contradicts reality. For example, a person who is very much alive can be considered by the law to be legally dead, while an inanimate object might be given rights denied the legally dead but actually alive person. A child, in the legal world, might not be considered to be a "person." In other words, the law can bring such things as corporations to life and treat them as though they had body and soul, while causing other entities, under certain conditions, to be treated as though they were dead, even though they are very much alive. We can find people to be legally guilty even when they are factually innocent, and the system itself is not troubled by this because factual innocence is not part of the legal world. We can define income in such a way that someone with an enviable salary, an exquisite home, and luxurious possessions will not have any legal income under the tax laws. A road on the island of Hawaii can be declared to be a link in the interstate highway system. A real emergency might not trigger a legal "state of emergency." Courts can argue that there is no "case or controversy" in a situation where doctors wish to give someone a blood transfusion but that person refuses.[60]

One of the great advantages in employing abstractions is that it increases the options that are available for ordering future experience. Relationships and legal duties can be established to promote almost any purpose. There is a much wider range of choice in considering what can be encouraged or discouraged than is possible in an environment in which all that exists are the actual contacts and experiences of individuals. The way in which legal relations are ordered can be very different from what exists in the real world. For example, "all men are created equal" can be the premise of a legal code, even though it is an obviously false description of reality. Corporations can be considered persons under the law, even though they have no body or soul. A person can own land without physically possessing it. There is, in other words, no need to find justification in the physical world for how we structure our legal world.

It is difficult to explain the abstract nature of some words or concepts because we often speak about them just as we would talk about something real. For example, we talk about "possessing" a right as though the process of possession is the same as possessing something tangible. Discussion of a contract may mistakenly identify the contract as being the paper document rather than the "meeting of the minds" or the agreement on which the paper is based. We can speak of the "*merger* of estates, of the *breaking* of contracts, of the *ripening* of obligations."[61] We can go to court to assert a right, but we cannot literally find a right with any of our senses. We can put our hands on the assets of a corporation but not on the corporation itself. We can drink Coca-Cola, but we cannot talk or write to the Coca-Cola Corporation, only to an employee of the corporation. Language shapes our thought about many of these concepts and, in some cases, works to hide their true nature from us.

What is often not understood is that the law is much more comfortable dealing with its own universe and deals with the real world only indirectly. Legal decisions do not depend on one's status in the real world but on a fictional counterpart in the world that law has created. For lawyers and judges, therefore, what exists before their eyes is less important than what exists in their minds, what the law tells them exists or does not exist in the abstract legal world. Their function is to determine whether a particular act would be lawful in the world of law, populated as it is by entities that have either no tangible existence or an abstract existence that differs from their real counterparts. If it is lawful in the legal world, then it will be lawful in the real world. If it is not permitted in the legal world, it will not be allowed in the real world, even if the activity in question might seem just and desirable.

In a common accident case, for example, a judge who evaluates the lawfulness of an individual's act is actually thinking about whether it would be lawful for the abstract individual existing in the legal world to commit the act. The only quality of the "individual," as it exists in tort law, is that it is "reasonable." When a judge asks, "What would a reasonable person do in the circumstances in which the defendant found himself," the judge is actually asking whether the abstract legal individual would have done what the real defendant did. One of the differences between lawyers and laypeople is that lawyers are acquainted with those things that are found in the legal world that do not exist in our world or that exist differently.

This example suggests the other main benefit of guiding behavior through abstractions, that law becomes more universal. The abstract individual who is the subject of some law can be without gender, without race, without wealth, and without religion. Similarly, all those unique qualities of particular individuals that emphasize differences among people can be ignored. As a result, law becomes more impersonal and applicable generally to all individuals. When there is a "concept of the individual as an independent entity equal to other individuals,"[62] it also becomes possible to equate equality with equal rights even though real equality in the conditions of life is lacking, to promise formal equality under the law while substantive equality is absent.

The heavy reliance on abstractions that is typical of modern liberal legal systems is not evident in all legal systems.[63] Except in Rome, reliance on abstract concepts was lacking in the ancient world. Law professor J. C. Smith has pointed out that these cultures "contain few abstract or theoretical concepts. Most concepts in such legal systems derive their meaning directly from, or in terms of sensed experience."[64] Similarly, anthropologists John Comaroff and Simon Roberts concluded that "even in societies in which people themselves speak easily about such matters and ostensibly have rough terminological counterparts for the term 'law,' there is rarely (if ever) a separate class of *legal* norms, functionally and conceptually distinguished from other types of precept or 'especially organized for jural purposes.' "[65] Thus ownership in ancient codes did not depend on property "rights" but required actual possession of the item in question. In such cultures, the phrase "possession is nine-tenths of the law" made much more sense than it does today. Ownership depended on actual possession and not on some legal rights that derived from a piece of paper. Transfer of ownership, therefore, required not the passing of "title" or the signing of a deed, but the "two parties would come upon the land, each with his witnesses, and the one would hand the other a twig or piece of turf which would symbolize the land passing from the possession of the one person to the other."[66] Similarly, contracts for the future performance of an action did not exist. Promises and agreements to do something at a future time were not legally enforceable. Commercial transactions required that the actual exchange of land, goods, or money take place. What was important was transfer of the goods and actual possession and not the performance of some abstract obligation.

Such societies, which were relatively static and undesirous of change, did not have a great need to develop abstract concepts with which to order future relationships and transactions. In addition, the lack of literacy in such cultures was a deterrent to fashioning a system of law that could be thought about apart from sensed experience. The form in which communication occurred was not a form that encouraged the use of abstractions. In an oral culture, there can be "no reference to 'dictionary definitions' . . . Instead, the meaning of each word is ratified in a succession of concrete situations, accompanied by vocal inflections and physical gestures, all of which combine to particularize both its specific denotation and its accepted connotative usages."[67] What was most important in oral cultures was to provide guideposts to appropriate behavior that could be remembered. Standards of conduct, therefore, were more likely to be found in stories and narratives than explicitly stated in abstract principles or rules. Particular traits of particular individuals acting in realistic situations would, it was hoped, be emulated. What was necessary was that points of reference be familiar and understandable in terms of common experience. Legal regulations, therefore, when framed for the use of either oral or craft–literate societies, are turned into case law or participial law: "If a man commits a certain act he shall do or suffer accordingly"; "If his ox shall gore another man he shall pay so and so"; or else, "The man doing a given act shall be declared without the law"; and so forth. In a theistic context, the law is addressed to the hearer as a personal command of the god: "Thou shalt not do so and so." The kind of legal statement that is avoided is the one that would say, "Murder is definable as a crime punishable by death"; "Ownership of property implies responsibility for its maintenance"; "Personal liability proportionate to the investment made"; and so forth. In short, in order to frame a legal directive, a situation is conceived and stated, cast in the form of an event or an action by a given agent, not in the form of a general principle within which a given case might fall. The law code of Hammurabi and the various Hebraic law codes incorporated in the Pentateuch all exhibit this kind of syntax.[68]

The language of the law in such societies certainly does not indicate a complete lack of conceptualization or an inability to think abstractly. But it does reveal a greater affinity with the finite than the infinite, with the concrete than the abstract. This outlook was not limited to law but permeated the culture. Plato and Aristotle, for example,

regarded the unlimited or infinite as aesthetically, philosophically, and even morally repugnant. To appreciate the Greek attitude, we need only stand before a Doric temple, whose geometry is so pleasingly complete, self-contained, and finite . . . Both Plato and Aristotle believed that the universe itself was finite; otherwise, it would have been unworthy of the name "cosmos," or ordered world.[69]

Writing and print contributed to the growth of a legal process that became increasingly dependent on abstract thought by providing a tangible form to something invisible and intangible. The principal effect of this was to reduce reliance on images, rhyme, rhythm, and mnemonic devices and to allow the development, study, analysis, revision, and refinement of concepts. Prior to the late Middle Ages, this process seems to have occurred only in Rome and not in other societies that had writing. As I have indicated earlier, however, societies that had writing often limited its use and restricted literacy. In these societies, writing did not replace the spoken word so much as work with it. Manuscript cultures remained, in the words of Walter Ong, "oral–aural."[70] It is not surprising that until printing brought about the expansion of literacy and the growth of materials of study, law was more a matter of appropriate behavior and custom than of abstract principles and that even when the focus was on justice, the context was often on "what justice does or how it behaves, not what it *is*."[71] Even in the centuries before Gutenberg, when the use of paper increased and writing was more common, written materials about law were "almost always essentially practical. It was generally something that told their brethren how an action could be begun, delayed, carried on, defeated, or a record of what had been done in the past, if that was likely to be useful for the future. Scientific arrangement was a secondary affair. Theoretical speculation scarcely existed."[72]

In her famous study of the methods used to enhance memory in ancient and medieval times, Frances Yates described the kind of permanent change for individuals and institutions that occurred with the shift "from image culture to word culture."[73] She recounts how, in Victor Hugo's *Notre Dame de Paris,*

> a scholar, deep in meditation in his study . . . gazes at the first printed book which has come to disturb his collection of manuscripts. Then . . . he gazes at the vast cathedral, silhouetted against the starry sky . . . "Ceci tuera cela," he says. The printed book will destroy the building. The parable which Hugo develops out of the comparison of the building, crowded with images, with the arrival in his library of a printed book might be applied to the effect on the invisible cathedrals of memory of the past of the spread of printing. The printed book will make such huge built-up memories, crowded with images, unnecessary. It will do away with habits of immemorial antiquity whereby a "thing" is immediately invested with an image and stored in the places of memory.[74]

Gregory the Great is reported to have stated that statues were "the books of the illiterate."[75] Such "books" facilitated memory by providing clear images. Print, however, assisted recall by very different means, in which the only images facing the reader were the shapes of the letters. This shift contributed not only to an enormous increase in the amount of information one could have access to, but also to a change in the kind of information that could easily be communicated. The saying "A picture is worth a thousand words" suggests that it is difficult, if not impossible, to communicate some messages verbally. Seeing the *Mona Lisa* and reading a description of it, for example, cannot possibly create the same effect or impact. But a thousand pictures might be inadequate for communicating a thought contained in a very few words. It would border on the futile, for example, to attempt to communicate what a right is through pictures. McLuhan argued for the different communicative powers of image and print by providing the following example:

> Suppose that, instead of displaying the Stars and Stripes, we were to write the word "American flag" across a piece of cloth and to display that. While the symbols would convey the same meaning, the effect would be quite different. To translate the rich visual mosaic of the Stars and Stripes into written form would be to deprive it of most of its qualities of corporate image and of experience . . . Perhaps this illustration will serve to suggest the change the tribal man experiences when he becomes literate. Nearly all the emotional and corporate family feeling is eliminated from his relationship with his social group. He is emotionally free to separate from the tribe and to become a civilized individual, a man of visual organization who has uniform attitudes, habits, and rights with all other civilized individuals.[76]

The enhanced ability of literate media to facilitate abstract thought may be more understandable if an analogy is used from the realm of religion. In the evolution of Western religion, as of Western law, emphasis on the abstract ultimately prevailed over the concrete.[77] It was not easy for the monotheistic ideal of an abstract god to replace a belief in gods with real forms. Here, too, the written word played an influential role. The prohibition in the Ten Commandments against the production of images suggests that the suppression of images was necessary to facilitate a change in the way in which the deity was to be imagined. Without graphic and tangible representations of the deity, the difficult task of accepting an invisible force would be easier. Similarly, during the Reformation, Calvin urged that the Second Commandment be observed and that the illiterate be taught to read, a program that was consistent with Calvinist religious thought.

While there is no "Second Commandment" in law that prohibits the use of images, one would not know this if one examined the books of the law. Legal literature has as few pictures as the prayer book of a person who follows the Bible literally. If actual prohibitions existed to ban pictures from the shelves of law libraries, there would not be fewer illustrations than exist today.[78] The law seems to have understood implicitly that fostering the abstract is easier when images are suppressed. Pictures would interfere with the decision-making process by focusing attention on aspects of life that are not part of the legal world. One would see real faces with expressions of pain or pleasure and be more tempted to consider the actual conditions or circumstances under which we live our lives. In the abstract legal world, we are equal before the law because the abstract individual is the same as all other abstract individuals. He or she is without gender, without emotion, and without economic advantages that lead us all to be different from one another. The legal person, unlike a real person, cannot be pathetic or sympathetic, wise or stupid, rich or poor. Except in unusual circumstances, these are not characteristics that have been given to the abstract individual because such traits are not supposed to affect decisions of lawfulness or liability.

How is it possible to make decisions on the basis of some faceless and amorphous nonbeing and ignore the real people who are involved in a case? Clearly, this is a difficult challenge that may often be ignored or avoided. What needs to be understood is that one of the forces which assists the use of such a decision-making process in the face of many temptations to act differently is a conditioning of the mind by the medium of print. Even with this mental conditioning, as the legal realists informed us, judging often involves mere lip service to the abstract legal world. Yet without the force exerted by the medium of print, the degree of legal decisions determined by people rather than by law would be even greater.

The extent to which images are suppressed in order to facilitate obedience to abstract legal principles is most obvious in law schools and in the training of those we wish to be most comfortable with this model. Law school education is less training in practical matters than in "thinking like a lawyer" and in conditioning one's mind to focus more on rules than on persons. The degree to which law schools have traditionally been successful has led some critics to charge law students with being "brain-dead"[79] and to equate legal education with brainwashing and thought-reform methods.[80] The cause is commonly attributed to the use of the Socratic method in class, often in a dehumanizing manner. It may be, however, that legal education is dehumanizing as a consequence of the use of materials in which real individuals retain their names, but no other facets of their identities are discernable from the judge's description of them. Persons in real or hypothetical legal cases are always abstracted persons about whom only a few legally relevant facts are known. In neither form are there any persons with whole personalities. Lawyers, therefore, "learn (by default perhaps) to deal with abstracted, selected facts, rather than real facts."[81]

Legal educators seem to have a subconscious awareness that socialization into the profession must come via print. Traditional casebooks and law reviews rarely contain a photograph breaking up the continuous pages of print. At a fundamental level, there would seem to be an essential facilitating link between liberal legal thought and the printed word. Bernard Diamond, a professor of law and psychiatry, has suggested that

> it is as if a deliberate effort were being made to dehumanize the law, to transform the law into an abstraction that has no relationship to an individual. I would like to see law reports illustrated with photographs of all the participants, including the victim, the defendant, the attorneys, and the judge. Perhaps then the student might understand that the legal process is concerned with real live human beings. To my knowledge, no modern law book is illustrated except those dismal anatomical texts used for reference by personal injury lawyers. This has not always been so. I own a 1562 Flemish criminal law book illustrated with many beautifully detailed engravings depicting every crime described in the book.[82]

Illustrations are not a part of traditional legal education because they would make it more difficult for law students to develop the habits of thought that are considered to be at the core of being a lawyer. Becoming a lawyer means, in part, that one gradually learns how to fit individual cases into large categories. Judgments about individual actions are made by seeing whether the behavior is consistent with what some broad standard or rule seems to require. Such judgments can be made only if one is willing and able to focus on some attributes of an individual and ignore other qualities. Very rarely in the legal process is the whole person judged or important to consider. The process of learning to think like a lawyer is made infinitely easier if illustrations are not used because the lawyer or judge has to be comfortable with the reduction or elimination of information. Illustrations or films may, in the eyes of a teacher, provide too much information about an individual, and students may be unwilling to ignore this "irrelevant" information. "Thinking like a lawyer" involves treating people on the basis of the legal category they may fall into. Reading opinions of appellate judges in which the discussion is about law and not about people is a much more suitable method of learning when the goal is to think abstractly about people and learn how to treat different people as though they were all the same.

Law students often discuss "hypothetical" cases and read "real" cases. Yet this is a largely irrelevant distinction. The characters in judicial opinions lose any unique qualities that they might actually possess. Judicial opinions refer to real people, but as these characters are embalmed in print, they lose their personalities. One admirer of McLuhan used the following example to illustrate how easily information can be lost as a real experience is described in print:

> While lecturing to a large audience in a modern hotel in Chicago, a distinguished professor is bitten in the leg by a cobra. The whole experience takes three seconds. He is affected through the touch of the reptile, the gasp of the crowd, the swimming sights before his eyes. His memory, imagination, and emotions come into emergency action. A lot of things happen in three seconds. Two weeks later he is fully recovered and wants to write up the experience in a letter to a colleague. To communicate this experience through print means that it must first be broken down into parts and then mediated, eyedropper fashion, one thing at a time, in an abstract, linear, fragmented, sequential way. This is the essential structure of print. And once a culture uses such a medium for a few centuries, it begins to perceive the world in a one-thing-at-a-time, abstract, linear, fragmented, sequential way. And it shapes its organizations and schools according to the same premises. The form of print has become the form of thought.[83]

Professor John Noonan has suggested that judges use abstractions as a mask to hide their own individuality and that of the people who appear before them. This mask, however, not only allows the judge to suppress his own feelings, but also restricts the outward vision of the judge so that rulings can be made without considering the real person who is affected. Noonan points out that "rules, not persons, are the ordinary subject matter of legal study . . . Little or no attention is given to the persons in whose minds and in whose interaction the rules have lived—to the persons whose difficulties have occasioned the articulation of the rule, to the lawyers who have tried the case, to the judges who have decided it."[84] Similarly, in attacking the exclusion of empathetic knowledge in the legal process, Lynne Henderson has written that

> legal decisions and lawmaking frequently have nothing to do with un-
> derstanding human experiences, affect, suffering—how people *do* live.
> . . . While emotion may generate laws via "politics," once those laws
> meet whatever criteria are necessary to constitute legitimacy in a sys-
> tem, they are cleansed of emotion under this vision of the Rule of
> Law. The law becomes not merely a human institution affecting real
> people, but rather The Law.[85]

Making decisions on the basis of abstract legal figures when the case involves real people is not an easy task. The legal realists asserted that such a process is not even the norm. Juries, either because of sympathy for the plaintiff or because of recognition that the defendant is a "deep pocket," may arrive at a verdict that is not justified by an application of abstract rules to abstract individuals for whom wealth or poverty is an unknown condition. Every case in which law and justice seem to be colliding or in which a procedural "technicality" seems to be standing in the way of a popular result illustrates the fact that the legal model, relying as it does on applying rules in an abstract world, is continually strug-gling with a model that would deal directly with the real person in the case. During the past several hundred years, one side in this struggle has benefitted more than the other from the form of com-munication that has guided legal thought. Using print as a censor, the law has moved in a direction that has seemed to be more natural than it actually is.

Electronic Media

If print has been a means for promoting abstract thought, for limiting the information that is considered relevant to decision making, and for substituting faceless beings for real people in the world of rules, can the electronic media continue to serve these functions as effectively? Much popular concern has been raised about the potentially dehumanizing impact of computers. It is feared that we will be treated as numbers rather than people, that crucial decisions will be made by machines, which necessarily lack feeling and compassion. Comparisons are made that stress the flexibility, informality, and personal relationships which purportedly characterized the precomputer age with the impersonal treatment we are often subjected to in various contexts today.

The problem with this line of argument is the assumption that computerized decision making, if it ever came to pass, would be replacing person-oriented decisions. Whatever the validity of this concern in the nonlegal context, such a development in the legal world would have to be described differently. In the legal process, at least, it would be more accurate to say that decision makers relying on and conditioned by print would be replaced by decision makers relying on and conditioned by the electronic media. The fear of dehumanization is that the use of computers will make us too legalistic and too rule oriented. It is assumed that the electronic media will foster the same habits of thought and the same practices as print, albeit more efficiently and rigorously. It is, however, as has been noted previously, unlikely that the electronic media are simply more powerful versions of print. A society in which all decisions are made on the basis of impersonal abstract rules requires, as a precondition, that we think in a manner which accepts this form of decision making as appropriate and desirable. Since the electronic media are very different from print, the model of decision making fostered by print will become weaker and progressively less appealing. Rather than strengthening the paradigm of print (and of law), the evolving forms of electronic communication may actually threaten and transform the print model.

One of the clear lessons of the history of printing is that we should be extremely wary of assuming that the early form of a new technology will be the same as the mature or developed form. The first printed books, for example, looked very much like manuscripts. The typeface used was similar to a written script.[86] Febvre and Martin concluded that

> the first printers, far from being innovators, took extreme care to produce exact imitations. The 42-line Bible, for example, was printed in a letter-type which faithfully reproduced the handwriting of the Rhenish missals. . . . How could they have imagined a printed book

other than in the form of the manuscripts on which they were in fact modeled? And would not the identity of the book and manuscript be the most obvious proof of their technical triumph, as well as the guarantee of their commercial success?[87]

We are still in an age in which video tries to emulate film while much of what emanates from computers strives to be similar to print. For example, desktop-publishing programs take pride in their ability to duplicate traditional typefaces. Word-processing programs feature justified margins to make the output from "printers" look more printlike. History is, in a sense, repeating itself as the technology stresses its ability to produce a product that looks familiar. The new technology seems to be able to do what the old did but with greater efficiency and at lower cost.

The ability to mimic print tends to mask how different the new technologies are. To explore the consequences of the electronification of communications, it is necessary to understand not what television and computers have been but what they are likely to become. It is, for example, important to view these two branches of electronic communication as being closely related to each other rather than, as many would think, as being separate and distinct entities. What is occurring, as our technologies become more sophisticated, as data from each are carried over the same wires, is that each is acquiring qualities possessed by the other. Computers, in addition to processing numbers and text, are becoming instruments that can provide sound, moving images, and information from distant places. They can do much of what television does, and more. Television, using videotape or signals transmitted over high-capacity cables rather than through the air, is also giving the viewer greater control over what appears on the screen. The technologies are converging and providing opportunities for obtaining, storing, and processing information that neither technology was capable of in its early form.

As the technologies evolve rapidly, we will move out of this introductory era and should be prepared for the development of novel forms of output. The ability of the electronic media to convert digital information to a form that can appeal to any of our senses provides it with a flexibility that was lacking in print. Textual information on paper will not disappear, and not every message will include text, pictures, motion, sound, and smell. But combinations that are now unfamiliar to us will begin to appear, and formats that have been restricted because of the technology of print and the limitations of existing cables will gradually surface.[88] We are currently in a phase in which a new guide has been provided to us, one that speaks some new languages and has different interests and capabilities. We are still being spoken to, however, in the language used by the last guide and are only gradually being introduced to the new interests and capabilities of the new technologies.

As limits on the form of information are relaxed, limits on thought are lifted as well.[89] The effort of the law to maintain an imageless body of knowledge that appeals to only our sense of sight will become more difficult as we are able to select what information is provided to us and what form it will assume. The information-reduction function of print that fostered the development and use of abstractions will be challenged as we are given more information to think about and some information that, like music, poetry, or drama, may touch us or move us in ways that are difficult to articulate. In this respect, the new media and the preprint media may have something in common. In the premechanical era, the

> scribe was in immediate physical contact with the book he produced; he felt the letters form under his pen. His tactile and muscular participation in making the words was far greater than that of a modern typist. The scribe also repeated the words as he copied and so brought a third sense into play in the craft of writing, as McLuhan emphasized. Words that were felt and heard as well as seen had an immediacy and reality that we can scarcely appreciate today. Abstraction in reading was similarly discouraged by the run-on style of writing and the need to vocalize each word.[90]

McLuhan had argued that print changed the perceptual orientation of Western culture. The written manuscript, which was largely a talking book because that was how most persons received information from a manuscript, became silent after printing. The book is still silent because computers and video are considered separate and independent technologies. Most of the technological fences between the print, sound, and image worlds are being demolished, however, and public understanding of the merging of video and computer technologies will grow rapidly as hardware and software that allow the manipulation of these previously separate fields are distributed. The silent and pictureless screen of text that is provided by most books or by word processors today will still be an option, perhaps even a favored one, but it will be one of many and may not receive the same degree of attention that print currently has in such fields as law, where sound and images would interfere with traditional habits of thought.

As we begin to employ and rely on media that are less capable than print of promoting the use of abstract concepts, we, like our distant ancestors, may be less willing than we are now to accept the abstraction in place of the real. The consequences of such a shift would be momentous because those abstractions that are central to the legal process would be less meaningful, less powerful, and less influential. Consider, for example, the concept of rights, which would, perhaps, be the most obvious victim of developments along the line described. During the past thirty years, important changes have occurred in the legal status of women, blacks, criminal defendants, students, veterans, prisoners, homosexuals, children, mental patients, illegal aliens, and various other groups. We have been experiencing, in the eyes of some, a "rights explosion" or "rights revolution" in the sense that old rights are being expanded, new rights are being created, and the number of cases in which rights are the central focus is increasing. Thus far, the new media appear to have encouraged this development by fostering links among previously isolated individuals and by publicizing problems and injustices widely. What is not often asked is what is occurring to the meaning and concept of rights. The law often provides a right to equal treatment rather than equal treatment, a right to pursue a claim in lieu of providing what is actually sought. While the number of rights seems to be growing, owing in part to the catalyzing power of the new media, how secure is the idea or concept of a right and a process in which rights are an acceptable alternative to the object of the right?

The answer to this question is critically important because if a right means something different or is valued differently in the future than it has been in the past, what has been acquired recently may not be as secure as it was originally. As a result of the shift in our means of communication, however, this is precisely what may occur. While attention is focused on the latest court battles over the claims of a particular group, a more subtle but perhaps more important shift is occurring in how rights are perceived and defined. We may, in other words, be experiencing a second "rights revolution" in which the meaning and value of rights are changing and the role of rights in the paradigm of law is becoming different.[91] Granted that a second revolution is under way in our thinking about rights, may it not be taking much of its force and direction from two facts? First, more and more information is available to us than previously. Second, this information is appearing in more and more radically different forms.

Rights are not a feature of every legal system in every historical period. A Japanese legal scholar, for example, has written that the concept of a right did not appear in Japanese thinking "until the end of the Tokugawa period (1603–1867). . . . The concept of a right is still too new to have struck a deep root in our conceptions. . . . It is different to assert one's own interests from asserting rights although it may appear to be the same."[92] Even in our legalistic culture, there has been a tension between law and reality, between the abstract and the concrete. As the new technologies evolve into a more mature form, we have to try to comprehend not only how groups use the new forms of communication to assert rights, but also whether the new media provide support for the idea of rights as well.

Professor Steven Lukes has argued that the use of abstractions was a significant move forward, but it must be transcended. He writes that the use of abstractions was

> a crucial weapon in the breaking down of traditional privileges and hierarchies, in the dissolution of separate and incommensurable social orders and ranks, and in the establishing of universal human claims in the form of legal rights. The formal legal framework of modern democratic societies is the guardian of the abstract individual. It provides for formal equality (before the law) and formal freedom (from illegal or arbitrary treatment). These are crucial and indispensable gains but, if we are to take equality and liberty seriously, they must be transcended. And that can only be achieved on the basis of a view of unabstracted individuals in their concrete, social specificity, who, in virtue of being *persons* all require to be treated and to live in a social order

which treats them as possessing dignity, as capable of exercising and increasing their autonomy, of engaging in valued activities within a private space, and of developing their several potentialities.[93]

The analysis I have provided suggests that the new media are pushing us in just this direction.

Conclusion

During 1987, as the United States celebrated the two hundredth anniversary of the Constitution's ratification, thousands of persons visited the National Archives in Washington, D.C., to see the document itself. Those making this pilgrimage were undoubtedly impressed with the pieces of parchment on display and with the specially controlled lighting conditions that would help preserve the fragile and yellowing documents. It would, therefore, probably have surprised most, if not all, of these visitors to learn that what they saw was not really the official Constitution. In effect, both the visitors to this shrine and the documents themselves were being kept "in the dark."[1] The document that has been on public display since 1876 and that is almost universally believed to be *the* Constitution actually has little or no legal significance.

Akhil Reed Amar, a professor of law at Yale University, has pointed out that the Constitution became the "supreme law of the land" not when it was signed in Philadelphia but when it was ratified "by the people."[2] The version of the Constitution actually distributed to the states and ratified by the people of the United States was not the manuscript copy that is on display but a printed version produced on September 28, 1787, eleven days after the parchment copy was signed. Fortunately, the print version of September 28 and the manuscript of September 17 seen by tourists contain the same words. They do differ in capitalization and punctuation, however, and courts would be bound to follow the print version if such differences were ever to affect the meaning of a phrase or the outcome of a case.

From the analysis presented in this book, it should not be a surprise that the Constitution is in print. The processes and values promoted by the Constitution are much more consistent with the practices and ideals of a print culture than one dependent on writing. Clauses that seem to have no connection to media or communication, such as the amendment procedure and the separation

266

of political and judicial branches of government, reflect habits of thought that were not likely to have been influential in the preprint era. Most obviously, the logistics of ratification and of creating uniform standards applicable to citizens and states were facilitated by the use of print.

We have, I believe, been as unaware of the print-oriented character of law as of the fact that our supreme law is a printed document. As the numerous references in court opinions and legal literature to our "written" Constitution indicate,[3] we tend not to distinguish writing from print. Similarly, we have displayed only limited sensitivity to the implications of widespread use of electronic communication. In this book, therefore, I have endeavored to focus some light on those facets of law where differences in the mode of communicating information are critical and where the adoption of new technologies of communication are likely to be significant. It is prudent to be a little tentative in drawing pictures of the future, particularly when the impact is occurring on several levels, but, as I have tried to show, the past may provide some trustworthy indications of where to look for change.

Research in the area of communications has not yet succeeded in explaining the exact relationship between a new technology and changes in institutional and personal life. Anthony Smith, who has identified many areas in which the new media can be expected to be influential, has written that

> our repertoire of working mental images does not seem at the present time to contain an apt metaphor or convenient cliché that sums up the flow of influence between a fresh technology and human society. We are free to borrow from economics the idea of the multiplier, or from scientific discourse Thomas Kuhn's idea of the paradigm collapse. Engineering and telecommunications are willing to lend us all manner of forces and thrusts, scatterings and pressures, but really nothing that provides a convincing and transposable conceptualization of the causal influences that pass between a new form of equipment and the organized minds and bodies of people living in society.[4]

In discussing law, which is a powerful force in its own right and which is an institution that can be looked at and defined in different ways, it would be foolhardy to predict a timetable for a series of changes it might undergo. But for an institution that is dependent on the communication of words and symbols, it would be equally foolhardy, if not more so, to ignore revolutionary technologies that have, at their center, enormous but uncharted power to manipulate words and symbols. What is most necessary is to be sensitive to the qualities of the new technologies, to the capabilities they provide, and to the constraints they place on us. The viability, effectiveness, and nature of law in the future depends on whether we understand the changes occurring to the law and are able to respond to them. As a skilled writer, sensitive to the power and constraints of language,[5] or as a creative artist, working to overcome the limits of a particular medium, a person interested in the future of law must also be cognizant of the particular qualities of modes of expression.

In Chapter 2, I noted that the blindfold worn by Justice symbolized not merely the law's desire to be impartial, but its need to limit and manage the use of information. Law is a process that cannot function if there is no restriction on the acquisition of information and no means for organizing and regulating the information that is acquired. It is, therefore, significant that the figure representing Law and Justice on many public buildings was attired differently in the preprint era. Prior to the sixteenth century, most statues of Justice did not include a blindfold, and "hundreds of images—statues, illustrated manuscripts, paintings—depicted Justice with eyes open."[6] This was a period, of course, when the law itself placed less emphasis on organizing and controlling information. By affecting the acquisition and use of information, print, in my view, has contributed to the legal blindfold and to the modern shape and form of the law. The development of new forms of communication in our era, therefore, places the goals, processes, institutions, concepts, and values of the law—its symbolic and real, its visible and invisible components—in a precarious position. As the traditional icon has its blindfold loosened and lifted, and as it then becomes freed to confront new sights (and sounds), all that is symbolized by a once-familiar figure of Justice will, ineluctably, be refashioned as well.

Notes

INTRODUCTION

1. Richard L. Abel, *The Politics of Informal Justice* (New York: Academic Press, 1982), p. 1.

2. Harold Berman, *Law and Revolution* (Cambridge, Mass.: Harvard University Press, 1983), p. 39.

3. Marshall McLuhan, *Understanding Media* (New York: McGraw-Hill, 1964), p. 161.

4. George Gerbner, "Trial by Television: Are We at the Point of No Return?" 63 *Judicature* 416, 418 (1980).

5. The power of stock exchanges to control trading is itself threatened by new technologies. See Adrian Hamilton, *The Financial Revolution* (New York: Free Press, 1986), pp. 42–49; see also Shoshana Zuboff, *In the Age of the Smart Machine* (New York: Basic Books, 1988).

6. Norbert Wiener, *The Human Use of Human Beings* (Boston: Houghton Mifflin, 1950), p. 143.

7. Harold Berman, "The Background of the Western Legal Tradition in the Folklaw of the Peoples of Europe," 45 *University of Chicago Law Review* 553, 563 (1978).

8. Marc Galanter, "The Legal Malaise: Or, Justice Observed," 19 *Law and Society Review* 537, 545 (1985).

9. George Bolling, *AT&T: Aftermath of Antitrust* (Washington, D.C.: National Defense University, 1983), p. 3.

10. H. L. A. Hart, *The Concept of Law* (Oxford: Oxford University Press, 1961), p. 121.

11. Iredell Jenkins, *Social Order and the Limits of Law* (Princeton, N.J.: Princeton University Press, 1980), p. 9.

12. Bonnie McDaniel Johnson and Ronald E. Rice, "Reinvention in the Innovation Process: The Case of Word Processing," in *The New Media: Communication, Research, and Technology,* ed. Ronald E. Rice (Beverly Hills, Calif.: Sage, 1984), p. 158.

13. William Seagle, *Law: The Science of Inefficiency* (New York: Macmillan, 1952). See also Samuel Gross, "The American Advantage: The Value of Inefficient Litigation," 85 *Michigan Law Review* 734 (1987).

14. This analogy is borrowed from Tony Schwartz, *The Responsive Chord* (Garden City, N.Y.: Doubleday [Anchor Press], 1974), 2.

15. Ethan Katsh, "The Supreme Court Beat: How Television Covers the U.S.

Supreme Court," 67 *Judicature* 6 (1983); Ethan Katsh and Stephen Arons, "How TV Cops Flout the Law," *Saturday Review,* March 19, 1977, pp. 11–18.

16. Quoted in David Riesman, *The Oral Tradition, the Written Word and the Screen Image* (Yellow Springs, Ohio: Antioch College, 1956), pp. 12–13.

17. McLuhan, *Understanding Media,* p. 23.

18. See particularly the writings of classicist Eric Havelock, *Preface to Plato* (Cambridge, Mass.: Harvard University Press, 1963) and *The Greek Concept of Justice* (Cambridge, Mass.: Harvard University Press, 1978); anthropologist Jack Goody, *Literacy in Traditional Societies* (New York: Cambridge University Press, 1968) and *The Logic of Writing and the Organization of Society* (Cambridge: Cambridge University Press, 1986); historian Elizabeth Eisenstein, *The Printing Press as an Agent of Change* (New York: Cambridge University Press, 1979); political scientist Ithiel de Sola Pool, *Technologies of Freedom* (Cambridge, Mass.: Harvard University Press, 1983); communications theorist Joshua Meyrowitz, *No Sense of Place* (New York: Oxford University Press, 1985); sociologist James Beniger, *The Control Revolution* (Cambridge, Mass.: Harvard University Press, 1986); and Walter Ong, *Interfaces of the Word: Studies in the Evolution of Consciousness and Culture* (Ithaca, N.Y.: Cornell University Press, 1977) and *Orality and Literacy* (London: Methuen, 1982).

19. Berman, *Law and Revolution,* p. 11.

20. Frederick Pollock and Frederick William Maitland, *The History of English Law Before the Time of Edward I,* 2nd ed. (Cambridge: Cambridge University Press, 1968), vol. 1, p. 25.

21. Oliver Wendell Holmes, *The Common Law* (Boston: Little, Brown, 1881), p. 5.

22. John F. A. Taylor, *The Masks of Society* (New York: Appleton-Century-Crofts, 1966), p. 4; see also Plutarch, *Lycurgus* 13.

23. Plato, *Phaedrus,* trans. R. Hackforth (Cambridge, Mass.: Harvard University Press, 1952), pp. 274–275.

CHAPTER 1

1. Oliver Wendell Holmes, *Speeches* (Boston: Little, Brown, 1934), p. 102.

2. *Burnett* v. *Coronado Oil and Gas Co.,* 285 U.S. 393 (1932).

3. Ellis Lewis, "The History of Judicial Precedent," 47 *Law Quarterly Review* 421 (1931).

4. C. K. Allen, *Law in the Making* (Oxford: Oxford University Press, 1964), p. 346.

5. William Seagle, *Law: The Science of Inefficiency* (New York: Macmillan, 1952), pp. 11–15.

6. Lon Fuller, *The Morality of Law* (New Haven, Conn.: Yale University Press, 1964), p. 39.

7. Ibid., pp. 33–34.

8. Ibid., p. 37.

9. Harold Berman and William Greiner, *The Nature and Functions of Law,* 4th ed. (Mineola, N.Y.: Foundation Press, 1980), p. 476.

10. Samuel Mermin, *Law and the Legal System* (Boston: Little, Brown, 1973), p. 5.

11. E. Adamson Hoebel, *The Law of Primitive Man* (New York: Atheneum, 1968), p. 275.

12. Eric Havelock, *Preface to Plato* (Cambridge, Mass.: Harvard University Press, 1963); Jonathan Spence, *The Memory Palace of Matteo Ricci* (New York: Viking, 1984); Frances Yates, *The Art of Memory* (London: Routledge and Kegan Paul, 1966).

13. See Chapter 4; see also Ithiel de Sola Pool, *Technologies of Freedom* (Cambridge, Mass.: Harvard University Press, 1983), p. 214; U.S. Congress, Office of Technology Assessment, *Intellectual Property Rights in an Age of Electronics and Information* (Washington, D.C.: Government Printing Office, 1986).

14. W. Warren Wagar, "Definitions and Origins," in *The Idea of Progress Since the Renaissance,* ed. W. Warren Wagar (New York: Wiley, 1969), p. 25.

15. Ecclesiastes 1:9.

16. Carl Becker, "Definitions and Origins," in *The Idea of Progress Since the Renaissance,* ed. W. Warren Wagar (New York: Wiley, 1969), p. 11.

17. Ruth Benedict, "The Growth of Culture," in *Man, Culture and Society,* ed. Harry Shapiro (New York: Oxford University Press, 1956), pp. 184–185.

18. Christopher R. Hallpike, *The Foundations of Primitive Thought* (New York: Oxford University Press, 1979), p. 102.

19. Peter Lawrence, *Road Belong Cargo* (Melbourne: Melbourne University Press, 1964), p. 33.

20. Hallpike, *Foundations of Primitive Thought,* p. 101.

21. Thomas Gladwin, *East Is a Big Bird: Navigation and Logic on Puluwat Atoll* (Cambridge, Mass.: Harvard University Press, 1970), p. 220.

22. John Gay and Michael Cole, *The New Mathematics and an Old Culture: A Study of Learning Among the Kpelle of Liberia* (New York: Holt, Rinehart and Winston, 1967), p. 22.

23. Havelock, *Preface to Plato,* p. 41.

24. Ibid., p. 29.

25. Ibid., pp. 29–30.

26. Eric Havelock, *The Greek Concept of Justice* (Cambridge, Mass.: Harvard University Press, 1978), p. 27.

27. See Chapter 2.

28. Robert M. Cover, "Roman Law," *Yale Law Report* (Fall 1986): 6.

29. Jack Goody and Ian Watt, "The Consequences of Literacy," in *Literacy in Traditional Societies,* ed. Jack Goody (New York: Cambridge University Press, 1968), p. 56.

30. "Ye shall not add unto the word which I command you, neither shall ye diminish from it" (Deuteronomy 4:2). A similar injunction can be found in Justinian's Code.

31. Jack Goody and Ian Watt, "The Consequences of Literacy," in *Literacy in Traditional Societies,* ed. Jack Goody (New York: Cambridge University Press, 1968).

32. Harold Innis, *The Bias of Communication* (Toronto: University of Toronto Press, 1951), p. 7.

272   NOTES

33. Elizabeth Eisenstein, *The Printing Press as an Agent for Change* (New York: Cambridge University Press, 1979), p. 109.

34. M. T. Clanchy, *From Memory to Written Record* (Cambridge, Mass.: Harvard University Press, 1979), pp. 21–22; Wendy Davies and Paul Fouracre, eds., *The Settlement of Disputes in Early Medieval Europe* (Cambridge: Cambridge University Press, 1986), p. 75.

35. Harold Berman, *Law and Revolution* (Cambridge, Mass.: Harvard University Press, 1983), pp. 121–122.

36. Geza Vermes, "Scripture and Tradition in Judaism: Written and Oral Torah," in *The Written Word: Literacy in Transition*, ed. Gerd Baumann (Oxford: Clarendon Press, 1986), pp. 84–87.

37. Margaret Aston, *The Fifteenth Century* (London: Thames & Hudson, 1968), p. 46.

38. Eduard Dijksterhuis, *The Mechanization of the World Picture* (Oxford: Oxford University Press, 1961), p. 167.

39. Barry Holtz, ed., *Back to the Sources: Reading the Classic Jewish Texts* (New York: Simon and Schuster, 1984).

40. Ibid., pp. 14–15.

41. Gershom Scholem, *The Messianic Idea in Judaism* (New York: Schocken, 1971), pp. 282–304.

42. Holtz, *Back to the Sources*, pp. 18–19.

43. Berman, *Law and Revolution*.

44. Ibid., pp. 121–123.

45. John P. Dawson, *The Oracles of the Law* (Ann Arbor: University of Michigan Press, 1968), p. 115.

46. Lloyd Fallers, *Law Without Precedent* (Chicago: University of Chicago Press, 1969), p. 312.

47. J. H. Baker, ed., *The Legal Profession and the Common Law: Historical Essays* (London: Hambledon Press, 1986), p. 473.

48. "Prologue," *The Canterbury Tales*, in *The Complete Poetical Works of Geoffrey Chaucer*, ed. John Tatlock and Percy MacKaye (New York: Macmillan, 1940).

49. George Sarton, *Six Wings* (Bloomington: Indiana University Press, 1957), p. 116.

50. Eisenstein, *Printing Press as an Agent for Change*, p. 109.

51. Ibid., p. 108.

52. Ibid., p. 703.

53. de Sola Pool, *Technologies of Freedom*, p. 213.

54. John Carter and Percival Muir, eds., *Printing and the Mind of Man* (London: Cassell, 1967).

55. Thomas Jefferson to George Whythe, January 16, 1796, quoted in Julian Boyd, "These Precious Monuments of . . . Our History", 22 *The American Archivist* 175–176 (1959). See also Sylvio Bedini, *Thomas Jefferson and His Copying Machines* (Charlottesville: University of Virginia Press, 1984).

56. Quoted in James Cochrane, *Dr. Johnson's Printer: The Life of William Strahan* (Cambridge, Mass.: Harvard University Press, 1964), p. 19, n. 2.

57. Eisenstein, *Printing Press as an Agent for Change*, pp. 109–110.

58. Arthur Goodhart, "Precedent in English and Common Law," 50 *Law Quarterly Review* 40, 62 (1934).

59. Lief Carter, *Reason in Law,* 2nd ed. (Boston: Little, Brown, 1984), p. 32.

60. Walter J. Ong, *Orality and Literacy: The Technologizing of the Word* (London: Methuen, 1982), p. 126.

61. Ellis Lewis, "The History of Judicial Precedent," 46 *Law Quarterly Review* 421 (1930); Allen, *Law in the Making,* p. 190; T. F. T. Plucknett, *A Concise History of the Common Law* (Boston: Little, Brown, 1956), p. 345.

62. Plucknett, *Concise History of the Common Law,* p. 347.

63. Allen, *Law in the Making,* p. 202.

64. Clanchy, *From Memory to Written Record,* p. 234.

65. Arthur Hogue, *Origins of the Common Law* (Bloomington: Indiana University Press, 1966), p. 191.

66. Quoted in Plucknett, *Concise History of the Common Law,* p. 343.

67. Lewis, "History of Judicial Precedent," 46 *Law Quarterly Review* 212.

68. Percy H. Winfield, *The Chief Sources of English Legal History* (Cambridge, Mass.: Harvard University Press, 1925), p. 147.

69. Lewis, "History of Judicial Precedent," 46 *Law Quarterly Review* 212.

70. Allen, *Law in the Making,* p. 201.

71. Lewis, "History of Judicial Precedent," 46 *Law Quarterly Review* 215.

72. Allen, *Law in the Making,* p. 201.

73. Plucknett, *Concise History of the Common Law,* p. 343.

74. Ibid., p. 347.

75. Ibid., p. 260.

76. Fallers, *Law Without Precedent,* p. 314.

77. Ibid., p. 273; Winfield, *Chief Sources of English Legal History,* p. 156.

78. Plucknett, *Concise History of the Common Law,* p. 270; William Holdsworth, "The Year Books," in Association of American Law Schools, *Select Essays in Anglo-American Legal History* (Boston: Little, Brown, 1908), vol. 2, pp. 96–122.

79. Plucknett, *Concise History of the Common Law,* p. 270.

80. Ellis Lewis, "The History of Judicial Precedent," 48 *Law Quarterly Review* 414 (1932).

81. Winfield, *Chief Sources of English Legal History,* p. 150.

82. A. W. B. Simpson, "The Source and Function of the Later Year Books," 87 *Law Quarterly Review* 94, 97 (1971).

83. Howard Graham, "Our Tong Maternall Marvelously Amendyd and Augmentyd: The First Englishing and Printing of the Medieval Statutes at Large, 1530–1533," 13 *U.C.L.A. Law Review* 58 (1965).

84. Winfield, *Chief Sources of English Legal History,* p. 156.

85. Ibid.

86. William Markby, "Elements of Law," in *Readings on the History and System of the Common Law,* ed. R. Pound and T. F. T. Plunknett (Rochester, N.Y.: Lawyers Cooperative, 1927), p. 125.

87. *Entick* v. *Carrington,* 10 St. Tr. 1030 (1765), cited in Peter Goodrich, *Reading the Law* (Oxford: Blackwell, 1986), p. 130.

88. *The Sovereignty of the Law: Selections from Blackstone's Commentaries,* ed. Gareth Jones (Toronto: University of Toronto Press, 1973), p. 51.

89. Quoted in William Holdsworth, *Some Lessons from Our Legal History* (New York: Macmillan, 1928), p. 18.

90. Jerome Frank, *Law and the Modern Mind* (Garden City, N.Y.: Doubleday, 1963), pp. 3–13.

91. "The great modern increase in the supply and the demand for news began in the early nineteenth century. Until then newspapers tended to fill out their columns with lackadaisical secondhand accounts or stale reprints of items first published elsewhere at home and abroad. The laws of plagiarism and of copyright were undeveloped. Most newspapers were little more than excuses for espousing a political position, for listing the arrival and departure of ships, for familiar essays and useful advice, or for commercial or legal announcements.

"Less than a century and a half ago did newspapers begin to disseminate up-to-date reports of matters of public interest written by eyewitnesses or professional reporters near the scene . . . " (Daniel Boorstin, *The Image* [New York: Harper & Row, 1964], p. 12).

92. Quentin Fiore, "The Future of the Book," in *The Future of Time,* ed. H. Yaker, H. Osmond, and F. Cheek (Garden City, N.Y.: Doubleday, 1971), pp. 479–497.

93. *Brown* v. *Board of Education,* 349 U.S. Reports 294, 301 (1954).

94. E. W. Ives, "The Origins of the Later Year Books," in *Legal History Studies, 1972,* ed. Dafydd Jenkins (Cardiff: University of Wales Press, 1975), pp. 138–141.

95. *The Collected Papers of Frederic William Maitland,* ed. H. A. L. Fisher (Cambridge: Cambridge University Press, 1911).

96. Seagle, *Law: The Science of Inefficiency.*

97. Symposium, "Law Libraries and Miniaturization," 66 *Law Library Journal* 395 (1973).

98. Jeffrey Pemberton, "The Linear File," *Database,* December 1986, p. 6.

99. Holdsworth, *Some Lessons from Our Legal History,* p. 19; see also Ronald Heiner, "Imperfect Decisions and the Law: On the Evolution of Legal Precedent and Rules," 15 *Journal of Legal Studies* 227 (1986).

100. Grant Gilmore, "Legal Realism: Its Cause and Cure," 70 *Yale Law Journal* 1037, 1041 (1961).

101. Thomas Young, "A Look at American Law Reporting in the 19th Century," 68 *Law Library Journal* 294, 304 (1975).

102. James High, "What Shall Be Done with the Reports?" 16 *American Law Review* 429, 434–435 (1882).

103. Some courts have responded to the problem by limiting the number of opinions that are published. See Robert S. Gerstein, " 'Law by Elimination': Depublication in the California Supreme Court," 67 *Judicature* 293 (1984).

104. Holdsworth, *Some Lessons from Our Legal History,* p. 22.

105. Karl Llewellyn, *The Bramble Bush* (Dobbs Ferry, N.Y.: Oceana Publications, 1960), p. 68.

106. Samuel Thorne, *Sir Edward Coke* (London: Selden Society, 1957).

107. Mirjan Damaska, "Structures of Authority and Comparative Criminal Procedure," 84 *Yale Law Journal* 480, 528 (1975).

108. Geoffrey Radcliffe, *Not in Feather Beds* (London: Harnish Hamilton, 1968), p. 216.

109. Craig Bradley, "The Uncertainty Principle in the Supreme Court," 1986 *Duke Law Journal* 1, 2 (1986).

110. See Milner Ball, "The Play's the Thing," 28 *Stanford Law Review* 81 (1975); see also Chapter 2, pp. 95–102.

CHAPTER 2

1. Laura Nader and Harry F. Todd, Jr., eds., *The Disputing Process: Law in Ten Societies* (New York: Columbia University Press, 1978), p. 1.

2. E. Adamson Hoebel, *The Law of Primitive Man* (New York: Atheneum, 1954), p. 329.

3. Karl Llewellyn, *The Bramble Bush* (Dobbs Ferry, N.Y.: Oceana Publications, 1960), p. 2.

4. Roscoe Pound, *An Introduction to the Philosophy of Law* (New Haven, Conn.: Yale University Press, 1954), p. 33.

5. Alan Watson, *The Nature of Law* (Edinburgh: Edinburgh University Press, 1977), p. 1.

6. Ibid., p. 43.

7. Robert Bolt, *A Man for All Seasons* (New York: Random House, 1960), p. 38.

8. *The American Heritage Dictionary of the English Language* (Boston: Houghton Mifflin, 1969).

9. Victor Li, *Law Without Lawyers* (Stanford, Calif.: Stanford Alumni Association, 1977), p. 25.

10. See, for example, William Golding, *Lord of the Flies* (New York: Coward McCann, 1962).

11. Thomas Hobbes, *The Leviathan,* ed. M. Oakeshott (New York: Macmillan, 1967), p. 100.

12. Henry Maine, *International Law* (New York, Holt, 1888), p. 8.

13. Paul Bohannon, *Law and Warfare: Studies in the Anthropology of Conflict* (Garden City, N.Y.: Natural History Press, 1967); Jean Buxton, "The Mandari of the Southern Sudan," in *Tribes Without Rulers,* ed. John Middleton and David Tait (London: Routledge and Kegan Paul, 1958), p. 88; Edward Winter, "The Aboriginal Political Structure of Bwamba," in ibid., p. 146.

14. Pascual Gisbert, *Preliterate Man* (Bombay: Manaktalas, 1967), p. x.

15. L. T. Hobhouse, *Social Development* (New York: Holt, 1924).

16. E. B. Tylor, *Anthropology* (London, 1946), vol. 2, p. 212.

17. Proverbs, 18:21.

18. Lloyd Fallers, *Law Without Precedent* (Chicago: University of Chicago Press, 1969).

19. David Tait, "The Territorial Pattern and Lineage System of Konkomba," in *Tribes Without Rulers,* ed. John Middleton and David Tait (London: Routledge and Kegan Paul, 1958), p. 187.

20. Robert Redfield, *The Primitive World and Its Transformations* (Ithaca, N.Y.: Cornell University Press, 1953), p. 13.

21. William Seagle, *The History of Law* (New York: Tudor, 1946), p. 33.

22. William Seagle, *Men of Law* (New York: Macmillan, 1947), pp. 3–4.

23. Paul Bohannon, "The Differing Realms of Law," 67 *American Anthropologist* 33, 36 (1965).

24. Stanley Diamond, "The Rule of Law versus the Order of Custom," in *The Rule of Law*, ed. Robert Paul Wolff (New York: Simon and Schuster, 1971), p. 120.

25. Leopold Pospisil, *Anthropology of Law* (New York: Harper & Row, 1971), p. 96.

26. Simon Roberts, *Order and Dispute* (New York: St. Martin's Press, 1979), p. 60.

27. Max Gluckman, "Gossip and Scandal," 4 *Current Anthropology* 307–316 (1963); Patricia Meyer Spacks, *Gossip* (Chicago: University of Chicago, 1985); Sissela Bok, *Secrets* (New York: Pantheon Books, 1982), pp. 89–101.

28. See Max Gluckman, *Politics, Law and Ritual in Tribal Society* (Oxford: Blackwell, 1971), p. 194.

29. Geer Van den Steenhoven, *Leadership and Law Among the Eskimos of the Keewatin District, Northwest Territory* (Rijswijk: Excelsior, 1962).

30. Roberts, *Order and Dispute*, p. 67.

31. Winter, "Aboriginal Political Structure of Bwamba," pp. 145–146.

32. Colin Turnbull, *The Forest People* (New York: Simon and Schuster, 1961), pp. 118–119.

33. Ibid., pp. 119–120.

34. American Bar Association, *Dispute Resolution Program Directory* (Washington, D.C.: American Bar Association, 1985).

35. P. H. Gulliver, *Social Control in an African Society* (Boston: Boston University Press, 1963), p. 299.

36. Lon Fuller, "Human Interaction and the Law," in *The Rule of Law*, ed. Robert Paul Wolff (New York: Simon and Schuster, 1971), p. 177.

37. Jack Goody, "Alternative Paths to Knowledge in Oral and Literate Cultures," in *Speech and Written Language: Exploring Orality and Literacy*, ed. Deborah Tannen (Norwood, N.J.: Ablex, 1982), p. 202.

38. Mary Douglas, *Purity and Danger* (London: Routledge and Kegan Paul, 1966), p. 86.

39. J. David Bolter, *Turing's Man* (Chapel Hill: University of North Carolina Press, 1984), pp. 134–135.

40. Clifford Geertz, "Deep Play: Notes on the Balinese Cockfight," 101 *Daedalus* 26 (1972).

41. Sherry Ortner, *Sherpas through Their Rituals* (New York: Cambridge University Press, 1978), pp. 6–9.

42. Hoebel, *Law of Primitive Man*, p. 261.

43. Ibid., p. 274.

44. "In old times proof was not an attempt to convince the judges; it was an appeal to the supernatural, and very commonly a unilateral act. The common modes of proof are oaths and ordeals . . . They have not come there to convince the court, they have not come there to be examined and cross-examined like modern witnesses, they have come there to bring upon themselves the wrath of God if what they say be not true" (F. W. Maitland, *The Forms of Action at Common Law* [Cambridge: Cambridge University Press, 1909], p. 15).

45. Susan Reynolds, "Law and Communities in Western Christendom," 25

American Journal of Legal History 205, 215 (1981); see also Robert Bartlett, *Trial by Fire and Water: The Medieval Judicial Ordeal* (Oxford: Oxford University Press, 1986).

46. Paul Hyams, "Trial by Ordeal: The Key to Proof in the Early Common Law," in *On the Laws and Customs of England: Essays in Honor of Samuel E. Thorne*, ed. Morris Arnold, Thomas Green, Sally Scully, and Stephen White (Chapel Hill: University of North Carolina Press, 1981), p. 97.

47. Hoebel, *Law of Primitive Man*, p. 99.

48. Quoted in Diamond, "Rule of Law Versus the Order of Custom," p. 120.

49. Peter Goodrich, *Reading the Law* (Oxford: Blackwell, 1986), p. 62.

50. Susan Reynolds, *Kingdoms and Communities in Western Europe, 900–1300* (Oxford: Oxford University Press, 1984), p. 36.

51. Seagle, *Men of Law*, p. 12. The importance of writing to law is similarly stressed in Goodrich, *Reading the Law*. Goodrich writes, for example, that "the law comes from books and it is the books of law that guarantee it permanence. ... The conjunction of writing and law is intrinsic to the foundational value of western legal order" (p. 218).

52. Julian Jaynes, *The Origins of Consciousness in the Breakdown of the Bicameral Mind* (Boston: Houghton Mifflin, 1976), p. 198.

53. A. S. Diamond, *Primitive Law, Past and Present* (London: Methuen, 1971), p. 177.

54. Claude Lévi-Strauss, *Tristes Tropiques* (London: Cape, 1973), p. 299.

55. Sally Falk Moore, *Power and Property in Inca Peru* (New York: Columbia University Press, 1958).

56. Godfrey Lienhardt, "The Western Dinka," in *Tribes Without Rulers*, ed. John Middleton and David Tait (London: Routledge and Kegan Paul, 1958), p. 114; Redfield, *Primitive World and Its Transformations*, p. 55.

57. John Gay and Michael Cole, *The New Mathematics and an Old Culture: A Study of Learning Among the Kpelle of Liberia* (New York: Holt, Rinehart and Winston, 1967), p. 14.

58. Barrington Moore, *Privacy: Studies in Social and Cultural History* (London: Sharpe, 1984), p. 9.

59. Jack Goody, "Literacy and the Non-Literate," *Times Literary Supplement* (London), May 12, 1972, pp. 539–540.

60. Elizabeth Eisenstein, *The Printing Press as an Agent of Change* (New York: Cambridge University Press, 1979), p. 313.

61. See Chapter 3.

62. John H. Kautsky, *The Politics of Aristocratic Empires* (Chapel Hill: University of North Carolina Press, 1982), p. 122.

63. H. F. Jolowicz, *Roman Foundations of Modern Law* (Oxford: Oxford University Press, 1957), p. 38.

64. Kautsky, *Politics of Aristocratic Empires*, p. 123.

65. Solomon Gandz, "Oral Tradition in the Bible," in *Jewish Studies in Memory of George A. Kohut*, ed. S. Baron and A. Marx (New York: Alexander Kohut Memorial Foundation, 1935), p. 256.

66. W. Simpson and J. Stone, *Law and Society in Evolution* (St. Paul, Minn: West, 1942), p. 2.

67. W. Michael Reisman, *Folded Lies* (New York: Free Press, 1979), p. 17.

68. Reynolds, "Law and Communities in Western Christendom," p. 224.

69. J. M. Kelly, *Studies in the Civil Judicature of the Roman Republic* (Oxford: Oxford University Press, 1976), p. 97.

70. Gandz, "Oral Tradition in the Bible," p. 248; an interesting historical review of the uses of writing is contained in Jack Goody, *The Interface Between the Written and the Oral* (Cambridge: Cambridge University Press, 1987), pp. 3–56.

71. Fritz Kern, *Kingship and Law in the Middle Ages* (Oxford: Blackwell, 1948), pp. 158–159.

72. For further clarification of these semantic problems, see John P. Dawson, *The Oracles of the Law* (Ann Arbor: University of Michigan Press, 1968), pp. 128–134; Harold D. Hazeltine, "General Preface" to Theodore F. T. Plucknett, *Statutes and Their Interpretation in the First Half of the Fourteenth Century* (Cambridge: Cambridge University Press, 1922).

73. Jolowicz, *Roman Foundations of Modern Law.*

74. Gandz, "Oral Tradition in the Bible," pp. 260–261. Similar attitudes were apparently present in ancient Greece; see Eric Havelock, *Preface to Plato* (Cambridge, Mass.: Harvard University Press, 1963), p. 55, n. 15.

75. Laura Nader, "The Anthropological Study of Law," 6 *American Anthropologist* 3, 18 (1965).

76. Eric Havelock, *The Liberal Temper in Greek Politics* (New Haven, Conn.: Yale University Press, 1957), p. 139.

77. A. K. R. Kiralfy, *Potter's Historical Introduction to English Law and Its Institutions* (London: Sweet & Maxwell, 1958), p. 313.

78. Ibid., p. 19.

79. M. T. Clanchy, *From Memory to Written Record* (Cambridge, Mass.: Harvard University Press: 1979), p. 29.

80. Ibid., p. 11.

81. Ibid., p. 19.

82. Ibid., p. 20.

83. Helen Cam, "An East Anglican Shire-Moot of Stephen's Reign," 34 *English Historical Review* 570 (1924).

84. Clanchy, *From Memory to Written Record,* p. 210.

85. Ibid., p. 32.

86. Ibid., p. 20.

87. Reynolds, "Law and Communities in Western Christendom," p. 207.

88. Ibid., p. 208.

89. Brian Stock, *The Implications of Literacy* (Princeton, N.J.: Princeton University Press, 1983), p. 58.

90. Reynolds, "Law and Communities in Western Christendom," p. 223.

91. William Stubbs, *Lectures on Medieval and Modern History* (Oxford: Oxford University Press, 1886), p. 119.

92. Clanchy, *From Memory to Written Record,* pp. 41–44.

93. William Holdsworth, *Some Makers of English Law* (Cambridge: Cambridge University Press, 1938), p. 11.

94. Harold Berman, *Law and Revolution* (Cambridge, Mass.: Harvard University Press, 1983), p. 451.

95. J. H. Baker, *An Introduction to English Legal History* (London: Butterworth, 1971), p. 9.

96. Dawson, *Oracles of the Law*, pp. 3–4.

97. Ralph Turner, *The English Judiciary in the Age of Glanvill and Bracton, c. 1176–1239* (Cambridge: Cambridge University Press, 1985), p. 34.

98. Ibid., p. 152.

99. Ibid., p. 39.

100. Clanchy, *From Memory to Written Record*, p. 221.

101. Paul Hyams, "Trial by Ordeal," p. 96.

102. William Holdsworth, *A History of English Law* (London: Methuen, 1966), vol. 3, p. 635.

103. George Adams, *Council and Courts in Anglo-Norman England* (New York: Russell & Russell, 1965), p. 139.

104. Ibid., p. 131–132.

105. Plucknett, *Statutes and Their Interpretation in the First Half of the Fourteenth Century*, p. 22.

106. Ibid., p. 1.

107. Ibid., p. 25.

108. Ibid., p. 104.

109. Ibid., p. 104.

110. Ibid., p. 68.

111. Ibid., p. 131.

112. William Holdsworth, *Sources and Literature of English Law* (Oxford: Oxford University Press, 1925), p. 41.

113. Ibid., p. 49.

114. Ibid., p. 22.

115. Hazeltine, "General Preface" to Plucknett, *Statutes and Their Interpretation in the First Half of the Fourteenth Century*, p. xvii.

116. Plucknett, *Statutes and Their Interpretation in the First Half of the Fourteenth Century*, p. 56.

117. Theodore F. T. Plucknett, *A Concise History of the Common Law* (Boston: Little, Brown, 1956), p. 338.

118. Plucknett, *Statutes and Their Interpretation in the First Half of the Fourteenth Century*, p. 103.

119. Helen Cam, *Law-Finders and Law-Makers in Medieval England* (London: Merlin Press, 1962), p. 14.

120. John Dawson, *A History of Lay Judges* (Cambridge, Mass.: Harvard University Press, 1960).

121. "It is a textbook commonplace that one of the most significant features of English legal history was the early establishment of the supremacy of the royal courts in London (for example, King's Bench, Common Pleas, Chancery, Star Chamber) over rival seignorial and local jurisdictions, but this generalisation must be kept in perspective. As late as 1628, Sir Edward Coke wrote that 'there be divers law within the realm of England', and then went on to list sixteen different varieties, only one of which he called the common law. This diversity of law was administered by an extremely large number of courts. In addition to the various royal jurisdictions, there were, among others, quarter sessions, county courts,

borough courts, manorial courts, stannary courts, pyepowder courts, and last, but hardly least, ecclesiastical courts. Some of these, especially the county and hundred courts, had already declined in importance by the time Elizabeth came to the throne, but others, most notably the courts associated with the manors (courts leet and baron) and the borough courts, were still vital institutions in most local communities" (C. W. Brooks, "Common Lawyers in England, c. 1558–1642," in *Lawyers in Early Modern Europe and America*, ed. W. R. Prest [New York: Holmes and Meier, 1981], p. 42).

122. Ralph Houlbrooke, *Church Courts and the People During the English Reformation* (Oxford: Oxford University Press, 1979); Paul Hair, ed., *Before the Bawdy Court: Selections from Church Court and Other Records Relating to the Correction of Moral Offences in England, Scotland and New England, 1300–1800* (New York: Barnes & Noble, 1972).

123. John A. F. Thomson, *The Transformation of Medieval England, 1370–1529* (London: Longman, 1983), p. 296.

124. Cam, *Law-Finders and Law-Makers in Medieval England*, p. 93.

125. Baker, *Introduction to English Legal History*, p. 15.

126. Hair, *Before the Bawdy Court*, p. 28.

127. G. R. Elton, *England, 1200–1640* (Ithaca, N.Y.: Cornell University Press, 1969), p. 57.

128. DeLloyd J. Guth, "Enforcing Late-Medieval Law: Patterns in Litigation During Henry VII's Reign," in *Legal Records and the Historian*, ed. J. H. Baker (London: Royal Historical Society, 1978), p. 80.

129. Ibid., p. 91.

130. Ibid., p. 94.

131. *Miller* v. *Cotton*, 5 Ga. 341, 349 (1848).

132. Roberto Unger, *Law in Modern Society* (New York: Free Press, 1978), p. 53.

133. Gerald Strauss, *Law, Resistance and the State: The Opposition to Roman Law in Reformation Germany* (Princeton, N.J.: Princeton University Press, 1986).

134. Holdsworth, *History of English Law*, vol. 4, p. 186.

135. Otto Brunner, *Land und Herrschaft. Grundfragen der terrritorialen Verfassungsgeschichte Osterreichs im Mittelalter*, 5th ed. (Vienna, 1965), p. 155, quoted in Strauss, *Law, Resistance and the State*, p. 40.

136. Howard Nenner, *By Colour of Law* (Chicago: University of Chicago Press, 1977), p. 15.

137. Holdsworth, *History of English Law*, vol. 4, p. 187.

138. Walter J. Ong, *Rhetoric, Romance, and Technology* (Ithaca, N.Y.: Cornell University Press, 1971), p. 3.

139. Stock, *Implications of Literacy*, p. 9.

140. Clanchy, *From Memory to Written Record*, p. 218.

141. Joshua 1:8.

142. Clanchy, *From Memory to Written Record*, p. 226.

143. H. J. Chaytor, *From Script to Print* (London: Sidgwick & Jackson, 1966), p. 4; Jack Goody has argued that writing involves changing "the channel of communicated language from an auditory to a visual one. You hear speech and see

writing; speaking with mouth, listening with ear; writing with hand, reading with eyes. To channel mouth-to-ear is added the channel hand-to-eye" (*Interface Between the Written and the Oral*, p. 186).

144. Plucknett, *Statutes and Their Interpretation in the First Half of the Fourteenth Century*, p. 165.

145. Howard Graham, "Our Tong Maternall Marvelously Amendyd and Augmentyd: The First Englishing and Printing of the Medieval Statutes at Large, 1530–1533," 13 *U.C.L.A. Law Review* 58 (1965).

146. Ibid., p. 77; H. S. Bennett, *English Books and Readers, 1475–1557* (Cambridge: Cambridge University Press, 1952), p. 79.

147. L. W. Abbott, *Law Reporting in England, 1485–1585* (London: Athlone Press, 1973), p. 229.

148. Graham, "Our Tong Maternall Marvelously Amendyd and Augmentyd," p. 71.

149. D. E. C. Yale, " 'Of No Mean Authority': Some Later Uses of Bracton," in *On the Laws and Customs of England: Essays in Honor of Samuel E. Thorne*, ed. Morris Arnold, Thomas Green, Sally Scully, and Stephen White (Chapel Hill: University of North Carolina Press, 1981), p. 388.

150. H. S. Bennett, *English Books and Readers, 1603 to 1640* (Cambridge: Cambridge University Press, 1970), p. 119.

151. Plucknett, *Concise History of the Common Law*, p. 381.

152. Abbott, *Law Reporting in England*, p. 227.

153. Berman, *Law and Revolution*, p. 77.

154. Eisenstein, *Printing Press as an Agent of Change*.

155. Ibid., p. 105.

156. Ibid., pp. 105–106.

157. C. P. Rodgers, "Humanism, History and the Common Law," 6 *Journal of Legal History* 129 (1985).

158. "It took the entire first century of printing to generate a truly satisfactory printed edition of the *Corpus iuris civilis* (Torelli, 1553) and the *Corpus iuris canonici* (Dionysius Gothefredus, 1583), so that the first generations to use printed legal texts had to use editions that were not intrinsically superior to any good manuscript except in price. Academic law was thus in the comically embarrassing position of a discipline proclaiming its devotion to a text that was simply not available in unassailable form. The discomfort was made even more exquisite by the fact that the jurists knew their foundation texts were faulty and believed they knew precisely where the remedy lay: in a locked shrine in Florence, where the *Urtext* of all European exemplars of the *Digest* could be found" (Steven Rowan, "Jurists and the Printing Press in Germany: The First Century," in *Print and Culture in the Renaissance*, ed. Gerald Tyson and Sylvia Wagonheim [Newark: University of Delaware Press, 1986], p. 76).

159. Frederic W. Maitland and Francis C. Montague, *A Sketch of English Legal History* (New York: Putnam, 1915), p. 109.

160. Holdsworth, *Sources and Literature of English Law*, p. 31.

161. Plucknett, *Concise History of the Common Law*, p. 234.

162. Samuel Thorne, ed., *On the Laws and Customs of England* (Cambridge, Mass.: Harvard University Press, 1964), p. 1.

282   NOTES

163. C. W. Brooks, "Litigants and Attorneys in the King's Bench and Common Pleas, 1560–1640," in *Legal Records and the Historian*, ed. J. H. Baker (London: Royal Historical Society, 1978), p. 45.

164. J. H. Baker, ed., *The Legal Profession and the Common Law: Historical Essays* (London: Hambledon Press, 1986), p. 473.

165. Brooks, "Litigants and Attorneys in the King's Bench and Common Pleas," p. 41.

166. C. W. Brooks, *Pettyfoggers and Vipers of the Commonwealth* (Cambridge: Cambridge University Press, 1986), p. 51.

167. Graham, "Our Tong Maternall Marvelously Amendyd and Augmentyd," p. 93.

168. W. Barlee, *A Concordance of All Written Lawes Concerning Lords of Mannours, Theire Free Tenentes and Copieholders* (London: Manorial Society, 1911).

169. Richard Solomon, "Computers and the Concept of Intellectual Copyright," in *Electronic Publishing Plus*, ed. Martin Greenberger (White Plains, N.Y.: Knowledge Industry Publications, 1985), p. 238.

170. This process can be seen in television broadcasts as well. The television set, when it "receives a signal," is creating a copy of something that is itself a copy of something that exists somewhere else. This might become clearer if we imagine what happens when one watches a prerecorded videotape that is being played on a videocassette recorder. The signal does not leave the videotape, but a copy of what is on the tape is sent to the television set and processed into a picture. Televisions, unlike VCRs, do not make permanent copies, but the process of "reception" is similar.

171. Solomon, "Computers and the Concept of Intellectual Copyright," pp. 235–236.

172. Alice LaPlante, "Liability in the Information Age," *InfoWorld*, August 18, 1986, p. 37.

173. Ithiel de Sola Pool, *Technologies of Freedom* (Cambridge, Mass.: Harvard University Press, 1983), p. 213.

174. Charles Krauthammer, "The Joy of Analog," *Time*, May 26, 1986, p. 84.

175. "Editor's Note," *New York Times*, August 22, 1986, p. B1.

176. American Express has recently stopped sending signed charge slips to holders of American Express cards along with their bill. Instead, members receive what looks like a reduced copy of the receipt. This copy is created by scanning the actual receipt, putting it into electronic form, and then using a laser printer to make a copy of the form. This is done to allow American Express to reap the benefits of the information on the hundreds of millions of charge slips processed each year and to market new products and services (John Markoff, "American Express Goes High-Tech," *New York Times*, July 31, 1988, sec. 3, p. 1).

177. James Beniger, *The Control Revolution: Technological and Economic Origins of the Information Society* (Cambridge, Mass.: Harvard University Press, 1986), p. 25.

178. Bolter, *Turing's Man*, pp. 162–163.

179. Jack Goody, *The Logic of Writing and the Organization of Society* (Cambridge: Cambridge University Press, 1986), p. 153.

180. Richard Susskind, "Expert Systems in Law and the Data Protection Adviser," 7 *Oxford Journal of Legal Studies* 145 (1987).

181. John Dickinson, "Legal Rules: Their Function in the Process of Decision," 79 *University of Pennsylvania Law Review* 833, 849 (1931).

182. Lynne Henderson, "Legality and Empathy," 85 *Michigan Law Review* 1574 (1987).

183. John Comaroff, "Talking Politics: Oratory and Authority in a Tswana Chiefdom," in *Political Language and Oratory in Traditional Society,* ed. Maurice Bloch (New York: Academic Press, 1975), p. 141.

184. Alexis de Toqueville, *Democracy in America* (New York: Knopf, 1945), p. 280.

185. Vilhelm Aubert, *In Search of Law* (Totowa, N.J.: Barnes & Noble, 1983), pp. 78–79.

186. Ibid.

187. Bruce Ackerman, *Reconstructing American Law* (Cambridge, Mass.: Harvard University Press, 1984), p. 97.

188. Fallers, *Law Without Precedent,* p. 13.

189. Roberts, *Order and Dispute,* pp. 20–21.

190. Nils Christie, "Crime Control as Drama," 13 *Journal of Law and Society* 1, 5 (1986).

191. Edward W. Cleary, "Evidence as a Problem in Communicating," 5 *Vanderbilt Law Review* 277, 282 (1952).

192. Quoted in Dennis Curtis and Judith Resnick, "Images of Justice," 96 *Yale Law Journal* 1727 (1987).

193. Ibid., p. 1728.

194. John Ziman, *Public Knowledge: The Social Dimension of Science* (New York: Cambridge University Press, 1968), p. 47–48.

195. Herbert Simon, "Applying Information Technology to Organization Design," 33 *Public Administration Review* 271 (1973).

196. Beniger, *Control Revolution,* p. 15.

197. Plato, *The Laws,* trans. and ed. Thomas L. Pangle (New York: Basic Books, 1980), 739c.

198. Edmund Carpenter and Marshall McLuhan, *Explorations* (Boston: Beacon Press, 1960), p. xi.

199. Jack Goody and Ian Watt, "The Consequences of Literacy," in *Literacy in Traditional Societies,* ed. Jack Goody (New York: Cambridge University Press, 1968), pp. 59–60.

200. Douglas, *Purity and Danger,* p. 77.

201. Joshua Meyrowitz, *No Sense of Place* (New York: Oxford University Press, 1985), p. 87.

202. Ibid., p. 89.

203. Ibid., p. 92.

204. Ibid., p. 88–89.

205. Vine Deloria, *God Is Red* (New York: Dell, 1973), p. 78.

206. See Chapter 3.

207. John Naisbitt, *Megatrends* (New York: Warner Books, 1982), p. 10.

208. While considerable publicity has been given to the issue of "hyperlexis" or the litigation explosion, the best statistical analysis of the problem casts doubt upon

its existence. See Marc Galanter, "Reading the Landscape of Disputes: What We Know and Don't Know (and Think We Know) About Our Allegedly Contentious and Litigious Society," 31 *U.C.L.A. Law Review* 4 (1983).

209. Franz Kafka, *Parables and Paradoxes* (New York: Schocken, 1961), p. 61.

210. Janice Roehl and Royer Cook, *The Multi-Door Dispute Resolution Program: Phase I Assessment, Preliminary Report* (Washington, D.C.: Institute for Social Analysis, 1985); James Finkelstein, "The D.C. Multi-Door Courthouse," 69 *Judicature* 305 (1986).

211. Frank Sander, "Varieties of Dispute Processing," 70 *Federal Rules Decisions* 79, 111 (1976).

212. "Toward the Multi-Door Courthouse—Dispute Resolution Intake and Referral," *NIJ Reports*, July 1986, p. 2.

213. Ibid., p. 2.

214. H. W. Arthurs, *Without the Law: Administrative Justice and Legal Pluralism in Nineteenth-Century England* (Toronto: University of Toronto Press, 1985), p. 89.

215. Judith Resnik, "Failing Faith: Adjudicatory Procedure in Decline," 53 *University of Chicago Law Review* 494, 536 (1986).

216. Robert Peckham, "The Federal Judge as a Case Manager: The New Role in Guiding a Case from Filing to Disposition," 69 *California Law Review* 770 (1981); Carrie Menkel-Meadow, "For and Against Settlement: Uses and Abuses of the Mandatory Settlement Conference," 33 *U.C.L.A. Law Review* 485 (1985).

217. Beniger, *Control Revolution*.

218. Ibid., p. 9.

219. Ibid., p. 10.

220. Anthony D'Amato, "Can/Should Computers Replace Judges?" 11 *Georgia Law Review* 1277 (1977).

221. Richard Susskind, "Expert Systems in Law: A Jurisprudential Approach to Artificial Intelligence and Legal Reasoning," 49 *Modern Law Review* 168 (1987).

222. Simon, "Applying Information Technology to Organization Design," p. 277.

223. Owen M. Fiss, "Against Settlement," 93 *Yale Law Journal* 1073 (1984).

224. Marc Galanter, "Justice in Many Rooms: Courts, Private Ordering, and Indigenous Law," 19 *Journal of Legal Pluralism* 1, 13 (1981).

225. Gulliver, *Social Control in an African Society*, p. 299.

226. Historical changes in the meaning of a court are examined in J. H. Baker, "The Changing Concept of a Court," in *The Legal Profession and the Common Law: Historical Essays*, ed. J. H. Baker (London: Hambledon Press, 1986), pp. 153–170.

CHAPTER 3

1. "The effort to coerce belief . . . is the hallmark of a feudal or totalitarian society" (Thomas Emerson, *The System of Freedom of Expression* [New York: Random House, 1970], p. 21). See J. B. Bury, *A History of Freedom of Thought*, 2nd ed. (New York: Oxford University Press, 1952); J. M. Robertson, *A Short History of Free-thought* (New York: Russell & Russell, 1957).

2. "In the future, which we seek to make secure, we look forward for a world founded upon four essential freedoms. The first is freedom of speech and expression" (address of President Franklin D. Roosevelt to Congress, January 6, 1941). Justice Benjamin Cardozo wrote, several years before Roosevelt, that freedom of speech is "the matrix, the indispensable condition, of nearly every other form of freedom" (*Palko* v. *Connecticut*, 302 U.S. 319, 327 [1937]). See also Edmund Cahn, "The Firstness of the First Amendment," 65 *Yale Law Journal* 464 (1956); Robert Bingham Downs, *The First Freedom: Liberty and Justice in the World of Books and Reading* (Chicago: American Library Association, 1960); Nat Hentoff, *The First Freedom: The Tumultuous History of Free Speech in America* (New York: Delacorte, 1979).

3. See Peter Stansky, ed., *On Nineteen Eighty-four* (San Francisco: Freeman, 1983); Irving Howe, ed., *1984 Revisited* (New York: Harper & Row, 1983); W. F. Bolton, *The Language of 1984* (Knoxville: University of Tennessee Press, 1984); William Steinhoff, *The Road to 1984* (London: Weidenfeld & Nicolson, 1975).

4. *George Orwell: The Lost Writings*, ed. W. J. West (New York: Arbor House, 1985).

5. Martin Esslin, who also worked for the BBC during World War II, concluded, "Much of the role of the mass media in *Nineteen Eighty-Four* also derives from Orwell's familiarity with the propaganda technique of Goebbels, the mastermind behind the German psychological warfare offensive. The German radio broadcasts of special announcements of victories were preceded by lengthy bursts of martial music and fanfares, in exactly the same manner as described in *Nineteen Eighty-Four*. There was a special unit in 200 Oxford Street devoted to the daily analysis of German propaganda, its lies and methods . . . The principles of Newspeak in *Nineteen Eighty-Four* certainly owe much to the study of German propaganda that formed part of the daily routine of those working in the British propaganda effort. The manipulation of the masses by the media in *Nineteen Eighty-Four* thus is clearly an amalgam of the practices Orwell had encountered before and during the war, and his own experience as a propagandist in the BBC's English-language service to India" ("Television and Telescreen," in *On Nineteen Eighty-Four*, ed. Peter Stansky [San Francisco: Freeman, 1983]). Marshall McLuhan asserted that the fact the "that Hitler came into political existence at all is directly owing to radio and public-address systems" (*Understanding Media* [New York, New American Library, 1964], p. 262). See also Oran J. Hale, *The Captive Press in the Third Reich* (Princeton, N.J.: Princeton University Press, 1964).

6. West, ed., *George Orwell*, p. 21.

7. Leo Bogart, "The Growth of Television," in *Mass Communications*, ed. W. Schramm (Urbana: University of Illinois Press, 1960), pp. 95–111.

8. The impetus for building the first electronic digital computer, ENIAC (Electronic Numerical Integrator and Computer), was to speed up the calculation of artillery firing tables during World War II (Jeremy Bernstein, *The Analytical Machine*, 2nd ed. rev. [New York: Morrow, 1981], p. 60).

9. ENIAC weighed 30 tons, was 80 feet long and 8 feet high, and ran on 18,000 vacuum tubes.

10. For a readable history of the development of the computer, see Bernstein, *Analytical Machine*.

11. David Owen, "Copies in Seconds," *The Atlantic,* November 1986, pp. 64–73. The first transistor radio, introduced in 1954, was also not a commercial success (Bernstein, *Analytical Machine,* p. 80).

12. George Orwell, "The Russian Regime," review of *Russia Under Soviet Rule* by N. de Basily, *New English Weekly,* January 12, 1939, in *The Collected Essays, Journalism and Letters of George Orwell,* ed. Sonia Orwell and Ian Angus (London: Secker & Warburg, 1968), vol. 1, p. 381.

13. William Kuhns, *The Post-Industrial Prophets: Interpretations of Technology* (New York: Weybright and Talley, 1971),

14. George Orwell, *1984* (New York: Harcourt, Brace, 1949), p. 176.

15. William Read, "The First Amendment Meets the Information Society," in *Telecommunications: Issues and Choices for Society,* ed. Jerry Salvaggio (New York: Longman, 1983), p. 85.

16. Ibid.

17. "Emile Durkheim, the great sociologist, once asked the question: How can it be that we feel more free, as the powers of the state have grown? He answered that it is only when the numerous state institutions are efficient and clearly defined that we know what is expected of us and what constraints bear upon us . . . Anarchy is not liberty, but slavery. It is very much through the extensive network of communication in industrial countries, reaching from the metropolis into every town, village, home and back again, that we can operate in ways that enable us to feel 'free' as individuals, though knowing that we are socially constrained. Liberty rests not only on a foundation of defined authority but also upon the operation of a two-way communication service" (Colin Cherry, "The Telephone System" in *The Social Impact of the Telephone,* ed. Ithiel de Sola Pool [Cambridge: MIT Press, 1977], pp. 124–125).

18. Jeffrey M. Blum, "The Divisible First Amendment: A Critical, Functionalist Approach to Freedom of Speech and Electoral Campaign Spending," 58 *N.Y.U. Law Review* 1273, 1275 (1983).

19. Raymond D. Gastil, *Freedom in the World: Political and Civil Liberties* (New York: Freedom House, 1980); David Bidney, ed., *The Concept of Freedom in Anthropology* (The Hague: Mouton, 1963); Carl Friedrich, ed., *Liberty* (New York: Atherton Press, 1962); William Mayton, "From a Legacy of Suppression to a 'Metaphor of the Fourth Estate,' " 39 *Stanford Law Review* 139, 140 (1986).

20. Donald Thomas, *A Long Time Burning: The History of Literary Censorship in England* (New York: Praeger, 1969), p. 7.

21. Sir Edmund Leach, quoted in M. I. Finley, "Censorship in Classical Antiquity," *Times Literary Supplement,* July 29, 1977, p. 923.

22. Pnina Lahav, ed., *Press Law in Modern Democracies: A Comparative Study* (New York: Longman, 1985), p. 1. See also David Weaver, Judith Buddenbaum, and Jo Ellen Fair, "Press Freedom, Media and Development, 1950–1979: A Study of 134 Nations," 35 *Journal of Communications* 104 (1985).

23. Herbert J. Muller, "Freedom and Justice in History," in *The Concept of Freedom in Anthropology,* ed. David Bidney (The Hague: Mouton, 1963), p. 273.

24. Dorothy Lee, *Freedom and Culture* (Englewood Cliffs, N.J.: Prentice-Hall, 1959), p. 53.

25. Alan F. Hattersley, *A Short History of Democracy* (Cambridge: Cambridge University Press, 1942), p. 16.

26. Eric Havelock, *The Greek Concept of Justice* (Cambridge, Mass.: Harvard University Press, 1978), p. 31.

27. Thomas I. Emerson, *Toward a General Theory of the First Amendment* (New York: Random House, 1963), pp. 4–15.

28. Hattersley, *Short History of Democracy*, p. 15.

29. E. Adamson Hoebel, *Man in the Primitive World* (New York: McGraw-Hill, 1958), p. 496. Pascual Gisbert similarly notes that "in this *sui generis*, perhaps 'natural', democracy not even the chief is formally recognized as such" (*Preliterate Man* [Bombay: Manaktalas, 1967], p. 78).

30. E. Adamson Hoebel, *The Law of Primitive Man* (New York: Atheneum, 1968), pp. 294–295; see also Colin Turnbull, *The Mountain People: A Study of the Pygmies of the Congo* (New York: Simon and Schuster, 1961).

31. "Right conclusions are more likely to be gathered out of a multitude of tongues, than through any kind of authoritative selection" (*United States* v. *Associated Press*, 52 F. Supp. 362, 372 [1943]).

32. Maurice Bloch, ed., *Political Language and Oratory in Traditional Society* (New York: Academic Press, 1975), p. 3.

33. Maurice Bloch, "Astrology and Writing in Madagascar," in *Literacy in Traditional Societies*, ed. Jack Goody (New York: Cambridge University Press, 1968), p. 288.

34. Stanley Diamond, *In Search of the Primitive* (New Brunswick, N.J.: Transaction Books, 1974), pp. 3–5; Kathleen Gough, "Literacy in Kerala," in *Literacy in Traditional Societies*, ed. Jack Goody (New York: Cambridge University Press, 1968), p. 153.

35. Interview with Georges Charbonnier, in *The Future of Literacy*, ed. R. Disch (Englewood Cliffs, N.J.: Prentice-Hall, 1973), p. 18.

36. M. T. Clanchy, *From Memory to Written Record* (Cambridge, Mass.: Harvard University Press, 1979), p. 7.

37. Jack Goody and Ian Watt, "The Consequences of Literacy," in *Literacy in Traditional Societies*, ed. Jack Goody (New York: Cambridge University Press, 1968), p. 58.

38. Harold Innis, *Empire and Communication* (Toronto: University of Toronto Press, 1950), p. 10.

39. Ben Bagdikian, *The Information Machines* (New York: Harper & Row, 1971), pp. 4–5.

40. Eugene Charlton Black, "The Eighteenth Century: Control and Revolution," in *Censorship: Five Hundred Years of Conflict* (New York: New York Public Library, 1984), p. 65.

41. David Reisman, *The Oral Tradition, the Written Word and the Screen Image* (Yellow Springs, Ohio: Antioch College, 1956), pp. 12–13. See also Chapter 6.

42. Goody and Watt, "Consequences of Literacy," p. 3.

43. Difficulties in determining and comparing literacy rates in different societies are examined in R. S. Schofield, "The Measurement of Literacy in Pre-Industrial England," in *Literacy in Traditional Societies*, ed. Jack Goody (New York: Cambridge University Press, 1968), pp. 311–325; see also Keith Thomas, "The Meaning of Literacy in Early Modern England," in *The Written Word: Literacy in Transition*, ed. Gerd Baumann (Oxford: Clarendon Press, 1986), pp. 97–132.

44. Finley, "Censorship in Classical Antiquity," pp. 923–924; see also J. David

Bolter, *Turing's Man* (Chapel Hill: University of North Carolina Press, 1984), p. 137; Natalie Zemon Davis, *Society and Culture in Early Modern France* (Stanford, Calif.: Stanford University Press, 1975).

45. Finley, "Censorship in Classical Antiquity," p. 925. See also M. I. Finley, *Economy and Society in Ancient Greece* (New York: Viking Press, 1981), p. 92.

46. Havelock, *Greek Concept of Justice.*

47. Jack Goody, ed., *Literacy in Traditional Societies* (New York: Cambridge University Press, 1968), p. 14.

48. It is interesting that the Tenth Commandment, the prohibition on perjury, is also related to communication and to an abuse of the spoken word.

49. Leonard Levy, *Emergence of a Free Press* (New York: Oxford University Press, 1985), p. 4.

50. Havelock, *Greek Concept of Justice,* p. 336.

51. M. I. Finley, *Politics in the Ancient World* (Cambridge: Cambridge University Press, 1983), pp. 29–31.

52. Eric Havelock, *Preface to Plato* (Oxford: Blackwell, 1963), pp. 3–19.

53. Plato, *The Republic,* trans. W. H. D. Rouse (New York: New American Library, 1956), 595E.

54. Plato, *Ion,* trans. W. H. D. Rouse (New York: New American Library, 1956), 540E.

55. Plato, *Phaedrus,* trans. B. Jowett (New York: Random House, 1937), 275A.

56. Plato, *The Republic,* trans. F. M. Cornford (New York: Oxford University Press, 1941), 557B.

57. Plato, *The Laws,* trans. and ed. Thomas L. Pangle (New York: Basic Books, 1980), p. 190.

58. Havelock, *Preface to Plato,* pp. 280–287.

59. Ibid., p. 56.

60. Plato, *The Apology,* trans. B. Jowett (New York: Random House, 1937), 446.

61. Havelock, *Greek Concept of Justice,* p. 321.

62. Max Radin, "Freedom of Speech in Ancient Athens," 48 *American Journal of Philology* 215, 218 (1927).

63. Goody and Watt, "Consequences of Literacy," p. 51.

64. Bolter, *Turing's Man,* p. 135.

65. F. M. Cornford, *Before and After Socrates* (Cambridge: Cambridge University Press, 1932), p. 41.

66. Thucydides, *History of the Peloponnesian Wars,* bk. II, chap. xxxvii.

67. W. T. Jones, *The Classical Mind* (New York: Harcourt, Brace & World, 1969), p. 62.

68. Radin, "Freedom of Speech in Ancient Athens," p. 215.

69. Leonard Levy, *Treason Against God: A History of the Offense Against Blasphemy* (New York: Schocken, 1981), p. 15.

70. Ibid., pp. 7–15.

71. Thomas P. Kasoulis, "Reference and Symbol in Plato's *Cratylus* and Kukai's *Shojijissogi,*" 32 *Philosophy East and West* 404–405 (1982).

72. Ithiel de Sola Pool, *Technologies of Freedom* (Cambridge, Mass.: Harvard University Press, 1983), p. 14.

73. Levy, *Treason Against God;* Moshe Carmilly-Weinberger, *Censorship and Freedom of Expression in Jewish History* (New York: Sepher-Hermon Press, 1977).

74. Paul F. Grendler, "The Advent of Printing," in *Censorship: Five Hundred Years of Conflict* (New York: New York Public Library, 1984), p. 29.

75. Rudolph Hirsch, "Pre-Reformation Censorship of Printed Books," in *The Printed Word,* ed. Rudolph Hirsch (London: Variorum Reprints, 1978), p. 100.

76. S. H. Steinberg, *Five Hundred Years of Printing,* 3rd ed. (Baltimore: Penguin Books, 1974), p. 260.

77. *Miami Herald* v. *Tornillo,* 418 U.S. 241 (1973).

78. Finley, "Censorship in Classical Antiquity," p. 923.

79. Michael Clapham, "Printing," in *A History of Technology: From the Renaissance to the Industrial Revolution,* ed. C. Singer, E. Holmyard, A. Hall, and T. Williams (Oxford: Oxford University Press, 1957), p. 377.

80. L. Febvre and H. Martin, *The Coming of the Book* (London: NLB, 1976), p. 262. Hirsch estimates that 40,000 titles or approximately 10 million books were published in the fifteenth century and that by the middle of the sixteenth century, 150,000 titles had been published in more than 60 million copies (Rudolph Hirsch, "Printing and the Spread of Humanism: The Example of Albrecht Von Eyb," in *The Printed Word,* ed. Rudolph Hirsch [London: Variorum Reprints, 1978], p. 25).

81. Margaret Aston, *The Fifteenth Century* (London: Thames and Hudson, 1968), p. 9.

82. Febvre and Martin, *Coming of the Book,* pp. 249–250.

83. Ibid.

84. Hirsch, "Pre-Reformation Censorship of Printed Books," p. 102. See also Febvre and Martin, *Coming of the Book,* p. 171.

85. Marianna Tax Choldin, *A Fence Around the Empire: Russian Censorship of Western Ideas under the Tsars* (Durham, N.C.: Duke University Press, 1985), p. 4.

86. Febvre and Martin, *Coming of the Book,* p. 172.

87. Henri-Jean Martin, "Publishing Conditions and Strategies in Ancien Régime France," in *Books and Society in History,* ed. Kenneth Carpenter (New York: Bowker, 1983), p. 57.

88. Elizabeth Eisenstein, *The Printing Revolution in Early Modern Europe* (New York: Cambridge University Press, 1983), p. 155.

89. Quoted in Hirsch, "Pre-Reformation Censorship of Printed Books," p. 102.

90. Febvre and Martin, *Coming of the Book,* p. 172.

91. Elizabeth Eisenstein, *The Printing Press as an Agent of Change* (New York: Cambridge University Press, 1979), pp. 310–313; Hirsch, "Printing and the Spread of Humanism," p. 25; John Wall, "The Reformation in England and the Typographical Revolution: 'By this printing . . . the doctrine of the Gospel soundeth to all nations,'" in *Print and Culture in the Renaissance,* ed. Gerald Tyson and Sylvia Wagonheim (Newark: University of Delaware Press, 1986), p. 208.

92. Eisenstein, *Printing Press as an Agent of Change,* pp. 306–307. It is interesting that Catholic forces in England almost a century later used the press to rebel against English Protestantism and that "the circulation of foreign printed texts opened the way for the great Catholic revival of the fifteen-eighties" (Leona Ros-

tenberg, *The Minority Press and the English Crown* [Nieuwkoop: De Graaf, 1971], p. 31).

93. Arthur G. Dickens, *Reformation and Society in Sixteenth Century Europe* (New York: Harcourt, Brace & World, 1968), p. 51.

94. Richard Friedenthal, *Luther: His Life and Times* (New York: Harcourt, Brace & World, 1967), pp. 109–110.

95. Frederick S. Siebert, *Freedom of the Press in England, 1476–1776* (Urbana: University of Illinois Press, 1952).

96. Ibid., p. 116.

97. Martin, "Publishing Conditions and Strategies in Ancien Régime France," pp. 57–58.

98. Hannah Arendt, *Between Past and Future: Eight Exercises in Political Thought* (New York: Viking, 1968), pp. 92–93.

99. Rostenberg, *Minority Press and the English Crown*, p. 4; see also Siebert, *Freedom of the Press in England*.

100. Siebert, *Freedom of the Press in England*, p. 249.

101. Joel Wiener, "Social Purity and Freedom of Expression," in *Censorship: 500 Years of Conflict* (New York: New York Public Library, 1984), p. 93.

102. Herbert Bricker, *Freedom of Information* (New York: Macmillan, 1949), p. 32.

103. Steinberg, *Five Hundred Years of Printing*, p. 264.

104. Febvre and Martin, *Coming of the Book* p. 144.

105. Robert Darnton, *The Literary Underground of the French Regime* (Cambridge, Mass.: Harvard University Press, 1982), pp. v–vi.

106. Febvre and Martin, *Coming of the Book*, p. 300.

107. Raymond Birn, "Book Production and Censorship in France, 1700–1715," in *Books and Society in History*, ed. Kenneth Carpenter (New York: Bowker, 1983), p. 156. See also David Pottinger, *The French Book Trade in the Ancien Régime, 1500–1791* (Cambridge, Mass.: Harvard University Press, 1958), pp. 54–81.

108. Siebert, *Freedom of the Press in England*, p. 260.

109. Ibid., p. 261.

110. Ibid., p. 263. See also William Holdsworth, *A History of English Law*, 2nd ed. (London: Methuen, 1937), pp. v–vi, 360–379.

111. Leonard W. Levy, *Emergence of a Free Press* (New York: Oxford University Press, 1985).

112. Leonard W. Levy, *Legacy of Suppression* (Cambridge, Mass.: Harvard University Press, 1960).

113. Leonard W. Levy, *Freedom of Speech and Press in Early American History: Legacy of Suppression* (New York: Harper & Row [Torchbook], 1963), p. xxi.

114. Levy, *Emergence of a Free Press*, p. x.

115. Ibid.

116. Levy, *Freedom of Speech and Press in Early American History*, pp. xi–xvii.

117. Levy, *Emergence of a Free Press*, p. xii.

118. Ibid., p. x.

119. Ibid.

120. Ibid., p. xi.
121. Brief for Respondents at 50, *Herbert* v. *Lando,* 99 S. Ct. 1635 (1979).
122. Arthur M. Schlesinger, *Prelude to Independence* (New York: Knopf, 1957). See also Isaiah Thomas, *The History of Printing in America,* 3rd ed. (New York: Weathervane Books, 1970).
123. Jeffrey Smith, *Printers and Press Freedom* (New York: Oxford University Press, 1988), p. 13.
124. Mayton, "From a Legacy of Suppression to a 'Metaphor of the Fourth Estate,' " p. 142.
125. Potter Stewart, "Or of the Press," 26 *Hastings Law Journal* 631, 636 (1975).
126. Steven Levy, *Hackers* (Garden City, N.Y.: Doubleday, 1984), p. 41.
127. Walter Wriston, chairman of Citicorp, quoted in Adrian Hamilton, *The Financial Revolution* (New York: Free Press, 1986), p. 32.
128. McLuhan, *Understanding Media.*
129. Emerson, *System of Freedom of Expression,* p. 12.
130. "Bennett Sees 'Bullying' of ABC by Soviets," *Washington Post,* January 12, 1986, p. A7.
131. Tom Shales, "Go-Ahead for ABC's Amerika," *Washington Post,* January 23, 1986, p. D1.
132. Dissatisfaction with more frequent appearances of Soviet representatives on American television news programs is discussed in Ted Smith, *Moscow Meets Main Street* (Washington, D.C.: Media Institute, 1988).
133. Joshua Meyrowitz, *No Sense of Place* (New York: Oxford University Press, 1985), p. 168.
134. Bagdikian, *Information Machines,* pp. 2–3.
135. Benjamin Compaine, "The Expanding Base of Media Competition," 35 *Journal of Communications* 81, 90 (1985).
136. Donald Shainor, *Behind the Lines: The Private War Against Soviet Censorship* (New York: St. Martin's Press, 1985), p. 80.
137. Finley, "Censorship in Classical Antiquity," pp. 923–924.
138. Shainor, *Behind the Lines,* p. 83.
139. David Goldfarb, "A Refusenik's Story," *New York Times Magazine,* December 28, 1986, p. 22.
140. Ibid., p. 3.
141. David Beam, "Atari Bolsheviks," *The Atlantic,* March 1986, pp. 28–32.
142. Linda Melvern, David Hebditch, and Nick Anning, *Techno-Bandits* (Boston: Houghton Mifflin, 1984), p. 29.
143. *New York Times,* September 30, 1985, p. B6.
144. Jane Leftwich Curry, trans. and ed., *The Black Book of Polish Censorship* (New York: Random House, 1984), p. 417.
145. Martin Krygier, "In Occupied Poland," *Commentary,* March 1986, pp. 15–23; Timothy Garton Ash, "Poland: The Uses of Adversity," *New York Review of Books,* June 27, 1985, pp. 5–10. See also Michael Kaufman, "Illicit Weekly Has Survived Polish Raids," *New York Times,* February 16, 1986, p. 7.
146. Roger Boyes, "Start of the Other Star Wars," *The Times* (London), November 12, 1985, p. 14.

147. David H. Bain, "Letter from Manila: How the Press Helped to Topple a Despot," *Columbia Journalism Review*, May–June 1986, pp. 27–36. An interesting analysis of the role of the traditional and the electronic media in the Iranian revolution is in Hamid Mowlana, "Technology versus Tradition: Communication in the Iranian Revolution," 29 *Journal of Communication* 107 (1979).

148. William Broad, "Civilians Use Satellite Photos for Spying on Soviet Military," *New York Times*, April 7, 1986, p. A1; see also U.S. Congress, Office of Technology Assessment, *Commercial Newsgathering from Space: A Technical Memorandum* (Washington, D.C.: Government Printing Office, 1987).

149. William Broad, "Private Cameras in Space Stir U.S. Security Fears," *New York Times*, August 25, 1987, p. C1; William Broad, "Soviet Offering to Sell Photographs Taken from Space," *New York Times*, July 14, 1987, p. C2.

150. "Photo Satellites Restricted by U.S.," *New York Times*, July 12, 1987, p. 22.

151. *United States* v. *Morison*, 604 F. Supp. 655 (1985), *affirmed*, 844 F.2d 1057 (1988).

152. See Reporters Committee for Freedom of the Press, *The News Media and the Law* (Washington, D.C.: Reporters Committee for Freedom of the Press).

153. *United States* v. *The Progressive, Inc.*, 467 F. Supp. 990 (W.D. Wisc.), *appeal dismissed*, 610 F. 2d. 819 (7th Cir., 1979).

154. Iver Peterson, "Scrambling of Signals Today Thwarts TV Dish Antennas," *New York Times*, January 15, 1986, p. A1; Richard Zacks, "Just When Satellite TV Was Taking Off, Someone Scrambled the Picture," *TV Guide*, December 21, 1985, p. 45; David Owen, "Satellite Television," *The Atlantic*, June 1985, pp. 45–62.

155. David E. Sanger, "U.S. to Curb Supercomputer Use by Soviet Scholars Working Here," *New York Times*, February 10, 1986, p. A1.

156. U.S. Congress, Office of Technology Assessment, *Defending Secrets, Sharing Data: New Locks and Keys for Electronic Information* (Washington, D.C.: Government Printing Office, 1987).

157. David Sanger, "Computer Code Shift Expected: Eavesdropping Fear Indicated," *New York Times*, April 15, 1986, p. D1.

158. U.S. Congress, Office of Technology Assessment, *Science, Technology and the First Amendment* (Washington, D.C.: Government Printing Office, 1988), p. 7.

159. de Sola Pool, *Technologies of Freedom*, p. 193.

160. Elizabeth Ferrarini, *Infomania* (Boston: Houghton Mifflin, 1985); Alfred Glossbrenner, *The Complete Handbook of Personal Computer Communications* (New York: St. Martin's Press, 1983).

161. Shoshana Zuboff, *In the Age of the Smart Machine* (New York: Basic Books, 1988), p. 9.

162. Ibid., p. 10.

163. Joseph F. Sullivan, "Cordless Phones Raise an Eavesdropping Issue," *New York Times*, March 11, 1986, p. B3.

164. John J. Fialka, "Study Sheds Light on Vulnerability of Computers to Electronic Spying," *Wall Street Journal*, October 18, 1985, p. 31; John Markoff, "Breach

Reported in U.S. Computers," *New York Times,* April 18, 1988, p. 1; John Markoff, "Top-Secret, and Vulnerable," *New York Times,* April 25, 1988, p. D1.

165. Marc U. Porat, "Communication Policy in an Information Society," in *Communications for Tomorrow: Policy Perspectives for the 1980s,* ed. Glen O. Robinson (New York: Praeger, 1978), pp. 3–60.

166. Martin Tolchin, "Russians Sought U.S. Banks to Gain High-Tech Secrets," *New York Times,* February 16, 1986, p. A1.

167. Kaarle Nordenstreng and Herbert Schiller, *National Sovereignty and International Communication* (Norwood, N.J.: Ablex, 1979), p. 62.

168. N. R. Kleinfield, "Turning McGraw-Hill Upside Down," *New York Times,* February 2, 1986, sec. 3, p. 1.

169. John Milton, *Areopagitica,* in *The Works of John Milton,* ed. William Haller (New York: Columbia University Press, 1931–38), vol. 4, p. 298.

170. *First National Bank of Boston* v. *Bellotti,* 435 U.S. 765, 783 (1978).

171. Kent Middleton and Roy Mersky, eds., *Freedom of Expression: A Collection of Best Writings* (Buffalo, N.Y.: Hein, 1981), p. v.

172. Andrew Pollack, "Free Speech Issues Surround Computer Bulletin Board Use," *New York Times,* November 12, 1984, p. A1; Martin Lasden, "Of Bytes and Bulletin Boards," *New York Times Magazine,* August 4, 1985, p. 34.

173. John Naisbitt, *Megatrends* (New York: Warner Books, 1982), pp. 1–35.

174. Alexander Bickel, "The 'Uninhibited, Robust, and Wide-Open' First Amendment," in *Where Do You Draw the Line?* ed. Victor Cline (Provo, Utah: Brigham Young University Press, 1974), p. 65. For a discussion of the relationship between the degree of press freedom and specific press laws, see Lahav, *Press Law in Modern Democracies,* pp. 344–345.

175. de Sola Pool, *Technologies of Freedom,* pp. 128–150.

176. Middleton and Mersky, *Freedom of Expression,* p. v; see also Robert H. Bork, "Neutral Principles and Some First Amendment Problems," 47 *Indiana Law Journal* 1, 3 (1971).

177. Lahav, *Press Law in Modern Democracies,* p. 1.

178. See, for example, Vincent Blasi, "The Checking Value in First Amendment Theory," 1977 *American Bar Foundation Research Journal* 521–649 (1977); Bork, "Neutral Principles and Some First Amendment Problems," pp. 1–35.

179. James Fruehling, ed., *Sourcebook on Death and Dying* (Chicago: Marquis, 1982).

180. Emerson, *Toward a General Theory of the First Amendment,* p. 47.

181. Blasi, "Checking Value in First Amendment Theory," p. 527.

182. Lillian BeVier, "The First Amendment and Political Speech: An Inquiry into the Substance and Limits of Principle," 30 *Stanford Law Review* 299 (1978).

183. Ronald Dworkin, *A Matter of Principle* (Cambridge, Mass.: Harvard University Press, 1985).

184. Ben Bagdikian, "The U.S. Media: Supermarket or Assembly Line?" 35 *Journal of Communications* 81 (1985).

185. Jerry Mander, *Four Arguments for the Elimination of Television* (New York: Morrow, 1978).

186. Franklyn S. Haiman, *Speech and Law in a Free Society* (Chicago: University of Chicago Press, 1981), p. 3.

CHAPTER 4

1. James Carlson, *Prime Time Law Enforcement* (New York: Pantheon, 1985); Ethan Katsh and Stephen Arons, "How TV Cops Flout the Law," *Saturday Review* March 19, 1977, pp. 11–18.

2. James Beniger, *The Control Revolution: Technological and Economic Origins of the Information Society* (Cambridge, Mass.: Harvard University Press, 1986).

3. See Edward Ploman and L. Clark Hamilton, *Copyright* (London: Routledge and Kegan Paul, 1980), p. 4.

4. H. J. Chaytor, *From Script to Print* (London: Sidgwick & Jackson, 1966), p. 123.

5. Ithiel de Sola Pool, *Technologies of Freedom* (Cambridge, Mass.: Harvard University Press, 1983), p. 14.

6. Elizabeth Eisenstein, *The Printing Press as an Agent of Change* (New York: Cambridge University Press, 1979), pp. 121–122.

7. Marc Drogin, *Anathema! Medieval Scribes and the History of Book Curses* (Totowa, N.J.: Allanheld & Schram, 1983), p. 18.

8. Aubert Clark, *The Movement for International Copyright in Nineteenth Century America* (Washington, D.C.: Catholic University Press, 1960), pp. 1–2.

9. T. F. T. Plucknett, "The Harvard Manuscript of Thornton's *alSumma*," 51 *Harvard Law Review* 1038, 1048 (1938).

10. Graham Pollard, "The *Pecia* System in the Medieval Universities," in *Medieval Scribes, Manuscripts and Libraries*, ed. M. B. Parkes and Andrew Watson (London: Scolar Press, 1978), p. 145.

11. Drogin, *Anathema!* p. 15.

12. Cyprian Blagden, *The Stationers' Company: A History, 1403–1959* (Cambridge, Mass.: Harvard University Press, 1960).

13. Lyman Patterson, *Copyright in Historical Perspective* (Nashville, Tenn.: Vanderbilt University Press, 1968), p. 6.

14. Ibid., p. 5.

15. Ibid., p. 6.

16. See Chapter 6.

17. J. David Bolter, *Turing's Man* (Chapel Hill: University of North Carolina Press, 1984), p. 166.

18. See, generally, U.S. Congress, Office of Technology Assessment, *Intellectual Property Rights in an Age of Electronics and Information* (Washington, D.C.: Government Printing Office, 1986).

19. de Sola Pool, *Technologies of Freedom*, p. 214.

20. Eisenstein, *Printing Press as an Agent of Change*, pp. 121–122.

21. Melville Nimmer, *Nimmer on Copyright* (New York: Bender, 1971), p. 33.

22. Anthony Smith, *Goodbye Gutenberg* (New York: Oxford University Press, 1980), pp. 314–315.

23. Office of Technology Assessment, *Intellectual Property Rights in an Age of Electronics and Information*, p. 130.

24. Mary Ann Buckles, "Interactive Fiction as Literature," *Byte*, May 1987, p. 140.

25. Judge Curtis Bok in *Commonwealth* v. *Gordon*, 66 Pa. D. & C. 101 (Philadelphia County Ct., 1949).

26. *Technical Report of the Commission on Obscenity and Pornography*, vol. 2 (Washington, D.C.: Government Printing Office, 1970), p. 71.

27. Norman St. John-Stevas, *Obscenity and the Law* (London: Secker & Warburg, 1956), p. 2.

28. Jeffrey Henderson, *The Maculate Muse: Obscene Language in Attic Comedy* (New Haven, Conn.: Yale University Press, 1975), p. 5.

29. Walter Kendrick, *The Secret Museum: Pornography in Modern Culture* (New York: Viking, 1987), p. 42.

30. *Lives of the Most Eminent Painters, Sculptors, and Architects*, 10 vols., trans. Gaston DaC. De Vere (London, 1912–1914), vol. 6, pp. 104–105. See also David Foxon, *Libertine Literature in England, 1660–1745* (New Hyde Park, N.Y.: University Books, 1965), p. 19.

31. Leonard W. Levy, *Treason Against God: A History of the Offense Against Blasphemy* (New York: Schocken, 1981), p. 15.

32. *United States* v. *Roth*, 77 S. Ct. 1304 (1957).

33. *Miller* v. *California*, 93 S. Ct. 2607 (1973).

34. Ibid.

35. Ibid.

36. *The Queen* v. *Read*, 11 Mod. Rep. 142 (1708), quoted in Edward De Grazia, *Censorship Landmarks* (New York: Bowker, 1969), p. 3.

37. *Technical Report of the Commission on Obscenity and Pornography*, vol. 2, p. 71.

38. Ibid., p. 66.

39. Kendrick, *Secret Museum*, p. 58.

40. *The Diary of Samuel Pepys*, ed. R. Latham and W. Matthews (Berkeley: University of California Press, 1976), vol. 9, pp. 57–59.

41. *United States* v. *Roth*, 77 S. Ct. 1304 (1957).

42. *Miller* v. *California*, 93 S. Ct. 2607 (1973).

43. Joshua Meyrowitz, *No Sense of Place* (New York: Oxford University Press, 1985), p. 60.

44. Ibid., p. 117.

45. Office of Technology Assessment, *Intellectual Property Rights in an Age of Electronics and Information*, p. 12.

46. Marshall McLuhan, quoted in Meyrowitz, *No Sense of Place*, p. v.

47. Kendrick, *Secret Museum*, p. 221.

48. "When the Court declared that obscenity is not a form of expression protected by the First Amendment, no distinction was made as to the medium of expression" (*Kaplan* v. *California*, 413 U.S. 115, 119 [1973]).

49. Marshall McLuhan, *Understanding Media* (New York: McGraw-Hill, 1964), p. 32.

50. *American Booksellers Association, Inc.* v. *Hudnut*, 598 F. Supp. 1316 (1984); David Copp and Susan Wendell, *Pornography and Censorship* (Buffalo, N.Y.: Prometheus Books, 1983); Catherine McKinnon, "Pornography, Civil Rights, and Speech," 20 *Harvard Civil Rights–Civil Liberties Law Review* 1 (1985); Thomas Emerson, "Pornography and the First Amendment: A Reply to Professor Mc-

Kinnon," 3 *Yale Law and Policy Review* 130 (1984); Andrea Dworkin, "Against the Male Flood: Censorship, Pornography and Equality," 8 *Harvard Women's Law Journal* 1 (1985); "Anti-Pornography Laws and First Amendment Values," 98 *Harvard Law Review* 460 (1984).

51. *FCC* v. *Pacifica Foundation*, 438 U.S. 726 (1978); Reginald Stuart, "F.C.C. Acts to Restrict Indecent Programming," *New York Times*, April 17, 1987, p. A1.

52. Oscar Wilde, *The Picture of Dorian Gray*, preface.

53. Attorney General's Commission on Pornography, *Final Report* (Washington, D.C.: Department of Justice, 1986).

54. Don Pember, *Privacy and the Press* (Seattle: University of Washington Press, 1972), p. ix.

55. The impetus for writing about the subject appears to have come from Warren, who objected to newspaper pictures and stories published about the Boston social scene, of which he was a part (Ibid., pp. 20–25). See also William Prosser, "Privacy," 48 *California Law Review* 383 (1960); Alpheus Mason, *Brandeis, A Free Man's Life* (New York: Viking, 1946).

56. Samuel Warren and Louis Brandeis, "The Right to Privacy," 4 *Harvard Law Review* 193, 195–196 (1890).

57. Richard Hixson, *Privacy in a Public Society* (New York: Oxford University Press, 1987), p. 29.

58. Esther Forbes, *Paul Revere: The World He Lived In* (Boston: Houghton Mifflin, 1942), p. 70.

59. Hannah Arendt, *The Human Condition* (Chicago: University of Chicago Press, 1958), p. 38.

60. Barrington Moore, *Privacy: Studies in Social and Cultural History* (Armonk, N.Y.: Sharpe, 1984), p. 82.

61. Alan Westin, *Privacy and Freedom* (New York: Atheneum, 1967); Irwin Altman, "Privacy Regulation: Culturally Universal or Culturally Specific?" 33 *Journal of Social Issues* 66 (1977).

62. Ferdinand Schoenman, "Privacy: Philosophical Dimensions of the Literature," in Ferdinand Schoenman, *Philosophical Dimensions of Privacy* (New York: Cambridge University Press, 1984), p. 1.

63. See Chapter 6.

64. Hixson, *Privacy in a Public Society*, p. xv.

65. Tom Gerety, "Redefining Privacy," 12 *Harvard Civil Rights–Civil Liberties Law Review* 233, 236 (1977).

66. Warren and Brandeis, "Right to Privacy," p. 193.

67. Irwin Altman, *The Environment and Social Behavior: Privacy, Personal Space, Territory and Crowding* (Monterey: Brooks/Cole, 1975), p. 50.

68. Steven Lukes, *Individualism* (Oxford: Blackwell, 1973), p. 62.

69. Edward Shils, "Privacy: Its Constitution and Vicissitudes," 36 *Law and Contemporary Problems* 281, 289 (1966).

70. *Olmstead* v. *United States*, 277 U.S. 438 (1928).

71. Moore, *Privacy*, p. 71.

72. Ibid., p. 73.

73. Sissela Bok, *Secrecy* (New York: Pantheon, 1982).

74. In 1987, operators of large databases refused a federal government request that they limit access to electronic databases and inform the government of the information requested by some subscribers (Bob Davis, "Federal Agencies Press Data-Base Firms to Curb Access to 'Sensitive' Information," *Wall Street Journal*, February 5, 1987, p. 23).

75. See U.S. Congress, Office of Technology Assessment, *Federal Government Information Technology: Electronic Surveillance and Civil Liberties* (Washington, D.C.: Government Printing Office, 1985).

76. Ruth Gavison, "Privacy and the Limits of Law," 89 *Yale Law Journal* 421, 430 (1980).

77. S. I. Benn and G. F. Gaus, "The Public and the Private: Concepts and Action" in *Public and Private in Social Life*, ed. S. I. Benn and G. F. Gaus (New York: St. Martin's Press, 1983), p. 8.

CHAPTER 5

1. Richard L. Abel, "The Transformation of the American Legal Profession," 20 *Law and Society Review* 7 (1986).

2. Julie Taylor, *Demographics of the American Legal Profession* (Cambridge, Mass.: Harvard Law School, 1983), p. 3.

3. Barbara Curran, "The Legal Profession in the 1980's: Selected Statistics from the 1984 Lawyer Statistical Report" (paper presented to the Law and Society Association, June 1984), p. 1.

4. *New York Times*, April 10, 1978, p. 56.

5. Curran, "Legal Profession in the 1980's," p. 2.

6. Ibid.

7. Taylor, *Demographics of the American Legal Profession*, p. 4.

8. Ibid., p. 8.

9. Curran, "Legal Profession in the 1980's," p. 5.

10. In spite of the civil rights movement, the number of black law students and lawyers has not increased nearly as much as those of women. Blacks make up 12 percent of the general population but only a little more than 2 percent of the legal profession. The number of black law students has increased from 3 percent in 1969 to more than 4 percent today. The number of all minorities accepted at law schools tripled from 1969 to 1974—from 2,900 to 10,000—but has been constant since then (Taylor, *Demographics of the American Legal Profession*, p. 8).

11. Ibid.

12. Ibid.

13. Abel, "Transformation of the American Legal Profession," p. 7; Richard Abel, "The Decline of Professionalism," 49 *Modern Law Review* 1 (1986); Richard Abel, "Law and Modernity," 49 *Modern Law Review* 545 (1986); Richard Abel, "The Rise of Professionalism," 6 *British Journal of Law and Society* 82 (1979).

14. Abel, "Transformation of the American Legal Profession," p. 14.

15. Ibid., p. 16.

16. In 1987, the hundred largest law firms had a median number of four branch

offices, and more than one-third of the lawyers in these firms worked in the branch offices, many of them overseas (James W. Jones, "The Challenge of Change: The Practice of Law in the Year 2000," 41 *Vanderbilt Law Review* 683, 687 [1988]).

17. Roscoe Pound, *The Lawyer from Antiquity to Modern Time* (St. Paul, Minn.: West, 1953), pp. 35–58.

18. Robert C. Palmer, "The Origins of the Legal Profession in England," 11 *Irish Jurist* 126–146 (1976).

19. Henry Fielding, *Joseph Andrews,* bk. 3, chap. 1.

20. Jack Goody, *The Logic of Writing and the Organization of Society* (Cambridge: Cambridge University Press, 1986), pp. 141–143.

21. "Representation in litigation was regarded in the beginning of English law, as in the beginnings in all systems, as something exceptional" (Pound, *The Lawyer from Antiquity to Modern Time,* p. 79); Robert Robson, *The Attorney in Eighteenth-Century England* (Cambridge: Cambridge University Press, 1959), p. 1.

22. *Henry VI, Part II,* act iv, sc. ii.

23. Luke 11:52.

24. *Henry VI, Part II,* act iv, sc. ii.

25. Luke 11:52.

26. C. W. Brooks, *Pettyfoggers and Vipers of the Commonwealth* (Cambridge: Cambridge University Press, 1986), p. 10.

27. E. W. Ives, "A Lawyer's Library in 1500," 85 *Law Quarterly Review* 104 (1969).

28. Denis Hay, "Fiat Lux," in *Printing and the Mind of Man,* ed. John Carter and Percival Muir (London: Cassell, 1967), p. xxiv.

29. L. Febvre and H. Martin, *The Coming of the Book* (London: NLB, 1976), p. 30.

30. Paper mills were not established in England until 1588. Michael Birks explains that "there is a simple explanation for the tardiness of Englishmen in building their own mills. The staple industry was the production of wool; few people wore clothing made of any other material, and until the fashion of wearing linen underwear became widely accepted there was not a sufficient supply of rags available to make the pulp" (*Gentlemen of the Law* [London: Stevens and Sons, 1960], p. 69).

31. Ibid., p. 74.

32. Percy Winfield, *The Chief Sources of English Legal History* (Cambridge, Mass.: Harvard University Press, 1925), p. 252.

33. Brian Abel-Smith and Robert Stevens, *Lawyers and the Courts* (London: Heinemann, 1967), p. 16.

34. J. H. Baker, ed., *The Legal Profession and the Common Law: Historical Essays* (London: Hambledon Press, 1986), p. 99.

35. Brooks, *Pettyfoggers and Vipers of the Commonwealth,* p. 12.

36. Ibid., p. 11.

37. Ibid., p. 11.

38. Herman Melville, "Bartleby," in *Billy Budd, Sailor, and Other Stories* (Baltimore: Penguin Books, 1967), p. 67.

39. A. W. B. Simpson, "The Source and Function of the Later Year Books," 87 *Law Quarterly Review* 94, 106 (1971).

40. Ibid., p. 98.

41. Wilfred Prest, *The Inns of Court under Elizabeth I and the Early Stuarts* (Totowa, N.J.: Rowman & Littlefield, 1972), p. 132.

42. "When we contemplate lawyers as a whole, we are bound to wonder whether these diverse men of law can properly be regarded as constituting a single profession" (J. H. Baker, "The English Legal Profession, 1450–1550," in *Lawyers in Early Modern Europe and America,* ed. W. R. Prest [New York: Holmes & Meier, 1981], p. 17).

43. Eliot Freidson, *Professional Powers* (Chicago: University of Chicago Press, 1986), p. 37.

44. Eliot Freidson, *Profession of Medicine* (New York: Dodd, Mead, 1970), pp. 71–72.

45. Michael Joseph, *Lawyers Can Seriously Damage Your Health* (London: Michael Joseph, 1984), p. 8.

46. U.S. Department of Labor, *Dictionary of Occupational Titles,* 4th ed. (Washington, D.C.: Government Printing Office, 1977).

47. Ernest Greenwood, "Attributes of a Profession," 2 *Social Work* 44–57 (1957).

48. Ibid., p. 45.

49. Freidson, *Professional Powers,* p. 26.

50. Peter Wright, "What Is a Profession," 29 *Canadian Bar Review* 748, 752 (1951).

51. Wilfrid Prest, *The Rise of the Barristers* (Oxford: Oxford University Press, 1986), p. 2.

52. Magali Sarfatti Larson, *The Rise of Professionalism: A Sociological Analysis* (Berkeley: University of California Press, 1977), p. xii.

53. Erving Goffman, *The Presentation of Self in Everyday Life* (Garden City, N.Y.: Doubleday, 1959), p. 46.

54. Freidson, *Professional Powers,* pp. 9–16.

55. Ibid., pp. 9–10.

56. Ibid., p. 9.

57. Winfield, *Chief Sources of English Legal History,* p. 91.

58. Febvre and Martin, *Coming of the Book,* p. 263.

59. Ibid. See also Miriam Usher Chrisman, *Lay Culture, Learned Culture: Books and Social Change in Strasbourg, 1480–1599* (New Haven, Conn.: Yale University Press, 1982).

60. William Seagle, *History of Law* (New York: Tudor, 1946), p. 14.

61. Ives, "A Lawyer's Library in 1500," p. 104.

62. C. P. Rodgers, "Humanism, History and the Common Law," 6 *Journal of Legal History* 129 (1985).

63. Winfield, *Chief Sources of English Legal History,* pp. 298–299.

64. Thurman Arnold, *The Symbols of Government* (New York: Harcourt, Brace & World, 1962), p. 57.

65. Harold Hyman, " 'No Cheers for the American Law School?' A Legal Historian's Complaint, Plea, and Modest Proposal," 71 *Law Library Journal* 227 (1978).

66. T. F. T. Plucknett, *A Concise History of the Common Law* (Boston: Little, Brown, 1956), p. 269.

67. Pound, *The Lawyer from Antiquity to Modern Time,* pp. 10–11.

300 NOTES

68. Christopher Columbus Langdell, "Harvard Celebration Speeches," 3 *Law Quarterly Review* 123, 124 (1887).
69. Plucknett, *Concise History of the Common Law*, p. 253.
70. This point is discussed more fully in Chapter 6.
71. Christopher Evans, *The Micro Millennium* (New York: Viking, 1979), p. 113.
72. Freidson, *Professional Powers*, p. 112.
73. Joshua Meyrowitz, *No Sense of Place* (New York: Oxford University Press, 1985), p. 79.
74. J. David Bolter, *Turing's Man* (Chapel Hill: University of North Carolina Press, 1984), p. 163.
75. Adam Hodgkin has suggested that "as the invention of printing led to the development of tables of contents, headlines, title pages, indices, or to the production of dictionaries, encyclopaedias, atlases, and gazettes, so the use of the computer will lead authors to present texts in new ways and surround them with a novel apparatus. The 'book' which is not merely written on a computer but *for* a computer, may be given a structure which has loops and branches and thereby subverts the linearity of the printed book. . . . For example, the novel *Hopscotch* by the Argentine novelist Julio Cortázar. This unusual work strains against the possibility of the printed book in a form which anticipates a serious possibility with computerized texts. There are two sets of page numbers. At the top of the page are the ordinary sequence of page numbers, numbers which correspond to the order in which leaves are bound, and at the foot of the page are placed the numbers which determine the alternative order in which the book could be read—if you find '123' at the bottom of the page you know that Cortázar intended you to turn to page 123, and so on. It may be contrived, experimental, or artificial to write a book, printed on paper, whose pages can be read in two different orders, but there are serious artistic or practical possibilities in books, written for a computer, whose order and structures can be modified or recomposed by the reader on the screen" ("New Technologies in Printing and Publishing," in *The Written Word: Literacy in Transition,* ed. Gerd Baumann [Oxford: Clarendon Press, 1986], pp. 158–159).
76. Adrian Hamilton, *The Financial Revolution* (New York: Free Press, 1986), p. 15.
77. Jones, "Challenge of Change," p. 689.
78. Tamar Lewin, "Law Firms Expanding in Scope," *New York Times,* February 11, 1987, p. D1.
79. John Wigmore, quoted in Pound, *The Lawyer from Antiquity to Modern Time,* p. 353.

1. Jerome Frank, *Law and Modern Mind* (New York: Coward-McCann, 1930).
2. James White, *When Words Lose Their Meaning* (Chicago: University of Chicago Press, 1984), p. 267.

3. Roberto Unger, *Law in Modern Society* (New York: Free Press, 1976).
4. Ibid., p. 50.
5. Ibid.
6. Ibid., p. 51.
7. Ibid., p. 52.
8. Ibid., p. 53.
9. Ibid.
10. Ibid., pp. 66–76.
11. Ibid., p. 66.
12. Charles Moore, ed., *The Status of the Individual in East and West* (Honolulu: University of Hawaii Press, 1964).
13. Meir Dan-Cohen, *Rights, Persons, and Organizations* (Berkeley: University of California Press, 1986), p. 13.
14. Richard McKeon, "The Individual in Law and in Legal Philosophy in the West," in *The Status of the Individual in East and West,* ed. Charles Moore (Honolulu: University of Hawaii Press, 1964), p. 453.
15. Louis Dumont, *Essays on Individualism* (Chicago: University of Chicago Press, 1986), p. 23.
16. James Carey, "Harold Adams Innis and Marshall McLuhan," 17 *Antioch Review* 5, 10 (1967).
17. Henry Maine, *Ancient Law* (New York: Scribner, 1864), p. 229.
18. Karl Polanyi, *The Great Transformation* (New York: Farrar and Rinehart, 1944), p. 46.
19. An insightful study of the modern class action that traces its origins to medieval conceptions of the group is Stephen Yeazell, *From Medieval Group Litigation to the Modern Class Action* (New Haven, Conn.: Yale University Press, 1987).
20. Arlene Saxonhouse, "Classical Greek Conception of Public and Private," in *Public and Private in Social Life,* ed. S. I. Benn and G. F. Gaus (New York: St. Martin's Press, 1983), p. 363.
21. Clifford Geertz, "On the Nature of Anthropological Understanding," 63 *American Scientist* 47–53 (1975).
22. Jakob Burekhardt, *The Civilization of the Renaissance in Italy,* trans. S. G. C. Middlemore, ed. B. Nelson and C. Trinkhaus (New York: Harper & Row, 1958), p. 143.
23. Richard Shweder and Edmund Bourne, "Does the Concept of the Person Vary Cross-Culturally?" in *Culture Theory,* ed. R. Schweder and R. Levine (New York: Cambridge University Press, 1984), pp. 158–199.
24. Walter Ullmann, *The Individual and Society in the Middle Ages* (Baltimore: Johns Hopkins University Press, 1966), p. 36.
25. Ibid., p. 48.
26. Ibid., p. 22.
27. Ibid., p. 36.
28. Alice Erh-Soon Tay and Eugene Kamenka, "Public Law—Private Law," in *Public and Private in Social Life,* ed. S. I. Benn and G. F. Gaus (New York: St. Martin's Press, 1983), p. 70.
29. David Riesman, "The Oral and Written Tradition," in *Explorations in Com-*

munications, ed. Marshall McLuhan and Edmund Carpenter (Boston: Beacon Press, 1960), p. 114.

30. Wendy Donager O'Flaherty, "The Uses and Abuses of Other People's Classics," *Federation Review,* September–October, 1986, p. 36.

31. Walter J. Ong, *Orality and Literacy: The Technologizing of the Word* (London: Methuen, 1982), p. 178.

32. Martin Hollis, "Of Masks and Men," in *The Category of the Person,* ed. Michael Carrithers, Steven Collins, and Steven Lukes (Cambridge: Cambridge University Press, 1985), p. 222.

33. Saxonhouse, "Classical Greek Conception of Public and Private," p. 363.

34. Ernst Goldschmidt, *The Printed Book of the Renaissance* (Amsterdam: Van Heusden, 1974), pp. 60–61.

35. Elizabeth Eisenstein, *The Printing Press as an Agent for Change* (New York: Cambridge University Press, 1979), p. 121.

36. Ibid., p. 132.

37. Harold Berman, "Conscience and Law: The Lutheran Reformation and the Western Legal Tradition," p. 8 (manuscript).

38. John Lyons, *The Invention of the Self* (Carbondale: Southern Illinois University Press, 1978).

39. Harold Berman, *Law and Revolution* (Cambridge, Mass.: Harvard University Press, 1983), pp. 29–30.

40. Alan MacFarlane, *The Origins of English Individualism* (Oxford: Blackwell, 1978), p. 5.

41. Ronald A. Rice, ed., *The New Media: Communication, Research, and Technology* (Beverly Hills, Calif.: Sage, 1984), p. 129.

42. Dan-Cohen, *Rights, Persons, and Organizations.*

43. Sherry Turkle has argued that "the computer . . . is a constructive as well as a projective medium. When you create in a programmed world, you work in it, you experiment in it, you live in it. The computer's chameleon-like quality, the fact that when you program it, it becomes your creature, makes it an ideal medium for the construction of a wide variety of private worlds and, through them, for self-exploration" (*The Second Self: Computers and the Human Spirit* [New York: Simon and Schuster, 1984], p. 15).

44. The first edition of *Computer-Readable Databases* in 1976 contained 301 databases; the 1979 edition, 528; the 1982 edition, 773; and the 1985 edition, 2,805 (see Martha Williams, Lawrence Lannom, and Carolyn Robins, *Computer-Readable Databases: A Directory and Data Sourcebook* [Chicago: American Library Association, 1985], p. viii).

45. *Statistical Abstract of the United States* (Washington, D.C.: Government Printing Office, 1988), p. 55.

46. Joseph Cantor, *Political Action Committees: Their Evolution, Growth and Implications for the Political System* (Washington, D.C.: Congressional Research Service, 1984).

47. S. Hiltz and M. Turoff, *The Network Nation* (Reading, Mass.: Addison-Wesley, 1978), p. xxv.

48. Yeazell, *From Medieval Group Litigation to the Modern Class Action.*

49. Ronald A. Rice, "Mediated Group Communication," in *The New Media:*

Communication, Research, and Technology, ed. Ronald A. Rice (Beverly Hills, Calif.: Sage, 1984), p. 129.

50. Joanne Lipman, "As Network TV Fades, Many Advertisers Try Age-Old Promotions," *Wall Street Journal,* August, 26, 1986, p. 1.

51. Paul Rubin, "Common Law and Statute Law," 11 *Journal of Legal Studies* 205, 213 (1982).

52. J. David Bolter, *Turing's Man* (Chapel Hill: University of North Carolina Press, 1984), p. 35.

53. Richard Flathman, *The Practice of Rights* (Cambridge: Cambridge University Press, 1976), p. 165.

54. Dan-Cohen, *Rights, Persons, and Organizations,* p. 164.

55. Ibid., p. 5.

56. Alvin Toffler, "The Future of Law and Order," *Encounter,* July 1973, p. 15.

57. Lon Fuller, *Legal Fictions* (Stanford, Calif.: Stanford University Press, 1967), p. 12.

58. F. H. Lawson, "The Creative Use of Legal Concepts," 32 *New York University Law Review* 913 (1957).

59. Ibid.

60. *Application of the President and Directors of Georgetown Hospital, Inc.,* 331 F. 2d 1010 (D.C. Cir. 1964).

61. Fuller, *Legal Fictions,* p. 12.

62. Kawashima Takeyoshi, "The Status of the Individual in the Notion of Law, Right, and Social Order in Japan," in *The Status of the Individual in East and West,* ed. Charles Moore (Honolulu: University of Hawaii Press, 1964), p. 440.

63. Ibid.

64. J. C. Smith, "The Unique Nature of the Concepts of Western Law," 46 *Canadian Bar Review* 191, 198 (1968).

65. John L. Comaroff and Simon Roberts, *Rules and Processes* (Chicago: University of Chicago Press, 1981), p. 9.

66. Smith, "The Unique Nature of the Concepts of Western Law," p. 202.

67. Jack Goody and Ian Watt, "The Consequences of Literacy," in *Literacy in Traditional Societies,* ed. Jack Goody (New York: Cambridge University Press, 1968), p. 29.

68. Eric Havelock, *The Greek Concept of Justice* (Cambridge, Mass.: Harvard University Press, 1978), p. 43.

69. Bolter, *Turing's Man,* p. 63.

70. Ong, *Orality and Literacy,* p. 119.

71. Havelock, *Greek Concept of Justice,* p. 14.

72. Percy Winfield, "Early Attempts at Reporting Cases," 159 *Law Quarterly Review* 316, 322 ((1924).

73. Eisenstein, *Printing Press as an Agent for Change,* p. 67.

74. Frances Yates, *The Art of Memory* (London: Routledge and Kegan Paul, 1966), p. 131.

75. Quoted in Eisenstein, *Printing Press as an Agent for Change,* p. 67.

76. Marshall McLuhan, *Understanding Media* (New York: McGraw-Hill, 1964), p. 85.

77. R. Godfrey Lienhardt, "Religion," in *Man, Culture and Society,* ed. Harry Shapiro (New York: Oxford University Press, 1956).

78. An exception to the de facto rule that pictures have no place in law reviews is Volume 96 of the *Yale Law Journal,* where pictures are included in several articles. This was, however, a special issue dedicated to the late Robert Cover, and the themes of the articles that contained the pictures are atypical of the content of law reviews. See also Howard Latin, Gary Tannehill and Robert White, "Remote Sensing Evidence and Environmental Law," 64 *California Law Review* 1300, 1310–1316 (1969), which contains the only color photographs I know of in a law-review article.

79. Arthur S. Miller, "Social Justice and the Warren Court," 11 *Pepperdine Law Review* 473, 475 (1984).

80. Victor Li, Introduction to Allyn Rickett and Adele Rickett, eds., *Prisoners of Liberation* (Garden City, N.Y.: Anchor Books, 1973).

81. Thomas Shaffer and Robert Redmount, "The Worship of the Disembodied Brain," *Barrister* 11 (1975).

82. Bernard Diamond, "Psychic Pressure," *Juris Doctor,* December 1976, p. 42.

83. John Culkin, "A Schoolman's Guide to Marshall McLuhan," in *McLuhan: Pro and Con,* ed. Raymond Rosenthal (New York: Funk and Wagnalls, 1968), p. 249.

84. John T. Noonan, Jr., *Persons and Masks of the Law* (New York: Farrar, Straus & Giroux, 1976), p. 6.

85. Lynne Henderson, "Legality and Empathy," 85 *Michigan Law Review* 1574 (1987).

86. Denis Hay, "Fiat Lux," in *Printing and the Mind of Man,* ed. John Carter and Percival Muir (London: Cassell, 1967), p. xxii.

87. L. Febvre and H. Martin, *The Coming of the Book* (London: NLB, 1976), pp. 77–78. See also Goldschmidt, *Printed Book of the Renaissance,* p. 13.

88. "Technological advances in voice synthesis, digital storage of audio and (in due course) voice recognition suggest that interactive audio information services—'heardata' or 'audiotex'—can be flexible and economical" (Martin C. J. Elton, "The Spoken and Printed Word in Electronic Communications," in *Electronic Publishing Plus,* ed. Martin Greenberger [White Plains, N.Y.: Knowledge Industry Publications, 1985], p. 27).

89. In discussing similar changes that a new form of communication might bring to the world of science, John Ziman has written: "The real issue is that the distinction between formal and informal scientific communications should not be blurred. The official scientific paper in a reputable journal is not an advertisement, or a news item. . . . it is written in a special impersonal form, in somewhat abstract language, within a strong convention of form and style. . . . A major achievement of our civilization is the creation of this form of communication, however clumsy or barbaric it may seem to those whose concerns are with poetry and feeling. . . . Word of mouth can never conform to these conventions. The choice of language is inevitably haphazard and elusive, and is always accompanied by gestures to convey the meaning. To publish verbatim the 'discussion' on a paper at a conference is to give unwarranted permanence and solidity to the contingent and transitory" (*Public Knowledge* [Cambridge: Cambridge University Press, 1968], pp. 110–111).

90. Bolter, *Turing's Man*, p. 137.

91. For a discussion of the evolution of paradigms, see Thomas Kuhn, *The Structure of Scientific Revolutions* (Chicago: University of Chicago Press, 1970).

92. Yosiyuki Noda, "The Character of the Japanese People and the Conception of Law," in *The Japanese Legal System*, ed. H. Tanaka (Tokyo: University of Tokyo Press, 1976), pp. 301–310.

93. Steven Lukes, *Individualism* (Oxford: Blackwell, 1973), p. 153.

CONCLUSION

1. Akhil Reed Amar, "Our Forgotten Constitution: A Bicentennial Comment," 97 *Yale Law Journal* 281 (1987).

2. Ibid., p. 286.

3. "It is of paramount importance to me that our country has a written constitution" (Hugo Black, *A Constitutional Faith* [1968], p. 3). *Marbury* v. *Madison*, 5 U.S. (1 Cranch) 137 (1803), which is permeated with the idea of the "writtenness" of the Constitution, is among the most-cited sources—for example, "the greatest improvement on political institutions, a written constitution . . . "

4. Anthony Smith, "The Influence of Television," 114 *Daedelus* 1 (1985).

5. See the writings of James B. White: *When Words Lose Their Meaning* (Chicago: University of Chicago Press, 1984); *The Legal Imagination: Studies in the Nature of Legal Thought and Expression* (Boston: Little, Brown, 1973); and "Thinking About Our Language," 96 *Yale Law Journal* 1960 (1987). In "Thinking About Our Language," White writes that "each of us is partly made by our language, which gives us the categories in which we perceive the world and which form our motives; but we are not simply that, for we are users and makers of our language too; and in remaking our language we contribute to the remaking of our characters and lives, for good or ill. . . . This is obviously the case with great artists and thinkers—their work changes the terms in which we think and talk, the ways in which we imagine and constitute ourselves . . . " (p. 1962).

6. Dennis Curtis and Judith Resnick, "Images of Justice," 96 *Yale Law Journal* 1727, 1755 (1987).

Bibliography

Abbott, Andrew. "Jurisdictional Conflicts: A New Approach to the Development of the Legal Professions." *American Bar Foundation Research Journal* 187 (1986).

Abbott, L. W. *Law Reporting in England, 1485–1585.* London: Athlone Press, 1973.

Abel, Richard. "The Decline of Professionalism." 49 *Modern Law Review* 1 (1986).

Abel, Richard. "Law and Modernity." 49 *Modern Law Review* 545 (1986).

Abel, Richard. *The Politics of Informal Justice.* New York: Academic Press, 1982.

Abel, Richard. "The Rise of Professionalism." 6 *British Journal of Law and Society* 82 (1979).

Abel, Richard. "The Transformation of the American Legal Profession." 20 *Law and Society Review* 7 (1986).

Abel, Richard, and Philip Lewis, eds. *Lawyers in Society.* Berkeley: University of California Press, 1988.

Abel-Smith, Brian, and Robert Stevens. *Lawyers and the Courts.* London: Heinemann, 1967.

Ackerman, Bruce. *Reconstructing American Law.* Cambridge, Mass.: Harvard University Press, 1984.

Adams, George. *Council and Courts in Anglo-Norman England.* New York: Russell & Russell, 1965.

Alfini, James. "Alternative Dispute Resolution and the Courts: An Introduction." 69 *Judicature* 252 (1986).

Allen, C. K. *Law in the Making.* Oxford: Oxford University Press, 1964.

Altman, Irwin. *The Environment and Social Behavior: Privacy, Personal Space, Territory and Crowding.* Monterey, Calif.: Brooks/Cole, 1975.

Altman, Irwin. "Privacy Regulation: Culturally Universal or Culturally Specific?" 33 *Journal of Social Issues* 66 (1977).

Amar, Akhil Reed. "Our Forgotten Constitution: A Bicentennial Comment." 97 *Yale Law Journal* 281 (1987).

American Bar Association. *Dispute Resolution Program Directory.* Washington, D.C.: American Bar Association, 1985.

American Booksellers Association, Inc. v. *Hudnut,* 598 F. Supp. 1316 (1984).

Anderson, David. "The Origins of the Press Clause." 30 *U.C.L.A. Law Review* 455 (1983).

"Anti-Pornography Laws and First Amendment Values." 98 *Harvard Law Review* 460 (1984).

Application of the President and Directors of Georgetown Hospital, Inc., 331 F. 2d 1010 (D.C. Cir. 1964).

Arendt, Hannah. *Between Past and Future: Eight Exercises in Political Thought.* New York: Viking, 1968.

Arendt, Hannah. *The Human Condition.* Chicago: University of Chicago Press, 1958.

Arnold, Thurman. *The Symbols of Government.* New York: Harcourt, Brace & World, 1962.

Arons, Stephen, and Ethan Katsh. "How TV Cops Flout the Law." *Saturday Review,* March 19, 1977, pp. 11–18.

Arthurs, H. W. *Without the Law: Administrative Justice and Legal Pluralism in Nineteenth-Century England.* Toronto: University of Toronto Press, 1985.

Ash, Timothy Garton. "Poland: The Uses of Adversity." *New York Review of Books,* June 27, 1985, pp. 5–10.

Aston, Margaret. *The Fifteenth Century.* London: Thames & Hudson, 1968.

Attorney General's Commission on Pornography. *Final Report.* Washington, D.C.: Department of Justice, 1986.

Aubert, Vilhelm. *In Search of Law.* Totowa, N.J.: Barnes & Noble Books, 1983.

Bagdikian, Ben. *The Information Machines.* New York: Harper & Row, 1971.

Bagdikian, Ben. "The U.S. Media: Supermarket or Assembly Line?" 35 *Journal of Communications* 81 (1985).

Bain, David H. "Letter from Manila: How the Press Helped to Topple a Despot." *Columbia Journalism Review,* May–June 1986, pp. 27–36.

Baker, C. Edwin. "Scope of First Amendment Freedom of Speech." 25 *U.C.L.A. Law Review* 964 (1978).

Baker, J. H. "The English Legal Profession, 1450–1550." In *Lawyers in Early Modern Europe and America.* Edited by W. R. Prest. New York: Holmes & Meier, 1981.

Baker, J. H. *An Introduction to English Legal History.* London: Butterworth, 1971.

Baker, J. H., ed. *The Legal Profession and the Common Law: Historical Essays.* London: Hambledon Press, 1986.

Ball, Milner. "The Play's the Thing." 28 *Stanford Law Review* 81 (1975).
Barron, Jerome. *Freedom of the Press for Whom?* Bloomington: Indiana University Press, 1973.
Bartlett, Robert. *Trial by Fire and Water: The Medieval Judicial Ordeal.* Oxford: Oxford University Press, 1986.
Baumann, Gerd, ed. *The Written Word.* Oxford: Clarendon Press, 1986.
Bauml, Franz. "Varieties and Consequences of Medieval Literacy and Illiteracy." 55 *Speculum* 237 (1980).
Beer, Lawrence. *Freedom of Expression in Japan.* Tokyo: Kodansha, 1984.
Beam, David. "Atari Bolsheviks." *The Atlantic,* March 1986, pp. 28–32.
Bedini, Sylvio. *Thomas Jefferson and his Copying Machines.* Charlottesville: University Press of Virginia, 1984.
Bell, Daniel. *The Coming of Post-Industrial Society.* New York: Basic Books, 1973.
Benedict, Ruth. "The Growth of Culture." In *Man, Culture and Society.* Edited by Harry Shapiro. New York: Oxford University Press, 1956.
Beniger, James. *The Control Revolution: Technological and Economic Origins of the Information Society.* Cambridge, Mass.: Harvard University Press, 1986.
Beniger, James. "Personalization of Mass Media and the Growth of Pseudo-Community." 14 *Communication Research* 352 (1987).
Benn, S. I., and G. F. Gaus, eds. *Public and Private in Social Life.* New York: St. Martin's Press, 1983.
Bennett, H. S. *English Books and Readers, 1475–1557.* Cambridge: Cambridge University Press, 1952.
Bennett, H. S. *English Books and Readers, 1603 to 1640.* Cambridge: Cambridge University Press, 1970.
Berman, Harold. "The Background of the Western Legal Tradition in the Folklaw of the Peoples of Europe." 45 *University of Chicago Law Review* 553 (1978).
Berman, Harold. "Conscience and Law: The Lutheran Reformation and the Western Legal Tradition." Manuscript.
Berman, Harold. *The Interaction of Law and Religion.* Nashville, Tenn.: Abington Press, 1974.
Berman, Harold. *Law and Revolution.* Cambridge, Mass.: Harvard University Press, 1983.
Berman, Harold, and William Greiner. *The Nature and Functions of Law.* 4th ed. Mineola, N.Y.: Foundation Press, 1980.
Bernstein, Jeremy. *The Analytical Machine.* 2nd ed. rev. New York: Morrow, 1981.
BeVier, Lillian. "The First Amendment and Political Speech: An Inquiry

into the Substance and Limits of Principle." 30 *Stanford Law Review* 299 (1978).

Bickel, Alexander. "The 'Uninhibited, Robust, and Wide-Open' First Amendment." In *Where Do You Draw the Line?* Edited by Victor Cline. Provo, Utah: Brigham Young University Press, 1974.

Bidney, David, ed. *The Concept of Freedom in Anthropology.* The Hague: Mouton, 1963.

Birks, Michael. *Gentlemen of the Law.* London: Stevens and Sons, 1960.

Birn, Raymond. "Book Production and Censorship in France, 1700–1715." In *Books and Society in History.* Edited by Kenneth Carpenter. New York: Bowker, 1983.

Black, Eugene Charlton. "The Eighteenth Century: Control and Revolution." In *Censorship: Five Hundred Years of Conflict.* New York: New York Public Library, 1984.

Blagden, Cyprian. *The Stationers' Company: A History, 1403–1959.* Cambridge, Mass.: Harvard University Press, 1960.

Blasi, Vincent. "The Checking Value in First Amendment Theory." 1977 *American Bar Foundation Research Journal* 521 (1977).

Bloch, M. "Astrology and Writing in Madagascar." In *Literacy in Traditional Societies.* Edited by Jack Goody. New York: Cambridge University Press, 1968.

Bloch, Maurice, ed. *Political Language and Oratory in Traditional Society.* New York: Academic Press, 1975.

Bloustein, Edward. "Privacy as an Aspect of Human Dignity: An Answer to Dean Prosser." 39 *New York University Law Review* 962 (1964).

Blum, Jeffrey M. "The Divisible First Amendment: A Critical, Functionalist Approach to Freedom of Speech and Electoral Campaign Spending." 58 *New York University Law Review* 1273 (1983).

Bogart, Leo. "The Growth of Television." In *Mass Communications.* Edited by W. Schramm. Urbana: University of Illinois Press, 1960.

Bohannon, Paul. "The Differing Realms of Law." 67 *American Anthropologist* 33 (1965).

Bohannon, Paul. *Law and Warfare: Studies in the Anthropology of Conflict.* Garden City, N.Y.: Natural History Press, 1967.

Bok, Sissela. *Secrets.* New York: Pantheon Books, 1982.

Bolling, George. *AT&T: Aftermath of Antitrust.* Washington, D.C.: National Defense University, 1983.

Bolter, J. David. *Turing's Man.* Chapel Hill: University of North Carolina Press, 1984.

Bolton, W. F. *The Language of 1984.* Knoxville: University of Tennessee Press, 1984.

Boorstin, Daniel. *The Americans: The Democratic Experience.* New York: Random House, 1973.

Boorstin, Daniel. *The Image*. New York: Harper & Row, 1964.

Bork, Robert H. "Neutral Principles and Some First Amendment Problems." 47 *Indiana Law Journal* 1 (1971).

Bowie, Norman. "The Law: From a Profession to a Business." 41 *Vanderbilt Law Review* 741 (1988).

Boyd, Julian. "These Precious Monuments of . . . Our History." 22 *The American Archivist* no. 2 (1959).

Boyes, Roger. "Start of the Other Star Wars." *The Times* (London), November 12, 1985, p. 14.

Bradley, Craig. "The Uncertainty Principle in the Supreme Court." 1986 *Duke Law Journal* 1 (1986).

Bricker, Herbert. *Freedom of Information*. New York: Macmillan, 1949.

Brief for Respondents. *Herbert* v. *Lando*, 99 S. Ct. 1635 (1979).

Broad, William. "Civilians Use Satellite Photos for Spying on Soviet Military." *New York Times*, April 7, 1986, p. A1.

Broad, William. "Private Cameras in Space Stir U.S. Security Fears." *New York Times*, August 25, 1987, p. C1.

Broad, William. "Soviet Offering to Sell Photographs Taken from Space." *New York Times*, July 14, 1987, p. C2.

Bronowski, Jacob. *The Origins of Knowledge and Imagination*. New Haven, Conn.: Yale University Press, 1978.

Brooks, C. W. "Common Lawyers in England, c.1558–1642." In *Lawyers in Early Modern Europe and America*. Edited by W. R. Prest. New York: Holmes & Meier, 1981.

Brooks, C. W. "Litigants and Attorneys in the King's Bench and Common Pleas, 1560–1640." In *Legal Records and the Historian*. Edited by J. H. Baker. London: Royal Historical Society, 1978.

Brooks, C. W. *Pettyfoggers and Vipers of the Commonwealth*. Cambridge: Cambridge University Press, 1986.

Brotman, Stuart. "Achieving Consensus at the FCC: Two Different Approaches to Establishing Cable Television Policy." *Negotiation Journal*, July 1987, p. 293.

Brown v. *Board of Education*, 349 U.S. 294 (1954).

Buckles, Mary Ann. "Interactive Fiction as Literature." *Byte*, May 1987, p. 140.

Buhler, Curt. *The Fifteenth Century Book*. Philadelphia: University of Pennsylvania Press, 1960.

Burckhardt, Jakob. *The Civilization of the Renaissance in Italy*. Translated by S. G. C. Middlemore and edited by B. Nelson and C. Trinkhaus. New York: Harper & Row, 1958.

Burnett v. *Coronado Oil and Gas Co.*, 285 U.S. 393 (1932).

Bury, J. B. *A History of Freedom of Thought*. 2nd ed. New York: Oxford University Press, 1952.

Buxton, Jean. "The Mandari of the Southern Sudan." In *Tribes Without Rulers*. Edited by John Middleton and David Tait. London: Routledge and Kegan Paul, 1958.

Cahn, Edmund. "The Firstness of the First Amendment." 65 *Yale Law Journal* 464 (1956).

Cam, Helen. "An East Anglican Shire-Moot of Stephen's Reign." 34 *English Historical Review* 570 (1924).

Cam, Helen. *Law-Finders and Law-Makers in Medieval England*. London: Merlin Press, 1962.

Cantor, Joseph. *Political Action Committees: Their Evolution, Growth and Implications for the Political System*. Washington, D.C.: Congressional Research Service, 1984.

Carey, James. "Harold Adams Innis and Marshall McLuhan." 17 *Antioch Review* 5 (1967).

Carlson, James. *Prime Time Law Enforcement*. New York: Pantheon, 1985.

Carmilly-Weinberger, Moshe. *Censorship and Freedom of Expression in Jewish History*. New York: Sepher-Hermon Press, 1977.

Carpenter, Edmund, and Marshall McLuhan. *Explorations*. Boston: Beacon Press, 1960.

Carr-Saunders, A. M., and P. A. Wilson. *The Professions*. London: Cass, 1964.

Carter, John, and Percival Muir, eds. *Printing and the Mind of Man*. London: Cassell, 1967.

Carter, Lief. *Reason in Law*. 2nd ed. Boston: Little, Brown, 1984.

Chaytor, H. J. *From Script to Print*. London: Sidgwick & Jackson, 1966.

Cherry, Colin. "The Telephone System." In *The Social Impact of the Telephone*. Edited by Ithiel de Sola Pool. Cambridge, Mass.: MIT Press, 1977.

Choldin, Marianna Tax. *A Fence Around the Empire: Russian Censorship of Western Ideas Under the Tsars*. Durham, N.C.: Duke University Press, 1985.

Chrisman, Miriam Usher. *Lay Culture, Learned Culture: Books and Social Change in Strasbourg, 1480–1599*. New Haven, Conn.: Yale University Press, 1982.

Christie, Nils. "Crime Control as Drama." 13 *Journal of Law and Society* 1 (1986).

Clanchy, M. T. *From Memory to Written Record*. Cambridge, Mass.: Harvard University Press, 1979.

Clapham, Michael. "Printing." In *A History of Technology: From the Renaissance to the Industrial Revolution*. Edited by C. Singer, E. Holmyard, A. Hall, and T. Williams. Oxford: Oxford University Press, 1957.

Clark, Aubert. *The Movement for International Copyright in Nineteenth Century America.* Washington, D.C.: Catholic University Press, 1960.

Cleary, Edward W. "Evidence as a Problem in Communicating." 5 *Vanderbilt Law Review* 277 (1952).

Cochrane, James. *Dr. Johnson's Printer: The Life of William Strahan.* Cambridge, Mass.: Harvard University Press, 1964.

Cohen, Morris. "Legal Forms." 31 *Yale Law Report* 25 (Spring 1985).

Cole, David. "Agon at Agora: Creative Misreadings in the First Amendment Tradition." 95 *Yale Law Journal* 857 (1986).

Colman, Rebecca. "Reason and Unreason in Early Medieval Law." 4 *Journal of Interdisciplinary History* 571 (1974).

Comaroff, John. "Talking Politics: Oratory and Authority in a Tswana Chiefdom." In *Political Language and Oratory in Traditional Society.* Edited by Maurice Bloch. New York: Academic Press, 1975.

Comaroff, John L., and Simon Roberts. *Rules and Processes.* Chicago: University of Chicago Press, 1981.

Commonwealth v. *Gordon,* 66 Pa. D. & C. 101 (Philadelphia County Ct., 1949).

Compaine, Benjamin. "The Expanding Base of Media Competition." 35 *Journal of Communications* 81 (1985).

Copp, David, and Susan Wendell. *Pornography and Censorship.* Buffalo, N.Y.: Prometheus Books, 1983.

Cornford, F. M. *Before and After Socrates.* Cambridge: Cambridge University Press, 1932.

Cover, Robert. "Nomos and Narrative." 97 *Harvard Law Review* 4 (1983).

Cover, Robert M. "Roman Law." *Yale Law Report,* Fall 1986, pp. 6–8.

Cowan, Geoffrey. *See No Evil.* New York: Simon and Schuster, 1979.

Cressy, David. *Literacy and the Social Order: Reading and Writing in Tudor and Stuart England.* Cambridge: Cambridge University Press, 1980.

Culkin, John. "A Schoolman's Guide to Marshall McLuhan." In *McLuhan: Pro and Con.* Edited by Raymond Rosenthal. New York: Funk and Wagnalls, 1968.

Curran, Barbara. "The Legal Profession in the 1980's: Selected Statistics From the 1984 Lawyer Statistical Report." Paper presented to the Law and Society Association, June 1984.

Curran, Barbara, Katherine Rosich, Clara Carson, and Mark Pucetti. *The Lawyer Statistical Report: A Profile of the Legal Profession in the 1980s.* Chicago: American Bar Foundation, 1985.

Curran, James, Michael Gurevitch, and Janet Woolacott. *Mass Communication and Society.* Beverly Hills, Calif.: Sage, 1979.

Curry, Jane Leftwich, trans. and ed. *The Black Book of Polish Censorship.* New York: Random House, 1984.

Curtis, Dennis, and Judith Resnick. "Images of Justice." 96 *Yale Law Journal* 1727 (1987).

D'Amato, Anthony. "Can/Should Computers Replace Judges?" 11 *Georgia Law Review* 1277 (1977).

Dabney, Daniel. "The Curse of Thamus: An Analysis of Full-Text Legal Document Retrieval." 78 *Law Library Journal* 5 (1986).

Damaska, Mirjan. "Structures of Authority and Comparative Criminal Procedure." 84 *Yale Law Journal* 480 (1975).

Dan-Cohen, Meir. *Rights, Persons, and Organizations.* Berkeley: University of California Press, 1986.

Darnton, Robert. *The Literary Underground of the French Regime.* Cambridge, Mass.: Harvard University Press, 1982.

Davies, Wendy, and Paul Fouracre, eds. *The Settlement of Disputes in Early Medieval Europe.* Cambridge: Cambridge University Press, 1986.

Davis, Bob. "Federal Agencies Press Data-Base Firms to Curb Access to 'Sensitive' Information." *Wall Street Journal,* February 5, 1987, p. 23.

Davis, Natalie Zemon. *Society and Culture in Early Modern France.* Stanford, Calif.: Stanford University Press, 1975.

Dawson, John. *A History of Lay Judges.* Cambridge, Mass.: Harvard University Press, 1960.

Dawson, John P. *The Oracles of the Law.* Ann Arbor: University of Michigan Press, 1968.

De Fleur, Melvin, and Sandra Ball-Rokeach. *Theories of Mass Communication.* New York: Longman, 1982.

Deloria, Vine. *God Is Red.* New York: Dell, 1973.

Dertouzos, Michael, and Joel Moses, eds. *The Computer Age: A Twenty-Year View.* Cambridge, Mass.: MIT Press, 1979.

de Sola Pool, Ithiel. *Technologies of Freedom.* Cambridge, Mass.: Harvard University Press, 1983.

Diamond, A. S. *Primitive Law, Past and Present.* London: Methuen, 1971.

Diamond, Bernard. "Psychic Pressure." *Juris Doctor,* December 1976, 42.

Diamond, Stanley. *In Search of the Primitive.* New Brunswick, N.J.: Transaction Books, 1974.

Diamond, Stanley. "The Rule of Law versus the Order of Custom." In *The Rule of Law.* Edited by Robert Wolff. New York: Simon and Schuster, 1971.

Dickens, Arthur G. *Reformation and Society in Sixteenth Century Europe.* New York: Harcourt, Brace & World, 1968.

Dickinson, John. "Legal Rules: Their Function in the Process of Decision." 79 *University of Pennsylvania Law Review* 833 (1931).

Dijksterhuis, Eduard. *The Mechanization of the World Picture.* Oxford: Oxford University Press, 1961.

Disch, R., ed. *The Future of Literacy.* Englewood Cliffs, N.J.: Prentice-Hall, 1973.

Dodds, E. R. *The Ancient Idea of Progress, and Other Essays on Greek Literature and Belief.* Oxford: Clarendon Press, 1973.

Douglas, Mary. *Purity and Danger.* London: Routledge and Kegan Paul, 1966.

Downs, Robert Bingham. *The First Freedom: Liberty and Justice in the World of Books and Reading.* Chicago: American Library Association, 1960.

Drogin, Marc. *Anathema! Medieval Scribes and the History of Book Curses.* Totowa, N.J.: Allanheld & Schram, 1983.

Duman, Daniel. "The Creation and Diffusion of a Professional Ideology in Nineteenth-Century England." 27 *Sociological Review* 113 (1979).

Duman, Daniel. *The English and Colonial Bars in the Nineteenth Century.* London: Croom Helm, 1983.

Duman, Daniel. *The Judicial Bench in England, 1725–1875.* London: Royal Historical Society, 1982.

Dumont, Louis. *Essays on Individualism.* Chicago: University of Chicago Press, 1986.

Dworkin, Andrea. "Against the Male Flood: Censorship, Pornography and Equality." 8 *Harvard Women's Law Journal* 1 (1985).

Dworkin, Ronald. *A Matter of Principle.* Cambridge, Mass.: Harvard University Press, 1985.

Economides, Kim, Mark Blacksell, and Charles Watkins. "The Spatial Analysis of Legal Systems: Toward a Geography of Law." 13 *Journal of Law and Society* 161 (1986).

Edelstein, Ludwig. *The Idea of Progress in Classical Antiquity.* Baltimore: Johns Hopkins University Press, 1967.

"Editor's Note." *New York Times,* August 22, 1986, p. B1.

Egan, Kieran. "Literacy and the Oral Foundations of Education." 57 *Harvard Educational Review* 445 (1987).

Eisenstein, Elizabeth. *The Printing Press as an Agent for Change.* New York: Cambridge University Press, 1979.

Elliot, Philip. *The Sociology of the Professions.* London: Macmillan, 1972.

Elton, G. R. *England, 1200–1640.* Ithaca, N.Y.: Cornell University Press, 1969.

Elton, Martin C. J. "The Spoken and Printed Word in Electronic Communications." In *Electronic Publishing Plus.* Edited by Martin

Greenberger. White Plains, N.Y.: Knowledge Industry Publications, 1985.

Emerson, Thomas. "Pornography and the First Amendment: A Reply to Professor McKinnon." 3 *Yale Law and Policy Review* 130 (1984).

Emerson, Thomas. *The System of Freedom of Expression.* New York: Random House, 1970.

Emerson, Thomas I. *Toward a General Theory of the First Amendment.* New York: Random House, 1963.

Evans, Christopher. *The Micro Millennium.* New York: Viking, 1979.

Fallers, Lloyd. *Law Without Precedent.* Chicago: University of Chicago Press, 1969.

FCC v. *Pacifica Foundation,* 438 U.S. 726 (1978).

Febvre, L., and H. Martin. *The Coming of the Book.* London: NLB, 1976.

Ferrarini, Elizabeth. *Infomania.* Boston: Houghton Mifflin, 1985.

John J. Fialka. "Study Sheds Light on Vulnerability of Computers to Electronic Spying." *Wall Street Journal,* October 18, 1985, p. 31.

Finkelstein, James. "The D..C Multi-Door Courthouse." 69 *Judicature* 305 (1986).

Finley, M. I. "Censorship in Classical Antiquity." *Times Literary Supplement,* July 29, 1977, p. 925.

Finley, M. I. *Economy and Society in Ancient Greece.* New York: Viking, 1981.

Finley, M. I. *Politics in the Ancient World.* Cambridge: Cambridge University Press, 1983.

Fiore, Quentin. "The Future of the Book." In *The Future of Time.* Edited by H. Yaker, H. Osmond, and F. Cheek. (Garden City, N.Y.: Doubleday, 1971).

First National Bank of Boston v. *Bellotti,* 435 U.S. 765 (1978).

Fiss, Owen M. "Against Settlement." 93 *Yale Law Journal* 1073 (1984).

Fitzgerald, Laura. "Towards a Modern Art of Law." 96 *Yale Law Journal* 2051 (1987).

Flaherty, David. *Privacy in Colonial New England.* Charlottesville: University Press of Virginia, 1972.

Flathman, Richard. *The Practice of Rights.* Cambridge: Cambridge University Press, 1976.

Flood, John. *The Legal Profession in the United States.* Chicago: American Bar Foundation, 1985.

Forbes, Esther. *Paul Revere: The World He Lived In.* Boston: Houghton Mifflin, 1942.

Foucault, Michel. *The Order of Things.* New York: Random House, 1970.

Foxon, David. *Libertine Literature in England, 1660–1745.* New Hyde Park, N.Y.: University Books, 1965.

Frank, Jerome. *Law and Modern Mind*. New York: Coward-McCann, 1930.

Franklin, Marc. "Suing Media for Libel: A Litigation Study." 1981 *American Bar Foundation Research Journal* 795 (1981).

Freidson, Eliot. *Profession of Medicine*. New York: Dodd, Mead, 1970.

Freidson, Eliot. *Professional Powers*. Chicago: University of Chicago Press, 1986.

Friedenthal, Richard. *Luther: His Life and Times*. New York: Harcourt, Brace & World, 1967.

Friedrich, Carl, ed. *Liberty*. New York: Atherton Press, 1962.

Friendly, Fred. *The Good Guys, the Bad Guys, and the First Amendment*. New York: Random House, 1975.

Friendly, Fred. *Minnesota Rag*. New York: Random House, 1981.

Friendly, Fred, and Martha Elliot. *The Constitution: That Delicate Balance*. New York: Random House, 1984.

Fruehling, James, ed. *Sourcebook on Death and Dying*. Chicago: Marquis, 1982.

Fuller, Lon. "Human Interaction and the Law." In *The Rule of Law*. Edited by Robert Paul Wolff. New York: Simon and Schuster, 1971.

Fuller, Lon. *Legal Fictions*. Stanford, Calif.: Stanford University Press, 1967.

Fuller, Lon. *The Morality of Law*. New Haven, Conn.: Yale University Press, 1964.

Galanter, Marc. "Justice in Many Rooms: Courts, Private Ordering, and Indigenous Law." 19 *Journal of Legal Pluralism* 1 (1981).

Galanter, Marc. "The Legal Malaise: Or, Justice Observed." 19 *Law and Society Review* 537 (1985).

Galanter, Marc. "Reading the Landscape of Disputes: What We Know and Don't Know (and Think We Know) About Our Allegedly Contentious and Litigious Society." 31 *U.C.L.A. Law Review* 4 (1983).

Gandz, Solomon. "Oral Tradition in the Bible." In *Jewish Studies in Memory of George A. Kohut*. Edited by S. Baron and A. Marx. New York: Alexander Kohut Memorial Foundation, 1935.

Ganley, Oswald, and Gladys Ganley. *To Inform or to Control?* New York: McGraw-Hill, 1982.

Gastil, Raymond D. *Freedom in the World: Political and Civil Liberties*. New York: Freedom House, 1980.

Gavison, Ruth. "Privacy and the Limits of Law." 89 *Yale Law Journal* 421 (1980).

Gay, John, and Michael Cole. *The New Mathematics and an Old Culture: A Study of Learning Among the Kpelle of Liberia*. New York: Holt, Rinehart and Winston, 1967.

Geertz, Clifford. "Deep Play: Notes on the Balinese Cockfight." 101 *Daedalus* 26 (1972).

Geertz, Clifford. "On the Nature of Anthropological Understanding." 63 *American Scientist* 47 (1975).

Gerbner, George. "Trial by Television: Are We at the Point of No Return?" 63 *Judicature* 416 (1980).

Gerety, Tom. "Redefining Privacy." 12 *Harvard Civil Rights–Civil Liberties Law Review* 233 (1977).

Gerstein, Robert S. " 'Law By Elimination': Depublication in the California Supreme Court." 67 *Judicature* 293 (1984).

Giedion, Siegfried. *Mechanization Takes Command.* New York: Norton, 1969.

Gilmore, Grant. "Legal Realism: Its Cause and Cure." 70 *Yale Law Journal* 1037 (1961).

Gisbert, Pascual. *Preliterate Man.* Bombay: Manaktalas, 1967.

Gladwin, Thomas. *East Is a Big Bird: Navigation and Logic on Puluwat Atoll.* Cambridge, Mass.: Harvard University Press, 1970.

Glossbrenner, Alfred. *The Complete Handbook of Personal Computer Communications.* New York: St. Martin's Press, 1983.

Gluckman, Max. "Gossip and Scandal." 4 *Current Anthropology* 307–316 (1963).

Gluckman, Max. *Politics, Law and Ritual in Tribal Society.* Oxford: Blackwell, 1971.

Goffman, Erving. *The Presentation of Self in Everyday Life.* Garden City, N.Y.: Doubleday, 1959.

Goldfarb, David. "A Refusenik's Story." *New York Times Magazine,* December 28, 1986, p. 22.

Goldschmidt, Ernst. *The Printed Book of the Renaissance.* Amsterdam: Van Heusden, 1974.

Goodhart, Arthur. "Precedent in English and Common Law." 50 *Law Quarterly Review* 40, 62 (1934).

Goodrich, Peter. "Literacy and the Languages of the Early Common Law." 14 *Journal of Law and Society* 422 (1987).

Goodrich, Peter. *Reading the Law.* Oxford: Blackwell, 1986.

Goody, Jack. "Alternative Paths to Knowledge in Oral and Literate Cultures." In *Speech and Written Language: Exploring Orality and Literacy.* Edited by Deborah Tannen. Norwood, N.J.: Ablex, 1982.

Goody, Jack. *The Interface Between the Written and the Oral.* Cambridge: Cambridge University Press, 1987.

Goody, Jack. "Literacy and the Non-Literate." *Times Literary Supplement* (London), May 12, 1972, pp. 539–540.

Goody, Jack. *The Logic of Writing and the Organization of Society.* Cambridge: Cambridge University Press, 1986.

Goody, Jack., ed. *Literacy in Traditional Societies*. New York: Cambridge University Press, 1968.

Graham, Howard. "Our Tong Maternall Marvelously Amendyd and Augmentyd: The First Englishing and Printing of the Medieval Statutes at Large, 1530–1533," 13 *U.C.L.A. Law Review* 58 (1965).

Graham, Howard, and John Heckel. "The Book that 'Made' the Common Law: The First Printing of Fitzherbert's *Le Graunde Abridgement*, 1514–1556." 51 *Law Library Journal* 100 (1958).

Greenawalt, Kent. "Speech and Crime." *American Bar Foundation Research Journal* 645 (1980).

Greenberg, Stanley. "Should the Courts Use Computerized Legal Databases?" 69 *Judicature* 322 (1986).

Greenberger, Martin, ed. *Electronic Publishing Plus* White Plains, N.Y.: Knowledge Industry Publications, 1985.

Greenwood, Ernest. "Attributes of a Profession." 2 *Social Work* 44 (1957).

Grendler, Paul F. "The Advent of Printing." In *Censorship: 500 Years of Conflict*. New York: New York Public Library, 1984.

Grey, Thomas. "The Constitution as Scripture." 37 *Stanford Law Review* 1 (1984).

Groskaufmanis, Karl. "What Films We May Watch: Videotape Distribution and the First Amendment." 136 *University of Pennsylvania Law Review* 1263 (1988).

Gross, Samuel. "The American Advantage: The Value of Inefficient Litigation." 85 *Michigan Law Review* 734 (1987).

Gulliver, P. H. *Social Control in an African Society*. Boston: Boston University Press, 1963.

Guth, DeLloyd J. "Enforcing Late-Medieval Law: Patterns in Litigation During Henry VII's Reign." In *Legal Records and the Historian*. Edited by J. H. Baker. London: Royal Historical Society, 1978.

Haiman, Franklyn S. *Speech and Law in a Free Society*. Chicago: University of Chicago Press, 1981.

Hair, Paul, ed. *Before the Bawdy Court: Selections from Church Court and Other Records Relating to the Correction of Moral Offences in England, Scotland and New England, 1300–1800*. New York: Barnes & Noble, 1972.

Hale, Oran J. *The Captive Press in the Third Reich*. Princeton, N.J.: Princeton University Press, 1964.

Hallpike, Christopher R. *The Foundations of Primitive Thought*. New York: Oxford University Press, 1979.

Hamilton, Adrian. *The Financial Revolution*. New York: Free Press, 1986.

Hart, H. L. A. *The Concept of Law*. Oxford: Oxford University Press, 1961.

Hattersley, Alan F. *A Short History of Democracy* Cambridge: Cambridge University Press, 1942.

Havelock, Eric. *The Greek Concept of Justice.* Cambridge, Mass.: Harvard University Press, 1978.

Havelock, Eric. *The Liberal Temper in Greek Politics.* New Haven, Conn.: Yale University Press, 1957.

Havelock, Eric. *Preface to Plato.* Oxford: Blackwell, 1963.

Hay, Denis. "Fiat Lux." In *Printing and the Mind of Man,* Edited by John Carter and Percival Muir. London: Cassell, 1967.

Hazeltine, Harold D. General Preface to *Statutes and Their Interpretation in the First Half of the Fourteenth Century,* by Theodore F. T. Plucknett. Cambridge: Cambridge University Press, 1922.

Heiner, Ronald. "Imperfect Decisions and the Law: On the Evolution of Legal Precedent and Rules." 15 *Journal of Legal Studies* 227 (1986).

Henderson, Jeffrey. *The Maculate Muse: Obscene Language in Attic Comedy.* New Haven, Conn.: Yale University Press, 1975.

Henderson, Lynne. "Legality and Empathy." 85 *Michigan Law Review* 1574 (1987).

Henderson, R. "Legal Literature and the Impact of Printing on the Legal Profession." 68 *Law Library Journal* 288 (1975).

Hentoff, Nat. *The First Freedom: The Tumultuous History of Free Speech in America.* New York: Delacorte, 1979.

High, R. "What Shall Be Done with the Reports?" 16 *American Law Review* 429 (1882).

Hiltz, S., and M. Turoff. *The Network Nation.* Reading, Mass.: Addison-Wesley, 1978.

Hirsch, Rudolph. *The Printed Word.* London: Variorum Reprints, 1978.

Hixson, Richard. *Privacy in a Public Society.* New York: Oxford University Press, 1987.

Hobbes, Thomas. *The Leviathan.* Edited by W. G. P. Smith. pt. I, ch. xiii. 1929.

Hobhouse, L. T., *Social Development.* New York: Holt, 1924.

Hoebel, E. Adamson. *The Law of Primitive Man.* New York: Atheneum, 1968.

Hoebel, E. Adamson. *Man in the Primitive World.* New York: McGraw-Hill, 1958.

Hogue, Arthur. *Origins of the Common Law.* Bloomington: Indiana University Press, 1966.

Holdsworth, William. *A History of English Law.* London: Methuen, 1966.

Holdsworth, William. *Some Lessons from Our Legal History.* New York: Macmillan, 1928.

Holdsworth, William. *Some Makers of English Law.* Cambridge: Cambridge University Press, 1938.

Holdsworth, William. *Sources and Literature of English Law*. Oxford: Oxford University Press, 1925.

Holdsworth, William. "The Year Books." In *Select Essays in Anglo-American Legal History*. By Association of American Law Schools. Boston: Little, Brown, 1908.

Hollis, Martin. "Of Masks and Men." In *The Category of the Person*. Edited by Michael Carrithers, Steven Collins, and Steven Lukes. Cambridge: Cambridge University Press, 1985.

Holmes, Oliver Wendell. *The Common Law*. Boston: Little, Brown, 1881.

Holmes, Oliver Wendell. *Speeches*. Boston: Little, Brown, 1934.

Holtz, Barry, ed. *Back to the Sources: Reading the Classic Jewish Texts*. New York: Simon and Schuster, 1984.

Houlbrooke, Ralph. *Church Courts and the People During the English Reformation*. Oxford: Oxford University Press, 1979.

Howe, Irving, ed. *1984 Revisited*. New York: Harper & Row, 1983.

Hunter, Dard. *Papermaking: The History and Technique of an Ancient Craft*. New York: Knopf, 1957.

Hyams, Paul. "Trial by Ordeal: The Key to Proof in the Early Common Law." In *On the Laws and Customs of England: Essays in Honor of Samuel E. Thorne*. Edited by Morris Arnold, Thomas Green, Sally Scully, and Stephen White. Chapel Hill: University of North Carolina Press, 1981.

Hyman, Harold. " 'No Cheers for the American Law School?' A Legal Historian's Complaint, Plea, and Modest Proposal." 71 *Law Library Journal* 227 (1978).

Innis, Harold. *The Bias of Communication*. Toronto: University of Toronto Press, 1951.

Innis, Harold. *Empire and Communication*. Toronto: University of Toronto Press, 1950.

Ives, E. W. "A Lawyer's Library in 1500." 85 *Law Quarterly Review* 104 (1969).

Ives, E. W. "The Origins of the Later Year Books." In *Legal History Studies, 1972*. Edited by Dafydd Jenkins. Cardiff: University of Wales Press, 1975.

Jacobstein, C. Myron. "Some Reflections on the Control of the Publication of Appellate Court Opinions." 27 *Stanford Law Review* 791 (1975).

Jaynes, Julian. *The Origins of Consciousness in the Breakdown of the Bicameral Mind*. Boston: Houghton Mifflin, 1976.

Jenkins, Iredell. *Social Order and the Limits of Law*. Princeton, N.J.: Princeton University Press, 1980.

Johnson, Bonnie McDaniel, and Ronald A. Rice. "Reinvention in the Innovation Process: The Case of Word Processing." In *The New*

Media: Communication, Research, and Technology. Edited by Ronald A. Rice. Beverly Hills, Calif.: Sage, 1984.

Jolowicz, H. F. *Roman Foundations of Modern Law.* Oxford: Oxford University Press, 1957.

Jones, Gareth, ed. *The Sovereignty of the Law: Selections from Blackstone's Commentaries.* Toronto: University of Toronto Press, 1973.

Jones, James W. "The Challenge of Change: The Practice of Law in the Year 2000." 41 *Vanderbilt Law Review* 683 (1988).

Jones, W. T. *The Classical Mind.* New York: Harcourt, Brace & World, 1969.

Kafka, Franz. *Parables and Paradoxes.* New York: Schocken, 1961.

Kaplan v. California, 413 U.S. 115 (1973).

Kasoulis, Thomas P. "Reference and Symbol in Plato's *Cratylus* and Kukai's *Shojijissogi.*" 32 *Philosophy East and West* 404 (1982).

Katsh, Ethan. "Communications Revolutions and Legal Revolutions: The New Media and the Future of Law." 8 *Nova Law Review* 633 (1984).

Katsh, Ethan. "Is Television Anti-law?: An Inquiry into the Relationship Between Law and Media." 7 *ALSA Forum* 26 (1983).

Katsh, Ethan. "The Medium Has a Message: Television, Israel, and the People of the Book." 30 *Judaism* 295 (1981).

Katsh, Ethan. "The Supreme Court Beat: How Television Covers the U.S. Supreme Court." 67 *Judicature* 6 (1983).

Katsh, Ethan. "Television: The Message, the Medium and Legal Values." In *Law and Society: Culture Learning Through Law.* Edited by Richard Vuylsteke. Honolulu: East-West Center, 1977.

Kaufman, Michael. "Illicit Weekly Has Survived Polish Raids." *New York Times,* February 16, 1986, p. 7.

Kautsky, John H. *The Politics of Aristocratic Empires.* Chapel Hill: University of North Carolina Press, 1982.

Kelly, J. M. *Studies in the Civil Judicature of the Roman Republic.* Oxford: Oxford University Press, 1976.

Kendrick, Walter. *The Secret Museum: Pornography in Modern Culture.* New York: Viking, 1987.

Kern, Fritz. *Kingship and Law in the Middle Ages.* Oxford: Blackwell, 1948.

Kevelson, Roberta. *The Law as a System of Signs.* New York: Plenum, 1988.

Kidder, Tracy. *The Soul of a New Machine.* Boston: Little, Brown, 1981.

Kiralfy, A. R. "Custom in Mediaeval English Law." 9 *Journal of Legal History* 27 (1988).

Kiralfy, A. K. R. *Potter's Historical Introduction to English Law and Its Institutions.* London: Sweet & Maxwell, 1958.

Kleinfield, N. R. "Turning McGraw-Hill Upside Down." *New York Times,* February 2, 1986, sec. 3, p. 1.

Kosinsky, Jerzy. *Being There.* New York: Harcourt Brace Jovanovich, 1970.

Krauthammer, Charles. "The Joy of Analog." *Time,* May 26, 1986, p. 84.

Krygier, Martin. "In Occupied Poland." *Commentary,* March 1986, pp. 15–23.

Kuhn, Thomas. *The Structure of Scientific Revolutions.* Chicago: University of Chicago Press, 1970.

Kuhns, William. *The Post-Industrial Prophets: Interpretations of Technology.* New York: Weybright and Talley, 1971.

Lahav, Pnina, ed. *Press Law in Modern Democracies: A Comparative Study.* New York: Longmar, 1985.

Landes, David. *Revolution in Time.* Cambridge, Mass.: Harvard University Press, 1983.

Langdell, Christopher Colubmus. "Harvard Celebration Speeches." 3 *Law Quarterly Review* 123 (1887).

LaPlante, Alice. "Liability in the Information Age." *InfoWorld,* August 18, 1986, p. 37.

Larson, Magali Sarfatti. *The Rise of Professionalism: A Sociological Analysis.* Berkeley: University of California Press, 1977.

Lasden, Martin. "Of Bytes and Bulletin Boards." *New York Times Magazine,* August 4, 1985, p. 34.

Lateef, Noel. "Keeping Up with Justice: Automation and the New Activism." 67 *Judicature* 213 (1983).

Latin, Howard, Gary Tannehill, and Robert White. "Remote Sensing Evidence and Environmental Law." 64 *California Law Review* 1300 (1969).

Laumann, Edward, and David Knoke. "The Increasingly Organizational State. *Society,* January–February 1988, p. 21.

Lawrence, Peter. *Road Belong Cargo.* Melbourne: Melbourne University Press, 1964.

Lawson, F. H. "The Creative Use of Legal Concepts." 32 *New York University Law Review* 913 (1957).

Lee, Dorothy. *Freedom and Culture.* Englewood Cliffs, N.J.: Prentice-Hall, 1959).

Levinson, L. Harold. "Making Society's Legal System Accessible to Society: The Lawyer's Role and Its Implications." 41 *Vanderbilt Law Review* 789 (1988).

Lévi-Strauss, Claude. *Tristes Tropiques.* London: Cape, 1973.

Levy, Leonard W. *Emergence of a Free Press.* New York: Oxford University Press, 1985.

Levy, Leonard W. *Legacy of Suppression: Freedom of Speech and Press in Early American History.* New York: Harper & Row [Torchbook ed.], 1963.

Levy, Leonard W. *Treason Against God: A History of the Offense Against Blasphemy.* New York: Schocken, 1981.

Levy, Steven. *Hackers.* Garden City, N.Y.: Doubleday, 1984.

Lewin, Tamar. "Law Firms Expanding in Scope." *New York Times,* February 11, 1987, p. D1.

Lewis, Anthony. "*New York Times* v. *Sullivan* Reconsidered: Time to Return to the Central Meaning of the First Amendment." 84 *Columbia Law Review* 603 (1983).

Lewis, Ellis. "The History of Judicial Precedent, Pt. 1." 46 *Law Quarterly Review* 212 (1930).

Lewis, Ellis. "The History of Judicial Precedent, Pt. 2." 46 *Law Quarterly Review* 421 (1930).

Lewis, Ellis. "The History of Judicial Precedent, Pt. 3." 47 *Law Quarterly Review* 421 (1931).

Lewis, Ellis. "The History of Judicial Precedent, Pt. 4." 48 *Law Quarterly Review* 414 (1932).

Li, Victor. Introduction to *Prisoners of Liberation.* Edited by Allyn Rickett and Adele Rickett. Garden City, N.J.: Anchor Books, 1973.

Li, Victor. *Law Without Lawyers.* Stanford, Calif.: Stanford Alumni Association, 1977.

Lieberman, Jethro, and James Henry. "Lessons from the Alternative Dispute Resolution Movement." 53 *University of Chicago Law Review* 424 (1986).

Lienhardt, R. Godfrey. "Religion." In *Man, Culture and Society.* Edited by Harry Shapiro. New York: Oxford University Press, 1956.

Lienhardt, R. Godfrey. "The Western Dinka." In *Tribes Without Rulers.* Edited by John Middleton and David Tait. London: Routledge and Kegan Paul, 1958.

Lipman, Joanne. "As Network TV Fades, Many Advertisers Try Age-Old Promotions." *Wall Street Journal,* August, 26, 1986, p. 1.

Llewellyn, Karl. *The Bramble Bush.* Dobbs Ferry, N.Y.: Oceana Publications, 1960.

Lloyd, Dennis. *The Idea of Law.* Baltimore: Penguin, 1964.

Lobingier, C. Sumner. "Precedent in Legal Systems." 44 *Michigan Law Review* 955 (1946).

Logan, Robert. *The Alphabet Effect.* New York: Morrow, 1986.

Lukes, Steven. *Individualism.* Oxford: Blackwell, 1973.

Lyon, Bryce. *A Constitutional and Legal History of Medieval England.* New York: Norton, 1980.

Lyons, John. *The Invention of the Self.* Carbondale: Southern Illinois University Press, 1978.

McDermott, Jo. "Another Analysis of Full-Text Legal Document Retrieval." 78 *Law Library Journal* 337 (1986).

MacFarlane, Alan. *The Origins of English Individualism.* Oxford: Blackwell, 1978.

McGovern, Francis. "Toward a Functional Approach for Managing Complex Litigation." 53 *University of Chicago Law Review* 440 (1986).

McKeon, Richard. "The Individual in Law and in Legal Philosophy in the West." In *The Status of the Individual in East and West.* Edited by Charles Moore. Honolulu: University of Hawaii Press, 1964.

McKinnon, Catherine. "Pornography, Civil Rights, and Speech." 20 *Harvard Civil Rights–Civil Liberties Law Review* 1 (1985).

McLuhan, Marshall. *The Gutenberg Galaxy.* Toronto: University of Toronto Press, 1962.

McLuhan, Marshall. *Understanding Media.* New York: New American Library, 1964.

Maine, Henry. *Ancient Law.* New York: Scribner, 1864.

Maine, Henry. *International Law.* New York: Holt, 1888.

Maitland, Frederic William. *The Collected Papers of Frederic William Maitland.* Edited by H. A. L. Fisher. Cambridge: Cambridge University Press, 1911.

Maitland, F. W. *The Forms of Action at Common Law.* Cambridge: Cambridge University Press, 1909.

Maitland, Frederic W., and Francis C. Montague. *A Sketch of English Legal History.* New York: Putnam, 1915.

Mander, Jerry. *Four Arguments for the Elimination of Television.* New York: Morrow, 1978.

Manheim, Jarol. "Can Democracy Survive Television?" 26 *Journal of Communications* 84 (1976).

Mann, Elizabeth. "Telephones, Sex, and the First Amendment." 33 *U.C.L.A. Law Review* 1221 (1986).

Mark, Gregory. "The Personification of the Business Corporation in American Law." 54 *University of Chicago Law Review* 1441 (1987).

Markoff, John. "Breach Reported in U.S. Computers." *New York Times,* April 18, 1988, p. 1.

Markoff, John. "Top-Secret, and Vulnerable." *New York Times,* April 25, 1988, p. D1.

Martin, Henri-Jean. "Publishing Conditions and Strategies in Ancien Régime France." In *Books and Society in History.* Edited by Kenneth Carpenter. New York: Bowker, 1983.

Martino, Antonio, and Fiorenza Natali. *Automated Analysis of Legal Texts.* Amsterdam: Elsevier Science, 1986.

Mason, Alpheus. *Brandeis, a Free Man's Life.* New York: Viking, 1946.

Mayton, William. "From a Legacy of Suppression to a 'Metaphor of the Fourth Estate.' " 39 *Stanford Law Review* 139 (1986).

Meadow, Robert, ed. *New Communication Technologies in Politics.* Washington, D.C.: Annenberg Schools' Washington Program, 1985.

Melody, William, Liora Salter, and Paul Heyer. *Culture, Communication, and Dependency: The Tradition of H. A. Innis.* Norwood, N.J.: Ablex, 1981.

Melvern, Linda, David Hebditch, and Nick Anning. *Techno-Bandits.* Boston: Houghton Mifflin, 1984.

Melville, Herman. "Bartleby." In *Billy Budd, Sailor and Other Stories.* Baltimore: Penguin, 1967.

Menkel-Meadow, Carrie. "For and Against Settlement: Uses and Abuses of the Mandatory Settlement Conference." 33 *U.C.L.A. Law Review* 485 (1985).

Mermin, Samuel. *Law and the Legal System.* Boston: Little, Brown, 1973.

Meyrowitz, Joshua. *No Sense of Place.* New York: Oxford University Press, 1985.

Miami Herald v. *Tornillo.* 418 U.S. 241 (1973).

Middleton, Kent, and Roy Mersky, eds. *Freedom of Expression: A Collection of Best Writings.* Buffalo, N.Y.: Hein, 1981.

Miller v. *California,* 93 S.Ct. 2607 (1973).

Miller, Arthur R. *The Assault on Privacy.* Ann Arbor: University of Michigan Press, 1971.

Miller, Arthur S. "Pretense and Our Two Constitutions." 54 *George Washington Law Review* 375 (1986).

Miller, Arthur S. *Social Change and Fundamental Law: America's Evolving Constitution.* Westport, Conn.: Greenwood Press, 1979.

Miller, Arthur S. "Social Justice and the Warren Court." 11 *Pepperdine Law Review* 473 (1984).

Milton, John. *Areopagitica.* In *The Works of John Milton.* Edited by William Haller. New York: Columbia University Press, 1931–1938.

Minow, Martha. "Interpreting Rights: An Essay for Robert Cover." 96 *Yale Law Journal* 1860 (1987).

Moore, Barrington. *Privacy: Studies in Social and Cultural History.* Armonk, N.Y.: Sharpe, 1984.

Moore, Charles, ed. *The Status of the Individual in East and West.* Honolulu: University of Hawaii Press, 1964.

Moore, Sally Falk. *Power and Property in Inca Peru.* New York: Columbia University Press, 1958.

Mowlana, Hamid. "Technology versus Tradition: Communication in the Iranian Revolution." 29 *Journal of Communication* 107 (1979).

Muller, Herbert J. "Freedom and Justice in History." In *The Concept of*

Freedom in Anthropology. Edited by David Bidney. The Hague: Mouton, 1963.

Mumford, Lewis. *Technics and Civilization.* New York: Harcourt, Brace, 1934.

Nader, Laura. "The Anthropological Study of Law." 6 *American Anthropologist* 3 (1965).

Nader, Laura, and Harry F. Todd, Jr., eds. *The Disputing Process: Law in Ten Societies.* New York: Columbia University Press, 1978.

Naisbitt, John. *Megatrends.* New York: Warner Books, 1982.

National Telecommunications and Information Administration. *Issues in Domestic Telecommunications: Direction for National Policy.* Washington, D.C.: Department of Commerce, 1985.

Nelson, Theodore. *Computer Lib.* Redmund, Wash.: Microsoft, 1987.

Nenner, Howard. *By Colour of Law.* Chicago: University of Chicago Press, 1977.

Nimmer, Melville. *Nimmer on Copyright.* New York: Bender, 1971.

Noda, Yosiyuki. "The Character of the Japanese People and the Conception of Law." In *The Japanese Legal System.* Edited by H. Tanaka. Tokyo: University of Tokyo Press, 1976.

Noonan, John T., Jr. *Persons and Masks of the Law.* New York: Farrar, Straus and Giroux, 1976.

Nora, Simon, and Alain Minc. *The Computerization of Society.* Cambridge, Mass.: MIT Press, 1980.

Nordenstreng, Kaarle, and Herbert Schiller. *National Sovereignty and International Communication.* Norwood, N.J.: Ablex, 1979.

Oettinger, Anthony. "Information Resources: Knowledge and Power in the 21st Century." *Science,* July 4, 1980, pp. 191–198.

O'Flaherty, Wendy Donager. "The Uses and Abuses of Other People's Classics." *Federation Review,* September–October, 1986, p. 36.

Oldham, James. "Law Reporting in the London Newspapers, 1756–1786." 31 *American Journal of Legal History* 177 (1987).

Olmstead v. *United States,* 277 U.S. 438 (1928).

Ong, Walter J. *Interfaces of the Word: Studies in the Evolution of Consciousness and Culture.* Ithaca, N.Y.: Cornell University Press, 1977.

Ong, Walter J. *Orality and Literacy: The Technologizing of the Word.* London: Methuen, 1982.

Ong, Walter J. *Rhetoric, Romance, and Technology.* Ithaca, N.Y.: Cornell University Press, 1971.

Ortner, Sherry. *Sherpas Through Their Rituals.* New York: Cambridge University Press, 1978.

Orwell, George. *George Orwell: The Lost Writings.* Edited by W. J. West. New York: Arbor House, 1985.

Orwell, George. *1984.* New York: Harcourt, Brace, 1949.

Orwell, George. "The Russian Regime." Review of *Russia Under Soviet Rule,* by N. de Basily. *New English Weekly,* January 12, 1939. In *The Collected Essays, Journalism and Letters of George Orwell.* Vol. 1. Edited by Sonia Orwell and Ian Angus. (London: Secker & Warburg, 1968).

Owen, David. "Copies in Seconds." *The Atlantic,* November 1986, pp. 64–73.

Owen, David. "Satellite Television." *The Atlantic,* June 1985, pp. 45–62.

Palko v. *Connecticut,* 302 U.S. 319, 327 (1937).

Palmer, Robert C. "The Origins of the Legal Profession in England." 11 *Irish Jurist* 126 (1976).

Patterson, Lyman. *Copyright in Historical Perspective.* Nashville, Tenn.: Vanderbilt University Press, 1968.

Pearson, Jessica. "An Evaluation of Alternatives to Court Adjudication." 7 *Justice Systems Journal* 420 (1982).

Peckham, Robert. "The Federal Judge as a Case Manager: The New Role in Guiding a Case from Filing to Disposition." 69 *California Law Review* 770 (1981).

Pember, Don. *Privacy and the Press.* Seattle: University of Washington Press, 1972.

Pemberton, Jeffrey. "The Linear File." *Database,* December 1986, p. 6.

Pepys, Samuel. *The Diary of Samuel Pepys.* Vol. 9. Edited by R. Latham and W. Matthews. Berkeley: University of California Press, 1976.

Peterson, Iver. "Scrambling of Signals Today Thwarts TV Dish Antennas." *New York Times,* January 15, 1986, p. A1.

"Photo Satellites Restricted by U.S." *New York Times,* July 12, 1987, p. 22.

Ploman, Edward, and L. Clark Hamilton. *Copyright.* London: Routledge and Kegan Paul, 1980.

Plucknett, Theodore F. T. *A Concise History of the Common Law.* Boston: Little, Brown, 1956.

Plucknett, Theodore F. T. "The Harvard Manuscript of Thornton's *alSumma.*" 51 *Harvard Law Review* 1038 (1938).

Plucknett, Theodore F. T. *Statutes and Their Interpretation in the First Half of the Fourteenth Century.* Cambridge: Cambridge University Press, 1922.

Polanyi, Karl. *The Great Transformation.* New York: Farrar and Rinehart, 1944.

Pollack, Andrew. "Free Speech Issues Surround Computer Bulletin Board Use." *New York Times,* November 12, 1984, p. A1.

Pollard, Graham. "The *Pecia* System in the Medieval Universities." In *Medieval Scribes, Manuscripts and Libraries.* Edited by M. B. Parkes and Andrew Watson. London: Scolar Press, 1978.

Pollock, Frederick, and Frederick William Maitland. *The History of English Law Before the Time of Edward I.* 2nd ed. Cambridge: Cambridge University Press, 1968.

Porat, Marc U. "Communication Policy in an Information Society." In *Communications for Tomorrow: Policy Perspectives for the 1980s.* Edited by Glen O. Robinson. New York: Praeger, 1978.

Pospisil, Leopold. *Anthropology of Law.* New York: Harper & Row, 1971.

Pottinger, David. *The French Book Trade in the Ancien Régime, 1500–1791.* Cambridge, Mass.: Harvard University Press, 1958.

Pound, Roscoe. *An Introduction to the Philosophy of Law.* New Haven, Conn.: Yale University Press, 1954.

Pound, Roscoe. *The Lawyer from Antiquity to Modern Time.* St. Paul, Minn.: West, 1953.

Pound, R., and T. Plucknett, eds. *Readings on the History and System of the Common Law.* Rochester, N.Y.: Lawyers Cooperative, 1927.

Prest, Wilfred. *The Inns of Court under Elizabeth I and the Early Stuarts.* Totowa, N.J.: Rowman & Littlefield, 1972.

Prest, Wilfred. *The Rise of the Barristers.* Oxford: Oxford University Press, 1986.

Price, Monroe. "Reexamining Intellectual Property Concepts: A Glimpse into the Future Through the Prism of *Chakrabarty.*" 6 *Cardozo Arts and Entertainment Law Journal* 443 (1988).

Probert, Walter. *Law, Language and Communication.* Springfield, Ill.: Thomas, 1972.

Prosser, William. "Privacy." 48 *California Law Review* 383 (1960).

Pylyshyn, Zenon. *Perspectives on the Computer Revolution.* Englewood Cliffs, N.J.: Prentice-Hall, 1970.

The Queen v. *Read.* 11 Mod. Rep. 142 (1708). In *Censorship Landmarks.* Edited by Edward De Grazia. New York: Bowker, 1969.

Rabban, David. "The Ahistorical Historian: Leonard Levy on Freedom of Expression in Early American History." 37 *Stanford Law Review* 795 (1985).

Rabban, David. "The Emergence of Modern First Amendment Doctrine." 50 *University of Chicago Law Review* 1205 (1983).

Rabban, David. "The First Amendment in Its Forgotten Years." 90 *Yale Law Journal* 514 (1981).

Radcliffe, Geoffrey. *Not in Feather Beds.* London: Hamish Hamilton, 1968.

Radin, Max. "Freedom of Speech in Ancient Athens." 48 *American Journal of Philology* 215 (1927).

Read, William. "The First Amendment Meets the Information Society." In *Telecommunications: Issues and Choices for Society.* Edited by Jerry Salvaggio. New York: Longman, 1983.

Redfield, Robert. *The Primitive World and Its Transformations*. Ithaca, N.Y.: Cornell University Press, 1953.

Reisman, W. Michael. *Folded Lies*. New York: Free Press, 1979.

Reporters Committee for Freedom of the Press. *The News Media and the Law*. Washington, D.C.: Reporters Committee for Freedom of the Press.

Resnik, Judith. "Failing Faith: Adjudicatory Procedure in Decline." 53 *University of Chicago Law Review* 494 (1986).

Resnik, Judith. "Tiers." 57 *Southern California Law Review* 840 (1984).

Reynolds, Susan. *Kingdoms and Communities in Western Europe, 900–1300*. Oxford: Oxford University Press, 1984.

Reynolds, Susan. "Law and Communities In Western Christendom." 25 *American Journal of Legal History* 205 (1981).

Rice, Ronald A., ed. *The New Media: Communication, Research, and Technology*. Beverly Hills, Calif.: Sage, 1984.

Riesman, David. "The Oral and Written Tradition." In *Explorations in Communications*. Edited by Marshall McLuhan and Edward Carpenter. Boston: Beacon Press, 1960.

Riesman, David. *The Oral Tradition, the Written Word and the Screen Image*. Yellow Springs, Ohio: Antioch College, 1956.

Roberts, Simon. *Order and Dispute*. New York: St. Martin's Press, 1979.

Robertson, J. M. *A Short History of Free-thought*. New York: Russell & Russell, 1957.

Robson, Robert. *The Attorney in Eighteenth-Century England*. Cambridge: Cambridge University Press, 1959.

Rodgers, C. P. "Humanism, History and the Common Law." 6 *Journal of Legal History* 129 (1985).

Roehl, Janice, and Royer Cook. *The Multi-Door Dispute Resolution Program: Phase I Assessment, Preliminary Report*. Washington, D.C.: Institute for Social Analysis, 1985.

Rosenthal, Raymond. *McLuhan: Pro and Con*. New York: Funk and Wagnalls, 1968.

Rostenberg, Leona. *The Minority Press and the English Crown*. Nieuwkoop: De Graaf, 1971.

Rowan, Steven. "Jurists and the Printing Press in Germany: The First Century." In *Print and Culture in the Renaissance*. Edited by Gerald Tyson and Sylvia Wagonheim. Newark: University of Delaware Press, 1986.

Rubin, Paul. "Common Law and Statute Law." 11 *Journal of Legal Studies* 205 (1982).

Rueschemeyer, Dietrich. *Lawyers and Their Society*. (Cambridge, Mass.: Harvard University Press, 1975).

Rutland, Robert. *"Well Acquainted with Books:" The Founding Fathers of 1787*. Washington, D.C.: Library of Congress, 1987.

Sanger, David. "Computer Code Shift Expected: Eavesdropping Fear Indicated." *New York Times,* April 15, 1986, p. D1.

Sanger, David E. "U.S. to Curb Supercomputer Use by Soviet Scholars Working Here." *New York Times,* February 10, 1986, p. A1.

Sarton, George. "The Quest for Truth: Scientific Progress During the Renaissance." In *The Renaissance: Six Essays.* New York: Harper & Row, 1962.

Sarton, George. *Six Wings.* Bloomington: Indiana University Press, 1957.

Saxonhouse, Arlene. "Classical Greek Conception of Public and Private." In *Public and Private in Social Life.* Edited by S. I. Benn and G. F. Gaus. New York: St. Martin's Press, 1983.

Schauer, Frederick. "Precedent." 39 *Stanford Law Review* 571 (1987).

Schlesinger, Arthur M. *Prelude to Independence.* New York: Knopf, 1957.

Schmidt, Benno. *Freedom of the Press vs. Public Access.* New York: Praeger, 1976.

Schoenman, Ferdinand. *Philosophical Dimensions of Privacy.* New York: Cambridge University Press, 1984.

Schofield, R. S. "The Measurement of Literacy in Pre-Industrial England." In *Literacy in Traditional Societies.* Edited by J. Goody. New York: Cambridge University Press, 1968.

Scholem, Gershom. *The Messianic Idea in Judaism.* New York: Schocken, 1971.

Schwartz, Tony. *The Responsive Chord.* Garden City, N.Y.: Anchor Press/Doubleday, 1974.

Seagle, William. *The History of Law.* New York: Tudor, 1946.

Seagle, William. *Law: The Science of Inefficiency.* New York: Macmillan, 1952.

Seagle, William. *Men of Law.* New York: Macmillan, 1947.

Shaffer, Thomas, and Robert Redmount. "The Worship of the Disembodied Brain." *Barrister* 11 (1975).

Shainor, Donald. *Behind the Lines: The Private War Against Soviet Censorship.* New York: St. Martin's Press, 1985.

Shils, Edward. "Privacy: Its Constitution and Vicissitudes." 36 *Law and Contemporary Problems* 281 (1966).

Shklar, Judith. *Legalism.* Cambridge, Mass.: Harvard University Press, 1964.

Shweder, Richard, and Edmund Bourne. "Does the Concept of the Person Vary Cross-culturally?" In *Culture Theory.* Edited by Richard Shweder and Robert LeVine. New York: Cambridge University Press, 1984.

Sidorsky, David, ed. *Essays on Human Rights.* Philadelphia: Jewish Publication Society, 1979.

Siebert, Frederick S. *Freedom of the Press in England, 1476–1776.* Urbana: University of Illinois Press, 1952.

Simon, Herbert. "Applying Information Technology to Organization Design." 33 *Public Administration Review* 271 (1973).

Simpson, A. W. B. "The Rise and Fall of the Legal Treatise." 48 *University of Chicago Law Review* 632 (1981).

Simpson, A. W. B. "The Source and Function of the Later Year Books." 87 *Law Quarterly Review* 94 (1971).

Smith, Anthony. *Goodbye Gutenberg.* New York: Oxford University Press, 1980.

Smith, Anthony. "The Influence of Television." 114 *Daedelus* 1 (1985).

Smith, J. C. "The Unique Nature of the Concepts of Western Law." 46 *Canadian Bar Review* 191 (1968).

Smith, Jeffrey. *Printers and Press Freedom.* New York: Oxford University Press, 1988.

Smith, Ted. *Moscow Meets Main Street.* Washington, D.C.: Media Institute, 1988.

Smolla, Rodney. *Suing the Press.* New York: Oxford University Press, 1986.

Solomon, Richard. "Computers and the Concept of Intellectual Copyright." In *Electronic Publishing Plus.* Edited by Martin Greenberger. White Plains, N.Y.: Knowledge Industry Publications, 1985.

Sontag, Susan. *On Photography.* New York: Farrar, Straus and Giroux, 1973.

Spacks, Patricia Meyer. *Gossip.* Chicago: University of Chicago, 1985.

Spence, Jonathan. *The Memory Palace of Matteo Ricci.* New York: Viking Penguin, 1984.

Spengler, Oswald. *The Decline of the West.* New York: Knopf, 1928.

St. John-Stevas, Norman. *Obscenity and the Law.* London: Secker & Warburg, 1956.

Stansky, Peter, ed. *On Nineteen Eighty-four.* San Francisco: Freeman, 1983.

Starr, Paul. *The Social Transformation of American Medecine.* New York: Basic Books, 1982.

Staudt, Ronald. "Computers at the Core of Legal Education." 35 *Journal of Legal Education* 514 (1985).

Steinberg, S. H. *Five Hundred Years of Printing.* 3rd ed. Baltimore: Penguin, 1974.

Steinhoff, William. *The Road to 1984.* London: Weidenfeld & Nicolson, 1975.

Sterling, Christopher. *Electronic Media: A Guide to Trends in Broadcasting and Newer Technologies, 1920–1983.* New York: Praeger, 1984.

Stevens, Robert. *Law School.* Chapel Hill: University of North Carolina Press, 1983.

Stewart, Potter. "Or of the Press." 26 *Hastings Law Journal* 631 (1975).

Stock, Brian. *The Implications of Literacy.* Princeton, N.J.: Princeton University Press, 1983.

Strauss, Gerald. *Law, Resistance and the State: The Opposition to Roman Law in Reformation Germany.* Princeton, N.J.: Princeton University Press, 1986.

Stuart, Reginald. "F.C.C. Acts to Restrict Indecent Programming." *New York Times,* April 17, 1987, p. A1.

Stubbs, William. *Lectures on Medieval and Modern History.* Oxford: Oxford University Press, 1886.

Subervi-Velez, Federico. "The Mass Media and Ethnic Assimilation and Pluralism." 13 *Communications Research* 71 (1986).

Sullivan, Joseph F. "Cordless Phones Raise an Eavesdropping Issue." *New York Times,* March 11, 1986, p. B3.

Surrency, Erwin. "The Beginnings of American Legal Literature." 31 *American Journal of Legal History* 207 (1987).

Surrency, Erwin. "English Reports Printed in America." 3 *Legal Reference Service Quarterly* 9 (1983).

Surrency, Erwin. "Law Reports in the United States." 25 *American Journal of Legal History* 45 (1981).

Susskind, Richard. "Detmold's Refutation of Positivism and the Computer Judge." 49 *Modern Law Review* 125 (1986).

Susskind, Richard. "Expert Systems in Law: A Jurisprudential Approach to Artificial Intelligence and Legal Reasoning." 49 *Modern Law Review* 168 (1987).

Susskind, Richard. "Expert Systems in Law and the Data Protection Adviser." 7 *Oxford Journal of Legal Studies* 145 (1987).

Symposium. "Law Libraries and Miniaturization." 66 *Law Library Journal* 395 (1973).

Symposium. "The Living McLuhan." 31 *Journal of Communication* 116–199 (1981).

Tait, David. "The Territorial Pattern and Lineage System of Konkomba." In *Tribes Without Rulers.* Edited by John Middleton and David Tait. London: Routledge and Kegan Paul, 1958.

Takeyoshi, Kawashima. "The Status of the Individual in the Notion of Law, Right, and Social Order in Japan." In *The Status of the Individual in East and West.* Edited by Charles Moore. Honolulu: University of Hawaii Press, 1964.

Tay, Alice Erh-Soon, and Eugene Kamenka. "Public Law–Private Law." In *Public and Private in Social Life.* Edited by S. I. Benn and G. F. Gaus. New York: St. Martin's Press, 1983.

Taylor, Julie. "Demographics of the American Legal Profession." Cambridge, Mass.: Harvard Law School, 1983.

Taylor, John F. A. *The Masks of Society*. New York: Appleton-Century-Crofts, 1966.

Technical Report of the Commission on Obscenity and Pornography. Vol. 2. Washington, D.C.: Government Printing Office, 1970.

Tefft, Stanton, ed. *Secrecy*. New York: Human Sciences Press, 1980.

Tocqueville, Alexis de. *Democracy in America*. Edited by Phillips Bradley. New York: Knopf, 1945.

Thomas, Donald. *A Long Time Burning: The History of Literary Censorship in England*. New York: Praeger, 1969.

Thomas, Isaiah. *The History of Printing in America*. 3rd ed. New York: Weathervane Books, 1970.

Thomson, John A. F. *The Transformation of Medieval England, 1370–1529*. London: Longman, 1983.

Thorne, Samuel. *Essays in English Legal History*. London: Hambledon Press, 1985.

Thorne, Samuel. *Sir Edward Coke*. London: Selden Society, 1957.

Thorne, Samuel, ed. *On the Laws and Customs of England*. Cambridge, Mass.: Harvard University Press, 1964.

Toffler, Alvin. "The Future of Law and Order." *Encounter*, July 1973, p. 15.

Tolchin, Martin. "Russians Sought U.S. Banks to Gain High-Tech Secrets." *New York Times*, February 16, 1986, p. A1.

Toth, Michael. "Asking the Way and Telling the Law: Speech in Medieval Germany." 16 *Journal of Interdisciplinary History* 667 (1986).

"Toward the Multi-Door Courthouse—Dispute Resolution Intake and Referral." *NIJ Reports*, July 1986, p. 2.

Turkle, Sherry. *The Second Self: Computers and the Human Spirit*. New York: Simon and Schuster, 1984.

Turnbull, Colin. *The Forest People*. New York: Simon and Schuster, 1961.

Turnbull, Colin. *The Mountain People: A Study of the Pygmies of the Congo*. New York: Simon and Schuster, 1961.

Turner, Ralph. *The English Judiciary in the Age of Glanvill and Bracton, c. 1176–1239*. Cambridge: Cambridge University Press, 1985.

Twining, William. *Legal Theory and Common Law*. Oxford: Blackwell, 1986.

Ullman, Walter. *The Individual and Society in the Middle Ages*. Baltimore: Johns Hopkins University Press, 1966.

Ungar, Sanford. *The Papers and the Papers*. New York: Dutton, 1972.

Unger, Roberto. *Law in Modern Society*. New York: Free Press, 1976.

United States v. *Roth*, 77 S.Ct. 1304 (1957).

United States v. *The Progressive, Inc.*, 467 F. Supp. 990 (W.D. Wisc.), *appeal dismissed*, 610 F. 2d. 819 (7th Cir., 1979).

United States v. *Morison*, 604 F. Supp. 655 (1985), *affirmed*, 844 F.2d 1057 (1988).

United States v. *Associated Press*, 52 F. Supp. 362 (1943).

U.S. Congress, Office of Technology Asessment. *Commercial Newsgathering from Space: A Technical Memorandum.* Washington, D.C.: Government Printing Office, 1987.

U.S. Congress, Office of Technology Asessment. *Defending Secrets, Sharing Data: New Locks and Keys for Electronic Information.* Washington, D.C.: Government Printing Office, 1987.

U.S. Congress, Office of Technology Asessment. *Federal Government Information Technology: Electronic Record Systems and Individual Privacy.* Washington, D.C.: Government Printing Office, 1986.

U.S. Congress, Office of Technology Assessment. *Federal Government Information Technology: Electronic Surveillance and Civil Liberties.* Washington, D.C.: Government Printing Office, 1985.

U.S. Congress, Office of Technology Assessment. *Intellectual Property Rights in an Age of Electronics and Information.* Washington, D.C.: Government Printing Office, 1986.

U.S. Congress, Office of Technology Assessment. *Science, Technology and the First Amendment.* Washington, D.C.: Government Printing Office, 1988.

Van den Steenhoven, Geer. *Leadership and Law Among the Eskimos of the Keewatin District, Northwest Territory.* Rijswijk: Excelsior, 1962.

Von Nessen, Paul. "Law Reporting: Another Case for Deregulation." 48 *Modern Law Review* 412 (1985).

Wagar, W. Warren, ed. *The Idea of Progress Since the Renaissance.* New York: Wiley, 1969.

Wall, John. "The Reformation in England and the Typographical Revolution: 'By this printing . . . the doctrine of the Gospel soundeth to all nations.' " In *Print and Culture in the Renaissance.* Edited by Gerald Tyson and Sylvia Wagonheim. Newark: University of Delaware Press, 1986.

Warren, Samuel, and Louis Brandeis. "The Right to Privacy." 4 *Harvard Law Review* 193 (1890).

Watson, Alan. *The Nature of Law.* Edinburgh: Edinburgh University Press, 1977.

Weaver, David, Judith Buddenbaum, and Jo Ellen Fair. "Press Freedom, Media and Development, 1950–1979: A Study of 134 Nations." 35 *Journal of Communications* 104 (1985).

Weizenbaum, Joseph. *Computer Power and Human Reason.* San Francisco: Freeman, 1976.

West, Robin. "Jurisprudence and Gender." 55 *University of Chicago Law Review* 1 (1988).

Westen, Peter. "The Rueful Rhetoric of 'Rights.' " 33 *U.C.L.A. Law Review* 977 (1986).

Westin, Alan. *Privacy and Freedom.* New York: Atheneum, 1967.

White, James. *The Legal Imagination: Studies in the Nature of Legal Thought and Expression.* Boston: Little, Brown, 1973.

White, James. "Thinking About Our Language." 96 *Yale Law Journal* 1960 (1987).

White, James. *When Words Lose Their Meaning.* Chicago: University of Chicago Press, 1984.

White, Lynn. *Medieval Technology and Social Change.* Oxford: Clarendon Press, 1966.

Whitehead, Alfred North. *Modes of Thought.* New York: Macmillan, 1969.

Wiener, Joel. "Social Purity and Freedom of Expression." In *Censorship: 500 Years of Conflict.* New York: New York Public Library, 1984.

Wiener, Norbert. *The Human Use of Human Beings.* Boston: Houghton Mifflin, 1950.

Williams, Martha, Lawrence Lannom, and Carolyn Robins. *Computer-Readable Databases: A Directory and Data Sourcebook.* Chicago: American Library Association, 1985.

Winfield, Percy. *The Chief Sources of English Legal History.* Cambridge, Mass.: Harvard University Press, 1925.

Winfield, Percy. "Early Attempts at Reporting Cases." 159 *Law Quarterly Review* 316 (1924).

Winter, Edward. "The Aboriginal Political Structure of Bwamba." In *Tribes Without Rulers.* Edited by John Middleton and David Tait. London: Routledge and Kegan Paul, 1958.

Wolfe, Tom. "What If He Is Right?" In *The Pump House Gang.* Edited by Tom Wolfe. New York: Farrar, Straus and Giroux, 1968.

Wood, Amanda. *Knowledge Before Printing and After: The Indian Tradition in Changing Kerala.* Oxford: Oxford University Press, 1985.

Wright, Peter. "What Is a Profession?" 29 *Canadian Bar Review* 748 (1951).

Yale, D. E. C. " 'Of No Mean Authority': Some Later Uses of Bracton." In *On the Laws and Customs of England: Essays in Honor of Samuel E. Thorne.* Edited by Morris Arnold, Thomas Green, Sally Scully, and Stephen White. Chapel Hill: University of North Carolina Press, 1981.

Yates, Frances. *The Art of Memory.* London: Routledge and Kegan Paul, 1966.

Yeazell, Stephen. *From Medieval Group Litigation to the Modern Class Action.* New Haven, Conn.: Yale University Press, 1987.

Young, Thomas. "A Look at American Law Reporting in the 19th Century." 68 *Law Library Journal* 294 (1975).

Zacks, Richard. "Just When Satellite TV Was Taking Off, Someone Scrambled the Picture." *TV Guide,* December 21, 1985, p. 45.

Ziman, John. *Public Knowledge: The Social Dimension of Science.* New York: Cambridge University Press, 1968.

Zuboff, Shoshana. *In the Age of the Smart Machine.* New York: Basic Books, 1988.

Index